"Today, understanding our past is more urgent than ever to inform our future. This book makes a fantastic job of discussing fundamental issues to make sense of history in organization studies. The book is a must-read for all academics who are interested in producing solid organizational studies historical accounts as well as to understand how history has been discussed in organization studies."

Professor **Rafael Alcadipani**, *Fundação Getúlio Vargas, FGV-EAESP, São Paulo*

"The authors in this volume venture audaciously into the interdisciplinary worlds of management studies and history. The outcome is a book which marks a serious advance in showing how business and management can incorporate history more dynamically in research, and benefit greatly as a result."

Professor **Geoffrey Jones**, *Isidor Straus Professor of Business History, Harvard Business School*

"This volume takes an important next step in the further development of the 'historical turn' in organization studies by bringing together theoretical, methodological and empirical insights. Through compelling narratives from all parts of society, it demonstrates how the interplay between history and organization studies advances our reflexivity and ability to engage in the future."

Professor **Majken Schultz**, *Centre for Organizational Time, Copenhagen Business School*

"There is a need for historical organization studies. This book not only explains why this is the case but also what it means. The rich collection of empirical examples helps us understand the various approaches that can be taken and how they can contribute to organization studies. Highly recommended reading!"

Professor **Eero Vaara**, *Hanken School of Economics and Saïd Business School, University of Oxford*

"This collection demonstrates the extent to which the promise of Historical Organization Studies–the interplay between creative historical research and innovative organizational theory–is becoming a reality. Along with an introduction by four leading scholars that maps out the intellectual terrain of the field, the chapters demonstrate the variety of different ways in which scholars are integrating history and theory to generate new insights about organizations and organizing. I would especially recommend the volume for early career researchers interested in learning about a dynamic and emerging field of organizational scholarship."

Professor **Dan Wadhwani**, *University of Southern California and Copenhagen Business School*

HISTORICAL ORGANIZATION STUDIES

We are now entering a new phase in the establishment of historical organization studies as a distinctive methodological paradigm within the broad field of organization studies. This book serves both as a landmark in the development of the field and as a key reference tool for researchers and students.

For two decades, organization theorists have emphasized the need for more and better research recognizing the importance of the past in shaping the present and future. By historicizing organizational research, the contexts and forces bearing upon organizations will be more fully recognized, and analyses of organizational dynamics improved. But how, precisely, might a traditionally empirically oriented discipline such as history be incorporated into a theoretically oriented discipline such as organization studies? This book evaluates the current state of play, advances it and identifies the possibilities the new emergent field offers for the future. In addition to providing an important work of reference on the subject for researchers, the book can be used to introduce management and organizational history to a student audience at both undergraduate and postgraduate levels.

The book is a valuable source for wider reading, providing rich reference material in tutorials across organizational studies, or as recommended or required reading on courses with a connection to business or management history.

Mairi Maclean is Professor of International Business in the School of Management, University of Bath, where she is Associate Dean for Faculty.

Stewart R. Clegg is Distinguished Professor of Management and Organization Studies at the University of Technology Sydney.

Roy Suddaby is the Winspear Professor of Management at the University of Victoria and a Research Professor at the University of Liverpool Management School.

Charles Harvey is Professor of Business History and Management at Newcastle University Business School and Director of the Centre for Research on Entrepreneurship, Wealth and Philanthropy (REWP).

HISTORICAL ORGANIZATION STUDIES

Theory and Applications

*Edited by Mairi Maclean, Stewart R. Clegg,
Roy Suddaby and Charles Harvey*

LONDON AND NEW YORK

First published 2021
by Routledge
2 Park Square, Milton Park, Abingdon, Oxon OX14 4RN

and by Routledge
52 Vanderbilt Avenue, New York, NY 10017

Routledge is an imprint of the Taylor & Francis Group, an informa business

© 2021 selection and editorial matter, Mairi Maclean, Stewart R. Clegg, Roy Suddaby and Charles Harvey, individual chapters, the contributors

The right of Mairi Maclean, Stewart R. Clegg, Roy Suddaby and Charles Harvey to be identified as the authors of the editorial material, and of the authors for their individual chapters, has been asserted in accordance with sections 77 and 78 of the Copyright, Designs and Patents Act 1988.

With the exception of Chapter 1, no part of this book may be reprinted or reproduced or utilised in any form or by any electronic, mechanical, or other means, now known or hereafter invented, including photocopying and recording, or in any information storage or retrieval system, without permission in writing from the publishers.

Chapter 1 of this book is available for free in PDF format as Open Access from the individual product page at www.routledge.com. It has been made available under a Creative Commons Attribution-Non Commercial-No Derivatives 4.0 license.

Trademark notice: Product or corporate names may be trademarks or registered trademarks, and are used only for identification and explanation without intent to infringe.

British Library Cataloguing in Publication Data
A catalogue record for this book is available from the British Library

Library of Congress Cataloging-in-Publication Data
Names: Maclean, Mairi, 1959- editor. | Clegg, Stewart, editor. | Suddaby, Roy, editor.
Title: Historical organization studies : theory and applications / edited by Mairi Maclean, Stewart R. Clegg, Roy Suddaby and Charles Harvey.
Description: 1 Edition. | New York : Routledge, 2020. | Includes bibliographical references and index.
Identifiers: LCCN 2020028021 (print) | LCCN 2020028022 (ebook) | ISBN 9780367471217 (hardback) | ISBN 9780367471224 (paperback) | ISBN 9781003033592 (ebook)
Subjects: LCSH: Organization–Research. | Organizational sociology–Research. | Organizational behavior–Research. | Organization–History.
Classification: LCC HD30.4 .H57 2020 (print) | LCC HD30.4 (ebook) | DDC 302.3/50722–dc23
LC record available at https://lccn.loc.gov/2020028021
LC ebook record available at https://lccn.loc.gov/2020028022

ISBN: 978-0-367-47121-7 (hbk)
ISBN: 978-0-367-47122-4 (pbk)
ISBN: 978-1-003-03359-2 (ebk)

Typeset in Bembo
by Taylor & Francis Books

CONTENTS

List of figures ix
Acknowledgements x
List of contributors xii

PART I
Introduction 1

1 Historical organization studies: Advancing new directions for organizational research 3
   Mairi Maclean, Charles Harvey, Roy Suddaby and Stewart R. Clegg

PART II
Conceptual advances 23

2 Writing the history of practices 25
   Alistair Mutch

3 Towards a theory of historical reflexivity 39
   Gabrielle Durepos and Russ Vince

4 The organization-as-iceberg as a counter-metaphor 57
   Richard Badham, Todd Bridgman and Stephen Cummings

5 Towards critical historical studies: An emancipatory ontology 77
   Christiane Chihadeh

6 Don't talk about history: Indigenous views about the past and their implication for organization studies   90
François Bastien, William M. Foster and Diego M. Coraiola

PART III
Theoretical applications   105

7 The Canadian Alouette women: Reclaiming their space   107
Stefanie Ruel, Linda Dyer and Albert J. Mills

8 The enduring presence of the founder: A historical and interdisciplinary perspective on the organizational identity of collection museums   131
Sonia Coman and Andrea Casey

9 Institutional entrepreneurship and the field of power: The emergence of the global hotel industry   149
Mairi Maclean, Charles Harvey and Roy Suddaby

10 'Remember Mackintosh!' Historical homology and historical affinity in the design of the Scottish parliament building   170
Ron Kerr and Sarah Robinson

11 Institutional change as historical confluence: The development of the nursing profession in Japan   188
Ken Sakai

12 Studying the processes of managerial legitimacy and control of former state-owned enterprises in post-communist societies: A longitudinal study   207
Anna Soulsby

PART IV
Conclusion   225

13 At the intersection of theory and history: A research agenda for historical organization studies   227
Stewart R. Clegg, Roy Suddaby, Charles Harvey and Mairi Maclean

Index   *242*

ILLUSTRATIONS

Figures

3.1	A model of historical reflexivity	40
4.1	Cartoon reproduced with permission from Jock Macneish	57
7.1	Canadian space princess (*The Ottawa Citizen*, 1961)	119
7.2	More Canadian space princesses (Brebner, 2014)	120
7.3	DRTE men interacting with Alouette artifact (Brebner, 2014)	121
7.4	Human computer (Brebner, 2014)	121
7.5	Two DRTE scalers (Brebner, 2014)	122
7.6	Doris Jelly (center) pictured with co-workers at DRTE (Jelly, 2019)	124
7.7	Pat Butler, photographer (Brebner, 2014)	124
8.1	Overview of research process	134
8.2	Social network graph	141
8.3	Attributes and values of collector, collection, and collection museum	145
11.1	Changes in academism and professionalism in Japanese nursing, 1960s–2010s	199

Tables

9.1	Entry barriers and time to opening in Europe, the Middle East and Africa (EMEA)	155
12.1	Interviewees and other key actors	211

ACKNOWLEDGEMENTS

Many people have helped, directly and indirectly, with this book, which grew out of the editors' having worked together at Newcastle University Business School, UK. Its inspiration lies in the scholarly fulcrum generated in the many colloquia, symposia, conferences and seminars on the creative fusion of history and organization theory held over the past few years. In particular, we wish to thank participants who attended the European Group for Organizational Studies' (EGOS) sub-theme on 'Historical organization studies: Realizing the potential', held at the EGOS colloquium in Edinburgh in July 2019, which ran as two parallel streams. The support of the conference organizers, especially John Amis, Chris Carter and Angelika Zierer, was invaluable. Discussions at previous EGOS colloquia, meetings of the Management History division of the Academy of Management and at annual conferences of the Association of Business Historians and the British Academy of Management sharpened and extended our thinking. We are grateful for the contributions of Richard Badham, Andrea Bernardi, Andrea Casey, Christiane Chihadeh, Eugene Choi, Sonia Coman, Diego Coraiola, Thomas Davis, Stephanie Decker, Gabrielle Durepos, Micki Eisenman, Lars Engwall, Bill Foster, Alex Gillett, Andrew Godley, Michael Heller, Guy Huber, Trevor Israelsen, Ron Kerr, Matthias Kipping, Ann Langley, Garence Marechal, Tom McGovern, Niall McKenzie, John Millar, Albert Mills, Alistair Mutch, Adam Nix, Andrew Perchard, Pamela Popielarz, Sarah Robinson, Stefanie Ruel, Ken Sakai, Andrew Smith, Christian Stutz, Sabina Siebert, Anna Soulsby, Scott Taylor, Kevin Tennent, Behlül Üsdiken and Nicholas Wong. The editors of key special issues that have advanced the debate are also deserving of thanks, in particular Mick Rowlinson, Rafael Alcadipani, Amon Barros, Emma Bell, Todd Bridgman, Stephen Cummings, Walter Friedman, John Hassard, Geoffrey Jones, Mads Mordhorst, Andrew Popp, Martin Ruef and Dan

Wadhwani. Thanks are due to Rebecca Marsh, Alanna Donaldson and Alex Atkinson of Routledge as well as Louise Smith for their kind assistance in the production of this book. We thank Tyne & Wear Archives & Museums for permission to use the photograph of the Tyne Bridge under construction. Finally, we would like to thank our families for their love and support.

CONTRIBUTORS

Richard Badham is Professor of Management at the Macquarie Business School, Sydney. His research interests in change, politics and the role of irony in organization studies inform his forthcoming publications *Power, Politics and Organizational Change* (Sage, 2020, with Dave Buchanan) and *Ironies of Organizational Change* (Elgar, 2020, with Brenda Santiago).

François Bastien is an assistant professor at the Peter B. Gustavson School of Business at the University of Victoria. As a Huron-Wendat from the Indigenous community of Wendake, Bastien has observed incongruities between Indigenous ways of organizing and contemporary colonial models. He aims to translate Indigenous knowledge and challenge colonial assumptions.

Todd Bridgman is Associate Professor in the School of Management, Victoria University of Wellington, New Zealand. Todd's research draws on critical management studies, management history and management education. He specializes in exploring the origins of management theories and challenging their representation in best-selling textbooks.

Dr Andrea Casey is an associate professor of human and organizational learning at George Washington University. Her research interests include organizational memory, history and identity and their relationship to organizational change and strategy.

Christiane Chihadeh is a lecturer in strategy at Manchester Metropolitan University. Her research interests include institutional and organizational change and historical organizational studies. These interests have evolved to incorporate ideas from cultural political economy, with an emerging focus on the concepts of the imaginary and of politics in organization studies.

Stewart Clegg is Distinguished Professor at the University of Technology Sydney and is a prolific contributor to central and peripheral areas in the field. His work displays a fascination with power relations and history as inseparable. Among his recent books is *Management, Organizations and Contemporary Social Theory* (Routledge, 2019, with Miguel Pinha e Cuhna).

Dr Sonia Coman (PhD, Art History, Columbia University) is the Anne van Biema Curatorial Fellow at the Smithsonian's Freer and Sackler Galleries, which together form the National Museum of Asian Art. Dr Coman's research interests include identity formation in cultural organizations and the history of art markets and collecting.

Diego M. Coraiola is an assistant professor of management at the Augustana Campus of the University of Alberta. His research focuses on institutional change, organizational mnemonics and the strategic uses of the past. His work has been published in the *Strategic Management Journal*, *Journal of Business Ethics* and *Business History*.

Stephen Cummings is Professor of Management at Victoria University of Wellington, New Zealand, having previously held research fellowships at Judge Business School and Wolfson College, University of Cambridge. He is author of *A New History of Management* (Cambridge University Press, 2017) and co-edited *The Oxford Handbook of Critical Management Studies* (2009).

Gabrielle Durepos is an associate professor at Mount Saint Vincent University in Halifax, Canada. Her research interests include historical organization studies. She is Associate Editor of *Academy of Management Learning and Education*, *Management Learning* and *Qualitative Research in Organizations and Management*. Her website URL is www.gabrielledurepos.com

Linda Dyer is a professor in the John Molson School of Business, Concordia University, and studies the interpersonal interactions between workers of diverse age groups. Her research focuses on the later stages of careers during which people decide whether and how to transfer their knowledge to others, which is of critical importance to multigenerational organizations.

William (Bill) M. Foster is Professor of Management at the Augustana Campus of the University of Alberta. He has published in journals such as *Journal of Management*, *Strategic Management Journal*, *Human Relations* and *Business History*. He is Editor-in-Chief of *Academy of Management Learning and Education* and serves on the editorial boards of *Academy of Management Review* and *Business History*.

Charles Harvey is a Professor of Business Strategy at Newcastle University Business School, UK. He holds a PhD in International Business from the University of

Bristol. His research focuses on the historical processes that inform contemporary business practice, entrepreneurial philanthropy and the exercise of power by elite groups in society.

Ron Kerr works at the University of Edinburgh. His research draws on critical sociology and focuses on issues of power in organizations. He has published on the role of Scottish banking elites in the global financial crisis, on historicizing corporate architecture and, more recently, on populist politics.

Mairi Maclean is Professor of International Business at the University of Bath, UK. She received her PhD from the University of St Andrews. Her research interests include historical organization studies, business elites and elite power from a Bourdieusian perspective, and entrepreneurial philanthropy. Her research has been funded by the Leverhulme Trust, Reed Charity and the ESRC.

Albert J. Mills is an 0.2 Professor of Innovation Management at the University of Eastern Finland. He is Co-chair of the International Board for Critical Management Studies and co-editor of *Qualitative Research in Organizations and Management*. His latest book (with Milorad Novicevic) is *Management and Organizational History: A Research Overview* (Routledge, 2020).

Alistair Mutch is Professor of Information and Learning at Nottingham Trent University. He uses historical approaches to engage with and develop the concept of institutional logics, as in his *Reshaping Institutional Logics: History, Substance and Practices* (Routledge 2019). He also works on the history of eighteenth-century Scotland.

Sarah Robinson is Professor in Management and Organisation Studies at Adam Smith Business School, Glasgow University. Having a degree in history, her work often uses historical approaches – for example, to cultural production and the role of power, resistance and identity within organizations – often drawing on the work of Pierre Bourdieu.

Stefanie Ruel is a lecturer in organizational behaviour at the Open University. After a 20-year career in the Canadian space industry, she identifies as a critical management studies scholar, focusing on intersectionality scholarship and addressing the exclusion and marginalization of complex individuals in STEM contexts.

Ken Sakai is an associate professor at the Graduate School of Economics and Management, Tohoku University, Japan. He earned his PhD from Hitotsubashi University. His recent research focuses on the interactions and longitudinal dynamics of power, agency and institution. His work has been published in journals such as *Business History*.

List of contributors   xv

Anna Soulsby is an associate professor of organizational behaviour at Nottingham University Business School, UK. Her research interests include organizational and managerial change in post-communist societies; longitudinal research methods; narratives and organizational and community history; and institutional theory. She has been conducting fieldwork in organizations in the Czech Republic since 1991.

Roy Suddaby is the Winspear Chair of Management at the Peter B. Gustavson School of Business, University of Victoria, Canada, and Professor of Management at the Carson School of Business, Washington State University, USA. He is an adjunct professor at Ritsumeikan University, Japan, and at IAE Business School in Argentina and is a Fellow of the Academy of Management.

Russ Vince is Professor of Leadership and Change at the School of Management, University of Bath, and Honorary Professor of Management at the University of St Andrews. He researches emotions in organizations, management learning and education, and leadership. Russ is a former editor-in-chief of the international academic journal *Management Learning*.

PART I
Introduction

1

HISTORICAL ORGANIZATION STUDIES

Advancing new directions for organizational research

Mairi Maclean, Charles Harvey, Roy Suddaby and Stewart R. Clegg

Introduction

Historical organization studies is 'organizational research that draws extensively on historical sources, methods and knowledge to promote historically informed theoretical narratives attentive to both disciplines' (Maclean, Harvey and Clegg, 2016: 609). Put simply, it seeks to blend history and organization studies. The present status of historical organization studies is that of an emergent academic movement rather than an established community of practice. For more than two decades, organization theorists have pointed to the need for more and better research that recognizes the importance of the past in shaping the present and influencing the future (Kieser, 1994; Zald, 1993). Some have identified a distinct 'historic turn' in organization studies, an epistemological shift led by scholars who perceive the field to have been constrained by its orientation towards contemporary cross-sectional studies covering limited periods of time (Clark and Rowlinson, 2004; Mills, Suddaby, Foster and Durepos, 2016). By *historicizing* organizational research, it is argued, the contexts and forces bearing upon organizations might be more fully recognized and analyses of organizational dynamics might be improved.

How, precisely, might organizational research be *historicized*? How might a traditionally empirically oriented discipline such as history be incorporated into a theoretically oriented discipline such as organization studies? How might the power of history be harnessed to advance the explanatory potential of organization theory? What might history tangibly contribute to our knowledge of management and organizations (Clegg, 2006; Clegg and Courpasson, 2007)? We are now embarking on a new stage in the establishment of historical organization studies as a distinctive epistemological and methodological approach that develops a historical research strategy within the broad field of organization studies. This book makes a timely intervention that advances the discussion while extending and deepening what has already been achieved. Hence, it offers a mixture of conceptual and theoretically informed empirical papers that help to define the field and to orient it further in future. In this way, the book serves both as a landmark in the development of the field and as an important milestone in building an emergent and strengthening community of scholars. It thereby contributes to the reimagining of historical organizational studies while advancing new directions for organizational research. This chapter takes stock by evaluating the current state of play, explores recent scholarly exemplars on theorized history, while looking at the possibilities offered for future research.

Advancing new directions

The integration of history with organization studies has been the topic of extensive debate in recent years. Indeed, the genesis of the present book lies in the European Group for Organizational Studies' (EGOS) sub-theme on 'Historical organization studies: Realizing the potential', held at the EGOS colloquium in Edinburgh in July 2019. The sub-theme was so successful and attracted so many papers that it ran as two parallel streams. It continued the momentum established by an EGOS standing working group on organizational history, in which participants, alongside members of the Management History division of the Academy of Management, worked energetically for several years. The fruits of that work have found expression in a number of ground-breaking publications and avenues for future exploration (Bucheli and Wadhwani, 2014; Kipping and Üsdiken, 2014; Maclean et al., 2016; Rowlinson, Hassard and Decker, 2014). These activities have been accompanied by a flurry of special issues in journals such as the *Academy of Management Review, Organization Studies, Management Learning, Organization*, the *Revista de Administração de Empresas* and the *Strategic Management Journal*. The notion of historical organization studies emerged from this scholarly fulcrum.

The first main contribution of this literature has been to specify the problems inherent in reconciling disciplinary traditions. In terms of history and organization studies, these are summarized by Rowlinson et al. (2014) as three epistemological dualisms: in organization studies, the prioritization of analysis, self-generated data and simple chronology differ fundamentally from the prioritization by historians of narrative, documentary sources and periodization. The second main contribution of this foundational literature is to demonstrate how these differences might fruitfully be overcome. Kipping and Üsdiken (2014) suggest three modes of correspondence between history and organization theory: history as a means of testing theory, history informing theoretical perspectives and history lending complexity to theorization.

Building on these insights, Maclean, Harvey and Clegg (2016; 2017) elaborate the idea of historical organization studies – organizational research that embeds organizing and organizations in their socio-historical context(s) to generate historically informed theoretical narratives attentive to both disciplines. These authors point out that there has been a good deal more longitudinal research in organization studies than is commonly acknowledged. They propose a typology entailing four differing conceptions of history in organizational research. First, history as evaluating, where history is used as a means of testing and refining theory and arguments. Such an approach recognizes that theory testing can benefit from a greater focus on context and temporality. It also acknowledges that, over time, events may be subject to reinterpretation and re-evaluation, the nature of history being that it is constantly open to debate. Second, history as explicating, where history is used in applying and developing theory to uncover the operation of transformative social processes. This entails employing historical data to probe theories that unearth causal mechanisms. Third, history as conceptualizing, where history is employed to generate new theoretical constructs, seeking to 'stretch the scope of explanations' (Lippmann and Aldrich, 2014: 128) by drawing lessons and generalizing inductively from empirical data and particular historical cases. Fourth, history as narrating, where history is used to explain the form and origins of significant contemporary phenomena (Maclean et al., 2016: 612). History as conceptualizing arguably offers the most scope for demonstrating conceptual originality in historical research, where theorization becomes more explicit, promoting the development of rich, robust historical scholarship. History as narrating nevertheless remains perhaps the most frequent mode of employing history in organizational research. As White (1987: 169) observes, 'Getting the "story" out of "history" was … a first step in the transformation of historical studies into a science'. For Ricoeur, narrative is humanizing, with history being a humanizing endeavour. So profound is the connection with narration that, for Ricoeur (1983: 177), history cannot depart from narrative 'without losing its historical character'. The production of a historical narrative is thus a composite process that implicates characters, events and authors in generating a unified, theoretically sensitive narrative analysis, in which theorization is largely implicit (Taylor, Bell and Cooke, 2009). Such an approach illuminates the nature of organizational history as historically constituted through language, replacing any conception of an objective historical reality with another, more open to social construction (Heller and Rowlinson, 2019; Maclean, Harvey, Sillince and Golant, 2018).

To accomplish historical organization studies, Maclean, Harvey and Clegg (2016; 2017) further identify five principles of historical organization studies designed to promote a closer union between history and organization theory. These are: dual integrity, pluralistic understanding, representational truth, context sensitivity and theoretical fluency (Maclean et al., 2016: 617). *Dual integrity* underscores the importance of both historical veracity and conceptual rigour, extending mutual respect to history and organization studies in uniting the two, such that each discipline informs and enhances the other without either becoming the driver of the other. We contend that historically informed theoretical narratives cognizant of both disciplines, the authenticity of which inheres in both theoretical interpretation and historical veracity, make a strong and singular claim to scholarly legitimacy. Given its centrality, *dual integrity* serves as an overarching 'master principle' for the remaining four. *Pluralistic understanding* signals an openness to alternatives and new ways of seeing, such that other kinds of understanding are accommodated in historical studies, embracing and reclaiming space for alterity within them and recognizing the richness that different perspectives bring. *Representational truth* denotes the congruence between evidence, logic and interpretation, to which authenticity and its construction are key, underlining the importance of 'ringing true' (Judt and Snyder, 2013). Representational truth underlines the vital relationship of trust researchers have not only with their audience but also with the subjects of their research (Taylor et al., 2009). As Rowlinson et al. (2014) observe, the fictionalization of organizations which is commonplace in organization studies prevents verification, emphasizing the importance of historical veracity in historical organization studies. *Context sensitivity* highlights attentiveness to historical specificities to promote a more contextualized appreciation of organizations which recognizes that these are moulded by the particular situational genesis from which they emerged (Aldrich, Ruef and Lippmann, 2020). The uniqueness of contextual conditions need not preclude generalizability. As Collingwood (1993: 396) argues persuasively, 'we learn by experience how to handle cases of influenza, without being held to the doctrine that all cases of influenza exactly resemble each other'. Finally, *theoretical fluency* points to the importance of mastering the relevant conceptual terrain, making more and better sense of historical cases by viewing them through an appropriate cognitive lens which enables scholars to see and understand better. Theoretical fluency encourages a more explicit theorization of temporal elements to develop insightful, substantive understanding of organizations and organizing, while recognizing that abstract concepts might be associated with case-specific, contextualized historical understanding.

We are now entering a new phase in establishing historical organization studies as a distinctive epistemological and methodological approach within the wide-ranging field of organization studies, concerned above all with putting *historical organization studies into action*. Scholars have been using organizational research in historical work for many years, but implicitly and largely unarticulated. As a singular type of reasoning it is now becoming more epistemologically and methodologically explicit (Suddaby, Coraiola, Harvey and Foster, 2020). Often what is dealt with is partial, very fragmentary data created for other purposes – 'shards created by the selection of materials, remainders left aside by an explication ... on the edges of discourses or in its rifts and crannies' (de Certeau, 1988: 4). The often fragmentary nature of the data, however, does not preclude meaningful insights being derived from the scrutiny of telling detail.

Such empirically founded research is not inimical to theory. Nor are theoretical approaches antithetical to organizational history, despite a longstanding aversion to theory on the part of some practising historians (Rowlinson et al., 2014). Historical organization studies aim to promote a structured dialogue between theoretical perspectives and empirical phenomena, fostering a fluid integration of theory with empirical observation (Harvey and Jones, 1990). Both theory and empirical research have much to offer the other. Although 'theory may help block out major dimensions of the narrative's plot, it still leaves a residue of events and aspects unexplained' (Hall, 1992: 185). Empirical research affords the 'thick description' of context to build and illuminate theory, which may provide an inductive foundation for elaborating theoretical insights (Geertz, 1973: 14). Delving into the historical, sociocultural specificities in which phenomena are embedded enhances historical understanding, which can lead to new theories. Without empirical depth, the danger is that organizational theory becomes disembodied from the practicalities of organizational existence (Sandberg and Tsoukas, 2011; Suddaby, Hardy and Huy, 2011). At the same time, empirical observation warns against the naïve assumption that contemporary phenomena are necessarily 'new' (Jones and Khanna, 2006). In a field as in thrall to the new as management and organization studies, such scepticism is acutely necessary.

More explicit theoretical narratives can bring contexts to life, uncovering how actors in the past have succeeded in navigating complexity (Langley, 1999; Lippmann and Aldrich, 2014). Theory can frame, energize and lend coherence to a research project (Hall, 1992). Theoretical interpretations can be refined and recalibrated through historical study and elucidation. Broader themes, such as sensemaking, can reach out to wider audiences. Shared perspectives offer a means for scholars from different backgrounds to have conversations, encouraging meaningful interdisciplinary dialogue between proponents of varying discourses and amplifying relevance. There is an evident tension between uniqueness and isomorphism in organizational research, between contextual specificities and universalist inclinations. Organizational case study research is founded on a premise of replication (Eisenhardt, 1989). Yet, as Deleuze (2004) has argued compellingly, human beings paradoxically copy in order to establish difference. Although historians have often been reluctant to acknowledge that there may be general mechanisms influencing organizational behaviour, it is in the productive *interplay* between theoretical perspectives and empirical observation that empirically founded organizational research has much to contribute.

Already, there are strong examples of original theorization based on historical analysis and historical sources. Suddaby, Foster and Quinn-Trank (2010) have put forward the construct of *rhetorical history* as a potentially valuable, rare, inimitable and malleable resource to affirm the importance of a company's history in shaping opinion and influencing action. This has implications for organizational remembering and identity work, casting light on the 'mnemonic manifestations' of past events and how these may impact on identity work across time (Judt and Snyder, 2013: 276; Suddaby et al., 2016). What is remembered and what is forgotten shape an organization's image and identity (Anteby and Molnár, 2012), opening up possibilities for the reuse of company mottos or artefacts for new purposes years later (Hatch and Schultz, 2017). Suddaby, Foster and Mills (2014) draw attention to the need for an enhanced sensitivity to the inherent historical nature of institutions in developing the notion of *historical institutionalism*. Such an approach acknowledges that, with time, organizations become infused with meaning in a way that transcends their initial purpose, and that institutionalization is in essence an intrinsically historical operation (Selznick, 1957). Durepos, Mills and Helms Mills (2008) advance the concept of *ANTi-History*, drawing on actor-network theory as a critical lens through which to consider the sociopolitical process of writing a company history, accentuating the importance of locating companies in the broader 'sociopasts' in which they originated. Mutch (2018) employs history as a means of reframing institutional logics through his work on taken-for-granted historical practices. Vaara and Lamberg (2016) emphasize the need to understand the *historical embeddedness* of strategic processes and practices. Harvey, Maclean et al. (2011) propose a *transactional model* of entrepreneurial philanthropy based on Bourdieu's capital theory in an examination of the life of Andrew Carnegie (see also Harvey, Maclean and Suddaby, 2019). Drawing similarly on Bourdieusian theory, Harvey, Press and Maclean (2011) explore how tastes are formed, transmitted, embedded and reproduced across generations. Gasparin, Green and Schinckus (2019) highlight *historical sensemaking* that emphasizes how individuals seek patterned means of making sense of events on the basis that 'historical time is an essential dimension of the sensemaking and sensegiving of human actors' (Wadhwani and Jones, 2014: 208). Wadhwani and Jones (2014) underline the role of *historical reasoning* as a way of illuminating key aspects of the entrepreneurial process by addressing temporal assumptions explicitly and reflexively. Stutz and Sachs (2018) underscore the potential for a reflexive historical lens to contribute to research on corporate social responsibility (CSR), developing a research strategy attuned to the normative agenda of CSR which they term the *reflexive historical case study*. Luyckx and Janssens (2020) explore the role of ideological *discursive strategies* in (de)legitimacy struggles in the Great Recession in Belgium (see also Maclean, Harvey, Sillince and Golant, 2014; Maclean, Harvey, Golant and Sillince, 2020). Perchard and McKenzie (2020) examine the contribution that historical perspectives and methods can make to elucidating organizational *path dependence* in the context of the British aluminium industry. Scholars have also begun to explore the *uses of the past* in organizing, investigating, for example, the enduring influence of organizational founders often long after their decease (Basque and Langley, 2018; Maclean, Harvey, Suddaby and O'Gorman, 2018; Wadhwani, Suddaby, Mordhorst and Popp, 2018).

Interest is beginning to be focused on how the Global South might contribute to an agenda which hitherto has remained resolutely western in orientation, dominated by western-style rationality and 'narrative imperialism' (Phelan, 2005), impeding ethnic diversity and leaving little room for engagement with 'the other' (de Certeau, 1988: 3). Recent special issues on the topic of historical organization studies have sought to grapple with this issue (Barros, Coraiola, Maclean and Foster, 2021; Durepos, Maclean, Alcadipani and Cummings, 2020). In novel fashion, Pio and Syed (2020) explore the contribution that ancient inscriptions in India, Aśokan (273–232 BC) stelae, can make to expand our understanding of management learning on diversity.

In related fashion, researchers have begun to reinvestigate the origins of management education globally, finding that the principles of American management were not always as readily absorbed elsewhere as is often believed, but were resisted and nuanced to accommodate different cultural actualities (Cooke and Alcadipani, 2015; Üsdiken, 1997). Maclean, Shaw, Harvey and Booth (2020) show how dynamic knowledge networks known as 'management research groups' advanced practice-based learning to provide effective solutions to shared problems in interwar Britain. Given that history is constitutive (Jenkins, 2003), reconsidering the origins of management education and practice around the world may recast our understanding of these in the present and future (Cummings and Bridgman, 2011; Cummings, Bridgman, Hassard and Rowlinson, 2017; Khurana, 2007).

Historical organization studies demand both methodological and epistemological rigour (Maclean, Harvey and Stringfellow, 2017). Dual integrity rests on sound and robust investigatory procedures which pay due regard to the exacting standards applied in both organizational research and in history, where each is seen as complementary to the other. Wider methodological reflection drawn from the former can enliven debate and entail historiographical reflexivity in the latter (Decker, Rowlinson and Hassard, 2020). The 'rules of evidence', of verification, must be respected and observed (White, 1987: 67). The alternative would be for historical organization studies to condone a dilution of methodological standards, which would flout our overarching principle of dual integrity. It is precisely owing to unease over a potential lowering of the exacting standards demanded by history that some business historians have been wary of promoting greater use of history in organization studies, concerned that a preoccupation with theory might be linked to a lack of respect for and sensitivity to history. Bruce (2020) argues that there is currently a battle ongoing for the heart and soul of management and organizational history. White (1987: 164) warns of the dangers of historical dilettantism:

> If one is going to 'go to history', one had better have an address in mind rather than go wandering around the streets of the past like a *flaneur*. Historical *flaneurisme* is undeniably enjoyable, but the history we are living today is no place for tourists.

Organization theorists have related epistemological concerns centring on the 'uncritical embracing of history as an explanation of organizational structure, processes, and outcomes' (Kieser, 1994: 608). Yet, as the examples of theorization founded on historical analysis illustrated above have shown, history can be used to generate new theory (Suddaby et al., 2011; 2020). Methodological transparency is fundamental not only to spark interdisciplinary conversations and so build audiences for scholarship, but also to the important task of scholarly legitimation (McKenzie, Gordon and Gannon, 2019; Smith and Umemura, 2019). Scholarly communities function according to agreed norms of publication (Suddaby et al., 2011), and attracting scholarly legitimacy rests on evidence of authenticity and relevance. Being relevant is the taken-for-granted fundament of organization studies as a discipline. Transparency in the use of methods of both disciplines is likely to enable scholars of historical organization studies to self-construct their own relevance, and to shape the field accordingly.

The fragmentary data on which organizational historians regularly draw is often located in archives. Archival analysis exemplifies 'the historian's empirical method of choice' (Cooke and Alcadipani, 2015: 483). Yet, despite increasing exhortations to take history seriously, management scholars who venture into archives to use the sources to be found there remain relatively few and far between (McKinlay, 2013). There are, of course, exceptions to this (Tennent, Gillett and Foster, 2020; Maclean, Shaw et al., 2020), including many of the chapters featured in this volume. Cummings et al. (2017) stress that archival work is demanding. Critical issues revolve around access, copyright and digitization, demanding skilful negotiation on the part of the organizational researcher. Archives involve layers of accessibility. Visitors accorded access enter unknown territory where they are dependent on the cooperation of archivists, who serve as key gatekeepers. Archives themselves are often incomplete (Cooke and Alcadipani, 2015). Moreover, they are not objective, disinterested places, but rather are implicated in power relations, being spaces where material has been selected and sifted through, where knowledge is produced and inscribed and discourse is formed (de Certeau, 1988; Foucault, 2002; Schwarzkopf, 2012). This underscores the importance of the *values* that organization scholars bring to history and that animate and frame their research (White, 1987: 164).

The assumptive epistemological historical dynamic that remains tacit and largely unacknowledged in much organizational research is uncovered and laid bare in historical organization studies (Suddaby et al., 2014). Attention to time and temporalities comes to the fore, illuminating past, present and projected futures (Hernes, 2014; Sewell, 2005). Braudel (1980) emphasizes the need to study very long expanses of time and to enquire what might be learned from these. An evolutionary approach of this nature can extend the scope of explication, casting light on the outcomes of long-lived historical processes. The long-run effects of specific courses of action may only be apparent over a lengthy timescale (Barton, Horváth and Kipping, 2016; Jones and Khanna, 2006), which is not to rid history of its messiness and contingency (Lippmann and Aldrich, 2014). Critical incidents and crucible events occur, take shape and emerge within 'these depths, this semistillness' that the *longue durée* frames (Braudel, 1980: 33). What Braudel (1980: 26) terms the 'dialectic of duration' implies long-lasting movements punctuated by shorter bursts of activity. Historians often begin from present concerns, such that the past represents a 'reconstitution of societies and human beings engaged in the network of human realities of today' (de Certeau, 1988: 11). Past and present are mutually implicated inasmuch as the 'function of history is to promote a profounder understanding of both past and present through the interrelation between them' (Carr, 1990: 68). History thus has a 'living role' to play whereby conceptualizations of past phenomena are subject to reinterpretation and re-evaluation over time as circumstances change and evolve (Ericson, Melin and Popp, 2015: 506). Although history is essentially backward-looking, in fact a forward-looking perspective gives scope for rethinking and reimagining, which may in turn enable alternative histories to develop and be written (Cummings and Bridgman, 2011;

Raff, 2013). It is in the interaction between these temporal perspectives – 'the dialectic of coming to be, having been, and making present' (Ricoeur, 1983: 61) – that the greatest scope resides for making meaningful contributions.

In other words, any historical project concerns not just history in the past but also history in the present and future, affecting the scope conditions wherein current and future choices are made (Schultz and Hernes, 2013; Wadhwani and Bucheli, 2014). Looking ahead to the prospects and challenges that historical organization studies must embrace, we collectively carve out space for new directions within the terrain of organizational research.

Historical organization studies in practice

Conceptual contributions

The writing of history, de Certeau (1988: xxvi) observes, concerns 'the study of writing as historical practice'. In Part II of our edited collection, Alistair Mutch explores whether it is possible to examine practices through historical study (Chapter 2). The study in question, founded on rich archival research, concerns the seemingly mundane practices performed in the rural parishes of the Churches of Scotland and England, which in turn shed light on differing ecclesiastical routines performed in the two churches. Although it is rare for organization theorists to examine organizations prior to the nineteenth century (Casson and Casson, 2013; Kieser, 1998; Newton, 2004), this comparative investigation delves into the intricacies and telling details of eighteenth-century church governance. Mutch points to the need to study practices as nouns, not verbs. What he finds is, first, that practices, even when identical in name, are moulded by specific temporal and spatial conjunctures. Second, he highlights that practices themselves have a history, albeit one which is often submerged in taken-for-granted routines that rarely emerge from the shadows of a past shrouding their sense. Where there is reification and solidification of past practices into rituals and routines, which are more available to scrutiny, the historical investigation of such practices is made possible. The great bulk of practice research, Mutch argues, fails to take account of the fact that routines are historically generated. Investigating them in this way may reveal novel, surprising aspects of the sociopolitical identities of the communities from which they took shape and form.

Critical history, according to Collingwood (1993: 386), can be applied to an infinite variety of topics, 'all of which become historical sources so far as historians can find ways of employing them as such'. In an innovative chapter on historical reflexivity (Chapter 3), Durepos and Vince blend emotion in organizations with a historical organization studies approach to focus on individual career achievement in the neo-liberal university, imbued with a logic of efficiency and productivity. Reflexivity, they assert, comprises an implicit historical aspect. Historical reflexivity is an iteratively reflective process whereby individuals create, both retrospectively and prospectively, nonlinear narratives of their past, present and future practices, animated by their own embodied history (Maclean, Harvey and Chia, 2012a). History is thus not only socially constructed, but also ontologically constitutive (Jenkins, 2003). In other words, we elaborate history as we engage in inscribing our lives. Durepos and Vince offer a more personal, reflexive take on historical organization studies that brings to the fore the lived experience of organizations. Their chapter is informed by a non-chronological conception of history, infused by emotion, which unsettles conventional ordering and implies a new relationship with past, present and future. Academics can recover meaning in their own lives, they conclude, by engaging in writing as a means of composing, and hence perhaps also discovering, the self.

Richard Badham, Todd Bridgman and Stephen Cummings take a novel approach to historical organization studies by critically exploring the genesis, history and evolution of a longstanding metaphor in organization theory, the iceberg, examining its continued relevance and reflexive use today (Chapter 4). It was de Certeau (1988: 312) who observed that metaphors used in history can signify many different things simultaneously, congealing into images whose meanings intersect: 'Through metaphor, a rhetorical means, and through ambivalence, a theoretical instrument, many things are in play in the same spot, transforming each spatial element into a volume where they intersect'. As a linguistic trope, the iceberg is suggestive of organizational silencing and the risks associated with speaking openly. It evokes unseen dangers obscured beneath the surface of organizational realities, the destructive effects of which can prove devastating. As such, its relevance at the time of writing, amid a global pandemic, is evident, where not only organizations but entire nations have been stopped in their tracks and 'shut down' by an invisible pestilence wreaking havoc with national health systems. This chapter provides a considered, reflective account of the iceberg-as-metaphor, in a bid to breathe new life into the discussion and improve its use in several ways: by recognizing the ambivalent endorsement the metaphor has garnered, by fostering an understanding of its openness and ambiguity and by illuminating present and past sensitivity to its limitations as a means of both 'seeing' and 'not seeing'. The iceberg draws attention to the layers beneath. As such, it attends to the necessity of plumbing those diverse emotions and politics that are often submerged, underlining the importance of pluralistic understanding, while warning of the danger of reifying assumptions.

In Chapter 5, Christiane Chihadeh explores the notion of historical consciousness in the production of critical historical studies, focusing on the relationship between the researcher, the practice of doing history and historical methods (Tennent et al., 2020). The subjectivity and reflexivity of the researcher, according to this viewpoint, are crucial. A critical realist approach that puts the emphasis on ontological foundations can encourage, she suggests, an emancipatory exploration of society and culture that enhances understanding of social issues. Informed by insights drawn from the work of Coraiola, Foster and Suddaby (2015), Chihadeh probes differing reconstructivist, constructivist and deconstructivist perspectives from history and the social sciences. Critical grounded theory is proposed as an apt methodology to operationalize historical research in a manner that expands interdisciplinary possibilities. Considered thus, archival ethnography illuminates the notion of serendipity as an endless process of discovery that emphasizes the emancipatory potential of the data collection process itself.

The act of division which separates past from present in modern historiography is taken to task by Bastion, Foster and Coraiola (Chapter 6), who focus on the richness and relevance of Indigenous cultures, where the past is understood as the shared, dynamic product of ongoing relations. In such mnemonic cultures, ways of knowing and making sense of the world are passed down through the oral tradition from generation to generation by elders who serve as stewards of knowledge and past experience. The importance of oral history may lie 'not in its adherence to facts but rather in its divergence from them, where imagination, symbolism, desire break in' (Portelli, 1981: 100), in this way fostering a re-enchantment of society (Suddaby, Ganzin and Minkus, 2017). The dialogue with 'the other' (de Certeau, 1988: 3) that western rationality, underpinned by socially constructed assumptions of linearity and continuous progress, has traditionally suppressed and the 'historic turn' has largely bypassed is championed by this chapter. Indigenous organizations, these authors observe, are unique and culturally embedded. In embracing Indigenous worldviews, where the relationship with nature and the environment is paramount and which chime with principles of pluralistic understanding, historical organization studies has much to gain. The legacy of colonization and its associated trauma is an enduring one (Barros and Wanderley, 2020). Hearing the voices of those silenced and excluded over centuries of western hegemony, bereft of agency and legitimacy, engages a moral imperative.

Theoretical applications

In Part III of our volume, Ruel, Dyer and Mills explore the act of gendered remembering in the context of the Canadian space programme of the 1960s, Alouette, which saw the launch of Alouette I and II satellites into space (Chapter 7). These authors assume a postmodern approach in examining the discursive processes at play in an organizational history in which white men exercised almost exclusive voice compared with the women who participated in the missions but were effectively silenced. Through exploring antenarratives – 'prospective (future-oriented) ways of sensemaking' (Boje, 2008: 13) – the authors aim to surface gendered subtexts to tease out different aspects in a study of silences, including who is performing them and the emotions which underpin and support them. The tacit 'meta-rules' (Mills and Murgatroyd, 1991) that inform such silences are probed in the partial tales of female participants in the programme. These include the assumption that women lacked interest in science, and that they should leave employment to marry or have children (Durepos, McKinlay and Taylor, 2017); moreover, the grand narratives that told epic tales of scientific prowess were naturally masculine in orientation, which fed into wider systems of domination and exclusion, serving the status quo. To honour the women concerned, bringing them out of the shadows cast in the past for scrutiny in the present and future, their anonymity is foregone so that they are no longer forgotten and silenced. In western cultures, 'the group (or the individual) is legitimized by what it excludes (this is the creation of its own space)' (de Certeau, 1988: 5). By conducting an important 'historical rescue and recovery' exercise, the authors enable the Alouette women to *reclaim* their space. They also bring to light a vital moral and social purpose in historical organization studies, furthering the development of feminist historiography that spotlights some inspirational women all too often ignored in received and hegemonic narratives.

Collection museums serve as microcosms whose guiding organizing principle is determined by the original collector-founder. Coman and Casey explore how the identity of a collection museum alters over time as well as to what degree it maintains ontological fealty to the collector-founder responsible for its genesis (Chapter 8). Drawing on emergent literature on collective memory (Halbwachs, 1950), organizational identity (Zundel, Holt and Popp, 2016), the discourse of history (Barthes, 1986) and institutional 'ghosts' (Orr, 2014), these authors examine how the identity of the founder comes to serve as a 'barometer' in the evolution of art history discourse, showing how founders' collection choices made many years previously are subsequently canonized. The empirical site of the research is the collection of Japanese ceramics assembled by American industrialist Charles Lang Freer (1854–1919), who legated his wide-ranging art collection to the Smithsonian Institution. In novel fashion, the chapter introduces a pioneering methodology that combines the use of archival methods commonly deployed in art history with social network analysis to contribute fresh insights on the interrelationships between the museum, its artefacts, the founder and the art markets in which they are located. The changing biographies of collections over time lead to 'afterlives' that are open to examination. It is the enmeshing of the founder's personal identity, perpetuated through institutional memory and storytelling, with the validation of seminal choices that results in her or his ongoing preservation in the museum's organizational identity.

Institutional entrepreneurship and the field of power are brought together by Maclean, Harvey and Suddaby, in Chapter 9, in their study of the creation of the global hotel industry in early-phase globalization – an example of collective agency in which Hilton played a formative part. Institutional researchers have largely failed to grapple with Bourdieu's (1996) construct of the field of power, despite its evident relevance for realizing a new organizational template. Drawing on rich archival data housed at the University of Houston, the chapter develops and refines understanding of the field of power in the context of institutional entrepreneurship. The field of power emerges not as a single, abstract entity, as it is commonly presented, but rather as intrinsically plural and highly differentiated, set within contrasting political milieus and jurisdictions in which Hilton strove to forge alliances with influential host-country elites (Maclean, Harvey and Press, 2006). These multidimensional *fields of power* were set apart not only by politics and governance regime but also by the alacrity with which they welcomed American business. The different temporalities which governed the opening of host-country hotels reflected the degrees of resistance and obstruction exhibited by local elites. The chapter also makes a methodological contribution. The rich historical case draws attention to deep institutional structures, the consequences of which may only be discernible over a lengthy period, highlighting links and interrelations otherwise unnoticed in an ahistorical account (Braudel, 1980; Heracleous and Barrett, 2001). Companies are composed of constructions, layers of sedimentation (Clegg, 1981), often concealing change from the observer. Considering the development of the global hotel industry from a historical perspective sheds light on how it evolved and unfolded in the long run. The received idea that global capitalism grew out of the efforts of US corporate leaders intent on exporting the American model (Djelic, 1998) is revised, revealing a new model more attuned to local specificities.

The field of cultural production comes to the fore in Kerr and Robinson's socio-historical study of the creation of the new Scottish parliament, a vital symbol of emergent nationhood (Chapter 10). The authors add to the literature on historical organization studies by developing a historical relational analysis that embraces Bourdieu's (1993) historical sociology, introducing the notions of historical homology and historical affinity. The chapter highlights the importance of the field of cultural production in national identity formation, contributing to the rebirth of a former democracy. Enric Miralles, the parliament's Catalan architect, drew inspiration from Charles Rennie Mackintosh and the Glasgow School of designers, seeking to key the new building to the Edinburgh landscape not as a monument to hegemonic power but as fundamentally democratic in ethos, while distinctively Scottish. The past provided a resource to be exploited, such that ancient Scottish symbols and emblems, including saltires, crow-stepped gables and a knot garden, became refashioned in contemporary style (Harvey, Press et al., 2011). Imagining the nation or 'nationizing' reveals itself as an ongoing process of (re)interpreting the past in which actors from the cultural field – including poets and novelists, as well as politicians and architects – take centre stage.

In his best-selling book *The Path*, Konosuke Matsushita, the founder of Panasonic, writes that 'achieving the status of a professional ... is not easy, and the effort required to maintain one's professionalism is likewise tremendous' (2010: 110). Sakai's chapter on the development of the nursing profession in Japan echoes this sentiment, chronicling the collective struggle of Japanese nurses over decades as they traversed the obstacle-strewn path to full professional recognition (Chapter 11). Sakai focuses on the interrelationship between institutional work and institutional outcomes from the 1880s to the present, charting an important shift in the nurses' relative power during this time. Drawing on archival data and interviews with nursing professionals, he shows how Japanese nurses, who at the outset of his study period were subordinate, low-status actors with limited capacity for agency, came to enjoy a relatively powerful position in Japanese healthcare. The changing power relations between nurses and doctors see the former expand their power to become recognized as critical partners of the latter. The chapter demonstrates the importance of adopting a wider understanding of agency and historical dynamics when studying institutional work. Writing during a worldwide pandemic, one can speculate whether nurses not only in Japan, but globally, might, alongside doctors, further expand the scope of their power in the future as the quintessential criticality of the tasks they perform and our total dependence upon them demonstrate the significance and salience of their vulnerability and bravery before the ravages of a pandemic.

In the penultimate chapter (Chapter 12) featuring theoretical applications, Soulsby examines processes of re-legitimation and control in a former state-owned enterprise in the Czech Republic, exploring the role of stories and collective sensemaking in building shared understanding and managerial legitimacy (Maclean, Harvey and Chia, 2012b). The speed of transformation experienced by Central and East European societies and organizations after the fall of the Berlin Wall in 1989 was spectacular, generating organizational dissonance (Hollinshead and Maclean, 2007). An organization's past nevertheless forms an important strategic resource through which organizational history can be (re)packaged for different constituencies (Ooi, 2001). The case study company concerned in Soulsby's study, anonymized as Volnské Strojírny a Slévárny (Vols), was visited by the author on multiple occasions from 1991 to 2011. It is unusual in organization studies for a company to be observed ethnographically over such a long period. However, this sustained fieldwork affords a rare level of insight, enhancing the author's capacity for *Verstehen* or interpretive understanding of the post-communist society in question (Soulsby, 2004; Weber, 1947). Equally, it is rare in historical work for an organization to be anonymized, given the importance of verification, though in organization studies this is the norm. The need to preserve the firm's anonymity in this case derives from the longitudinal nature of the study, the author having given her word early in the process not to disclose its identity. Soulsby traces the evolving reputation of the finance director from organizational 'hero' to 'villain' according to the company's changing fortunes. In doing so, she highlights the importance of control of the 'official' history; the preservation of archives and artefacts and command of formal public documents emerging as critical to retaining control of the ongoing historical narrative.

The book concludes with a chapter written by the editors that reiterates the importance of dual integrity by considering two recent treatments of the East India Company. One is by the historian William Dalrymple, the other by the social scientist Stewart Clegg, who is also an editor of this book. The difference between analyses largely oriented either to conceptualization or narration of history is underscored, as is the usefulness of the historian's labour for the social scientists' craft. Maintaining the focus on dual integrity, a history of the present is sketched prior to consideration of a history of the future that the present pandemic may be shaping. It is one that in many respects may afford a radical disjuncture with past organizational practices, indicating possible contours defining the history of the future.

Conclusion

In writing this book, we strive to be a catalyst both for developing the field and building a community of scholars with a shared interest in enacting historical organization studies. We recommend a greater porosity of boundaries to embrace varied ways of doing history in organization studies, as delineated above. Disciplinary boundaries are themselves 'artefacts of power' whose dominant paradigms resist redrawing to admit unorthodoxy and change (Steinmetz, 2007: 1). Interest in research combining theory with historical sources and methods is nevertheless plainly on the rise. The 'historic turn' can also be employed to generate a sense of belonging. Following its success as a political project, it is time, we suggest, to fulfil the promise of historical organization studies. The moment is now ripe to showcase what historical organization studies can contribute to research across a variety of domains, including strategy (Vaara and Lamberg, 2016; Suddaby et al., 2020), institutional entrepreneurship and institutional work (Mutch, 2007; Popp and Holt, 2013), organizational identity (Anteby and Molnár, 2012; Zundel et al., 2016) and Bourdieusian historical sociology (Harvey, Maclean et al., 2011; Harvey, Press et al., 2011). The chapters in this edited collection advance this agenda in several ways: First, as critical and theoretical research to extend and deepen what has already been accomplished; second, as empirically founded research with a theoretical focus. Further, as a collection, they help to map the terrain of this new direction in organizational research. Together, they demonstrate interdisciplinary breadth and intellectual curiosity (Holt and den Hond, 2013), aspiring to be 'analytical, creative, and bold' (Friedman and Jones, 2011: 1).

The narrative to this point suggests that history and organization studies have largely been separate worlds. This book moves beyond separate-world research to showcase reflexive empirical chapters on theorized history from both early career and more established scholars that exemplify historical organization studies in action, serving as an important landmark in the development of new directions. Our hope is that the studies it features will encourage other researchers of history and organization studies to get involved, to see how they might join and contribute to this stimulating agenda.

The front cover of this book shows the Tyne Bridge being built in Newcastle in 1928,[1] a bridge under construction, in the process of becoming, that was to become a prototype for the much larger Sydney Harbour Bridge, for which the steel was shipped from Middlesbrough in the north-east, by Dorman, Long & Co. Ltd. Our project, in many ways, began in Newcastle, where the four editors previously worked together and where, in June 2014, many authors featured in this volume gathered at the Association of Business Historians annual conference. We have been struck by just how appropriate the metaphor of the bridge is for our project of historical organization studies. Our project aims to bridge the gap between history and organization studies, bringing benefits to scholars from both disciplines. It seeks to suture together fragmented notions of past, present and future, in a process of becoming, mutually connected by the possibility of envisioning different potential futures. Bridges can sometimes be shrouded in fog or mist, like the haar that blows in off the North Sea, immortalized in Lindisfarne's 'fog on the Tyne', wholly or partially concealing their structure. We hope that this volume will provide a conceptual bridge that helps to bring some clarity to the exciting project of historical organization studies, still under construction and in a process of becoming, on which we have collectively embarked.

Note

1 Courtesy of Tyne & Wear Archives & Museums.

References

Aldrich, H.E., Ruef, M. and Lippmann, S. (2020). *Organizations evolving* (3rd edn). Cheltenham: Edward Elgar.
Anteby, M. and Molnár, V. (2012). Collective memory meets organizational identity: Remembering to forget in a firm's rhetorical history. *Academy of Management Journal*, 55 (3): 515–540.
Barros, A., Coraiola, D., Maclean, M. and Foster, W.M. (2021). History, memory, and the past in management and organization studies. *Revista de Administração de Empresas*, forthcoming.
Barros, A. and Wanderley, S. (2020). Decolonialism and management (geo)history: Is the past also a place? In Bruce, K. (ed.) (2020). *Handbook on research on management and organizational history*. Cheltenham: Edward Elgar, 192–211.
Barthes, R. (1986). *The rustle of language*. Berkeley and Los Angeles: University of California Press.
Barton, D., Horváth, D. and Kipping, M. (2016). Re-imagining capitalism for the long term. In Barton, D., Horváth, D. and Kipping, M. (eds.), *Re-imagining capitalism*. Oxford: Oxford University Press, 1–14.
Basque, J. and Langley, A. (2018). Invoking Alphonse: The founder figure as a historical resource for organizational identity work. *Organization Studies*, 39 (12): 1685–1708.
Boje, D. (2008). *Storytelling organizations*. London: Sage.
Bourdieu, P. (1993). *The field of cultural production*. Cambridge: Polity.
Bourdieu, P. (1996). *The state nobility: Elite schools in the field of power*. Cambridge: Polity.
Braudel, F. (1980). *On history*. Chicago: University of Chicago Press.
Bruce, K. (ed.) (2020). *Handbook on research on management and organizational history*. Cheltenham: Edward Elgar.
Bucheli, M. and Wadhwani, R.D. (eds.). (2014). *Organizations in time: History, theory, methods*. Oxford: Oxford University Press.
Carr, E.H. (1990). *What is history?* (2nd edn). London: Penguin Books.
Casson, M. and Casson, C. (2013). *The entrepreneur in history: From medieval merchant to modern business leader*. Basingstoke: Palgrave.
Clark, P. and Rowlinson, M. (2004). The treatment of history in organisation studies: Towards an 'historic turn'? *Business History*, 46 (3): 331–352.
Clegg, S.R. (1981). Organization and control. *Administrative Science Quarterly*, 26 (4): 545–562.
Clegg, S.R. (2006). The bounds of rationality: Power/history/imagination. *Critical Perspectives on Accounting*, 17 (7): 847–863.
Clegg, S.R. and Courpasson, D. (2007). The end of history and the futures of power. *Twenty-First Century Society*, 2 (2): 131–154.
Collingwood, R.G. (1993). *The idea of history*. Oxford: Oxford University Press.
Cooke, B. and Alcadipani, R. (2015). Toward a global history of management education: The case of the Ford Foundation and the São Paulo School of Business Administration, Brazil. *Academy of Management Learning & Education*, 14 (4): 482–499.

Coraiola, D., Foster, W.M. and Suddaby, R. (2015). Varieties of history in organization studies. In McLaren, P.G., Mills, A.J. and Weatherbee, T.G. (eds.), *The Routledge companion to management and organizational history*. Abingdon: Routledge, 206–221.
Cummings, S. and Bridgman, T. (2011). The relevant past: Why the history of management should be critical for our future. *Academy of Management Learning & Education*, 10 (1): 77–93.
Cummings, S., Bridgman, T., Hassard, J. and Rowlinson, M. (2017). *A new history of management*. Cambridge: Cambridge University Press.
De Certeau, M. (1988). *The writing of history*. New York: Columbia University Press.
Decker, S., Rowlinson, M. and Hassard, J. (2020). Rethinking history and memory in organization studies: The case for historiographical reflexivity. *Human Relations*. In press.
Deleuze, G. (2004). *Difference and repetition*. London: Continuum International.
Djelic, M.-L. (1998). *Exporting the American model*. Oxford: Oxford University Press.
Durepos, G., Maclean, M., Alcadipani, R. and Cummings, S. (2020). Historical reflections at the intersection of past and future: Celebrating 50 years of management learning. *Management Learning*, 51 (1): 3–16.
Durepos, G., McKinlay, A. and Taylor, S. (2017). Narrating histories of women at work: Archives, stories, and the promise of feminism. *Business History*, 59 (8): 1261–1279.
Durepos, G., Mills, A.J. and Helms Mills, J. (2008). Tales in the manufacture of knowledge: Writing a company history of Pan American World Airways. *Management and Organizational History*, 3 (1): 63–80.
Eisenhardt, K.M. (1989). Building theories from case study research. *Academy of Management Review*, 14 (4): 532–550.
Ericson, M., Melin, L. and Popp, A. (2015). Studying strategy as practice through historical methods. In Golsorkhi, D., Rouleau, L., Seidl, D. and Vaara, E. (eds.), *Strategy as practice* (2nd edn). Cambridge: Cambridge University Press, 506–519.
Foucault, M. (2002). *The archaeology of knowledge*. London: Routledge.
Friedman, W.A. and Jones, G. (2011). Business history: Time for debate. *Business History Review*, 85 (Spring): 1–8.
Gasparin, M., Green, W. and Schinckus, C. (2019). Shaping success through creative failure: A historical sensemaking analysis of the computerisation of the UK financial market. *Business History*, 1–22.
Geertz, C. (1973). *The interpretation of cultures*. New York: Basic Books.
Halbwachs, M. (1950). *La mémoire collective*. Paris: PUF.
Hall, J.R. (1992). Where history and sociology meet; Forms of discourse and sociohistorical inquiry. *Sociological Theory*, 10 (2): 164–193.
Harvey, C. and Jones, G. (1990). Business history in Britain into the 1990s. *Business History*, 32 (1): 5–16.
Harvey, C., Maclean, M., Gordon, J. and Shaw, E. (2011). Andrew Carnegie and the foundations of contemporary entrepreneurial philanthropy. *Business History*, 53 (3): 424–448.
Harvey, C., Maclean, M. and Suddaby, R. (2019). Historical perspectives on entrepreneurship and philanthropy. *Business History Review*, 93 (3): 443–471.
Harvey, C., Press, J. and Maclean, M. (2011). William Morris, cultural leadership and the dynamics of taste. *Business History Review*, 85 (2): 245–271.
Hatch, M.J. and Schultz, M. (2017). Toward a theory of using history authentically: Historicizing in the Carlsberg Group. *Administrative Science Quarterly*, 62 (4): 657–697.
Heller, M. and Rowlinson, M. (2019). Imagined corporate communities: Historical sources and discourses. *British Journal of Management*, 1–17.
Heracleous, L. and Barrett, M. (2001). Organizational change as discourse: Communicative actions and deep structures in the context of information technology implementation. *Academy of Management Journal*, 44 (4): 755–778.

Hernes, T. (2014). *A process theory of organization*. Oxford: Oxford University Press.
Hollinshead, G. and Maclean, M. (2007). Transition and organizational dissonance in Serbia. *Human Relations*, 60 (10): 1551–1574.
Holt, R. and den Hond, F. (2013). Sapere aude. *Organization Studies*, 34 (11): 1587–1600.
Jenkins, K. (2003). *Re-thinking history*. London: Routledge.
Jones, G. and Khanna, T. (2006). Bringing history (back) into international business. *Journal of International Business Studies*, 37 (4): 453–468.
Judt, T. with Snyder, T. (2013). *Thinking the twentieth century*. London: Vintage Books.
Khurana, R. (2007). *From higher aims to hired hands*. Princeton: Princeton University Press.
Kieser, A. (1994). Crossroads – why organization theory needs historical analyses – and how these should be performed. *Organization Science*, 5 (4): 608–620.
Kieser, A. (1998). From freemasons to industrious patriots: Organizing and disciplining in 18th century Germany. *Organization Studies*, 19 (1): 47–71.
Kipping, M. and Üsdiken, B. (2014). History in organization and management theory: More than meets the eye. *Academy of Management Annals*, 8 (1): 535–588.
Langley, A. (1999). Strategies for theorizing from process data. *Academy of Management Review*, 24 (4): 691–710.
Lippmann, S. and Aldrich, H.E. (2014). History and evolutionary theory. In Bucheli, M. and Wadhwani, R.D. (eds.), *Organizations in time: History, theory, methods*. Oxford: Oxford University Press, 124–146.
Luyckx, J. and Janssens, M. (2020). Ideology and (de)legitimation: The Belgian public debate on corporate restructuring during the Great Recession. *Organization*, 27 (1): 110–139.
Maclean, M., Harvey, C. and Chia, R. (2012a). Reflexive practice and the making of elite business careers. *Management Learning*, 43 (4): 385–404.
Maclean, M., Harvey, C. and Chia, R. (2012b). Sensemaking, storytelling and the legitimization of elite business careers. *Human Relations*, 65 (1): 17–40.
Maclean, M., Harvey, C. and Clegg, S.R. (2016). Conceptualizing historical organization studies. *Academy of Management Review*, 41 (4): 609–632.
Maclean, M., Harvey, C. and Clegg, S.R. (2017). Organization theory in Business and Management History: Current status and future prospects. *Business History Review*, 91 (3): 457–481.
Maclean, M., Harvey, C., Golant, B.D. and Sillince, J.A.A. (2020). The role of innovation narratives in accomplishing organizational ambidexterity. *Strategic Organization*, 1–29.
Maclean, M., Harvey, C. and Press, J. (2006). *Business elites and corporate governance in France and the UK*. Basingstoke: Palgrave Macmillan.
Maclean, M., Harvey, C., Sillince, J.A.A. and Golant, B.D. (2014). Living up to the past? Ideological sensemaking in organizational transition. *Organization*, 21 (4): 543–567.
Maclean, M., Harvey, C., Sillince, J.A.A. and Golant, B.D. (2018). Intertextuality, rhetorical history and the uses of the past in organizational transition. *Organization Studies*, 39 (12): 1733–1755.
Maclean, M., Harvey, C. and Stringfellow, L.J. (2017). Narrative, metaphor and the subjective understanding of historic identity transition. *Business History*, 59 (8): 1218–1241.
Maclean, M., Harvey, C., Suddaby, R. and O'Gorman, K. (2018). Political ideology and the discursive construction of the multinational hotel industry. *Human Relations*, 71 (6): 766–795.
Maclean, M., Shaw, G., Harvey, C. and Booth, A. (2020). Management learning in historical perspective: Rediscovering Rowntree and the British interwar management movement. *Academy of Management Learning & Education*, 19 (1): 1–20.

Matsushita, K. (2010). *The path*. New York: McGraw Hill.
McKenzie, N.G., Gordon, J. and Gannon, M. (2019). A spirit of generosity: Philanthropy in the Scotch whisky industry. *Business History Review*, 93 (3): 529–552.
McKinlay, A. (2013). Following Foucault into the archives: clerks, careers and cartoons. *Management and Organizational History*, 8 (2): 137–154.
Mills, A.J. and Murgatroyd, S.J. (1991). *Organizational rules: A framework for understanding organizations*. Maidenhead: Open University Press.
Mills, A.J., Suddaby, R., Foster, W.M. and Durepos, G. (2016). Revisiting the historic turn 10 years later: Current debates in management and organizational history. *Management and Organizational History*, 11 (2): 67–76.
Mutch, A. (2007). Reflexivity and the institutional entrepreneur: A historical exploration. *Organization Studies*, 28 (7): 1123–1140.
Mutch, A. (2018). Practice, substance, and history: Reframing institutional logics. *Academy of Management Review*, 43 (2): 242–258.
Newton, T. (2004). From freemasons to the employee: Organization, history and subjectivity. *Organization Studies*, 25 (8): 1363–1387.
Ooi, C.-S. (2001). Persuasive histories: Decentering, recentering and the emotional crafting of the past. *Journal of Organizational Change Management*, 15 (6): 606–621.
Orr, K. (2014). Local government chief executives' everyday hauntings: Towards a theory of organizational ghosts. *Organization Studies*, 35 (7): 1041–1061.
Perchard, A. and McKenzie, N.G. (2020). Aligning to disadvantage: How corporate political activity and strategic homophily create path dependence in the firm. *Human Relations*, 1–29.
Phelan, J. (2005). Who's here? Thoughts on narrative identity and narrative imperialism. *Narrative*, 13 (3): 205–210.
Pio, E. and Syed, J. (2020). Stelae from ancient India: Pondering anew through historical empathy for diversity. *Management Learning* 51 (1): 109–129.
Popp, A. and Holt, R. (2013). The presence of entrepreneurial opportunity. *Business History*, 55 (1): 9–28.
Portelli, A. (1981). The peculiarities of oral history. *History Workshop Journal*, 12 (1): 96–107.
Raff, D.M.G. (2013). How to do things with time. *Enterprise and Society*, 14 (3): 435–466.
Ricoeur, P. (1983). *Time and narrative: Vol. 1*. Chicago: University of Chicago Press.
Rowlinson, M., Hassard, J. and Decker, S. (2014). Strategies for organizational history: A dialogue between historical theory and organization theory. *Academy of Management Review*, 39 (3): 250–274.
Sandberg, J. and Tsoukas, H. (2011). Grasping the logic of practice: Theorizing through practical rationality. *Academy of Management Review*, 36 (2): 338–360.
Schultz, M. and Hernes, T. (2013). A temporal perspective on organizational identity. *Organization Science*, 24 (1): 1–21.
Schwarzkopf, S. (2012). What is an archive – and where is it? Why business historians need a constructive theory of the archive. *Business Archives*, 105: 1–9.
Selznick, P. (1957). *Leadership in administration: A sociological interpretation*. Berkeley and Los Angeles: University of California Press.
Sewell, W.H. (2005). *Logics of history: Social theory and social transformation*. Chicago: University of Chicago Press.
Smith, A.D. and Umemura, M. (2019). Prospects for a transparency revolution in the field of business history. *Business History*, 61 (6): 1–23.
Soulsby, A. (2004). Who is observing whom? Fieldwork roles and ambiguities in organisational case study research. In Clark, E. and Michailova, S. (eds.), *Fieldwork in transforming societies: Understanding methodology from experience*. Basingstoke: Palgrave Macmillan, 39–56.

Steinmetz, G. (2007). The relations between sociology and history in the United States: The current state of affairs. *Journal of Historical Sociology*, 20 (1/2): 1–12.

Stutz, C. and Sachs, S. (2018). Facing the normative challenges: The potential of reflexive historical research. *Business and Society*, 57 (1): 98–130.

Suddaby, R., Coraiola, D., Harvey, C. and Foster, W.M. (2020). History and the microfoundations of dynamic capabilities. *Strategic Management Journal*, 41: 530–556.

Suddaby, R., Foster, W.M. and Mills, A.J. (2014). Historical institutionalism. In Bucheli, M. and Wadhwani, R.D. (eds.), *Organizations in time: History, theory, methods*. Oxford: Oxford University Press, 100–123.

Suddaby, R., Foster, W.M. and Quinn-Trank, C. (2010). Rhetorical history as a source of competitive advantage. In Baum, J.A.C. and Lampel, J. (eds.), *Globalization of strategy research*, 27: 147–173. London: Emerald.

Suddaby, R., Foster, W.M. and Quinn-Trank, C. (2016). Organizational re-membering: Rhetorical history as identity work. In *The Oxford handbook of organizational identity*. Oxford: Oxford University Press, 297–316.

Suddaby, R., Ganzin, M. and Minkus, A. (2017). Craft, magic and the re-enchantment of the world. *European Management Journal*, 35 (3): 285–296.

Suddaby, R., Hardy, C. and Huy, Q.N. (2011). Introduction to special topic forum: Where are the new theories of organization? *Academy of Management Review*, 36 (2): 236–246.

Taylor, S., Bell, E. and Cooke, B. (2009). Business history and the historiographical operation. *Management and Organizational History*, 4 (2): 151–166.

Tennent, K.D., Gillett, A.G. and Foster, W.M. (2020). Developing historical consciousness in management learners. *Management Learning*, 51 (1): 73–88.

Üsdiken, B. (1997). Importing theories of management and organization: The case of Turkish academia. *International Studies of Management and Organization*, 26 (3): 33–46.

Vaara, E. and Lamberg, J.-A. (2016). Taking historical embeddedness seriously: Three historical approaches to advance strategy process and practice research. *Academy of Management Review*, 41 (4): 633–657.

Wadhwani, R.D. and Bucheli, M. (2014). The future of the past in management and organization studies. In Bucheli, M. and Wadhwani, R.D. (eds.), *Organizations in time: History, theory, methods*. Oxford: Oxford University Press, 3–30.

Wadhwani, R.D. and Jones, G. (2014). Schumpeter's plea: Historical reasoning in entrepreneurship theory and research. In Bucheli, M. and Wadhwani, R.D. (eds.), *Organizations in time: History, theory, methods*. Oxford: Oxford University Press, 192–216.

Wadhwani, R.D., Suddaby, R., Mordhorst, M. and Popp, A. (2018). History as organizing: Uses of the past in organization studies. *Organization Studies*, 39 (12): 1663–1683.

Weber, M. (1947). *The theory of social and economic organization*. New York: Oxford University Press.

White, H. (1987). *The content of the form: Narrative discourse and historical representation*. Baltimore: Johns Hopkins University Press.

Zald, M.N. (1993). Organization studies as a scientific and humanistic enterprise: Toward a reconceptualization of the foundations of the field. *Organization Science*, 4 (4): 513–528.

Zundel, M., Holt, R. and Popp, A. (2016). Using history in the creation of organizational identity. *Management and Organizational History*, 11 (2): 211–235.

PART II
Conceptual advances

2

WRITING THE HISTORY OF PRACTICES

Alistair Mutch

This chapter draws on the idea of historical organization studies – 'organizational research that draws extensively on historical data, methods, and knowledge to promote historically informed theoretical narratives attentive to both disciplines' (Maclean, Harvey and Clegg, 2016: 609) in order to address the question of the degree to which it is feasible to investigate practices through historical investigations. It does so in order to address the focus on practices that is promulgated by Roger Friedland (2014) in his formulation of institutional logics. The chapter begins with a discussion of the place of practices in institutional logics, distinguishing practices as nouns from practise as a verb. The relative neglect of practices in historical work is explored, drawing on some observations by Foucault (2009). The historical problems posed by the nature of practices are then discussed, followed by an example that draws on both secondary and archival work, the ecclesiastical visitation. Such practices are discussed across both time periods and denominations within Western Christianity, building in particular on work carried out on the records of the Church of Scotland. The conclusion then argues that historical investigation of practices is not only feasible but also necessary in order to ground conceptualizations of logics.

The institutional logics perspective, one that has gained in influence in institutional studies of organizational life, was first presented by Roger Friedland and Robert Alford in 1991. Their starting point was a desire to 'bring society back in', as the title of their essay announced. Society, they argued, could be conceptualized as comprising a number of institutional spheres, each with its own logics and possessing relative autonomy. For them, institutions are combinations of symbolic constructions and material practices that give meaning to the ways in which people engage in their social and organizational life. They are few in number, operate at the societal level and are enduring in character. This perspective has been developed, most notably in the work of Patricia Thornton, William Ocasio and Michael

Lounsbury (2012), and their notion of logics as decomposable and modular has found considerable traction in the organizational literature. It has, however, been critiqued, notably by Friedland (2012) and Mutch (2019). The details of such critiques are not the concern of this chapter, but one relevant observation is the relatively thin use of history in their formulations. Friedland has taken the logics perspective in a different direction, one which influences the current discussion. He draws on an Aristotelian notion of substance as 'the foundation, or essence, of a thing that cannot be reduced to its accidental properties that attach to it nor to the materiality of its instances' (Friedland, 2009: 55). For him, 'Institutions have logics. An institutional logic is a bundle of practices organized around a particular substance and its secondary derivatives from which the normativity of those practices is derived' (Friedland, 2009: 61). Further, 'institutional substances cannot be directly observed, but are immanent in the practices that organize an institutional field, values never exhausted by those practices, practices premised on faith' (Friedland, 2009: 61). It follows from this formulation that an exploration of practices is central to the enterprise.

Defining and exploring practices

This chapter distinguishes between practise, as a verb, and practices, as nouns. Practise in the former sense is widely used, especially given the influence of practice theory in the work of social theorists such as Pierre Bourdieu and Anthony Giddens. In order to illustrate the distinction, we can examine the argument put forward by the sociologist Margaret Archer. In her discussion, practice is that which obtains, as distinct from official formulations. That is, the focus is on what persons actually do, as opposed to what they are told to do or what they 'ought' to do. Thus, Archer contrasts what Roman Catholics do in relation to sexual practices (contraception, extra-marital sex) with the official position on such practices. She then goes on to question the degree to which membership of the Catholic faithful depends on shared knowledge or understanding of those official positions. 'Every Sunday', she observes, 'it is the duty of the faithful to say the Creed but, were it broken down into its component propositions, the most diverse array of understood meanings would result' (Donati and Archer 2015: 174). I argue that the saying of the Creed is the practice, and it is the saying – rather than the understanding – that is important. This becomes clearer when we take a comparative perspective. Creeds are a statement of official doctrines, boiled down from more abstruse theological debates. Other branches of Christianity also incorporate the recitation of such creeds into their liturgical practices, notably the Church of England in its Book of Common Prayer. In turn, this should be seen in the context of a wider practice, which is that of a specification for conducting services of worship. To be sure, such practices can be contested, but other Christian denominations reject both the recitation of creeds and tightly structured forms of worship. As opposed to creeds, those in the Reformed Protestant tradition have catechisms (Mutch, 2017b). The faithful are expected to understand these and, indeed, to recite them, but not as part of an act of worship. Rather, they are used for education and, in particular, as a test for worthiness to participate in an important practice, that of communion. The opposition to structured worship then becomes an article of faith in itself; a badge of commitment to a set of beliefs and practices, as with the Presbyterian commitment to extempore prayers. This is not to say that such denominations do not have forms of structure in their services, but, for the present purpose, the contrast points up the importance of specified practices in Roman Catholic liturgical practice and, from this, identification with the faith through participation in taken-for-granted ways of acting.

Foucault, in his study of the practice of auricular confession, noted that:

> The history of ecclesiastical institutions has been written. The history of religious doctrines, beliefs, and representations has been written. There have also been attempts to produce the history of real religious practices, namely, when people confessed, took communion, and so on. But it seems to me that the history of the techniques employed, of the reflections on these pastoral techniques, of their development, application, and successive refinements, the history of the different types of analysis and knowledge linked to the exercise of pastoral power, has never really been undertaken.
>
> *(Foucault, 2009: 150)*

Examining practices in a historical context poses distinct challenges. The nature of those challenges is exemplified by looking at how contemporary social scientists investigate practices (Decker et al, 2018). There is a stream of research that explores routines in organizations (Feldman, 2000; Feldman and Pentland, 2003; Pentland and Feldman, 2005). With the starting point that the performance of routines often departs from how they are laid down in procedure manuals, modes of investigation that prioritize qualitative, in-depth exploration of situated practices are employed. Some form of observation is often preferred, given that interviews are often imperfect means of eliciting the specificities of practices. Much performance is tacit in nature, meaning that participants might not be aware of the nuances that an observer might tease out. All these considerations pose challenges for the historical reconstruction of practices, given that access to observe is impossible. The closest, perhaps, that historians have come is in employing oral historical methods (Tosh, 2000: 193–210). Although they are subject to the problems of faulty recall and forgetfulness that plague all retrospective accounts, oral history has proved valuable in reconstructing work practices. It is often the very mundane practices that are best recalled, especially when they have been ingrained as part of daily activities. Sometimes this can be the only means of recovering practices that have not made it into the formal historical record. In the early twentieth century, for example, farm servants in the north of Lancashire were hired on an annual basis at hiring fairs. These can be reconstructed from newspaper accounts, but such accounts do not reveal 'runaway' hirings of those immediately dissatisfied with the bargain they had struck – especially if what had been offered did not live up to the initial promise – who could legitimately seek a new place (Mutch, 1991). However, such accounts are dependent on living informants, which places severe limitations on historical reach. It might seem, then, that historical practices are largely irrecoverable, tantalizingly beyond our reach.

There are, however, concerns about the exploration of routines in organization studies that suggest that historical work still has much to offer. The resource intensiveness of observational techniques can mean that only relatively small sweeps of time can be explored. Sometimes, the episodic nature of such enquiries raises doubts about whether the 'routine' element of practices is being missed. This is compounded by the focus on the unique nature of specific performances. As Sennett argues in his critique of Erving Goffman's sensitive observation of how roles are performed,

> [e]ach of the 'scenes' in his purview is a fixed situation. How the scene came into being, how those who play roles in it change the scene by their acts, or, indeed, how each scene may appear or disappear because of larger historical forces at work in the society – to these questions Goffman is indifferent.
>
> (Sennett, 2002: 35–36)

In addition, the observer, no matter how careful and sensitive, has access to only one aspect of a routine that by its nature involves a network of other actors and their material props. Informants, that is, may have only partial access to the social world they inhabit. The reasons they give to explain aspects of that social world may be plausible but misleading. Comparative lawyers have debated the question of understanding legal systems from the outside. On one account, such attempts are doomed to failure, as the formal rules and practices evident to outsiders hide the informal understandings only available to insiders. However, against this, James Whitman (2013) has traced the history of dignitary law in the German legal system, contrasting it with US equivalents. The focus on human dignity in German provisions has no equivalence in the USA, he notes. German jurists, when asked about the roots of anti-hate speech laws, point to the legacy of fascism. However, Whitman, exploring the historical evolution of laws protecting human dignity in the German system, points to their origins in the aristocratic duelling culture of the nineteenth century. 'Interviewing local informants', he concludes, 'is a very poor way of fully understanding what is going on in European dignitary law. The participants themselves do not understand where their system came from, nor why it takes the form it takes' (Whitman 2013: 334).

One interesting example of how a historian has risen to the challenge of finding evidence to shed light on historical practices is that supplied by the historian of English localities, Keith Snell (2006). He was interested in exploring the changing nature of identification with place, especially changes in the attachment to place in English rural life brought about by increased social and geographical mobility. In order to explore this, he hit upon an unusual source: memorial inscriptions on gravestones. Reasoning that carving letters on gravestones was an expensive operation and one involving limited space, he argued that this necessitated a selection process. The choice of words to describe the deceased could therefore give an indication of changing patterns of attachment to place. Inscriptions that gave a place of residence, or used phrases such as 'of this parish', would seem to indicate a degree of attachment, a public statement that being from a place was worthy of commemoration. Using a sample of more than 16,000 gravestones in 87 burial grounds, he was able to show that this attachment persisted until the turn of the twentieth century, when mentions of place began to be replaced by reference to more personal qualities, such as the relation to other family members. As he notes, memorial inscriptions provide evidence that, 'People were once described, given an identity, and their behaviour even accounted for, by their place and their occupation in it, however parochial that might be' (Snell, 2006: 492). This imaginative use of what otherwise would seem mundane and taken-for-granted, of interest only to genealogists, indicates that historical sources can come in a range of forms. Often, for the historian, it is the mundane document, that which was produced as a by-product of operations, that is of most value.

Of course, much depends here on accidental survivals. In the eighteenth-century Church of Scotland, there was the practice of visitations (Mutch, 2015). Here, a committee would be formed to visit a parish and pose a series of questions to the minister, other church officials and heads of household. A complementary and integral part of this practice was the 'revision' of parish records. This involved the reading of parish registers, both of decisions made and monies spent, in order to produce a report. Often, we only have the summary of such inspections and the recommendations that ensued. On many occasions, it seems that the results were given in verbal feedback and not minuted, and so are lost to us. But, in one case, a chance survival gives us considerable insight into not just the operation of the practice, but also the wider logic that it embodied. Bound into the eighteenth-century session register of Dailly in the presbytery of Ayr is a set of working notes, written in small script on scraps of paper. These clearly represent the thinking of those charged with revising session registers in about 1733. The writer of the notes picked up 43 separate items of concern, all carefully cross-referenced to the pages of the register. He found 14 cases where the sederunt (that is, the record of attendance) had not been recorded and a further three where the session did not either open or close with prayer. In other words, these were matters of very detailed recording, as opposed to matters of principle, and one gets the impression of a very pernickety reviser. At one point, for example, it was observed that two elders were ordained without an edict being moved, but, when one turns to the minutes, it is found that the edict had been served and recorded previously. The same obtains when four examples were found where communion had been intimated but it had not been recorded as celebrated. In a further eight cases, the reviser was concerned that sentences of discipline being satisfied were recorded without a session being constituted, although it seems that this was often simply a record of the completion of a previously recorded decision. This level of attention to detail suggests something of what lay behind the bland notes about verbal representations. The revision of records, that is, could be a very thorough process that must have played a part in engendering a particular style of record keeping, almost obsessive in its attention to detail (Mutch, 2015: 72).

The practices to be examined and the logic that they instantiate are, therefore, those of religion. There is, of course, a voluminous literature on the relationship between a religious logic, premised ultimately on faith, and economic forms of logic, most notably that engendered by Weber (McKinlay and Mutch, 2015). Discussions of the relationship between Protestantism and the rise of capitalism have focused on the empirical warrant for Weber's assertions, as well as on the very nature of those assertions. However, debates have tended to focus on belief, most notably the doctrine of predestination and the elect. Such debates rumble on with little sign of conclusion, but the work examined here was animated by a different approach (Mutch, 2009). It asked, drawing on insights from both Foucault and new institutional theory, whether we should be examining the practices involved in the performance of religious faith. These practices were seen to take two principal forms. Rituals, such as prayer and its embodied performance, were seen to perform religion, to call it into being. But behind those rituals stood routines, routines of governance and accountability. Such routines were surfaced by asking the question, what did it take for ritual performances to be enacted? The subsequent research engendered by this alternative conceptualization took as its prime focus the taken-for-granted practices of the Presbyterian Church of Scotland, with a comparative but slightly less-developed contrast with equivalent practices (or lack of) in the Anglican Church of England (Mutch, 2011, 2012b, 2013, 2015).

The contrast developed here raises questions about the nature and value of comparative history. Some historians are suspicious about such endeavours, arguing that they neglect specificities within different societies (Gorski, 2018). However, there are two responses to such critiques. One is to acknowledge, with Ludmilla Jordanova, the 'constant attention to the concepts and categories, the frameworks, analytical procedures and theoretical ideas that making systematic comparisons demands' (Jordanova, 2019: 3). In the present case, the primary focus is on the routines that distinguish local practices of governance as outlined above. The second justification is that provided by Paul Veyne, when he observes that,

> if in order to study a civilization, we limit ourselves to reading what it says itself – that is, to reading sources relating to this one civilization – we will make it more difficult to wonder at what, in this civilization, was taken for granted.
>
> *(Veyne, 1984: 7)*

Comparative work, that is, can be of great value when we are considering routine practices in making what appears to be taken for granted strange.

My own research on ecclesiastical routines forms the basis for the next section, which inevitably generates a high degree of self-citation. It draws a series of contrasts between Scottish and English practices of local church governance in the eighteenth century. The contrasts are based on published work derived from extensive archival research. I use references to my published work to point to places where the argument presented here in outline is fleshed out in more detail. To avoid overburdening the text with detailed archival references, I cite instead the outlet where such material was used. It is important at the outset to point out that the evidence base for such contrasts is much stronger for Scotland than for England, for reasons that will become clearer below. However, the point for the current purpose is to show the possibilities of researching practices in historical time periods, the challenges of doing so and the gains that can be realized.

Contrasting governance and accountability routines

To put some initial boundaries around the object of enquiry, the contrasts are drawn between practices in, respectively, the Church of England and the Church of Scotland. Although other Christian denominations were active in the period, both the churches were officially established by law and were the bodies to which the majority of the faithful adhered. Further, it was their practices that were most widespread and that coloured secular activities to the greatest extent. In addition, the research resulting in the identification of contrasting practice was carried out in rural parishes, excluding the impact of other secular activities and, more importantly, representing the heartlands of each church, their 'ideal type' of church governance. As their organizational structures formed the context in which local practices operated, it is important to outline these. The Church of Scotland was Presbyterian in both theology and ecclesiology. At the local level, each parish had a kirk 'session', a body of some six or so men (and they were always men in this period) ordained as elders to serve for life. The kirk session had to be chaired or 'moderated' by the clerical incumbent, the minister. The proceedings of the session were recorded in registers of discipline, which were subject to the scrutiny of the presbytery. The presbytery comprised several parishes (usually between 10 and 15) and was composed of parish ministers plus selected elders. In turn, the presbyteries, which usually met monthly, were grouped in regional synods, which met twice a year to consider matters of policy. The presbytery also chose delegates, both a minister and an elder, to attend the annual general assembly. Meeting in Edinburgh, this body debated church policy and acted as a final court of appeal. Thus, the Church of Scotland had a carefully designed system of accountability and responsibility. By contrast, the Church of England had an Episcopalian polity. That is, authority flowed down from the two archbishops (Canterbury and York) through a hierarchy of bishops, each of which had oversight of a collection of parishes grouped into a diocese. Dioceses were of varying size, but generally were beyond the capacity of personal oversight, and so a structure of archdeacons had responsibility for groups of parishes. Within these parishes, however, clerical incumbents (rectors or vicars, depending on their appropriation of the tithes (tenths) on agricultural produce for their support) had a considerable degree of autonomy. They owed their livings to local patrons and often, at this time, held multiple such livings. Their parish affairs were governed by churchwardens.

There were generally two wardens, one selected by the 'people' (often the better-off parishioners) and one by the incumbent. They served an annual term of office and were formally responsible to the 'vestry', a meeting of the better-off inhabitants. Church wardens had responsibility for the maintenance of the fabric of the church and order within it. Some, although not all, were also responsible for poor relief (Tate, 1983). By contrast, all kirk sessions in this period were responsible for poor relief, as well as the maintenance of discipline.

Already, one can see some significant differences in formal structure between the two churches, which at the theological level were both Protestant. As noted above, arrangements in the Church of Scotland were predicated on accurate and comprehensive record keeping. This even extended to provision for the archiving of such documents in university libraries (Mutch, 2012a). The consequence is that, although there are gaps, a considerable volume of material, amounting to some 4 million pages, has survived, preserved in the National Records of Scotland in Edinburgh. By contrast, record keeping and preservation in England were patchy and fragmented. Often, survival owed a great deal to chance, as with the following declaration in the parish book of Hickling, Nottinghamshire:

> This book having been held for many years by the late Mr William Collishaw, formerly Churchwarden, and on his death having come into the custody of his son, Mr Thos Wm Collishaw, was handed by the latter to the Rector, Revd Canon Skelton, for preservation in the Church Chest this 8th day of May 1895.
>
> *(Mutch, 2011: 84)*

Surviving records are held in county record offices across the country, often subject to local procedures for classification and categorization. The observations for England that follow are based on the records that survive for one district in Nottinghamshire, comprising some 50 parishes. This is clearly far from representative of practice across the country, and so it has been supplemented by diaries kept by clerical incumbents and, more rarely, by a serving churchwarden, for the period (Mutch, 2017a). The survival of records for Scotland in such volume and in one location made the research process far more straightforward and comprehensive, hence the imbalance in coverage already alluded to. However, these patterns of survival in themselves tell us much about the status of record keeping in both polities.

The differing patterns of record survival also sensitize us to the need to consider the form as well as the content of such records. In Scotland, records of meetings were held in bound registers which generally featured margins containing a note of the content, one which could be used both to cross-refer to other records and to enable the progress of a particular issue. In the earlier part of the period, the margin often contained financial details such as the amount of money collected (Mutch, 2016a). Over time, these figures moved into a separate part of the register and then into a separate book of account (Mutch, 2012a). Such books of account were generally organized with income, or the 'charge', on one page and expenditure, or 'discharge', on the facing page. Such forms of presentation enabled both a cross-reference to the relevant decision and a means of calculating the balance. Such consistency of format was absent in England. In the sample of records examined, very few vestry minutes survive, and those that do were often fragmentary, on separate sheets of paper. Accounts, too, varied wildly in format. Very frequently, no transaction details have survived, with accounting statements being simply a bald statement of the concluding balance. Sometimes this was composed of an amount collected offset by the total expended, but in one parish, Whysall, the minute for one year was simply 'William Case in Hand on the Church account 15s 7d' (Mutch, 2011: 79).

What such records can give us an indication of is the structure of meetings. In Scotland, such meetings were generally at monthly intervals, and minutes start by recording attendance. Indeed, sessions failing to record attendance were subject to censure when registers were 'revised'. At one of these meetings, accounts were reviewed and a balance was struck. By the end of the century, such meetings happened at least half yearly, generally in June and December, and in a small number of cases quarterly. At such meetings, a balance was struck and decisions were taken about the distribution of funds. By contrast, meetings in England were generally annual events, at which accounts were 'given up'. Other meetings were held on an ad hoc basis. Attendance was limited to those of the 'principal inhabitants' who chose to attend. Thomas Turner, shopkeeper and diary keeper of East Hoathley, East Sussex, provides a vivid account of such meetings:

> After dinner I went down to Jones's to the vestry ... Wm. Piper was chosen overseer, Jos. Fuller electioner; Jn. Cayley churchwarden, Jos. Durrant electioneer ... We had several warm arguments at our vestry today and several volleys of execrable oaths oftentime resounded from almost all sides of the room, a most rude and shocking thing at public meetings.
>
> (Vaisey, 1984: 204)

Absent from such meetings, in a pattern which is commonly confirmed by other clerical diaries of the period, was the clerical incumbent. The famous clerical diary keeper Parson James Woodforde of Weston Longville, Norfolk, was renowned for recording the smallest details of his life, down to the meals he ate. However, he rarely mentions parish meetings and appears to have only attended one (Mutch, 2017a). By contrast, Scottish kirk sessions could not meet unless the minister was present to take the chair.

From the surviving records, it is possible to draw some conclusions about the financial consequences of the practices outlined. In Scotland, of a total of 1,052 annual balances examined, only 38, or just over 4 per cent, were negative (that is, expenditure exceeded income; Mutch, 2015: 117). In stark contrast, of the 672 balances examined for Nottinghamshire, 53 per cent were negative (Mutch, 2015: 159). This meant that, in Nottinghamshire, churchwardens were frequently out of pocket at the end of their term of office, often having to wait some time to recoup their losses. In turn, this meant that only wealthier inhabitants could afford to take office in anticipation of potential losses. By contrast, the corporate and enduring nature of the Scottish kirk session meant that practices such as budgeting and forecasting expenditure and income were feasible.

One final observation can be made about the location of these practices. When Turner makes reference to 'Jones's', he meant the village public house. Other sources indicate that parish meetings were frequently held in pubs, and that some of the parish money was spent on a meal for attendees. For example, in Edwalton in 1726, we find the entry, 'Paid for ale when these accounts was given up 2s 6d' (Mutch, 2011: 79). By contrast, meetings in Scotland were either in the church or, exceptionally, in the manse (the minister's house), and they certainly did not involve sociability. One minister, George Skene Keith, could thus proudly announce, in an explicit contrast to English practice, that, 'The Elders, or Churchwardens, receive no recompence – not even a dinner from the funds of the Church Session, which are applied solely to the relief of the poor' (Keith, 1811: 179).

Moving from the local level to viewing churches as national organizations, we can observe efforts to regulate and examine local activities through the medium of visitations. Forms of visitation had been inherited from the traditions of Roman Catholicism, but they were adapted to meet the very different structures of the two churches (Mutch, 2017b). In the Church of England, churchwardens were responsible for replying to sets of questions coming from their bishop and enacted by the archdeacon. However, several writers on the church in the eighteenth century have commented on the ineffectiveness of church discipline as expressed in the annual archdeacon's visitations. They note the frequent recording of '*omnia bene*' (all is well) in churchwardens' returns to the questions posed by archdeacons before their visitations (Spaeth, 2000: 64–72; Gregory and Chamberlain, 2003: 160, 183, 232). In other words, visitations became formulaic rituals. By contrast, visitations were carried out in more active fashion in Scotland. Here, they were the responsibility of the presbytery, which established committees to visit parishes on a rolling basis. In practice, this proved too exacting, and attention shifted to the revision of records, both registers of discipline and books of account.

What one can conclude from these evident contrasts is that there were very different logics of governance and accountability at work in the two countries, embedded and enacted in taken-for-granted practices. In Scotland, accountability was systemic, based on a careful specification of roles and responsibilities and supported by detailed record keeping (Mutch, 2014). By contrast, in England, the practices indicate a personal logic of accountability, shaped by custom and tradition, in which trust was placed in the character of officeholders (Mutch, 2013). If we pull out still further, we can see that such practices articulated with the wider logics at work in both societies. Scotland preserved its own systems of education and law, as well as religion, after the Treaty of Union with England in 1707. The education system aspired, based on the Reformation settlement that established Presbyterianism, to provide basic education in every parish, principally to enable the faithful to read the scriptures. The benign, if unintended, consequence was high levels of literacy. The legal system was one which owed a great deal to Roman law, in which legal processes featured extensive written documents. Both the legal and the educational systems thus complemented and fostered the focus on the written word that was such an important part of Presbyterian church governance (Mutch, 2012b). By contrast, English law was a common law tradition, based on judge-made law rather than the written system of Roman law. The education system was patchy and fragmented (Simon, 1960). At its apex were the universities of Oxford and Cambridge, with their focus on education in the classics as the source of the formation of character. The focus on character gelled well with local systems of governance.

This brief comparative outline of the routines that lay behind the rituals of the established Churches of England and Scotland in the eighteenth century highlights two important features of practices. The first is that practices, even if they have the same name, vary in content across time and space. The involvement of lay members of the church, which varied according to the ecclesiological commitments of different denominations, was a particular differentiator in imparting distinctive content to practices that otherwise appeared to have similar form. The second is that practices themselves have a history (Mutch, 2016b). They do not simply emerge from performance. They are, of course, adjusted to meet the demands of that performance, as the framers of formal guidance cannot envisage all the combinations of circumstances that performance will confront. But that performance is often guided by explicit formulations that, in their turn, draw on historically shaped understandings. The practice, for example, of framing visitation visits through the issuing of centrally determined questionnaires has a long historical pedigree, even if the content evolved. Those performing routines, that is, draw on the resources they find most readily to hand.

Conclusion

Of course, as the historian of the English Civil War David Underdown observes, 'Historians cannot be direct observers of the rituals they analyse, cannot sit, as it were, at the ringside of the Balinese cock-fight' (1987: 44). Here, he is referencing the famous work of the anthropologist Clifford Geertz and his excavation of the layers of meaning revealed by careful observation of cock fights in Bali. Likewise, we cannot see how the actors in the practices we have examined reacted. Even where, as in the early visitations in Scotland, a full written account is present, this cannot convey the whispered conversations between the visitors or the force with which they may have conveyed their decisions. As we know, speech is not all, and the written record of it is insufficient: tone of voice or body language may radically alter meaning and reception. As one commentator observed about Scottish visitations, looking back from the end of the nineteenth century,

> These inquisitions did vastly more harm than good. They were dangerous weapons to put in the hands of every malcontent who had a grudge to gratify

or a fanatical grievance to express, with the risk of making a clergyman's life a burden to him and his congregation a terror.

(Graham, 1899: 334)

Our understanding of how such practices operate in the present can help us understand such dynamics, even if it is impossible to observe them. It is here that the tempered exercise of the historical imagination is unavoidable.

However, the historian has available other forms of evidence which can help us get a sense of the context in which practices such as visitations operated. Graham's account, cited above, was derived from a singular conception of the clergyman's position based on a very limited set of sources. The wider availability of archival material enables us to correct the many misleading assertions in his account and get a more measured picture of the practice of visitation and its importance in manifesting the logic of this particular instantiation of religious faith. As Underdown observes, while unable to engage in direct observation, awareness of the importance of mundane practices means that historians are:

increasingly aware that a civic or parish ritual – a mystery play, a Rogationtide procession – or a festive gathering – a midsummer revel, a football match, an election riot – may reveal important features of the social and religious, and even perhaps the political, identity of a community.

(Underdown, 1987: 44)

It is here that comparative work can be of great value when we are considering routines that otherwise appear as 'natural'. It enables us to bring the mundane into sharper focus, given that the same challenges can be addressed in very different ways.

Practices are a central part of Friedland's formulations. A closer examination of practices as emergent from human activity but, once emergent, solidified into rituals and routines, enables the investigation of the historical development of such practices. Developments in organizational theory have brought routines out of the shadows, foregrounding their potential to act as generative systems. However, much of this work fails to take account of the historical shaping of such routines, not only in their own internal development but also in the variable historical contexts in which they have been practised. A key dimension revealed by historical comparisons is the differential involvement of actors in their operation. It is practices in which actors engage, but practices can in turn entangle actors in the wider ramifications of their logics.

References

Decker, S., Üsdiken, B., Engwall, L. and Rowlinson, M. (2018). Special issue introduction: Historical research on institutional change. *Business History*, 60 (5): 613–627.

Donati, P. and Archer, M. (2015). *The relational subject*. Cambridge: Cambridge University Press.

Feldman, M. (2000). Organizational routines as a source of continuous change. *Organization Science*, 11 (6): 611–629.
Feldman, M. and Pentland, B. (2003). Reconceptualizing organizational routines as a source of flexibility and change. *Administrative Science Quarterly*, 48: 94–118.
Foucault, M. (2009). *Security, territory, population: Lectures at the Collège de France 1977–1978*. Basingstoke: Palgrave Macmillan.
Friedland, R. (2009). Institution, practice and ontology: Towards a religious sociology. *Research in the Sociology of Organizations*, 27: 45–83.
Friedland, R. (2012). Book review: Patricia H. Thornton, William Ocasio and Michael Lounsbury, The Institutional Logics Perspective: A New Approach to Culture, Structure, and Process. *M@n@gement*, 15 (5): 582–595.
Friedland, R. (2014). Divine institution: Max Weber's value spheres and institutional theory. *Research in the Sociology of Organizations*, 41: 217–258.
Friedland, R. and Alford, R. (1991). Bringing society back in: Symbols, practices, and institutional contradictions. In Powell, W. and DiMaggio, P. (eds.), *The new institutionalism in organizational analysis*. Chicago: University of Chicago Press, 232–266.
Gorski, P. (2003). *The disciplinary revolution: Calvinism and the rise of the state in early modern Europe*. Chicago: University of Chicago Press.
Gorski, P. (2018). After positivism: Critical realism and historical sociology. *Political Power and Social Theory*, 34: 23–45.
Graham, H. (1899). *Social life in Scotland in the eighteenth century*. London: Adam & Charles Black.
Gregory, J. and Chamberlain, J. (2003). *The national church in local perspective: The Church of England and the regions, 1660–1800*. Woodbridge: Boydell.
Jordanova, L. (2019). *History in practice* (3rd edn). London: Bloomsbury.
Keith G, (1811). *General view of the agriculture of Aberdeenshire*. Aberdeen: A. Brown.
Maclean, M., Harvey, C. and Clegg, S. (2016). Conceptualizing historical organization studies. *Academy of Management Review*, 41 (4): 609–634.
McKinlay, A. and Mutch, A. (2015). 'Accountable Creatures': Scottish Presbyterianism, accountability and managerial capitalism. *Business History*, 57 (2): 1–16.
Mutch, A. (1991). The 'farming ladder' in North Lancashire, 1840–1914: Myth or reality. *Northern England*, 27 (1): 162–183.
Mutch, A. (2009). Weber and church governance: Religious practice and economic activity. *Sociological Review*, 57 (4): 586–607.
Mutch, A. (2011). Custom and personal accountability in eighteenth century south Nottinghamshire church governance. *Midland History*, 36 (1): 69–88.
Mutch, A. (2012a). Data mining the archives: The emergence of separate books of account in the Church of Scotland 1608–1800. *Scottish Archives*, 18: 78–94.
Mutch, A. (2012b). Theology, accountability and management: Exploring the contributions of Scottish Presbyterianism. *Organization*, 19 (3): 95–111.
Mutch, A. (2013). 'Shared Protestantism' and British identity: Contrasting church governance practices in eighteenth-century Scotland and England. *Social History*, 38 (4): 456–476.
Mutch, A. (2014). 'To bring the work to greater perfection': Systematising governance in the Church of Scotland 1696–1800. *Scottish Historical Review*, 93 (2): 240–261.
Mutch, A. (2015). *Religion and national identity: Governing Scottish Presbyterianism in the eighteenth century*. Edinburgh: Edinburgh University Press.
Mutch, A. (2016a). Marginal importance: Scottish accountability and English watchfulness. *Church History and Religious Culture*, 96 (1–2):155–178.
Mutch, A. (2016b). Bringing history into the study of routines: Contextualizing performance. *Organization Studies*, 37 (8): 1171–1188.

Mutch, A. (2017a). Administrative practices and the 'middling sort': Place, practice and identity in 18th century rural England. In Kidd, A. and Tebbutt, M. (eds.), *Identity, place and people – essays in public and social history*. Manchester: Manchester University Press, 19–38.

Mutch, A. (2017b). Practices and morphogenesis. *Journal of Critical Realism*, 16 (5): 499–513.

Mutch, A. (2018). Practice, substance and history: Reframing institutional logics. *Academy of Management Review*, 43 (2): 242–258.

Mutch, A. (2019). History contra memory: Response to Wang, Steele, and Greenwood. *Academy of Management Review*, 44 (2), 476–479.

Pentland, B. and Feldman, M. (2005). Organizational routines as a unit of analysis. *Industrial and Corporate Change*, 14 (5): 793–815.

Sennett, R. (2002). *The fall of public man*. London: Penguin.

Simon, B. (1960). *Studies in the history of education: 1780–1870*. London: Lawrence & Wishart.

Snell, K. (2006). *Parish and belonging: Community, identity and welfare in England and Wales, 1700–1950*. Cambridge: Cambridge University Press.

Spaeth, D. (2000). *The church in an age of danger: Parsons and parishioners, 1660–1740*. Cambridge: Cambridge University Press.

Tate, W. (1983). *The parish chest: A study of the records of parochial administration in England*. Chichester: Phillimore.

Thornton, P., Occasio, W. and Lounsbury, M. (2012). *The institutional logics perspective: A new approach to culture, structure, and process*. Oxford: Oxford University Press.

Tosh, J. (2000). *The pursuit of history*. Harlow: Longman.

Underdown, D. (1987). *Revel, riot and rebellion: Popular politics and culture in England 1603–1660*. Oxford: Oxford University Press.

Vaisey, D. (ed) (1984). *The diary of Thomas Turner 1754–1765*. Oxford: Oxford University Press.

Veyne, P. (1984). *Writing history: Essay on epistemology*. Middletown, CT: Wesleyan University Press.

Whitman, J. (2013). The neo-Romantic turn. In Legrand, P. and Munday, R. (eds.), *Comparative legal studies: Traditions and transitions*. Cambridge: Cambridge University Press, 312–344.

3
TOWARDS A THEORY OF HISTORICAL REFLEXIVITY

Gabrielle Durepos and Russ Vince

Introduction

Researchers in the field of 'historical organization studies' (HOS) (Maclean, Harvey and Clegg, 2016) have hinted at the role of *reflexivity* in history research (Stutz and Sachs, 2018; Barros, Carneiro and Wanderley, 2018). However, the benefits of merging ideas of reflexivity with history remain unexplored and theoretically under-developed. In this chapter, we propose the concept of *historical reflexivity*. This idea stems from an assumption that history is both socially constructed knowledge of the past (Jenkins, 1991) and ontologically enactive. In other words, we perform history as we compose our lives in the present, which shapes visions for the future and of the past (Durepos, 2015).

The increased attention to history in organization studies is evident in the proliferation of research on the history of organizations and management thought, narratives and memory (Mills, 2006; Wren and Bedeian, 2017; Bowden, 2018; Rowlinson, Casey, Hansen and Mills, 2014). A variety of methods have been developed to undertake this research, including: microhistory (Novicevic, Marshall, Humphreys and Seifried, 2018), rhetorical history (Suddaby, Foster and Quinn Trank, 2010), archival ethnography (Decker, 2014), historical hermeneutics (Taylor, 2015) and ANTi-History (Durepos, 2015). A central concern in the field has been to outline the role that studying the past of organizations can play in developing ideas and innovations for organizations in the future (Cummings, Bridgman, Hassard and Rowlinson, 2017; Lawrence, 1984). Despite this concern, there is no extant historically sensitive framework that theoretically connects the past, present and future.

In contrast to mainstream histories, which are ontologically realist and epistemologically positivist and privilege reason and rationality (Bowden, 2018), historical reflexivity recognizes the everyday practice of histories rather than relying on the historian as keeper of the past (Kalela, 2012; Trouillot, 1995). This idea is inspired by the extent to which notions of reflexivity and history already inform one another. For example, reflecting on history as past and present is central to the practice of reflexivity. Conversely, reflexivity has been drawn upon by postmodern HOS researchers to expose and problematize 'historical truths' and reveal them as one of many 'situated knowledges'. We feel that merging history with reflexivity in an explicit way holds promise to help HOS mature as a community of practice.

We define historical reflexivity in the following terms:

a   Historical reflexivity is an iterative process of reflection in which people create nonchronological narratives of their past, present and future practices, informed by their embodied history.
b   Some narratives feature comprehensions (we apprehend, experience and realize), whereas others feature compositions (we accomplish, make happen and enact). The process is iterative in the sense that the focus is on the co-creation of narratives of comprehension and composition, with an understanding that alterations to each shift our embodied history. Embodied history is a sedimentation of narratives over time, which become adopted, accepted as given, and consequently seem natural. Therefore, their ongoing historicity is forgotten or ignored.
c   Historical reflexivity opens the possibility for people to simultaneously invent historical narratives for change and guard historical narratives that sustain established order. These narratives connect with emotions that are surfaced through the 'unsettling' practice of reflexivity. As a theoretical construct, historical reflexivity invites scholars to question the impact of emotions and nonchronological histories on our knowledge of taken-for-granted aspects of individual and social practice.

We explain and develop this definition in the following sections of the chapter. First, we map our theoretical development of historical reflexivity through a description of the literatures on HOS, emotion in organizations and reflexivity that inform our definition. Using these literatures, we construct a theoretical model of historical reflexivity (see Figure 3.1). We discuss and illustrate each element of our model in detail. We then illustrate the model with an example of 'faculty career achievement' in the corporatized university. In the concluding section of the chapter, we consider the utility of our theoretical model for HOS and discuss some implications for research and practice.

Theory development

We provide a summary of the areas of existing knowledge that create our theoretical model. This gives the reader an introduction to both the current state of knowledge and the functioning of our theory in relation to knowledge development. Effective theories in organization studies generally have two primary

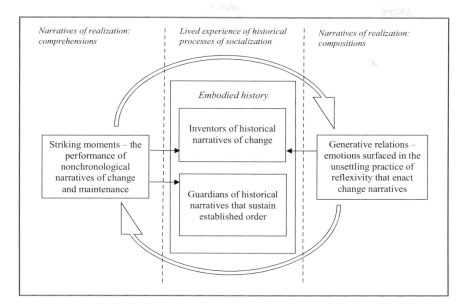

FIGURE 3.1 A model of historical reflexivity

characteristics: they should be original and useful. The originality of a theory stems from the creation of insights that reveal new ways of understanding. The utility of a theory recognizes that such insights need to be practical and applicable. Theoretical development, therefore, aims to be prescient; it is focused on 'the process of discerning what we need to know' (Corley and Gioia, 2011: 23). Theory captures the intersection between its explanatory power to inform and guide, its relevance to current and emerging issues and its role in the discovery of novel connections (Clancy and Vince, 2018). Simply put, 'a good theory explains, predicts and delights' (Sutton and Staw, 1995: 378).

Our theoretical model is built by making links between three aspects of knowledge that are currently separate. First, HOS is a field of 'organizational research that draws extensively on historical data, methods, and knowledge, embedding organizing and organizations in their sociohistorical context to generate historically informed *theoretical narratives* attentive to both disciplines' (Maclean et al., 2016: 609; our emphasis). However, these narratives are not exclusively located in how the past informs the present. They can be nonchronological in the sense that they are created from aspects of the past and the present, as well as (spoken and unspoken) desires concerning the future. We, therefore, require theory that helps us to recognize how people in organizations comprehend and perform history nonchronologically, as well as how we compose our lives in the present and connect with our lived experience of organizations.

Second, our lived experience is created and sustained through our emotional, as well as rational, responses to organizations. Contemporary research into emotions and organizations provides a range of insights about the emotional nature of such responses.

For example, they might arise from powerful, internalized feelings of self-hatred (Petriglieri and Stein, 2012) or envy (Stein, 2016). They may evolve from social emotions, which are emotions that reflect the state of social relations and hold people together in organizational processes – for example, social feelings of shame (Creed et al., 2014) or fear (Gill and Burrow, 2018). They may arise out of moral emotions that lead people to care about a social environment and, therefore, to support and improve its integrity – for example, notions of patient care that influence surgeons' field-level maintenance of professional practice (Wright, Zammuto and Liesch, 2017; see Chapter 11 by Ken Sakai in this volume), or the anger that motivates people's involvement with a human rights organization (Rodgers, 2010). We think that knowledge about emotions in organizations can be significant, especially because the role of emotions is increasingly noticed in the field of history (Boddice, 2018) but has been neglected in HOS. We argue for a theory that unsettles a need for a neutral, disembodied historian who draws on historical data dispassionately to construct an *emotion-free* narrative. Our theory offers a counter-perspective, that history is intimately connected to lived experience; it is produced in daily actor practices and relations that reveal an *emotion-full* narrative of organizational contexts.

Third, emotion-full narratives of lived experience are grounded in reflexivity, which involves 'questioning what we, and others, might be taking for granted – what is being said and not said – and examining the impact this has or might have' (Cunliffe, 2016b: 741). Reflexivity concerns our wish to comprehend the nature of the knowledge we produce and that produces us. It is about our lived experience of *being* reflexive, both for ourselves and in relation to others. Reflexivity is bound up with praxis. It suggests a 'need for self-conscious and ethical action based on a critical questioning of past actions and of future possibilities' (Cunliffe, 2016a: 749). A likely outcome of such action and reflection on the past and future is emotions of insecurity that are 'unsettling', both of self and other. Being unsettled can both open up opportunities for new ways of working and provoke resistance from the established order in support of current ways of working. Applied to an organizational context, reflexivity encourages us to unsettle what and how we know and disrupt the systems of domination that prevent us from knowing more or knowing differently. We, therefore, require theory that is capable of supporting an understanding of lived experiences in organizations which perceives people both as the inventors of historical narratives for change and as the guardians of enduring historical narratives that are associated with the maintenance of the prevailing order.

In summary, our development of a theory of historical reflexivity is built from three connected themes that link HOS: emotions in organizations, and being personally and relationally reflexive. Such a theory aims to:

- help us to anticipate how people in organizations comprehend and perform history nonchronologically, as well as how we compose narratives of our lives in the present and connect with our lived experience of organizations.
- help us to produce emotion-full narratives of the ways in which history is intimately connected to people's lived experience, as it is produced in everyday practice.

- help us to pinpoint a historical perspective on being reflexive. This involves our experience as inventors of historical narratives of change and as guardians of historical narratives that are associated with established order.

Historical reflexivity focuses on the process of 'unsettling' in relation to the past, present and future. For example, practising historical reflexivity can help us question assumptions of progress that impose a 'chronological order' on events, with the assumption that the next event is an improvement on the previous one. Historical reflexivity unsettles the notion of progress by exposing it as provisional and nonchronological. We present a novel view of the relationship between historical perceptions (as recursive) and the ongoing questioning of underlying assumptions. We show how this can inform and support practices that unsettle assumptions and invite possibilities for change.

Towards a theory of historical reflexivity

Our theoretical model of historical reflexivity is presented visually in Figure 3.1. We explain and develop each of the main components of our model in more detail, as well as showing how these components work together.

Our explanation of historical reflexivity highlights two interlinked 'narratives of realization'. Here, we are using the ambiguity of the verb *to realize* to make a link between nonchronological history and reflexivity. There are two senses to this verb. Realize means, first, to understand (to comprehend) and, second, to make happen (to compose). These meanings also connect history and reflexivity in the sense that they suggest a process of *being in history* rather than looking back on it chronologically. Our model, therefore, mirrors frameworks for learning that are based on the continuous interplay of reflection and action (Kolb, 1983), as well as frameworks of scholarship that emphasize the inseparable link between theory and practice. In the midst of narratives of realization are historical processes of socialization, or 'structuring structures' (Bourdieu, 1977: 72), which are frames of cognition, perception, preference, language and action that incline persons towards specific forms of organizational order. Structuring structures are bound up with emotions – for example, 'shame, humiliation, timidity, anxiety, guilt' (Bourdieu, 2004: 340) – which contribute to both the subversion and the reproduction of institutional order (Vince and Mazen, 2014). Structuring structures and their associated process of socialization, as Bourdieu (1990: 56) notes, can become 'embodied history' in that they are internalized, accepted as given, with their ongoing historicity forgotten or ignored.

Narratives of realization: comprehension

Historical reflexivity invokes a nonchronological history rather than one organized around chronological time. Although the HOS literature offers various options to emplot reflection and narratives of the past as history (i.e. give a structure that sets events in a given 'order'), historical reflexivity is aligned with the postmodern HOS idea that chronology in historical analysis is imposed and achieved, rather than given in the natural unfolding of things (White, 1985). Our notion of historical reflexivity suggests that an ongoing connection between time and history imposes a progressive order that is not necessarily representative of events or their consequences (individual or collective). This raises a question concerning the practicalities of historical reflexivity: what tools do we need to articulate a nonchronological view of history, one that can unsettle time-ordered chronology rather than one that remains dependent on it?

We answer this question by considering the performance of nonchronological narratives as they apply to efforts to change or maintain those structures that structure. We think that moments are not tied together in time, but rather reflect the present or resonate with the past, depending on their intensity. Therefore, narratives of realization associated with comprehension are performed through practical reflexivity on 'striking moments' (Corlett, 2013) in our lives (our being) through which we get a sudden or emerging insight, one that suggests new connections in relation to existing patterns of events (Cunliffe, 2002). Such moments confront us with realization. These are felt moments, when both conscious and unconscious emotions surface and give tone, significance and shape to practical reflexivity. The instances that are relived in striking moments do not present themselves in the chronological order in which they were initially experienced. Striking moments arise from noticing what would otherwise remain unnoticed about thought processes unfolding over time, values that are within and beyond their time, and shared connections with the future. For example, Reynolds and Vince (2020) reflexively engage with 27 papers, which is the sum of their collective scholarship within one journal, *Management Learning*, over a period of 50 years. This unusual act of reflexive enquiry produces anachronisms (things that are out of their time), uncanny resonances between past and present, and anticipatory connections that imagine and predict future possibilities.

Although some striking moments evoke sentiments of plausibility, others can lead to emotional and cognitive disconnects and discomfort. Striking moments have the potential to surface discord between what were once internalized, unconscious and accepted mental patterns and dispositions that are now consciously felt. These moments can be jarring because they are an opportunity for an emotional dissonance to surface between the sensemaking of what is, what was and what can or should be. Striking moments have the capacity to disrupt our emotional and behavioural steadiness. This instability can be characterized by experiencing the pleasant excitement of plausibility or the unpleasant emotions of hurt, anger and pain in reconciling both real and imagined past, present or future events. We think that striking moments can occur at individual and collective levels of engagement. In both cases, it is the power of these reflexive moments that unsettles expectations and supports insightful, imaginative and predictive possibilities. Striking moments are important because they emphasize the possibility of different connections to what is apparent and the potential to become conscious of contextually specific elements of underlying processes of socialization.

Narratives of realization: composition

Historical reflexivity emphasizes the power of our emotional lives and our capacity to construct emotional narratives that are both informed by our past and intimately connect our present and futures. Although striking moments highlight immediate or emerging narratives of conscious realization, not all moments of realization are conscious. Our conceptualization of historical reflexivity also implies connection to a broader idea, that each person is, at every moment, under the influence of their entire history (Ford and Harding, 2009). This acknowledges the complexities of our individual and relational lives, that we are connected to histories that are both real and imagined, to relations, contexts and emotions that continuously combine and recombine into new configurations. This has been referred to by the psychoanalytic theorist Christopher Bollas as 'psychic genera ... clusters of internal intensity that are created when related ideas, images, and feelings are attracted together' (Nettleton, 2017: 15).

For our theoretical model, we take from this the importance of the generative nature of associative relations and the fundamental role of emotions (both conscious and unconscious) as a creative aspect of reflexive engagement in organizations. Our lived experience of organizations does not only stimulate defences against emotions. It also offers us glimpses of the importance of our organizational dreamworlds (Gabriel, 1995; Vince, 2018) and the receptiveness and creativity of an *associative* mind. For example:

> The creation of the dream is not only a remarkable aesthetic accomplishment; it is the most sophisticated form of thinking we have. A dream can think hundreds of thoughts in a few seconds, its sheer efficiency breathtaking. It can think past, present and imagined future in one single image and it can assemble the total range of implicit affects within the day experience.
>
> *(Bollas, 2007: 73)*

The idea of the creativity of an associative mind is important for HOS because one's sense of self and other in organizations is formed unknowingly (as well as knowingly) within a social and political context and outside distinctions between past, present and future. Historical reflexivity seeks to identify the generative nature of associative relations that arise from a nonchronological perspective on history, and that 'we are all part of a matrix of relations in a social group, where certain ways of perceiving reality are impressed on individuals without proper conscious awareness of that influence' (Stamenova and Hinshelwood, 2018: 2). We consider these 'generative relations', as we call them, to be capable of both unsettling narratives of order and creating possibilities for change. We illustrate this theme in our upcoming example.

Historical reflexivity offers HOS the option to consider a perspective that is additional to the idea that organizational history is best understood through the rational analysis undertaken by unbiased historians. It supports a choice to analyse history as it is produced in daily actor practices and to continue to develop the neglected role of emotions in HOS (Stoler, 2009; Boddice, 2018). Histories are performed in daily practices by emotive humans, and those emotions profoundly influence what can be realized through our actions (Vince, 2006).

Embodied history

We contend that there is an ongoing relationship between everyday practice and processes of socialization that become 'embodied history, internalized as a second nature and so forgotten as history' (Bourdieu, 1990: 56). 'Embodied history', as it is conceptualized in historical reflexivity, is an example of a nonchronological history, where past, present and future combine to assist *both* with the internalization of organizational order *and* with the questioning of assumptions that underpin order. Historical narratives serve dual, contradictory purposes. They function both as narratives that maintain established order and narratives of potential change.

Historical reflexivity is connected to our being within a social and political context, to historical processes of socialization and to the possibility of unsettling them. Our narratives of realization, whether about comprehension or composition, are structuring structures that act upon us to generate and organize practices and representations. However, our acts anticipate the future at the same time as they are framed by previous experience, affording opportunities for 'questioning what we, and others, might be taking for granted – what is being said and not said – and examining the impact this has or might have' (Cunliffe, 2016b: 741). Cunliffe's (2016a: 749) insight into the process of reflexivity is important exactly because it is based on concurrent 'critical questioning of past actions and of future possibilities' that can give rise to striking moments and generative relations. A likely outcome of such reflection and action on the past and future is emotions of insecurity that are 'unsettling', both of self and other. Being unsettled can open up possibilities for new ways of being and provoke resistance within an established order in support of current ways of thinking.

In the context of our lived experience of processes of socialization, organizational actors are often free to think differently within the constraints of having to think the same. Reflexivity implies interrogation of contradictory purposes, questioning both our freedoms and constraints within a given organizational order. Reflexivity invites persons to 'deconstruct our own constructions of realities, identities, and knowledge, and highlight the intersubjective and indexical nature of meaning' (Cunliffe, 2003: 989). Such questioning of personal and social constructions is important because, if our thoughts are internalized and accepted, they come to iteratively inform our being – in relation to self, to others and to society. Reflexivity (certainly in the sense of 'deconstructing our own constructions') pushes us to reconsider who we are, as well as what we do, but always in the context of an established order. Our view is that striking moments of lived experience are bound together with generative relations in a process of unsettling established order.

These three intersecting components of our theoretical model provide the basis for the definition of historical reflexivity in the introduction to this chapter.

To restate this: historical reflexivity is an iterative process of reflection in which people create nonchronological narratives of their past, present and future practices, informed by their embodied history. Some narratives feature comprehensions (we apprehend, experience and realize), whereas others feature compositions (we accomplish, make happen and enact). In the following section of the chapter, we give an example of historical reflexivity to illustrate the utility of our theory within HOS.

Illustrating historical reflexivity: faculty career achievement in the corporatized university

We show historical reflexivity through an exploration of how 'faculty career achievement' (Berg and Seeber, 2016; Bateson, 1989) is realized in the corporatized university (Parker, 2018; Alvesson, Gabriel and Paulsen, 2017). In the process of historical reflexivity, people create narratives of realization that feature comprehensions and compositions. In the following example, we engage in our own historical reflexivity to reflect on how we *comprehend* career success and *compose* our academic careers in an intensified neoliberal university context.

To begin, we share our description of the corporatized university context. Informed by this context, we illustrate our narrative of comprehension with a focus on our striking moments. Our striking moments feature our emotions that are unsettled as we come to grips with a clock whose intensification has become naturalized and justified by a neoliberal ideology. We highlight how our emotions connect nonchronological events: all within one instant, we (re)live deep connections to our past, present and future. We come to realize that a consequent impact of the neoliberal university is a growing sense of researcher alienation and loss of meaningful research. The uncomfortable comprehension of faculty career achievement that is informed by an enterprising attitude propels us to invent narratives for change. These are featured in our composition: we rethink notions of academic career achievement by adopting an attitude of improvisation. We suggest the need to reclaim meaningful research and offer that academic achievement may lie in the craft of writing, itself. Throughout our example, we suggest that the sedimentation of our narratives of comprehension and composition overtime makes up and also shifts our embodied history. Because historical reflexivity is not a passive exercise, you, as reader, are invited to envisage your own notion of academic success and react to ours. Doing so may prompt you to invent your own historical narratives for change or guard narratives that sustain an established norm.

The corporatization of the North American and UK university over the past two decades has been lamented by many (Parker, 2018; Berg and Seeber, 2016; Alvesson et al., 2017). Though the university may have once been shielded from a neoliberal ideology, its infrastructure, practices and organizational culture have suffered owing to changes brought about by an intensified managerialism. As Berg and Seeber (2016: 3–4) note, 'our work has changed due to the rise in contractual positions, expanding class sizes, increased use of technology, [and] downloading of clerical tasks onto faculty'. The atmosphere of evaluation, evidenced by a rise in the need for accountability to the university via periodic progress reports, has intensified in light of institutional pressures of accreditation. These changes – and others, including a decrease in full-time tenured positions and an increase in demand for research output and service contribution – intensify pressures on faculty to *achieve* (Frost and Taylor, 1996). If achievement is measured by quantity of publications, then the goal is increasingly met. Alvesson et al. (2017) note that not only are academic publications on the rise, but also the number of academics. In this context, achievement is described as 'world-class performance' (Walsh, 1996: 481), language that highlights a global competitive mindset, as opposed to a global community. This neoliberal ideology is reminiscent of a normalized belief in justifying all decisions and actions based on a capitalist logic of efficiency, reason and rationality, as well as assessing survival through economic metrics. The instrumentality fuelled by this belief system has garnered an attitude of consumerism towards education, transforming students into customers and faculty into employees, a fundamental alteration of the relationship.

These changes have meant a significant university reformation, leading to large impacts on the day-to-day lived experience of academics. For example, those once blessed with sentiments of flexibility, creativity and empowerment associated with tenure may now experience tenure as 'working all the time ... because academic work by its very nature is never done' (Berg and Seeber, 2016: 3). Consequently, definitions, experiences and reflections on success and achievement in faculty careers have been reshaped. Anecdotal comments from our colleagues reveal that this new measure of success reeks of entrepreneurialism: faculty who adopt an ideology, attitude and work ethic akin to that of an entrepreneur to map their research, teaching and service have, respective to the new measuring stick, better chances for success.

Our historical reflexivity begins by imagining striking moments that we (our colleagues and ourselves) may experience in light of this current work context. We focus specifically on striking moments because they are the space in which narratives of comprehension are woven. Striking moments are sudden but fleeting glimpses of realizations where new connections are made between elements and associations once deemed unproblematic, normalized and taken for granted (Corlett, 2013). For example, reflection on tenure and academic success can trigger striking moments in which sudden perception is offered through connecting existing ideas, events or phenomena. Striking moments can happen anywhere, including during hallway conversations, and to anyone, such as early- or late-career academics. These days, the conversations are mostly rushed, because everyone is busy, having adopted a mindset of squeezing maximum productivity from each minute of the day. This efficiency, where the logic is to reduce the waste of time to maximize output, is redolent of neoliberalism. It creates a particular image of time, the clock, the intensification of work and, thus, the intensification of the clock. It seems that, if we do more with less time, the returns move us up one notch on the measuring stick of success. In that moment, questions are triggered: 'Wasn't the anxiety of the clock supposed to change post-tenure? Why did we think it would?' This can lead to sudden emotions of excitement, anxiety, worry, fear and happiness as we fuse and relive, nonchronologically, the various clocks that make up the enterprising academic career: the tenure clock, the PhD viva clock, the comprehensive examinations clock, the biological reproduction clock (Bateson, 1989), the I must pick up my children clock, the stomach clock ... I am hungry ... and is it not time for a vacation? More questions on the clock surface: 'Why does she want to meet at 5pm and not 7pm, I told her this cuts into my writing block, which took me two weeks to create. Do I bother to take the time to explain it, again? Will her reaction be too time consuming? Why do I feel so guilty about this? This thought process is taking up too much time and affecting my focus. Be strategic!' These striking moments connect nonchronological events through emotion. Historical reflexivity suggests that we may never be fully aware of the entire menu of the unconscious acting upon us or where the emotions come from. As Bollas (2007) notes, the unconscious is generative: it fuels associations between seemingly disparate elements, and we are continually under its influence.

Striking moments unsettle emotions. For example, the flexibility that came with tenure and evoked emotions of happiness, contentment and joy may now also come with emotions of anxiety, tensions and worry owing to intensified work schedules. Interestingly, the corporatization of academia discourages reflection on emotions associated with an intensified work space and pace. Berg and Seeber (2016: 2) explain that:

> Academic training includes induction into a culture of scholarly individualism and intellectual mastery; to admit struggle undermines our professorial identity. The academy as a whole has been reticent in acknowledging its stress; to talk about the body and emotion goes against the grain of an institution that privileges the mind and reason.

For aspiring *enterprising* academics, a significant amount of effort is needed to match inward emotions to those prescribed by the university. This makes us question the extent to which our conventional understanding of career achievement has overlooked the growing dissonance between 'inward' feelings and 'conventions of expression' (Boddice, 2018: 63). For example, hallway conversations with early career colleagues reveal a growing sentiment of shame when they admit failure in being efficiently creative. Some are genuinely confused; shouldn't the process of writing unleash happiness and excitement? These dissonances in emotion can lead to what Boddice (2018: 75) calls 'emotional suffering'. What examining striking moments allows us to do is surface and unsettle emotions so we can become acutely attuned to their presence and influence. In our own historical reflexivity, striking moments surface the emotional regime of the neoliberal university, which allows us to critically examine it. The outcome is an emergent narrative of comprehension in which the neoliberal university prescribes an emotional regime akin to that of a corporate environment.

Alvesson et al. (2017: 12) comment that the neoliberal university has led to the 'proletarianization of contemporary academics'. Not only is the academic labour force growing exponentially, but so is its research output. The enterprising work ethic supports the collective opinion that playing the publishing game is, by default, the means to manufacture the academic career. However, this neoliberal condition comes with severe compromises for the research. At an individual level, both the process and content of research come to have little intrinsic meaning and value. A growing condition of alienation haunts the academic, where there is potential to become so divorced from one's labour that meaningless becomes the norm. At a collective level, the value of the research to society is not always evident. As Alvesson et al. (2017: 5) note, meaningless research is 'a serious social problem'.

The narrative of realization above features reflections in which we come to comprehend, in a nonchronological and emotionally saturated way, our construction of academic career achievement. Exploring our narratives of comprehension directs our attention to embodied history and helps surface aspects of it vis-à-vis our lived experience. For example, in pointing to our embodied pasts, we may ask whether it was always like this. We recognize that our careers are not long enough for us to know what it used to be and felt like. Engaging in historical reflexivity allows us to acknowledge that, as narratives of comprehension are realized over time, they sediment and shift our embodied history. This opens up possibilities: an altered embodied past may frame and prompt the asking of different questions. We may wonder, as did Bateson (1989), whether the design of our lives must be rethought.

So far, we have focused on the illustration of narratives of comprehension and less on narratives of composition. However, engaging in historical reflexivity in practice would imply a co-creation and interaction of both narratives of realization. This is to highlight that the narratives of comprehension featured above have consequences for narratives of composition, and vice versa. Having noted the separation as heuristic only, we illustrate narratives of composition.

Narratives of composition sharpen our focus on generative relations. This helps us appreciate at least three aspects of composition. First, the emotions that unfold to connect nonchronological events are performative. Second, we can and should be creative in how we compose the problem or subject of our critique; we have agency in that moment. Third, and most relevant for our upcoming example, historical reflexivity is an act of composition. The process invites the composition of thought, emotion and reflection on past events undertaken in the present and with the potential to shape future action.

Our project of historical reflexivity prompted a desire to rethink notions of academic career achievement. Central to this is a redefinition of academic norms of success and failure that follow the neoliberal, ready-made model of academic achievement. Ultimately, this involves a reconfiguration of the academic identity away from being 'article-producing technicians' (Alvesson et al., 2017: 88). Rather, we explore what generative action is prompted when we adopt a mindset of composing an academic life.

Bateson (1989) teaches us that central to composition is a celebration of agency, improvisation, aesthetics and creativity. Composition problematizes that we can begin with a pre-formulated ending in mind. It cautions us against mindless and 'stubborn struggle[s] toward a single goal' (Bateson, 1989: 1). Composition provokes creative flows, with an emphasis on the need to be attentive and identify with those flows to discover their shape along the way. Composition connotes invention through configuring the familiar and unfamiliar elements of our lives into novel forms. This means embracing a continuous combination and recombination of both real and imagined emotions, as well as aspects of dreamworlds, relationships, contexts and histories. It involves recognizing the generative nature of those relations as a creative aspect of both individual and organizational reflexive engagement. Becoming attuned to composition invites examining resultant configurations, appreciating their aesthetics value and recognizing that within them lies possibility for action. Adopting this mindset towards the academic career would tempt us to discover the structure and meaning of success in a fluid way. Our academic careers and notions of success would be discovered along the way, as they are made – thus, in the course of their creation. We may even reconfigure academic accomplishment as the act of creating the career itself. In doing so, we may reconnect with our writing and research to reclaim meaning.

Alvesson et al. (2017) describe the idea of meaningful research by distinguishing between research that is meaningful to society and that which is meaningful to the ego or identity. Fundamental to reclaiming meaning in research is a need to create and demonstrate the value of academic knowledge to society. This implies a need for academics to question what common good the research serves. Beyond adding value to society, the research process itself, as well as the subjects explored, can and should be meaningful to the researcher. Research has the capacity to evoke curiosity, challenge and excitement within academics. These emotions can make one come alive, infuse one with purpose and give a sense of worth. It can help us identify with the process of doing the research and fulfil a sense of identity or even 'reinstate identity as a crucial part of the research' (Alvesson et al., 2017: 100).

There are a range of options on offer for academics to reclaim meaning in their lives and academic ventures. For one, embracing a style of writing that is audience-centric, doing research that is interesting and that can draw and retain audience attention is central to the process of recovering meaning. Beyond this, we argue meaning can be reclaimed when academics embrace that writing is the process in which the self is composed. Our point is that, in writing research articles, which multiply over the years to eventually populate pages on a CV and represent the collective of our research over time, we compose the academic self. Saying this implies that our CVs are more than a list of articles. Rather, they are a representation of and a comment on a particular academic identity. As Reynolds and Vince (2020: 140) showed in their historical reflexivity, the history of their publications is a 'representation of thought processes unfolding over time, of values that are within and beyond their time, and a shared connection with the future' of their field. As Alvesson et al. (2017: 93) note, 'we are – or become – our intellectual trajectories (or standstills)'. It is not possible to predict in the present moment what our CVs will feature in, say, 10 years. For example, what will our list of articles reveal about the subjects we are passionate about, the relationships we forged, the lands to which we travelled for conferences and the students we met along the way who shaped us? What can each piece of research expose about those feelings of uncertainty and vulnerability with which we grappled as we experimented with ideas? It is in those experiences, in the process of writing and forging the content, that we also write our self-concept. In writing the research, we write the self. We compose the academic identity in an improvisatory and creative way. The composition *is* the accomplishment. When we look back to our 'patchwork of achievements', we can begin to understand it as the composition, rather than a pursuit of 'the model of single-track ambition' toward a prescribed goal (Bateson, 1989: 15). These compositions are generative in that they are capable of both unsettling narratives of order and creating possibilities for change.

In our example of comprehending and composing faculty career achievement, we have sought to illustrate historical reflexivity as an iterative process where realizations of comprehension and composition layer on top of one another and become so taken for granted that their historicity is overlooked. In other words, our embodied history is a sedimentation of narratives of realization, over time. Each sedimentation presents a shift in our embodied history.

Contributions and conclusions

To create our theoretical model of historical reflexivity, we summarized and combined select aspects of the extant literatures on HOS, reflexivity and emotions in organizations. We did this to give the reader an introduction to both the current state of knowledge in these areas and the functioning of our theory in relation to knowledge development. Effective theories in organization studies generally have two primary characteristics: they should be original and useful. The originality of a theory stems from the creation of insights that reveal new ways of understanding. The utility of a theory recognizes that such insights need to be practical and applicable. Theoretical development, therefore, aims to be prescient; it is focused on 'the process of discerning what we need to know' (Corley and Gioia, 2011: 23). Theory captures the intersection between its explanatory power to inform and guide, its relevance to current and emerging issues and its role in the discovery of novel connections (Clancy and Vince, 2018). We believe that historical reflexivity is original and holds potential to be useful to workers, managers, students and (not just) academics. For the sake of its use value as a theory in HOS, we see its contribution as threefold.

First, historical reflexivity attunes us to (what we see is) a novel connection between reflexive practice, the present as well as a future-oriented HOS. The rise of history research in organization studies has been premised on the promise of how history can inform innovation – thus, new ways of organizing in the future (Cummings et al., 2017). No theoretical framework has been developed in HOS that connects reflexive practice to present and future action. The value of any framework lies in its potential to guide reflexivity, as well as theoretically connect the past, present and future. Historical reflexivity provides the conceptual means to undertake a nonchronological analysis by recognizing that the past, present and future are all implicated in how we make sense of managing and organizing in the present. Historical reflexivity helps us realize the potential of history by developing new ways to look back *that are connected to* looking forward.

Second, historical reflexivity addresses current and emerging theoretical concerns in HOS in at least two ways. First, historical reflexivity makes explicit the potential of history in the theorization and practice of reflexivity. Reflexivity has a 'historical' component. The extent to which current theorizations of history can inform the practice of reflexivity remains unrealized. This is because a theorized study of the past is not explicit in current theorizations of reflexivity. Historical reflexivity makes explicit the role of 'history' in the process of reflexivity. As a framework, it seeks to realize the potential of history in reflexive practice by theorizing the role of history in the process of reflexivity. Second, historical reflexivity addresses the emergent theoretical gap of the role of emotions in HOS. The role of emotions in historical thought is a novel area of study in the field of history (Boddice, 2018), but has thus far been neglected in HOS. Historical reflexivity helps us to develop insights into the role of emotions in the organization of reflection.

Third, historical reflexivity holds the capacity to explain, inform and guide how we make sense of what becomes taken for granted. The practical value of reflexivity is that it identifies and 'unsettles' what becomes assumed emotions, knowledge, relations and structures (Cunliffe, 2003). Although explanations of reflexivity hint at the role of the past, present and future in the process of unsettling (Pollner, 1991; Cunliffe, 2016a), this aspect of reflexivity is underrealized. Our framework of historical reflexivity focuses on the process of 'unsettling' and its relationship to the past, present and future. For example, practising historical reflexivity can unsettle assumptions of progress, which imposes a 'chronological order' on events, with the assumption that the next event is an improvement on the former. Historical reflexivity unsettles the notion of progress by exposing it as provisional and nonchronological. It presents a novel view of the relationship between historical perceptions (as recursive) and the ongoing questioning of underlying assumptions.

As with any other practice, historical reflexivity comes with methodological warnings. Cunliffe (2003: 991) notes that any reflexive study can flirt with, on the one hand, being informative and stimulating while, on the other, being unenlightening and hollow. We encourage those historical reflexivity studies that are educational and enlightening. As a final point, we hope that discussions about historical reflexivity can adopt a tone and a style that are reflexive in and of themselves. Those who practise historical reflexivity can surface the *content* and engage in the *process* reflexively by putting themselves within the reflexive frame, thus as part of the constructing process.

References

Alvesson, M., Gabriel, Y. and Paulsen, R. (2017). *Return to meaning: A social science with something to say*. Oxford: Oxford University Press.

Barros, A., Carneiro, A.d.T. and Wanderley, S. (2018). Organizational archives and historical narratives: Practicing reflexivity in (re)constructing the past from memories and silences. *Qualitative Research in Organizations and Management*, 14 (3): 280–294.

Bateson, M. C. (1989). *Composing a life*. New York: Grove Press.

Berg, M. and Seeber, B.K. (2016). *The slow professor: Challenging the culture of speed in the academy*. Toronto: University of Toronto Press.

Boddice, R. (2018). *The history of emotions*. Manchester: Manchester University Press.

Bollas, C. (2007). *The Freudian moment*. London: Karnac.

Bourdieu, P. (1977). *Outline of theory of practice*. Cambridge: Cambridge University Press.

Bourdieu, P. (1990). *The logic of practice*. Stanford, CA: Polity Press.

Bourdieu, P. (2004). *Science of science and reflexivity*. Cambridge: Polity Press.

Bowden, B. (2018). *Work, wealth and postmodernism: The intellectual conflict at the heart of business endeavor*. Switzerland: Palgrave Macmillan.

Clancy, A. and Vince, R. (2018). Theory as fantasy: Emotional dimensions to grounded theory. *British Journal of Management*, 43 (2): 174–184.

Corlett, S. (2013). Participant learning in and through research as reflexive dialogue: Being 'struck' and other effects of recall. *Management Learning* 44 (5): 453–469.

Corley, K.G. and Gioia, D.A. (2011). Building theory about theory building: What constitutes a theoretical contribution? *Academy of Management Review*, 36 (1): 12–32.

Creed, W.E.D., Hudson, B.A., Okhuysen, G.A. and Smith-Crowe, K. (2014). Swimming in a sea of shame: Incorporating emotion into explanations of institutional reproduction and change. *Academy of Management Review*, 39 (3): 275–301.

Cummings, S., Bridgman, T., Hassard, J. and Rowlinson, M. (2017). *A new history of management*. Cambridge: Cambridge University Press.

Cunliffe A.L. (2002). Reflexive dialogical practice in management learning. *Management Learning*, 33 (1): 35–61.

Cunliffe, A.L. (2003). Reflexive inquiry in organization research: Questions and possibilities. *Human Relations*, 56 (8): 983–1003.

Cunliffe, A.L. (2016a). Republication of 'On becoming a critically reflexive practitioner'. *Journal of Management Education*, 40 (6): 747–768.

Cunliffe, A.L. (2016b). 'On becoming a critically reflexive practitioner' Redux: What does it mean to 'be' reflexive? *Journal of Management Education*, 40 (6): 740–746.

Decker, S. (2014). Solid intentions: An archival ethnography of corporate architecture and organizational remembering. *Organization*, 21 (4): 514–542.

Durepos, G. (2015). ANTi-History: Toward amodern histories. In McLaren, P.G., Mills, A. J. and Weatherbee, T. (eds), *The Routledge companion to management and organizational history*. New York: Routledge, 153–180.

Ford, J. and Harding, N. (2009). More than identity? Christopher Bollas and the aesthetics of leadership. University of Bradford Working Paper No 09/14 (August). ISSN 2048-2495X.

Frost, P. and Taylor, S. (eds) (1996). *Rhythms of academic life*. California: Sage.

Gabriel, Y. (1995). The unmanaged organization: Stories, fantasies and subjectivity. *Organization Studies*, 16 (3): 477–501.

Gill, M.J. and Burrow, R.D. (2018). The function of fear in institutional maintenance: Feeling frightened as an essential ingredient in haute cuisine. *Organization Studies*, 39 (4): 445–465.

Jenkins, K. (1991). *Re-thinking history*. London: Routledge.
Kalela, J. (2012). *Making history: The historian and uses of the past*. London: Palgrave Macmillan.
Kolb, D. (1983). *Experiential learning: Experience as the source of learning and development*. London: Prentice Hall.
Lawrence, B.S. (1984). Historical perspective: Using the past to study the present. *Academy of Management Review*, 9 (2): 307–312.
Maclean, M., Harvey, C. and Clegg, S.R. (2016). Conceptualizing historical organization studies. *Academy of Management Review*, 41 (4): 609–632.
Mills, A. (2006). *Sex, strategy and the stratosphere*. New York: Palgrave.
Nettleton, S. (2017). *The metapsychology of Christopher Bollas: An introduction*. London: Routledge.
Novicevic, M., Marshall, D.R., Humphreys, J. and Seifried, C. (2018). Both loved and despised: Uncovering a process of collective contestation in leadership identification. *Organization*, 26 (2) 236–254.
Parker, M. (2018). *Shut down the business school*. London: Pluto Press.
Petriglieri, G. and Stein, M. (2012). The unwanted self: Projective identification in leaders' identity work. *Organization Studies*, 33 (9): 1217–1235.
Pollner, M. (1991). Left of ethnomethodology: The rise and decline of radical reflexivity. *American Sociological Review*, 56 (3): 370–380.
Reynolds, M. and Vince, R. (2020). The history boys: Critical reflections on our contributions to management learning and their ongoing implications. *Management Learning*, 51 (1), 130–142.
Rodgers, K. (2010). 'Anger is why we're all here': Mobilizing and managing emotions in a professional activist organization. *Social Movement Studies*, 9 (3): 272–291.
Rowlinson, M., Casey, A., Hansen, P. and Mills, A. (2014). Narratives and memory in organizations. *Organization*, 21 (4): 441–446.
Stamenova, K. and Hinshelwood, R.D. (2018). *Methods of research into the unconscious: Applying psychoanalytic ideas to social science*. London: Routledge.
Stein, M. (2005). The Othello conundrum: The inner contagion of leadership. *Organization Studies*, 26 (9): 1405–1419.
Stoler, A.L. (2009). *Along the archival grain: Epistemic anxieties and colonial common sense*. Princeton: Princeton University Press.
Stutz, C. and Sachs, S. (2018). Facing the normative challenges: The potential of reflexive historical research. *Business and Society*, 57 (1), 98–130.
Suddaby, R., Foster, W. and Quinn Trank, C. (2010). Rhetorical history as a source of competitive advantage. In Baum, J.A.C. and Lampel, J. (eds), *Globalization of strategy research*, 27. London: Emerald, 147–173.
Sutton, R.I. and Staw, B.M. (1995). What theory is not. *Administrative Science Quarterly*, 40 (3): 371–384.
Taylor, S. (2015). Critical hermeneutics for critical organizational history. In McLaren, P.G., Mills, A.J. and Weatherbee, T. (eds), *The Routledge companion to management and organizational history*. New York: Routledge, 143–152.
Trouillot, M.-R. (1995). *Silencing the past: Power and the production of history*. Boston: Beacon Press.
Vince, R. (2006). Being taken over: Managers' emotions and rationalizations during a company takeover. *Journal of Management Studies*, 43 (2): 343–365.
Vince, R. (2018). Institutional illogics: The unconscious and institutional analysis. *Organization Studies*, 40 (7): 953–973.
Vince, R., and Mazen, A. (2014). Violent innocence: A contradiction at the heart of leadership. *Organization Studies*, 35 (2): 189–207.

Walsh, J. (1996). Embracing change: We get by with a lot of help from our friends. In Frost, P. and Taylor, S. (eds), *Rhythms of academic life*. California: Sage, 481–483.
White, H. (1985). *The tropics discourse: Essays in cultural criticism*. Baltimore: Johns Hopkins University Press.
Wren, D.A. and Bedeian, A. (2017). *The evolution of management thought* (7th edn.). New York: John Wiley.
Wright, A.L., Zammuto, R.F. and Liesch, P.W. (2017). Maintaining the values of a profession: Institutional work and moral emotions in the emergency department. *Academy of Management Journal*, 60 (1): 200–237.

4

THE ORGANIZATION-AS-ICEBERG AS A COUNTER-METAPHOR

Richard Badham, Todd Bridgman and Stephen Cummings

Introduction

Within organization studies, the iceberg metaphor has become what Lakoff and Turner (1989) describe as an entrenched or unconsciously conventional

FIGURE 4.1 Cartoon reproduced with permission from Jock Macneish

metaphor. We argue, however, it is far from 'dead'. Appearances of the metaphor as a tired cliché can be deceptive. Announcements of its death are greatly exaggerated and, we will argue, unfortunate. Adopting a more dynamic approach to metaphors (Mueller, 2008), we represent the iceberg image as part dead and part alive. We make the case for turning it from a '*sleeping*' (low-activation) metaphor to one that is '*waking*' (high-activation). We argue further for its refinement and employment as a '*generative*' metaphor. In line with Donald Schon (1979), this is an argument for its use as a creative and reflective 'projective model'. We then advocate exploring its value as a generative *counter-metaphor* to (overly) rational model of organizations (Barrett and Cooperrider, 1990). Conservative or protective uses of the iceberg metaphor work within the confines of the rational systems metaphor, advocating a re-engineering of its informal component. Unreflexive adherents to an alternative fluid/process perspective dismiss the iceberg image without examining the ways of seeing and non-seeing embodied in both metaphors. In contrast, we argue for adopting and extending its reflexive and self-critical use as a counter-metaphor. In so doing, this chapter takes a novel approach to historical organization studies. It provides a critical analysis of the genesis, history and evolution of a familiar metaphor as support for its continued relevance and reflexive use in the present.

Iceberg as sleeping metaphor

> Try thinking about the corporate culture as an iceberg. Recognize that what you see on the surface is based on a much deeper reality. Recognize that the visible elements of the culture may be sustained by all kinds of hidden values, beliefs, ideologies and assumptions – questioned and unquestioned, conscious and unconscious. As a manager, recognize that it may not be possible to change the surface without changing what lies below.
>
> *(Morgan, 1989: 157–158)*

The standard narrative

Ever since the 1970s, the organization-as-iceberg metaphor has remained a staple diet in management education. It has been widely deployed within studies of organizational development (French and Bell, 1973, 1978), organizational culture (Knights and Willmott, 2006), organizational systems (Monat and Gannon, 2015), organizational change (Senior and Swailes, 2016) and organizational accidents (Sun, Paez, Lee, Salem and Daraiseh, 2006; Swuste, Gulijk and Zwaard, 2010). Its prevalence is well established within management student textbooks (Hellriegel and Slocum, 2011; Knights and Willmott, 2006; Mullins and Christy, 2010; Senior and Swailes, 2016), management consultancy rhetoric and practice (Rick, 2014, 2015), linguistic and cross-cultural introductions to the 'dual iceberg' (Collier, 2013; Cummins, 2001) as well as practitioner simplifications for disseminating complex system thinking (Kim, 1999). It has recently resurfaced in

'Theory U' approaches to organizational learning and development (Scharmer and Kaufer, 2013).

In most popular introductions to organizational behaviour (Hellriegel and Slocum, 2011: 479–480; Mullins and Chrysty, 2010: 4–9), and similarly popular introductions to change management (Senior and Fleming, 2006: 138–139), the iceberg figures prominently as a means of refocusing attention onto: the 'covert, behavioural' as well as the 'overt, formal' dimension of organizations; the powerful impact the former elements have; the dangers of failing to understand and attend to their consequences (as they are 'often hidden and resistant to change' (Hellriegel and Slocum, 2011: 479)); and the difficulties in detection given that the characteristics are 'mainly hidden', 'rarely talked about' and one has to 'guess' at how large it is and its significance. In popular parlance, the implication of the iceberg metaphor is to highlight the 'hidden' nature of the tacit, informal and covert dimensions of organizational life, and the 'dangerous' consequences of a failure to appreciate its depth and significance. As Senior and Fleming (2006: 139) note, the 'difficulties in detecting the extent and characteristics of the hidden part of the iceberg are analogous to the difficulties encountered in examining and understanding the more informal, hidden aspects of organizational behaviour', and, as Mullins and Chrysty (2010: 4) remark, citing Hellriegel, Slocum and Woodman (1998: 5), 'What sinks ships isn't always what sailors can see, but what they can't see'. Rick (2014; 2015) reinforces the *Titanic* icon in warning that seemingly well-planned and structured 'unsinkable' change interventions often founder after 'collision' with the less visible and insufficiently considered bulk of the organization that lies beneath the surface.

A more complex story

Beneath this surface view, however, lies a more complex picture. It is a picture that makes the iceberg metaphor more interesting and its use more complex and problematic.

The nature of its content

From a historical standpoint, the nature and origins of the metaphor are shrouded in ambiguity and misrepresentation. Its origins are regularly attributed to the anthropologist Edward Hall in his book *Beyond Culture* (1976), drawing on his work from the 1950s, yet there is no mention of the iceberg metaphor in that book. Moreover, Hall's brief reference to the metaphor was in another, earlier book, *Silent Language* (1959: 86), and it was to critique the concept. In Hall's words, although the 'iceberg analogy was commonly used when teaching this theory [levels of culture] to students and laymen alike', 'it soon turned out this theory was inadequate'. The iceberg metaphor in organizational development was popularized by Wendell French and Cecil Bell (1973) as a two-level image focused on culture. Yet Stan Herman, the attributed author of the metaphor, employed a three-level image with a stronger focus on the importance of power and influence (Herman, 1971, 2018). The organization as culture image is frequently attributed to Edgar Schein (Knights and Willmott, 2006), yet Schein never used the term iceberg and is critical of it (Schein in Brighton, 2015). As he recently noted, 'I did not like it because the basic assumptions that I consider the DNA of culture are neither so huge nor so static' (Schein, 2020).

Similarly, some attribute the origins of the iceberg metaphor in organizational learning and system dynamics to the work of Peter Senge in *The Fifth Discipline* (2006). Yet Senge made no mention of it. The precise origins of the metaphor in systems theory are unclear (Cavana, Goodman and Maani, 2018; Cunliff and Monat, 2018), and many systems thinkers are critical of its oversimplification (Cunliff in Cunliff and Monat, 2018; Hitchins, 2018). Images of the iceberg within this literature also vary considerably in terms of number of levels, what lies above and below the 'surface' and whether the iceberg refers to levels of causation or perspective (Cunliff, 2008). Finally, within organizational health and safety, the iceberg metaphor is often attributed to the German safety scholar Heinrich in his writings in 1927–1929. Yet he, also, never used the term, and the nature of the iceberg metaphor shifts over time in critical discussions of alternative views of causes and costs of injuries and accidents (Swuste, 2018; Swuste et al., 2010). Each of these literatures rarely, if ever, refers to the others.

Part of the current 'sleeping' nature of the iceberg metaphor is the uncritical acceptance of its overly simplified and inaccurate history. This chapter provides a more considered and reflective account in the belief that this may help to re-energize discussion and improve the use of the metaphor in three ways.

First, by acknowledging the *ambivalent support* given to the image from the outset. As Hall, its early critic, notes, its somewhat misleading and overly simplistic bipolar categorisation also made it accessible to traditional mindsets. It allowed the making of important distinctions and raised important issues around what it was and was not possible to talk about (Hall, 1959, 1966, 1976).

Second, by encouraging an appreciation of its *openness and ambiguity* as a possible contribution to its generative content and employment. Consideration of the historically diverse views of what lies above and below the 'waterline', and where to draw that line and its significance, opens up such issues for valuable discussion.

Finally, by highlighting historical and current sensitivity to the *limitations* of the image. This can be used to support a reflective and creative discussion of its nature and role as both a 'way of seeing' and 'way of not seeing'.

The significance of its context

Attention to the context of the iceberg's resonance and use is also of significance in exploring the appeal it has, the opposition it generates and its future use.

Its popularization in the 1970s was in an era of 'systems rationalism' (Barley and Kunda, 2010). This underlay support for its capacity to shift discussion of individual- and group-level characteristics and developments to organization-wide phenomena and to do so with an eye on systematic characteristics and scientific diagnosis. This was also an era marked by greater awareness of the limitations of overly rational views of individuals and organizations and the importance of sensemaking and politics in enacting organizational realities (Burns, 1961; Cohen, March and Olsen, 1972; Colville, Brown and Pye, 2012; Dalton, 2017; Meyer and Rowan, 1977; Weick, [1969] 1979). Finally, this period was characterized by multiple critiques of organizational life, from the emptiness of the corporate gamesman (Maccoby, 1978) and the rising culture of narcissism (Lasch, 1979) to the limitations of organization man (Whyte, 1956) and the dysfunctionalities of emotional labour (Hochschild, 1983). It was also the era of protests against the Vietnam War, corporate imperialism, global inequality and underdevelopment. The iceberg metaphor's pointing to the 'dangers' that lie beneath the surface of organizational life and the importance of understanding, sympathizing and collaborating with different values and perceptions resonated with this context.

In the current era, we have witnessed a variety of constructivist 'turns' in organizational studies, greater recognition of complexity and turbulence, and increased attention to agility and adaptability in fluid and changing conditions. In contrast, the frozen appearance of an iceberg metaphor appears to align it with outdated 'ice cube' models of change (Cummings, Bridgman and Brown, 2016; Kanter, Stein and Jick, 1992). Its rigid, object-like character appears anachronistic in an era in which it is more popular to highlight fluidity and narrative interpretation (Bennett, 2013a, 2013b; MacQueen, 2020). Moreover, its hierarchical and threatening character appears out of tune with emphases on networks, empowerment, collaboration, appreciative enquiry and generative dialogue (Schein in Brighton, 2015).

At the same time, however, there is widespread awareness that, despite such developments, overly rational views of individuals and organizations continue to dominate (Brunsson, 2014; Mccabe, 2016; March, 2007; Rowan, 2002). Despite the rhetoric, there is heightened sensitivity to continuing bureaucratic inertia, corporate grandiosity, functional stupidity and 'bullshit'; enduring systemic inequalities and discrimination; absence of intelligent, creative and responsible leadership; and widespread organizational silencing and dangers in 'speaking up' (Buchanan and Badham, 2020). The iceberg metaphor simply and directly speaks to such issues through the stark contrast it draws between rational legitimation and formal rhetoric, on the one hand, and the realities of uncertainty, hypocrisy, emotion and power, on the other. As we will illustrate below, the iceberg image can act as a clear and simple sensitizing concept and useful reminder of the pernicious effect of neglecting such realities, in a way that more refined and esoteric concepts and images fail to do. If the latter is the case, and alternative challenges to over-rational models have so far failed to resonate, then this ambiguous and ambivalent appeal of the iceberg metaphor raises interesting and important issues and challenges.

All quiet on the metaphor front

For a metaphor that is so commonly recognized and widely used in management education, one that raises a number of interesting and thorny issues, there has been a remarkable absence of any discussion or debate about its significance within organization studies. The metaphor rarely appears in formal academic discussions of the role of metaphors within organizational behaviour and change (Cornelissen, Oswick, Christensen and Phillips, 2008; Jacobs and Heracleous, 2006; Maclean, Harvey and Stringfellow, 2017; Marshak, 1993; Morgan, 2006; Palmer and Dunford, 1996). It is significant that the metaphor is absent from Gareth Morgan's celebrated *Images of Organization* (2006), although he does deploy it as a creative aid in his summary of tools in *Creative Organization Theory* (1989). Without explanation, French and Bell (1973) dropped the use of the 'iceberg' metaphor in their third, 2008 edition. No reference is made to the iceberg metaphor in contemporary overviews of perspectives on organizational theory (Hatch, 2013; Westwood and Clegg, 2003), organizational culture (Alvesson and Sveningsson, 2016; Giorgi, Lockwood and Glynn, 2015) and organizational change (Hughes, 2019; Stouten, Rousseau and De Cremer, 2018). Some popular extensive introductory textbooks on organization behaviour, culture and change do not include the iceberg (Buchanan and Huczynski, 2019; Burnes, 2017; Hayes, 2020).

In this chapter, we attempt to contribute to addressing this gap by exploring the potential, issues and challenges involved in 'waking up' this metaphor from its slumber and deploying it as a generative counter-metaphor to (overly) rational models and myths of organizational life.

Iceberg as generative metaphor

THATCHER: The Labour party iceberg manifesto, one tenth of its socialism visible, nine tenths beneath the water [laughter].
KINNOCK: In a way she was right, it's a bit of an iceberg manifesto. It's really cool, and it is ah very tough, and it is totally unsinkable.

(Wilson, 2015: 780)

The iceberg metaphor is inevitably generative. It creates by analogy ('seeing as') a variety of possible 'ways of seeing' and 'ways of not seeing' organizational life. But this generativity can be used in different ways and for different ends. For the purposes of this chapter, we approach this issue of generativity in relation to both the *content of metaphor* and the *context of its use*.

Generative content of the iceberg metaphor

Encouraging the view of organizations as an 'iceberg' reaffirms yet challenges the significance of the rational nature of organizational life. At an immediate level, it points to the existence of a prominent and visible rational 'tip', evident in formal structures, official rhetoric and public displays. Yet it also takes a 'deeper' look at the human dimensions of organization that are ignored, obscured or repressed by this 'surface' view. It combines this bipolar image with encouragement to go beneath the 'waterline'. It implies that it is important to achieve a greater understanding of what lies 'below' and take this into account in situations when opportunities and threats are missed through being misled by a partial focus on the more obvious 'tip'. Like the popular idiom that emerged in the 1960s, the 'tip of the iceberg', this metaphor highlights that in organizational life 'there is more to this than meets the eye'. It also warns us of the *Titanic*-like results of ignoring the foundering of organizational initiatives on neglected cultural, political and emotional conditions that lie beneath the organization's rational surface.

The power of this dimension of the iceberg metaphor lies in its resonance with broader, deeper and highly emotive imagery about modern life and culture. As Black (1993: 26; original emphasis), emphasizes, an active metaphor always requires:

> the receiver's cooperation in perceiving what lies *behind* the words used, and 'strong' metaphors have a high degree of background resonance and implicative elaboration i.e. how far the interpretative response can reach will depend upon the complexity and power of the metaphor-theme in question: Some metaphors, even famous ones, barely lend themselves to implicative elaboration, while others, perhaps less interesting, prove relatively rich in background implications. For want of a better label, I shall call metaphorical utterances that support a high degree of implicative elaboration *resonant*.

Without such resonance, Black notes, a metaphor is akin to an 'unfunny joke'. The failure of alternative counter-metaphors such as 'garbage can', 'irrational organization', 'wonderland' or 'rhizome' to catch on may be attributable to such a lack of popular resonance.

Four images embedded within significant modern social imaginaries (Taylor, 2004) underlie the strong cultural resonance of the iceberg metaphor. These images are intertwined with, and underlie, common characterizations of the iceberg as highlighting the contrast between the formal and informal in organizational life, the dangers of deeper, irrational factors that underlie the veneer of rationality and the *Titanic*-like hubris that leads to us ignoring such factors.

The first image is what we commonly recognize as a 'double plot' in social life (Gusfield, 2000): on the one hand, the socially approved expectations and technical requirements of the roles we play in society; on the other hand, our distance from such roles, the strain of shutting off other thoughts and behaviours in order to conform, and, consequently, our ambivalence towards them. As Burns (1961: 261–262) emphasizes, organizational members are confronted by a 'dual linguistic and moral code' as 'co-operators in a common enterprise and rivals for the material and intangible rewards of successful competition with each other' (see also Buchanan and Badham, 2020). The lived experience of our organizational self consequently lies not in official pronouncements of our corporate role, but in our responses to them (Kunda, 2006).

A second image is modern appreciation of the predictable irrationality of human beings (Ariely, 2009). As Aronson (1989: 134) observed, 'Man likes to think of himself as a rational animal. However, it is more true that he is a rationalizing animal, that he attempts to appear reasonable to himself and others'. As Hall (1959: 83–84) put it, the work of Sigmund Freud marked an important development in our modern conception of human behaviour:

> No longer was man considered to be entirely rational, ruled by logic. No longer could he be conceived of as an elegantly tooled machine run from the higher centres of the brain. Man became much less predictable but much more interesting when he was viewed as a battleground of conflicting drives and emotions, many of them hidden. After Freud it became common to think of man as a being who existed on a number of different levels at once.

Although Freud never used a phrase that is commonly attributed to his work, an 'iceberg theory of the mind' (Green, 2019), his ideas lent themselves to and reinforced such a basic image, with a focus on conscious rationality as the tip and unconscious irrationality below the surface.

A third image combines the latter two in widespread understanding and concern about the 'dark' side of modernity (Alexander, 2013). The idea that there are dangerous depths within the project of modernity, and that this is, in part, both caused and perpetuated by 'rational' repression, is an underlying component of the cultural fault-lines within the modern consciousness (Childs, 2008). Although the formal structure and rhetoric of organizations continue to be dominated by the 'rational myth' (Badham, 2017; Brunsson, 2014; Edelman and Talesh, 2011; Mccabe, 2016; Rowan, 2002), equally widespread are competing 'social imaginaries' (Taylor, 2004) or 'orders of worth' (Boltanski and Thevenot, 2006; Jagd, 2011) Not only do these prioritize values other than efficiency and profits (e.g. individualism, freedom, equality, community), they also warn about the dangers of subordinating life to instrumental rationality and institutional hierarchy (Alexander, 2013; Alvesson and Spicer, 2016; Badham and King, 2020).

A fourth image is different to the other three, in the sense that it is tightly linked to a symbolic event. It merits separate consideration because of its powerful mythical illustration of scepticism about modern technological hubris – this is the imagery of the fate of the *Titanic*. Although possibly inaccurate, but not too far from the truth, one historian asserted that the three most written-about subjects of all time are Jesus, the American Civil War and the *Titanic*. As exemplified in the satirical newspaper headline quoted at the head of the next section, the *Titanic* (with a name drawn from the classical Greek race of superbeings, the Titans), is a symbol of mankind's hubris (Mendelsohn, 2012). As employed in many introductions to the iceberg in organization behaviour and change, the dangers of underestimating the size and significance of the iceberg are illustrated by the image of the sinking of the *Titanic* (Rick, 2015).

As a result of its alignment with this background imagery, the organization-as-iceberg metaphor creates a simple, resonant and emotive 'way of seeing' organizations. It acknowledges how we are seduced into noticing and focusing on rational appearances. It points to the significance and importance of what we intuitively (as cultural 'moderns') recognize as a more human dimension of organizational life, one that runs counter to the formally rational. Finally, recommendations to 'flip the iceberg' can build on the idea that the rational 'tip' is a small, visible part of something larger without being restricted by seeing what 'lies below' as primarily dangerous.

Generative process for the iceberg metaphor

A generative process for applying the iceberg metaphor uses the metaphor in a creative and reflective manner. One of the most distinctive features of past use of the iceberg metaphor is the *absence* of any generative process in its use. The term is commonly employed, praised or condemned with little serious or systematic consideration of its multiple uses and diverse implications and the costs or benefits of its reflective use. This gap can be addressed in two ways. First, by drawing on relatively standard views of what is involved in the reflective and generative use of metaphors (Cornelissen et al., 2008; Jacobs and Heracleous, 2006; Palmer and Dunford, 1996). Second, by drawing on a more comprehensive and nuanced history of the iceberg metaphor in order to inform such a use. We shall address seven key issues that the generative use of the iceberg metaphor needs to be reflexive about and explore.

Overlap and difference

First, there is the degree to which the similarities and differences between an 'actual' iceberg and an 'actual' organization affect its usefulness as a creative tool. This needs to be sensitive to the fact that this 'overlap' is not objectively given but shaped by views and uses of the iceberg metaphor itself. Icebergs, for example, may be viewed as too fixed and rigid to be a useful image of an organization, and yet they may also be viewed as relevant as they are more alive and fluid in nature than has been recognized in the past (Wessel, 2018).

Ambiguity and complexity

Second is the ambiguous, imprecise and complex nature of the iceberg image, something that, if ignored, may simply confuse thought and action or, if deliberately deployed, may be valuable as a way of establishing a shared understanding and direction. The iceberg image, embedded in bipolar, explicit/implicit views of culture, faces Hall's original challenge: 'Like many other abstractions about culture, this one leaves us with the feeling, "Where do we go from here?"' (Hall, 1959: 86). This can be seen as a sign of weakness, hence the popularity in the 1980s (following the 1970s rise in popularity of the iceberg image) of more refined models such as McKinsey's 7S model, Johnson and Scholes' cultural web, Galbraith's STAR model or Nadler-Tushman's congruence model, and so on. At the same time, however, as Hall points out, the 'bipolar' distinction can be valuable in making new distinctions, enabling us to see behaviour on two levels and resonating with 'American' prejudices for polarized thinking. We might also add that it provides a general orientation for challenging over-rational expectations and views of organization, in ourselves as well as others, without restricting how we follow up this insight by employing any of a variety of models.

Prescription and description

Third is the interrelation between views of the iceberg as a description of how individuals and organizations view themselves and prescriptions for how they should be viewed (Cornelissen et al., 2008). On the one hand, the iceberg metaphor describes an over-preoccupation with the formal, cognitive and rational surface within organizations and their members. On the other hand, it prescribes paying greater attention to the 'bulk' of symbolic, emotive and political issues and relations on the advice that it is dangerous to do otherwise. Paying attention to the level at which this image, or its counter, *is* present in organizations, or the degree to which its insights should be present and attended to, is a significant component of its reflective use.

Literal and figurative dynamics

Fourth are the manner and degree to which the iceberg is presented as a sensitizing and motivating image or a more or less accurate description of the realities of organizational life. A focus on the former highlights its usefulness as a stimulus and provocation, whereas attending to the latter is more concerned with its empirical accuracy and analytic power. Despite preferences of some analysts for one or the other, a reflective view does not treat this as an either/or question.

Insights and blindness

Fifth, insights and blindness are the ways in which the iceberg metaphor represents a way of seeing and not-seeing. Supporters of the metaphor (Cunliff, 2008) and those who find it useful (Clegg, Kornberger, Pitsis and Mount, 2019; Mullins and Christy, 2010; Senior and Swailes, 2016) frequently point to its valuable role in highlighting the significance of informal, tacit and non-rational forces in an organization. Its critics emphasize that it is rigid, object-like and negative in its portrayal of culture and its impact (Bennett, 2013a; Brighton, 2015; MacQueen, 2020). The creative focus and deployment of the concept address these and other potential implications as part of discussions of the relevance of the image.

Opportunities and challenges in use

Sixth are the cultural and political factors that support or oppose the effective deployment of the iceberg metaphor as a means for challenging overly rational views of organization. On the one hand, the iceberg image resonates with routine observations about the existence of formal and informal dimensions to organizational life, its apparent object-like character appeals to objectivist prejudices, and its unitary character reinforces mechanistic and organic managerial assumptions about organizational goals. It is only reasonable to assume that these elements may contribute to its credibility and may be highlighted or deployed in the use of the image in an overly rational and unreflective manner. On the other hand, the iceberg metaphor portrays the bulk of organizational issues as not belonging to the rational 'tip'; includes feelings, identities and diverse political interests 'inside' the system that is being looked at rather than outside; and these elements can be used to challenge the more traditional and conservative use of the image. Both of these potentials can be, and should be, explored in regard to both the content of the metaphor and its likely or possible contextual uses.

Similarities, differences and irony

Seventh are the differences as well as the similarities between icebergs and organizations. Rather than simply illustrating similarities (e.g. observable surface 'tip', hidden 'depths', 'dangers' of neglecting the 'bulk' beneath etc.), the differences can be highlighted as a basis for disrupting existing perceptions (e.g. are organizations 'frozen' in this way, can we separate 'above and below the surface' issues in a mechanistic way, are cultures and politics potentially enabling and supportive as well as obstructive and dangerous etc.?). Alternative elaborations of the iceberg metaphor can also be involved, drawing on more fluid images of the life cycle of icebergs, the life forms they include, the flipping that sometimes occurs, what the world looks like from the perspective of the iceberg rather than those viewing or dealing with it, and so on. These can be used as an ironic counter to the ways that the iceberg has been viewed and deployed in organizations and organization studies. Such reversals are illustrated in the quote at the beginning of this section.

Iceberg as counter-metaphor

> World's largest metaphor hits iceberg – Titanic: Representation of man's hubris, sinks in North Atlantic.
>
> (The Onion, *1999*)

Countering metaphors

The resonance and powerful effect of the iceberg metaphor as counter-metaphor come from its use of a variety of, admittedly overlapping, methods for countering metaphor (Underhill, 2012) and making counter-claims (Gabriel, 2016) against dominant ideologies and viewpoints.

Countering metaphors can employ a variety of strategies (Eubanks, 2000; Underhill, 2012) including:

- Ascription of metaphors;
- Negating, contrasting or mirroring metaphors; and
- Foregrounding, paradoxical and ironic metaphorical strategies.

Ascription

Ascription involves revealing the metaphor underlying a perspective, thereby opening up contrast, reflection and criticism. The embedded nature of rational systems models means that the use and influence of metonymic elaborations often go unnoticed, such as 'function', 'role', 'health', 'survival', 'fit', 'alignment', 'heart', 'stomach', 'brain', 'processing', 'oiling', 'wheels', 'cogs', 'nuts and bolts', 'hard-wired', 'software', 'short circuits', and even 'purpose', 'goals' and 'objectives'. The iceberg metaphor 'short-circuits' the use of such terminology in a number of ways. The term is clearly, and often self-consciously, a metaphorical image, implicitly highlighting its own role and that of others. Without denying that system assumptions are made, the metaphor relegates the use of associated terms and forms of thought to the superficial. This results from the persuasive part-tacit, part-strategic metonymic elaborations such as the 'tip of the iceberg', the need to go beneath the 'surface' or below the 'waterline', the desirability of 'plumbing the depths', being aware of the 'dangers that lurk below' and so on.

Negating, contrasting or mirroring metaphors

This involves dismissal, creating alternative, contrasting metaphors and inverting or reversing the original. In one sense, the iceberg metaphor can be seen as negating, as it dismisses simple rational systems thinking as ignoring the most important features of organizational life. It also directly counters rational strategic system metaphors by contrasting them with an alternative metaphor that highlights the systemic informal, as well as formal, dimensions of an organization. As an inversion or reversal, the iceberg performs the above activity by portraying as fundamental and primary what the rational strategic model ignores as the 'bulk' of what goes on in organizations, and it inverts what it takes to be most important to be secondary and less significant.

Foregrounding, paradoxical and ironic strategies

Foregrounding involves illuminating some features and hiding or de-emphasizing others, whereas paradoxical metaphors highlight the existence of two opposite terms in tension in relation to one image, and irony involves using satire and parody to ridicule the dominant metaphor, through exaggeration, distortion or extension. The iceberg image clearly foregrounds the informal, uncertain, emotive and political dimensions of organizational life at the expense of the formal, certain, cognitive and unitary. It does to such a degree that those responsible for developing and using the concept are frequently at pains to emphasize that the formal tip still has relevance (Herman, 2018), stressing that concentrating on issues below the surface is not to 'ignore or deny the legitimacy' of those above (Herman, 1971: 603). As a paradoxical metaphor, the iceberg challenges the view of organizations as rational systems, yet includes emotions and politics in what could be understood as a broader and more comprehensive system view. As Herman (1971: 602) puts it: 'feelings are indeed facts' and they are 'in the system'. The ironic twist embodied in the iceberg metaphor is exemplified in the *Titanic* quote at the start of this section. The hubris of mankind's (or the organization's) excessive faith in rationality, technology and control is parodied by equating this with a surface and superficial distraction with an immediately obvious tip, while, ironically, only increasing the disastrous likelihood of 'sinking' after collision with what this outlook ignores or denies.

Counter-troping and reversing dominant tropes

Within this process, counter-tropes involve creating alternative tropes or reversing the dominant trope, through ridicule or novel elaborations (Steinitz, 2015). In order to reverse a dominant trope, the use of the iceberg metaphor needs to be embedded in a process that Sillince and Golant (2017), developing the insights of Oswick, Keenoy and Grant (2002), describe as 'cycling between irony and metaphor'. In this process, one metaphor is not simply counterposed to another as an alternative perspective, but used in an overturning or reversal of an established metaphor in order to open up the space for alternatives. Despite such authors pointing to this phenomenon, it has rarely been elaborated in any detail. The most extended analysis is provided by Kenneth Burke in his argument for the rhetorical power of adopting a 'perspective by incongruity' (Burke, 1935; George, 2018). In order to challenge an attitude-laden perspective, Burke argues, it is necessary to get 'buy-in' to an alternative. In order to do so, he recommends and outlines a 'corrective' rather than a 'debunking' approach, one that opens up creativity and imagination rather than offering a counter-dogma and set of prescriptions. This process involves verbal 'atom cracking' by challenging dominant perspectives, attitudes and associated metaphors on their own terms, using, converting, twisting and challenging their established 'pieties' and 'prejudices'.

Burke outlines five key dimensions of this process: (i) identifying the existing 'dramatic vocabulary' (e.g. metaphors, images and related attitudes associated with the rational model, and the 'representative anecdotes' that capture them); (ii) adopting a 'corrective' orientation towards critique, drawing on or framing any questioning or exposure in terms of the original concepts, images and prejudices (e.g. use of the 'system' model against itself, drawing on popular bipolar imagery of organizational life); (iii) creating a 'jolt' through portraying the ideas and images in the original metaphor in an 'incongruous fashion' (e.g. the neglect of, and danger of ignoring, the 'bulk' of the organization beneath the surface); (iv) bringing about a 'conversion' through incongruous vocabulary that 'converts downwards' what are held in high esteem or 'converts upwards' what are put down (e.g. the dominant formal structures and rhetoric become a superficial 'tip', and the 'soft' issues become the crucial support and potentially dangerous 'bulk'); (v) merges categories that are held to be exclusive or divides those that are held to be inclusive (e.g. uncertainty, emotion and politics are included 'within' the organizational system, and rational thought now points to the 'limits' of rationality); and (vi) adopting a 'comic frame' that emphasizes the partiality, entrapments, foibles and over-inflated expectations and dramas embedded in all perspectives, and the fallibility and folly of those who adhere to them (e.g. using a simple concrete metaphor suggests the partiality of this and other contrasting images, and reminders about the iceberg foster an expectation, appreciation of and adaptation to the irrationalities of organizational life).

Conclusion

> Understanding the reality of covert culture and accepting it on a gut level comes neither quickly nor easily, and it must be lived rather than read or reasoned.
>
> *(Hall, 1976: 58)*

In 'The War is Over, the Victors have Lost' (1992) and *Management and Don Quixote*, March notes laconically that, despite narrow disciplinary recognition of the limitations of the overly rational managerial image of organizations, its continuing influence remains in business schools and organizations as its 'justifications and explanations of action have been sanctified, they are accepted as morally and pragmatically obvious, they are taught as sacred dogma' (March, 2007: 1).

If we take seriously the case for developing critical and reflective practice (Reynolds and Vince, 2016; see also Chapter 3 of this volume, by Durepos and Vince), practical wisdom (Schwartz and Sharpe, 2011), phronesis (Flyvbjerg, 2001) or metis (Chia and Holt, 2008; Scott, 1999) in management education, this represents a significant challenge. How do we provide an effective embodied metaphor (Jacobs and Heracleous, 2006) to counter a dominant, pervasive, culturally pernicious and institutionally sanctioned rational myth, with its attendant images, metaphors and licensing stories?

So far, alternative metaphors have failed to gain traction. As even their supporters acknowledge, direct counter-metaphors such as 'garbage can', 'irrational organization', 'unmanaged organization' and 'wonderland' have not become strongly integrated into the assumptions and practices of strategy, operations, finance and even organizational behaviour (Brunsson, 2014; March, 1992; Mccabe, 2016).

This is our starting point, and the rationale for exploring possible counter-metaphors and the particular case of the iceberg. However, given the tenor of the times, in the first instance, the iceberg metaphor seems uniquely unsuitable for resuscitation. The traditional organizational development 'ice cube' model of change as a process of unfreezing, moving and refreezing has been frequently parodied (Kanter et al., 1992) and widely condemned (Cummings et al., 2016), and, by implication, so has 'iceberg' imagery. In a more 'processual' era, preferences are frequently expressed for more fluid metaphors. This frequently involves using rivers, tributaries, permanent white water, currents and undercurrents, beaches and waves, as well as imagery of kayaks, surfers and sailing ships. These are designed to help capture the challenges of navigating unpredictable emergence, turbulence and complexity (Badham, 2013; Es, 2011; MacQueen, 2020; Pettigrew, 1979; Schein and Schein, 2019; Vaill, 1989). As these assumptions became more embedded in contemporary discourse, the iceberg metaphor began to look rather like a tired cliché from an early modern era, worthy of little interest. Given this situation, one may reasonably ask, why bother to 'waken' a sleeping metaphor like the iceberg? We believe there are three main reasons.

First, the iceberg metaphor resonates strongly with established cultural imagery. It has an accessible persuasiveness that makes it memorable as a heuristic and useful as a reminder. Second, there *is* a danger in appealing to established prejudices. If used unreflexively and inappropriately, the iceberg metaphor can end up reinforcing overly static, reified and narrowly managerial and systemic views of an organization. Its critics are correct in this observation. However, there is nothing to prevent the generative employment of the iceberg metaphor. Our argument is for its use as 'counter-discourse' that opens up and creates discursive space, as people and ideas previously silenced are provided with vehicles and opportunities to speak up and 'talk back' (Moussa and Scapp, 1996). As a 'practical theory', this involves the use of the iceberg metaphor to counter the dominant reflex, gut-feel, overly rational response to events in our thoughts and actions. Third, the iceberg metaphor can, somewhat ironically, be productively used in conjunction with fluid imagery. Arguments for alternative fluid images may be made without reflection on their own partiality, ignore the role of rhetoric and drama in making an 'evidence-based' case for their superiority, and relapse into or subordinate them to a traditional rationalistic imperative to be agile and adaptive to align with a turbulent environment. The iceberg metaphor can act as a useful heuristic and ongoing reminder about the ingrained habits and institutional expectations that make such uses both likely and problematic. In addition, the iceberg metaphor can be elaborated in a more fluid manner and be reflectively self-critical about its potential blindness to fluidity and process. Geologists, historians, novelists and poets have pointed to the process of iceberg formation, travel and melting, the teeming life within the iceberg and its ever-changing and productive character, the adoption of the iceberg's 'point of view' rather than those who fear colliding with it, and the changing views of the iceberg over time as a result of shifting trade routes and contemporary climate change. All of these can be used to elaborate the metaphor in different ways. At the same time, once the iceberg metaphor has opened up the importance of going below the surface and challenging the rational tip, it is possible to move into a generative discussion about what metaphors, images and metrics might be used to capture the phenomena that the iceberg points to. This includes the added value of a variety of fluid images, contrasts between shadow and legitimate organizations, frontstage and backstage performances, organizations as domination, warfare or theatre, and so on. Pointing to the partial nature of the iceberg's generative content can be part of a generative process for its use.

In developing these points and arguing for the iceberg as a generative counter-metaphor, this chapter makes the case for its use in opening up creativity and imagination rather than replacing one dogmatic viewpoint by another. As a counter-trope, narrative or discourse, the aim is to contribute to Weick's (2007: 15) version of a desirable educational agenda for managers. As Karl Weick put it, 'To drop the tools of rationality is to gain access to lightness … Knowledge involves acquiring. Wisdom involves dropping. Sensitivity to that difference is part of what I think it means to reconfigure management education'.

References

Alexander, J. (2013). *The dark side of modernity*. Cambridge: Polity.
Alvesson, M., and Spicer, A. (2016). *The stupidity paradox*. London: Profile Books.
Alvesson, M., and Sveningsson, S. (2016). *Changing organizational culture: Cultural change work in progress*. New York: Routledge.
Ariely, D. (2009). *Predictable irrationality: The hidden forces that shape our decisions*. New York: Harper-Collins.
Aronson, E. (1989). The rationalizing animal. In Leavitt, H., Pondy, L. and Boje, D. (eds), *Readings in managerial psychology*. Chicago: University of Chicago Press, 134–144.
Badham, R. (2013). *Short change: An introduction to managing change*. Sumy, Ukraine: Business Perspectives.
Badham, R.J. (2017). Reflections on the paradoxes of modernity: A conversation with James March. In Smith, W.K., Lewis, M.W., Jarzabkowski, P. and Langley, A. (eds), *The Oxford handbook of organizational paradox*. Oxford: Oxford University Press, 1–24.
Badham, R., and King, E. (2020). Mindfulness at work: A critical review. *Organization*, 1–30.
Barley, S.R., and Kunda, G. (2010). Design and devotion: Surges of rational and normative ideologies of control in managerial discourse. *Administrative Science Quarterly*, 37 (3): 363–399.
Barrett, F.J., and Cooperrider, D.L. (1990). Generative metaphor intervention: A new approach for working with systems divided by conflict and caught in defensive perception. *The Journal of Applied Behavioral Science*, 26 (2): 219–239.
Bennett, M.J. (2013a). Culture is not like an iceberg. Retrieved January 28, 2020, from www.idrinstitute.org/2013/05/06/culture-not-like-iceberg/
Bennett, M.J. (2013b). The ravages of reification: Considering the iceberg and cultural intelligence, towards de-reifying intercultural competence. In *File IV, Colle Val D'Elsa,*. https://doi.org/10.1017/CBO9781107415324.004
Black, M. (1993). More about metaphor. In Ortony, A. (ed.), *Metaphor and thought*. Cambridge: Cambridge University Press, 19–34.
Boltanski, L., and Thevenot, L. (2006). *On justification: Economies of worth*. Princeton: Princeton University Press.
Brighton, D. (2015). Destroy the iceberg. Retrieved January 31, 2020, from https://brightonleadership.com/2015/10/06/destroy-the-iceberg/

Brunsson, N. (2014). The irrational organization: Irrationality as the basis for organizational action and change. *Management*, 2 (2): 141–144.
Buchanan, D., and Badham, R. (2020). *Power, politics and organizational change* (3rd edn.). London: Sage.
Buchanan, D., and Huczynski, A. (2019). *Organizational behaviour*. London: Pearson.
Burke, K. (1935). *Permanence and change*. New York: New Republic.
Burnes, B. (2017). *Managing change*. Harlow: Pearson.
Burns, T. (1961). Micropolitics: Mechanisms of institutional change. *Administrative Science Quarterly*, 6 (3): 257–281.
Cavana, B., Goodman, M., and Maani, K. (2018). Personal communication.
Chia, R., and Holt, R. (2008). The nature of knowledge in business schools. *Academy of Management Learning and Education*, 7 (4): 471–486.
Childs, P. (2008). *Modernism* (2nd edn). London: Routledge.
Clegg, S., Kornberger, M., Pitsis, T., and Mount, M. (2019). *Managing and organizations: An introduction to theory and practice* (5th edn.). London: Sage.
Cohen, M.D., March, J.G., and Olsen, J.F. (1972). A garbage can model of organizational choice. *Administrative Science Quarterly*, 17 (1): 1–25.
Collier, A. (2013). Culture is not like an iceberg. Retrieved July 30, 2018, from www.idrinstitute.org/2013/05/06/culture-not-like-iceberg/
Colville, I., Brown, A.D., and Pye, A. (2012). Simplexity: Sensemaking, organizing and storytelling for our time. *Human Relations*, 65 (1): 5–15.
Cornelissen, J.P., Oswick, C., Christensen, L.T., and Phillips, N. (2008). Metaphor in organizational research: Context, modalities and implications for research - Introduction. *Organization Studies*, 29 (1): 7–22.
Cummings, S., Bridgman, T., and Brown, K. (2016). Unfreezing change as three steps. *Human Relations*, 69 (1): 33–60.
Cummins, J. (2001). *Negotiating identities*. San Francisco: Californian Association for Bilingual Education.
Cunliff, E.D. (2008). Connecting systems thinking and action. *The Systems Thinker*, 15 (2): 1–13.
Cunliff, E., and Monat, J. (2018). Personal communication.
Dalton, M. (2017). *Men who manage*. (2nd edn). London: Routledge.
Edelman, L., and Talesh, S. (2011). To comply or not to comply, that isn't the question: How organizations construct the meaning of compliance. In Parker, C. and Neilsen, V. (eds.), *Explaining compliance*. Cheltenham: Edward Elgar, 103–122.
Es, R. van. (2011). *Diagnosing change*. Deventer, Netherlands: Vakmedianet.
Eubanks, P. (2000). *A war of words in the discourse of trade*. Carbondale and Edwardsville: Southern Illinois University Press.
Flyvbjerg, B. (2001). *Making social science happen*. Cambridge: Cambridge University Press.
French, W., and Bell, C. (1973). *Organization development: Behavioral science interventions for organization development*. Englewood Cliffs, NJ: Prentice Hall.
Gabriel, Y. (2016). Narrative ecologies and the role of counter-narratives. In Frandsen, S., Kuhn, T. and Lundholt, M. (eds), *Counter narratives and organization*. London: Routledge, 208–226.
George, A. (2018). *Kenneth Burke's permanence and change: A critical companion*. Columbia, SC: University of South Carolina Press.
Giorgi, S., Lockwood, C., and Glynn, M.A. (2015). The many faces of culture: Making sense of 30 years of research on culture in organization studies. *Academy of Management Annals*, 9 (1): 1–54.

Green, C. (2019). Where did Freud's iceberg metaphor of mind come from? *History of Psychology*, 22 (4): 369–379.
Gusfield, J.R. (2000). *Performing Action*. New Brunswick and London: Transaction.
Hall, E.T. (1959). *The silent language*. New York: Doubleday.
Hall, E.T. (1966). *The hidden dimension*. New York: Doubleday.
Hall, E.T. (1976). *Beyond culture*. New York: Doubleday.
Hatch, M. (2013). *Organization theory: Modern, symbolic and post-modern perspectives*. Oxford: Oxford University Press.
Hayes, J. (2020). *The theory and practice of managing change*. London: Red Globe.
Hellriegel, D., and Slocum, J. (2011). *Organizational behavior* (13th edn). Mason, Ohio: Cengage Learning.
Hellriegel, D., Slocum, J., and Woodman. R. (1998). *Management*. Nashville: South-Western Publishing.
Herman, S. (1971). What is this thing called organization development? *Personnel Journal* 50 (8), 595–603.
Herman, S. (2018). Personal communication.
Hitchins, D. (2018). Personal communication via Jamie Monat.
Hochschild, A.R. (1983). *The managed heart: Commercialization of human feeling*. Berkeley: University of California Press.
Hughes, M. (2019). *Managing and leading change*. London: Taylor & Francis.
Jacobs, C.D., and Heracleous, L.T. (2006). Constructing shared understanding: The role of embodied metaphors in organization development. *Journal of Applied Behavioral Science*, 42 (2): 207–226.
Jagd, S. (2011). Pragmatic sociology and competing orders of worth in organizations. *European Journal of Social Theory*, 14 (3): 343–359.
Kanter, R.M., Stein, B.A., and Jick, T.D. (1992). *The challenge of organizational change: How companies experience it and leaders guide it*. New York: Free Press.
Kim, D. (1999). *Introduction to systems theory*. New York: Pegasus Communications.
Knights, D., and Willmott, H. (2006). *Introducing organizational behaviour and management*. London: Thomson Learning.
Kunda, G. (2006). *Engineering culture: Control and commitment in a high-tech corporation*. Philadelphia: Temple University Press.
Lakoff, G., and Turner, M. (1989). *More than cool reason: A field guide to poetic metaphor*. Chicago: University of Chicago Press.
Lasch, C. (1979). *The culture of narcissism: American life in an age of diminishing expectations*. New York: W.W. Norton.
Maccoby, M. (1978). *The gamesman: Winning and losing the career game*. New York: Bantam.
Maclean, M., Harvey, C., and Stringfellow, L.J. (2017). Narrative, metaphor and the subjective understanding of historic identity transition. *Business History*, 59 (8): 1218–1241.
MacQueen, J. (2020). *The flow of organizational culture: New thinking and theory for better understanding and process*. London: Palgrave Macmillan.
Mccabe, D. (2016). 'Curiouser and curiouser!': Organizations as Wonderland – a metaphorical alternative to the rational model. *Human Relations*, 69 (4): 945–973.
March, J. G. (1992). The war is over and the victors have lost. *Journal of Socio-Economics*, 21 (3): 261–267.
March, J.G. (2007). *Management and Don Quixote*. France: HEC, You Tube. Retrieved from www.youtube.com/watch?v=bztgYMoTEjM.
Marshak, R.J. (1993). Managing the metaphors of change. *Organizational Dynamics*, 22 (1): 44–56.

Mendelsohn, B.D. (2012). UNSINKABLE: Why we can't let go of the Titanic, 1–16. Retrieved from www.newyorker.com/magazine/2012/04/16/unsinkable-3.
Meyer, J.W., and Rowan, B. (1977). Institutionalized organizations: Formal structure as myth and ceremony. *American Journal of Sociology*, 83 (2): 340–363.
Monat, J.P., and Gannon, T.F. (2015). What is systems thinking? A review of selected literature plus recommendations. *American Journal of Systems Science*, 4 (1): 11–26.
Morgan, G. (1989). *Creative organization theory*. Newbury Park: Sage.
Morgan, G. (2006). *Images of organization*. London: Sage.
Moussa, M., and Scapp, R. (1996). The practical theorizing of Michel Foucault: Politics and counter-discourse. *Cultural Critique*, 33 (Spring): 87–112.
Mueller, C. (2008). *Metaphors dead and alive, sleeping and waking: A dynamic view*. Chicago: University of Chicago Press.
Mullins, L., and Christy, G. (2010). *Management and organizational behaviour*. London: Pearson.
Oswick, C., Keenoy, T., and Grant, D. (2002). Metaphor and analogical reasoning in organization theory: Beyond orthodoxy. *Academy of Management Review*, 27 (2): 294–303.
Palmer, I., and Dunford, R. (1996). Conflicting uses of metaphors: Reconceptualizing their use in the field of organizational change. *Academy of Management Review*, 21 (3): 691–717.
Pettigrew, A.M. (1979). On studying organizational cultures. *Administrative Science Quarterly*, 24 (4): 570–581.
Reynolds, M., and Vince, R. (2016). *Organizing reflection*. Abingdon: Routledge.
Rick, T. (2014). Organizational culture is like an iceberg. Retrieved January 19, 2020, from www.torbenrick.eu/blog/culture/organizational-culture-is-like-an-iceberg/
Rick, T. (2015). The iceberg that sinks organizational change. Retrieved January 19, 2020, from www.torbenrick.eu/blog/change-management/iceberg-that-sinks-organizational-change/
Rowan, B. (2002). Rationality and reality in organizational management: Using the coupling metaphor to understand educational (and other) organizations - a concluding comment. *Journal of Educational Administration*, 40 (6): 604–611.
Scharmer, O., and Kaufer, K. (2013). *Leading from the emerging future*. San Francisco: Berrett-Koehler.
Schein, E. (2020). Personal communication.
Schein, E.H., and Schein, P. (2019). *The corporate culture survival guide*. Hoboken and San Francisco: Wiley.
Schon, D. (1979). *Displacement of concepts*. London: Tavistock.
Schwartz, B., and Sharpe, K. (2011). *Practical wisdom: The right way to do the right thing*. New York: Riverhead Books.
Scott, J. (1999). *Seeing like a state*. New Haven: Yale University Press.
Senge, P. (2006). *The fifth discipline: The art and practice of the learning organization* (2nd edn). London: Random House.
Senior, B., and Fleming, J. (2006). *Organizational change*. London: Prentice Hall.
Senior, B., and Swailes, S. (2016). *Organizational change* (5th edn). Harlow: Pearson Education.
Sillince, J.A.A., and Golant, B.D. (2017). The role of irony and metaphor in working through paradox during organizational change. In Smith, W.K., Lewis, M.L., Jarzabkowski, P. and Langley, A. (eds), *The Oxford handbook of organizational paradox*. Oxford: Oxford University Press, 260–276.
Steinitz, J. (2015). *What's metaphor got to do with it? Troping and counter-troping in Holocaust victim language*. University of Iowa. Retrieved from http://ir.uiowa.edu/etd/1910
Stouten, J., Rousseau, D.M., and De Cremer, D. (2018). Successful organizational change: Integrating the management practice and scholarly literatures. *Academy of Management Annals*, 12 (2): 752–788.

Sun, L., Paez, O., Lee, D., Salem, S., and Daraiseh, N.M. (2006). Estimating the uninsured costs of work-related accidents, part I: A systematic review. *Theoretical Issues in Ergonomics Science*, 7 (3): 227–245.
Swuste, P. (2018). Personal communcation.
Swuste, P., Gulijk, C. Van, and Zwaard, W. (2010). Safety metaphors and theories, a review of the occupational safety literature of the US, UK and The Netherlands, till the first part of the 20th century. *Safety Science*, 48 (8): 1000–1018.
Taylor, C. (2004). *Modern social imaginaries*. Durham and London: Duke University Press.
Underhill, J. (2012). *Ethnolinguistics and cultural concepts*. Cambridge: Cambridge University Press.
Vaill, P. (1989). *Managing as a performing art*. San Francisco: Jossey-Bass.
Weick, K. ([1969] 1979). *The social psychology of organizing*. Reading: Addison-Wesley.
Weick, K.E. (2007). Drop your tools: On reconfiguring management education. *Journal of Management Education*, 31 (5): 5–16.
Wessel, L. (2018). The base of the iceberg: It's big and teeming with life. *Knowable Magazine*, 20–21.
Westwood, R., and Clegg, S.R. (eds.) (2003). *Debating organization: Point-counterpoint in organization studies*. Oxford: Blackwell.
Whyte, W.H. (1956). *The organization man*. New York: Simon & Schuster.
Wilson, J. (2015). Political discourse. In Tannen, D., Hamilton, H. and Schiffrin, D. (eds), *Handbook of discourse analysis*. Chichester: Wiley-Blackwell, 775–795.

5

TOWARDS CRITICAL HISTORICAL STUDIES

An emancipatory ontology

Christiane Chihadeh

Introduction

Interest in historical awareness, which has become increasingly central to the discussion of the use of history in organization studies, has emanated from studies that have sought to bring the work of organizational and management theorists closer to that of more traditional business historians and historians more generally (Booth and Rowlinson, 2006; Bucheli and Wadhwani, 2014; Clark and Rowlinson, 2004; Maclean, Harvey and Clegg, 2016; 2017; Rowlinson, Hassard and Decker, 2014; Seixas, 2004; Suddaby, 2016; Wadhwani, Suddaby, Mordhorst and Popp, 2018). Such an endeavour has not sought to claim that one discipline is superior to another, but rather to explicate the importance and lucrativeness of the role history can play in our efforts to better understand organizations and more broadly, theories of organizing (Wadhwani et al., 2018).

Renewed interest in the historic turn in organization studies through historical consciousness and uses of the past literature has given prominence to the epistemological and ontological foundations of the way in which the notion of 'knowing' is to be understood. Knowing here refers to the way actors recognize and position themselves within time and how they reflect upon and interpret their past, to better understand their present and perceive their possible futures (Koselleck, 2004). What is more, Wadhwani et al. (2018: 1664) argue that the uses of the past perspective furthers this idea of knowing and takes into account the way in which 'organizational actors themselves produce and use history for purposes in the present'. The discussion has promoted an apparent concern with the way in which organization studies uses and engages with history, perhaps reflecting the notion of bridging disciplines to bring them closer together. A key aspect of the uses of the past literature is the apparent multiplicity of possible interpretations of the past; organizational actors may make multiple interpretations and interactions with the past (Wadhwani et al., 2018). A view of history beyond the normative or path-dependent process it was once perceived to be is thus enabled (Nelson and Winter, 1982; North, 1990).

The apparent malleability of the use and interpretation of the past undoubtedly enables research agendas to develop further, and historical research to be incorporated more regularly in traditionally organization-focused journals. The position of the researcher in the production of historical narratives and in the historical research process more generally is raised by this apparent malleability in interpretation. If the idea of knowing is important both epistemologically and ontologically for the organizational actor, then it must also be of importance to the researcher. If we are to draw upon Seixas's (2004) original discussion of the five principles of historical consciousness, we find an emphasis on the relationship between the researcher and history, the practice of history and, more practically, a concern with the methods, findings and empirics. These latter points not only highlight the need for historical consciousness to bring history more prominently into organization studies, but also allow researchers to understand the foundational tools and processes involved in producing historical research and historical narratives. These discussion points also feature in Rowlinson et al.'s (2014) elaboration of the organizational critique of archival sources and historical narratives and ensuing dualisms of explanation, evidence and temporality.

Focusing on the ontological and epistemological foundations of historical awareness or historical consciousness (Suddaby, 2016; Wadhwani et al., 2018) in management and organizational history provides the basis for my discussion. I will suggest ways in which a critical realist approach (with a focus upon ontological foundations) can help further our abilities to produce critical historical studies. In the following sections, I will review the literature pertaining to accepted approaches and varieties of history in organization studies, placing these discussions in the wider turns that have occurred in the organizations discipline. Next, discussion will focus more upon the deconstructivist approach to history, delving further into Munslow's (2006a) ontological typologies and suggesting, in fact, that deconstruction is only the first step in producing critical knowledge. These ideas will be further elaborated through an assessment of the deconstructivist approach not solely viewed as a history that offers a form of fictional writing (Rowlinson and Hassard, 2014), but as an approach with properties that are viable for an emancipatory ontology of historical reality. Discussion then turns to a critical realist approach to history in organization studies where I suggest the possibilities for furthering the critical element of historical studies through the emancipation of knowledge and an emancipatory discussion of society and culture. I will explore these possibilities of emancipatory and critical history by making reference to both feminist and Marxist history. Finally, the chapter concludes with the suggestion of a possible research process through critical grounded theory and the retroductive research movement emanating from critical realism.

Various ontologies of history: Tracing developments and current approaches

Coraiola, Foster and Suddaby (2015) provide some insights into the divide between history and the (social) sciences in management and organizational history as one that predominantly stems from varying ontological and epistemological positions. The authors go on to outline three perspectives concerning the nature of historical reality when defining history: a reconstructivist ontology, a constructivist ontology and a deconstructivist ontology. These distinctions of historical reality are built upon Munslow's (2006a; 2006b) discussion of ontological positions concerning the nature of historical reality. The varying approaches to history have been outlined by others (Rowlinson and Hassard, 2014) in an endeavour that seeks better to understand the production and use of history in organizations and organizing; these approaches can also be placed into wider contexts of development which trace the development and evolution of the use of history in organization studies (Üsdiken and Kieser, 2004; Üsdiken and Kipping, 2014).

Reconstructing history

The *reconstructivist ontology* of historical reality is an approach in which historians attempt to produce truthful assessments of historical accounts and narratives. The reconstructivist assumptions can be classified as a purer and more scientific approach to history inasmuch as historians within this paradigm adhere to the notion of the objective researcher. As such, their end goal is to produce a version of history based on factual truth; here, the researcher's own perspectives and inference of the past have no merit in the production of the historical narrative, as this is not information which would be obtainable from the sources being consulted (Coraiola et al., 2015). Historians adhering to a reconstructivist ontology endeavour to write about the past as it really happened, utilizing language as a tool to represent the past in terms legitimated by archival data and other events and action that have attained the status of empirical facts or artefacts that can (or ought to be) verified (Coraiola et al., 2015). Within the reconstructivist ontology, historians produce narrative accounts, and there is some recognition of the importance of interpretation in historical writing by those adhering to this paradigm. Such historians concede that historical narratives are an interpretive reconstruction from given sources that are impartially selected and critically evaluated (Coraiola et al., 2015). Drawing on earlier discussions in this chapter outlining the notion of knowing or what can be known (Wadhwani et al., 2018), then the reconstructivist historian's relationship with what can be known distinguishes them as an 'impartial observer' (Coraiola et al., 2015: 209). The commitment to the facts and impartiality in their interpretation represent a distinct epistemology.

Constructing history

The *constructivist ontology* encompasses multiple perspectives in the approach to historical research, but the most significant way in which it differs from the reconstructivist approach is acknowledgement that it is not possible to recount the past factually (Coraiola et al., 2015). For constructivists, knowledge of the past is always bounded by research questions, which are formulated and based upon knowledge gathered from existing sources. The importance of context in the production of history is recognized by constructivist historians; however, there also exists commitment to historical narratives not being narrative fiction, acknowledging that, for the most part, to some degree, historical knowledge and writing correspond to the reality of the past (Coraiola et al., 2015). Where those historians operating under the reconstructivist paradigm adopt an inductive and objective approach to history, historians within the constructivist paradigm adopt a more deductive approach akin to those employed within the social sciences, assuming or acknowledging that history studies require theoretical and conceptual underpinnings. Doing this places emphasis on the role of the researcher; it makes historical accounts contingent on the types of question a researcher's theoretical understanding is able to pose to sources (Coraiola et al., 2015; Munslow, 2006b).

Although a fair degree of diversity exists within the constructivist ontology, it is possible to define two major strands of thought. There is agreement upon the fact that historical sources are the primary way to access the past and produce historical interpretations, but disagreement arises when constructivist historians are questioned about the nature of historical sources. Coraiola et al. (2015) identify the two main strands of thought as the *practical realist constructivists*, whom they liken to Marxists, and, in contrast, the *post-empiricists*. The former are most closely aligned with the discussion above; for them, theoretical questions drive the way in which the historical case or problem is addressed; the latter differ slightly through the way in which a narrative approach is embraced such that the linguistic turn is incorporated into their conception of historical reality.

A shift from constructivist history to deconstructivist history

A *deconstructivist ontology* of history differs from the both the reconstructivist and constructivist ontologies inasmuch as it is characterized by postmodern thought. The impact of this on the discussion of history is to position the narrative as central to knowing what can be known in organization studies. Coraiola et al. (2015: 211) argue that, from this approach, 'history is understood as a narrative of a narrative and what we know about the past is merely a text that has been created and produced by historians'. What can be inferred from this is that those working with a deconstructivist ontology are producing a particular historical account of the past, not necessarily a factual account of the past. There is an apparent shift away from what could be considered more scientific history towards history as occurring in a similar realm to fictional writing (Rowlinson and Hassard, 2014).

The differentiating feature of the deconstructivist ontology is the lack of distinction between history and literature, which results in the general acceptance of history as a narrative representation of the past in the present, allowing historical narratives to become politicized and ideological. Those historians operating within a deconstructivist ontology leave themselves potentially open to criticism concerning the storyline and forms of language employed within the construction of the narrative (Munslow, 2006a).

Where the reconstructivist ontology implies an inductive style of reasoning and a constructivist ontology implies a deductive style of reasoning, Munslow (2006a: 62) argues that, within a deconstructivist ontology, historians use sources as 'meaningful historical explanations'. The implication is that the sources are not used to represent the past as it actually occurred; rather, the style of reasoning employed by historians within a deconstructivist ontology is to disclose a possible past through the application of various lenses to the sources utilized (Coraiola et al., 2015). From this perspective, the past does not come alive from the sources themselves but emanates from the positioning and framing employed by the historian, where 'the written historical narrative is the formal *re-presentation*' of historical content (Munslow, 2006a: 27). What emerges is a number of possible representations of, and possibilities for the existence of the past and the sources available for engagement.

Despite the apparent freedom deconstructionism appears to afford the historical researcher, there appear to be few examples of studies that adopt such an ontological approach. Those studies that do incorporate a deconstructivist approach have becomes vehicles for important cultural discussions. A clear example includes Mills's (2006) presentation of the history of gender in relation to organizational culture within the commercial airline industry. Despite engaging with documents typically found within corporate archives, Mills (2006) was able to produce a series of mini ethnographies, presenting a narrative concerning the way in which the airline industry had become gendered over a period of time, drawing upon influences from feminist research, gender and history consecutively (Rowlinson and Hassard, 2014). Although Mills's study represents a more scientific approach in some ways, particularly with the emphasis upon periodization and, to some extent, causal relationships, his ability to draw upon other disciplines for theoretical inspiration allowed for a more deconstructivist version of history. What emerged was a rich discussion of gender over time with emancipatory capabilities.

A critical realist ontology for historical organizational studies

In working towards an outline of a critical historical approach and eventually suggesting a retroductive research process, it is worth briefly reminding ourselves of some of the core premises of critical realism (particularly a critical realist ontology). Critical realism (CR) encompasses a stratified ontology distinguishing between the real, the actual and the empirical levels of discussion. The empirical domain is the level to which actors have direct access: it is the level of actors' sensations, impressions and perceptions of reality (Leca and Naccache, 2006). The domain of the actual comprises events (detected or not) in which phenomena can occur, regardless of whether actors perceive or experience them. These events are not transferred into the domain of the empirical until actors have interacted with or interpreted them, thus transforming them into experience (Bhaskar, 1978). Finally, the domain of the real encompasses the generative mechanisms and causal powers underlying events (Leca and Naccache, 2006).

The real particularly relates to 'naturally necessary' features; these can be casual properties or the possibilities of action offered by a material object or social network (Sum and Jessop, 2013). The real here can also comprise the vulnerability of social relations, which in some cases may be observable, whereas in others may not be a reality. The latter point relates to the way in which real causal and generative mechanisms, which can exist outside consciousness and awareness, can become manifest in a particular way within a particular context. These manifestations are grasped by actors who can then go on to construct multiple meanings for and of them, depending on their level of social understanding (Bhaskar, 1978). Emphasis is placed on the consideration of time and space and the importance of understanding the wider context and circumstance of particular events and the generative mechanisms at play (Archer, 1995; 1998). The empirical level of discussion is related to those events that are actualized. Both the empirical and the actual pose questions about the real (Jessop and Sum, 2006; Sum and Jessop, 2013).

CR goes beyond a more positivist ontology of cause–effect; instead, the acknowledgement of the real is in essence a 'regulative idea', rather than a reality to which we have direct access (Sum and Jessop, 2013: 10). Within CR, there is reliance on a method of retroduction as 'an open process that switches among concept building, retroductive moments, empirical inquiries, conceptual refinement, further retroduction, and so on' (Sum and Jessop, 2013:10). For adherents of CR, the real world is theory-laden, and the starting point for any enquiry is discursively constituted. A movement is implied from outlining a problem in a simple one-sided perspective to an account that encompasses complexity as a synthesis of multiple determinants and real mechanisms that makes connections between the actual and the empirical (Jessop and Sum, 2006; Sum and Jessop, 2013).

The application of the critical realist approach (particularly a critical realist ontology) with emphasis on the domain of the *real* has long animated points of difficulty and contention for researchers across the social sciences. Domingues (2018) explores this notion of the real within a wider critique of the Bhaskarian perspective of CR, arguing that Bhaskar perhaps places too much emphasis on mechanisms as 'things', prompting a consideration of mechanisms relating to the level of the real as processes. In Bhaskar's stratified ontology, mechanisms produce events and exist independently and enduringly beyond these events. Considering mechanisms of the domain of the real in a more process-like manner allows for understanding that existing processes may generate new and additional processes (Domingues, 2018).

Suggesting a critical approach: Critical grounded theory and a retroductive research process

In this section, I will begin to outline critical grounded theory (CGT) as an appropriate methodology or research process for the operationalization of archival and historical research. The section is structured so that the origins of CGT are clear, and so too is its basis within the critical realist realm of discussion. Belfrage and Hauf (2017) show theory building to be derived from fieldwork and interview data on which I shall build to argue for CGT's appropriateness for historical fieldwork (archival data collection and triangulation with other, arguably more secondary, data sources, e.g. the media and organization strategy statements). CGT is based on a critical realist ontology that counteracts naivety in claims that research can be neutral; put more simply, it mitigates against the notion that we enter into research with no preconceived ideas (as per grounded theory). Such an approach is particularly useful in the development of a methodology for a historically inclined research project where the phenomenon under scrutiny has already occurred and some knowledge of events will already be possessed by the researcher (whether this be a partial interest or great depths of knowledge).

The notion of a critical adaptation of grounded theory may seem slightly contradictory, particularly as grounded theory per Glaser and Strauss (1967) is rooted within the positivist science tradition. However, I will highlight the arguments put forward by Belfrage and Hauf (2015; 2017) to demonstrate the ways in which, by aligning them with CR, grounded theory tools can be integrated into theoretical frameworks for historical and archival organization studies. Grounded theory arose out of an apparent dissatisfaction with logical positivism and the need to provide a method that allowed for the qualitative production of results that were as reliable as those produced within quantitative studies (similar to some of the premises for the shift from a more reconstructivist to deconstructivist ontology discussed earlier within the chapter).

Glaser, as a naïve realist, saw pure induction as the only way to produce knowledge, and, despite grounded theory being an interpretivist and qualitative approach, this naïve realism remained (Belfrage and Hauf, 2015). The original view of pure induction is somewhat limiting as it implies that theory is already present within data or phenomena, and thus the role of the researcher employing grounded theory methods is that of discovery and nothing more (Belfrage and Hauf, 2015; Glaser and Strauss, 1967). Herein lies the naivety of such a perspective rejected by critical realists. Grounded theory, since its inception, has moved away from more positivist versions of induction, and it is now recognized among grounded theorists that initial observations are theory-laden and influenced by 'pre-concepts' or proto-theories (Belfrage and Hauf, 2017), as befits historical research.

The move away from pure induction is clearly represented by a schism between Glaser and Strauss, with Glaser adhering to the purist line. Since their formulation of grounded theory, Strauss has moved into a more post-positivist paradigm less opposed to recognizing the presence and use of existing theories within the formulation of research (Strauss and Corbin, 1990). Strauss and Corbin (1990) developed techniques within grounded theory in two ways: first, they used coding as a way in which the movement from data to codes to categories is facilitated. Second, they employed the 'conditional matrix' tool, which is related to that of the coding paradigm, as a tool that can aid a researcher in locating 'the phenomenon under study within a broader structural context and analyse the interrelations between micro and macro conditions on a variety of scales' (Belfrage and Hauf, 2015: 331). These tools contribute to the notion that research, whether employing grounded theory or not, is laden with preconceived notions and conceptualizations that need to be accounted for and addressed within the research process.

Strauss's move away from his initial conceptions of grounded theory with Glaser allows researchers from differing paradigmatic backgrounds to use grounded theory more openly; for example, Charmaz (2006) applies a more constructivist approach within critical grounded theory to capture notions of meaning-making. Jessop and Sum (2006) argue that our existing knowledge of the world is never free from some form of theoretical conditioning; as a result, a researcher does not enter a field of study without pre-existing theoretical assumptions. Where CR speaks to historical studies is in its recognition of social agendas, which stands in contrast to the more positivist agenda of the initial conceptions of grounded theory. Positivist theory seeks to explain social phenomena. Critical realists, in contrast, seek to understand social phenomena.

In employing CGT, the researcher is sensitive to context and the societal issues that exist within it; Belfrage and Hauf (2017: 9) submit that the 'choice of research problem is explicitly driven by moral and/or social concerns in an ambition to produce critical knowledge to enable social emancipation'. The research problem, therefore, emanates from critical observations and experiences of a social issue that requires some form of explanation, understanding and change (Belfrage and Hauf, 2017; Sum and Jessop, 2013).

Illustrating the application of a retroductive research process

CGT essentially sheds light on a retroductive research process that can prove fruitful when embarking on historical organizational studies from an emancipatory perspective. CGT goes some distance in addressing the notion of situated historical research offered by Wadhwani and Decker (2018). In recognizing the position of a situated historical researcher, the significance placed upon specific actions and events becomes more prominent. This not only accounts for the retrospective nature of historical research, but also the role the researcher has to play in the interpretation of history and the past (Bucheli and Wadhwani, 2014). In recognizing a historical researcher's situated position, relationships to the period or phenomena under study become more transparent, with benefits for illustrating and producing historical knowledge and narratives of the past (Wadhwani and Decker, 2018). Equally important, however, is the idea that historical research can also provide an alternative perspective on events. What is crucial to understand is that

CGT not only allows the researcher to be present in the research process, but also, in some ways, calls for the presence of the researcher to guide historical study. The retroductive research process (related to CGT) takes into account the position of the researcher and the role the research has to play in the production and dissemination of a historical narrative. Belfrage and Hauf (2017) outline a nine-step research process, which is not unidirectional but allows the research to progress in a linear fashion while also moving iteratively, back and forth, between the various phases of process as needed, with the ultimate goal of reaching an emancipatory discussion of social phenomena.

The CGT research process is primarily driven by a moral or social issue with the aim of producing critical (historical) knowledge with the goal of social emancipation, bringing to contemporary historical consciousness issues omitted or glossed over in conventional historiography. Thus, the role of the researcher is immediately determined and defined as one who is not objectively removed (as per the reconstructivist ontology of historical reality), but is in fact 'an active member of society ridden with social antagonisms and relations of exploitations, dominations and exclusion' (Belfrage and Hauf, 2017: 259). The purpose of the researcher is to address contemporary issues and uncover some of their historical grounds of exploitation, domination and exclusion. Such grounds can form the basis for the deconstruction of the 'naturalness' of present conditions. The initial phase of the CGT research process relates to the preliminary stages of interpretation of the research problem wherein the researcher consults hegemonic discourses relevant to the study. These pertain to the notion of proto-theories or proto-concepts, which distinguish CGT as a research process (Belfrage and Hauf, 2017). These hegemonic discourses can be found, for example, through media resources, existing literature, academic scholarship and policy documents (among other sources). The task is to perform the initial collection, preparation and evaluation of the discursive materials.

From this initial collection, the authors discuss a retroductive movement by which the researcher can turn to existing theories compatible with the assumptions of CR. Retroduction is described as the 'ongoing two-way, spiral movement between the abstract and the concrete, between theoretical and empirical work, that involves both an interpretive and a causal dimension of explanation' (Belfrage and Hauf, 2015: 334–335). Retroduction involves both a deductive and an inductive moment: the deductive moment involves creating soft hypotheses from existing theoretical concepts, not with the goal of testing them scientifically, but with the aim of putting them into 'dialogue' with observations made in the field. The inductive moment involves the researchers' immersion in the field, working initial data into emerging conceptualizations, refining initial proto-theories or preconceptions and deepening understanding, as well as reconstructing existing theory (Belfrage and Hauf, 2015; Jessop and Sum, 2006).

The next stage involves turning what has been learned through the retroductive movement into initial conceptualizations that guide the researcher through a phase of ethnographic fieldwork. Here, the initial conceptualizations formulated help guide the researcher through their fieldwork, with Belfrage and Hauf (2017) primarily focusing on more ethnographic methods of study, but this ethnographic notion can also be applied to archival and historical research. Ethnohistory speaks to the serendipity of finding sources (Jordanova, 2006), where serendipity becomes an unfolding process of discovery. Serendipity in archival research is an iterative and ongoing process of knowledge creation that happens in the archives (Popp and Fellman, 2017) through archival discovery, as outlined by Ketelaar (2001). Archival research is often discussed in conjunction with qualitative ethnographic studies in organization and management studies, essentially acting as a mode of triangulation. I want to approach ethnography in a slightly different manner, in terms of archival ethnography. What I hope to highlight is the way in which qualitative researchers employing ethnography immerse themselves within a field. Such immersion can also be done within the archives; indeed, this was already briefly discussed through reference to Mills's (2006) study of the gendered airline industry. I am proposing approaching documents within the archive in a similar manner to the way in which the participant is approached within in the field. Rowlinson et al. (2014) discuss ethnographic history in conjunction with organizational ethnography; the authors highlight three key criteria in conducting a traditional ethnographic study. They see the researcher as someone who observes and talks to people, employs a narrative form of writing and convinces the reader of the authority of the study. These criteria can be employed within ethnographic history. It has been claimed that ethnographers have to construct their texts from the field, whereas the text utilized by historians comes packaged, in the sense that the information required is provided neatly by the archive (Van Maanen, 1988). What is key is that, during this phase of the retroductive research process, the data collection process is potentially emancipatory in that it 'provides space, time and potentially voice to social problems' (Belfrage and Hauf, 2017: 259), affording the researcher the opportunity to develop further the initial proto-theories or pre-concepts through examining empirical findings.

The final movement within the CGT spiral is the process by which the researcher continuously and retroductively develops understanding of a social issue or problem. The emerging conceptualizations that are formed and their subsequent interpretations are continuously compared with already existing accounts, existing perhaps in written text but also as a result of earlier research processes. What emerges from the process serves to make the initial considerations of the researcher more complex, refined and rich (Belfrage and Hauf, 2017), especially in terms of emancipatory considerations. Although the latter stages heavily involve reflexivity in the production of CGT, I would argue that CGT is reflexive in its consciousness of the social issue or problem throughout the process. What emerges from the retroductive process are various potential outcomes starting from 'deepening or broadening' and establishing 'new conceptual connections', 'refinement', 'reconstruction of theory' or 'challenges to existing theory' (Belfrage and Hauf, 2017: 260). These outcomes are all properties or features of emancipatory critical and social studies which serve to deepen our understanding of social relations and provide new forms and lenses for understanding of social relations and thus the possible identification of social alternatives.

CGT speaks to historical research in various manners; Belfrage and Hauf (2015) highlight CGT as a process by which we can deepen our knowledge by improving understanding of historically specific cases. CGT can also broaden knowledge through the addition of variations in knowledge, echoing the sentiments of Welch, (2000), who argues that archival data has the potential to challenge existing theories as well as enable developmental explanation. Belfrage and Hauf (2015) also argue that CGT can serve as a way to connect projects and to challenge the explanatory value of middle-range concepts. The idea of connecting projects is significant when consideration is given to the difficulties researchers within organization and management studies face when trying to employ historical research methods; CGT can serve to strengthen the transdisciplinary capacities of archival research.

Discussion and conclusions

Throughout this chapter, there has been a concern for the way in which history can be accessed by a researcher and, thus, how this knowledge can be presented and known for others to access. The nature of the relationship between the historical researcher, data and the production of historical narratives is often discussed as fundamental in alleviating the tension that exists between organization theorists and scholars whose interest is in producing historical research (Maclean et al., 2016; 2017). Although this divide has narrowed in recent years, with the greater awareness of historical consciousness and the integration of the uses of the past literature into top-flight organization and management journals, there is still some way to go in explicating a research process or methodology that furthers this transparency and dialogues between the disciplines.

This chapter briefly took the reader through some of the varieties of ontologies relating to the nature of historical reality, which sought to build upon the premise of a deconstructivist ontology of history, embracing the possibility of multiple interpretations of the past and going beyond either a deductive or an inductive approach to history. I have argued for the emancipatory capabilities CR offers to the study of history. In this emancipatory sense, the historically situated researcher should aim to shed light on wider social and cultural issues as embedded within the past. The latter point develops some of the ideas of those scholars who work within the culturalist turn relating to historical studies, using theories of organization or organizing in conjunction with knowledge from wider disciplines (such as feminist theories), to make comments concerned with wider social and cultural processes of societies.

I have endeavoured to discuss history as an emancipatory process through the introduction of critical grounded theory and a retroductive research process for historical organization studies and for historical studies more generally. Drawing from a critical realist ontology, there is an apparent focus on the notion that some past structures or mechanisms remain fixed or observable, but there is room for interpretation and continuous learning in the research process in which the researcher becomes crucial. Even where real mechanisms of an ontology are concerned, some level of interpretation on the researcher's behalf is required, as knowledge is imperfect until discovered, and not everything can be known.

Traditional grounded theory encompasses discovery and endeavours to achieve knowledge production wholly from discovery in the field; critical grounded theory recognizes that the researcher enters the field with some preconceived idea or understanding of a topic. The same is generally true for historical researchers who have entered the field with some idea of the information they may collect, even if serendipity still occurs during the research process. The critical grounded theory research process accounts for the retroductive nature of a research project. Continuous learning and refinement are necessary and encouraged in order to produce narratives that culminate in some form of social emancipation. Whether this emancipation relates to the development of theory or challenging existing beliefs, it holds some benefit for the wider society by expanding practical consciousness of issues with the fruits of historical theoretical consciousness. Regardless of the ontological and epistemological underpinnings of historical organization studies and historical research more generally, the historian remains responsible for the production and dissemination of the historical narrative.

References

Archer, M. (1995). *Realist social theory: The morphogenetic approach.* Cambridge: Cambridge University Press.
Archer, M. (1998). Introduction: Realism in the social sciences. In Archer, M., Bhaskar, R., Collier, A., Lawson, T. and Norrie, A. (eds), *Critical realism essential readings.* Oxford: Routledge.
Belfrage, C.A. and Hauf, F. (2015). Operationalizing cultural political economy: Towards critical grounded theory. *Journal of Organizational Ethnography,* 4 (3): 324–340.
Belfrage, C. and Hauf, F. (2017). The gentle art of retroduction: Critical realism, cultural political economy and critical grounded theory. *Organization Studies,* 38 (2): 1–21.
Bhaskar, R. (1978). *A realist theory of science* (2nd edn). Leeds: Leeds Books.
Booth, C. and Rowlinson, M. (2006). Management and organizational history: Prospects. *Management and Organizational History,* 1 (1): 5–30.
Bucheli, M. and Wadhwani, R.D. (2014). *Organizations in time: History, theory, methods.* Oxford: Oxford University Press.
Charmaz, K. (2006). *Constructing grounded theory: A practical guide through qualitative analysis.* Thousand Oaks, CA: Sage.
Clark, P. and Rowlinson, M. (2004). The treatment of history in organisation studies: Towards an 'historic turn'? *Business History,* 46 (3): 331–352.
Coraiola, D.M., Foster, W.M. and Suddaby, R. (2015). Varieties of history in organization studies. In McLaren, P.G., Mills, A.J. and Weatherbee, T.G. (eds), *The Routledge companion to management and organizational history.* Abingdon: Routledge, 206–221.
Domingues, J.M. (2018). *Emancipation and history: The return of social theory.* Chicago: Haymarket Books.
Glaser, B.G. and Strauss, A.L. (1967). *The discovery of grounded theory: Strategies for qualitative research.* New York: Aldine.
Jessop, B. and Sum, N.-L. (2006). *Beyond the regulation approach: Putting capitalist economies in their place.* Cheltenham: Edward Elgar.

Jordanova, L. (2006). *History in practice* (2nd edn). London: Hodder Education.
Ketelaar, E. (2001). Tacit narratives: The meanings of archives. *Archival Science*, 1: 131–141.
Koselleck, R. (2004). *Futures past: On the semantics of historical time*. New York: Columbia University Press.
Leca, B. and Naccache, P. (2006). A critical realist approach to institutional entrepreneurship. *Organization*, 13 (5): 627–651.
Maclean, M., Harvey, C. and Clegg, S.R. (2016). Conceptualizing historical organization studies. *Academy of Management Review*, 41 (4): 609–632.
Maclean, M., Harvey, C. and Clegg, S.R. (2017). Organization theory in business and management history: Current status and future prospects. *Business History Review*, 91 (3): 457–481.
Mills, A. (2006). *Sex, strategy and the stratosphere: Airlines and the gendering of organizational culture*. New York: Palgrave Macmillan.
Munslow, A. (2006a). *Deconstructing history* (2nd edn). New York: Routledge.
Munslow, A. (2006b). *The Routledge companion to historical studies* (2nd edn). London: Routledge.
Nelson, R.R. and Winter, S.G. (1982). *An evolutionary theory of economic change*. Cambridge, MA: Harvard University Press.
North, D.C. (1990). A transaction cost theory of politics. *Journal of Theoretical Politics*, 2 (4): 355–367.
Popp, A. and Fellman, S. (2017). Writing business history: Creating narratives. *Business History*, 59 (8): 1242–1260.
Rowlinson, M. and Hassard, J. (2014). History and the cultural turn in organization studies. In Bucheli, M. and Wadhwani, R.D. (eds), *Organizations in time: History, theory, methods*. Oxford: Oxford University Press, 147–169.
Rowlinson, M., Hassard, J. and Decker, S. (2014). Research strategies for organizational history: A dialogue between historical theory and organization theory. *Academy of Management Review*, 39 (3): 250–274.
Seixas, P. (2004). Introduction. In Seixas, P. (ed.), *Theorizing historical consciousness*. Toronto: University of Toronto Press, 3–24.
Strauss, A. and Corbin, J. (1990). *Basics of qualitative research: Grounded theory procedures and techniques*. Newbury Park, CA: Sage.
Suddaby, R. (2016). Toward a historical consciousness: Following the historic turn in management thought. *M@n@gement*, 19 (1): 46–60.
Sum, N.-L. and Jessop, B. (2013). *Towards a cultural political economy: Putting culture in its place in political economy*. Cheltenham: Edward Elgar.
Üsdiken, B. and Kieser, A. (2004). Introduction: History in organisation studies. *Business History*, 46 (3): 321–330.
Üsdiken, B. and Kipping, M. (2014). History and organization studies: A long-term view. In Bucheli, M. and Wadhwani, R.D. (eds), *Organizations in time: History, theory, methods*. Oxford: Oxford University Press, 33–56.
Van Maanen, J. (1988). *Tales of the field: On writing ethnography*. Chicago: University of Chicago Press.
Wadhwani, R.D. and Decker, S. (2018). Clio's toolkit: The practice of historical methods in organization studies. In Mir, R. and Jain, S. (eds), *The Routledge companion to qualitative research in organization studies*. New York: Routledge, 113–128.
Wadhwani, R.D., Suddaby, R., Mordhorst, M. and Popp, A. (2018). History as organizing: Uses of the past in organization studies. *Organization Studies*, 39 (12): 1663–1683.
Welch, C. (2000). The archaeology of business networks: The use of archival records in case study research. *Journal of Strategic Marketing*, 8(2): 197–208.

6

DON'T TALK ABOUT HISTORY

Indigenous views about the past and their implication for organization studies

François Bastien, William M. Foster and Diego M. Coraiola

> "The collection of individual memories about the past ... exists in stories and [are] passed on over time, linking the past, present and future."
>
> *(Cree elder)*

Introduction

Many scholars have advocated for a 'historical turn' in research about organizations (e.g. Clark and Rowlinson, 2004; Kieser, 1994; Mills, Suddaby, Foster and Durepos, 2016; Zald, 1993). These conversations about the impact of the past in organizations have led to noteworthy developments. Kieser (1994), for one, explicitly claimed that organizational structures are rooted in past decisions and argued for a better understanding of the past in explaining elements of organizations in the present. Suddaby, Foster and Quinn Trank (2010), taking a more managerial approach, argue that the ability to effectively manage history leads to competitive advantage. From this perspective, the past is understood as a dynamic resource that is at the disposal of skilled actors in the present (Foster, Coraiola, Suddaby, Kroezen and Chandler, 2017). Similarly, Anteby and Molnár (2012) suggested that, 'who an organization is' and 'what it can do' is not determined just by its actions, but also by how it manages its own history.

As such, there have been significant advances in both organization studies and organizational history since the first discussions of the historic turn. These two streams of literature—history as a constraint on choice and history as an enabler of choice—have been combined into historical organization studies (Maclean, Harvey and Clegg, 2016) and generated relevant insights about history, memory and the past through empirical explorations of coffee shops (Foster, Suddaby, Minkus and Wiebe, 2011), breweries (Hatch and Schultz, 2017) and the wine industry (Voronov, De Clercq and Hinings, 2013). Nevertheless, a current limitation of these studies is that most of our understanding about history remains embedded in western assumptions of rationality in which history is seen to be both linear and causal. That is, organization scholars have moved beyond the assumption that organizations have a history to an understanding that history is something organizations do when they narrate their pasts. Notwithstanding, organizational narratives are usually framed as a chronological sequence of events that implies a direct and linear causality between past and present. More critically, historical narratives, in the western cultural account, are inexorably linked to myths of progress (Meyer, Boli and Thomas, 1987).

Different cultures have different conceptions of history. More importantly, societies vary in their awareness of the past and their past relationships (Pocock, 1962). Nevertheless, in management and organization studies, history, memory and the past have largely reinforced western assumptions and worldviews (Coraiola and Murcia, 2020; Kipping and Üsdiken, 2014). More specifically, the debates in the field have been dominated by Anglo-Saxon knowledge, with colonizing effects on other geographies (Wanderley and Barros, 2019). We are thus particularly deaf to discussions about organizations outside western nations. Our contention is that indigenous worldviews can offer a distinct perspective that so far has not been captured by the historic turn. In other words, the field of historical organization studies can benefit from the inclusion of indigenous worldviews.

Our discussions advocate for a move away from a western perspective that emphasizes a linear understanding of history and suggest a new avenue for theorizing the importance of the past for organizing. To do so, we first explore why history, in the western cultural account, is problematic for indigenous peoples. Second, we analyze how indigenous approaches to the past can illuminate our understanding of management and organizations. In so doing, we hope to generate interest and debate among scholars in both business history and organization studies that can evolve into practical suggestions for both indigenous and western organizations.

Historical consciousness in the western cultural account

Historical consciousness in organization studies describes how management scholars explore the elements of what constitutes history in organizations (Suddaby, 2016; Tennent, Gillett and Foster, 2020). The push for this 'historical turn' (Clark and Rowlinson, 2004) has led to relevant new insights. Rhetorical history (Suddaby et al., 2010) is used today to elaborate how social actors use the past (Schultz and Hernes, 2013; Wadhwani, Suddaby, Mordhorst and Popp, 2018) to 'make history' and shape outcomes that exist in the present (Godfrey, Hassard, O'Connor, Rowlinson and Ruef, 2016; Rowlinson, Booth, Clark, Delahaye and Procter, 2010). This deliberate and strategic construction of the past presumes that history is an interpretive device for imposing culture (Said, 1979), creating community (Anderson, 1983) and shaping strategy (Suddaby et al., 2010).

Still—for some—the past remains objectifiable in the way that it can constrain choices made by actors in the present (Mills et al., 2016). One explicit distinction lies in the way that the past is conceptualized as a sequence of stable and linear events. Vaara and Lamberg (2016), for instance, argued that strategic practices are embedded in historical conditions, mechanisms, and causality. Barney (1995) similarly emphasized how competitive advantage can derive from unique historical circumstances. Organizations have legacies that derive from specific elements such as location, culture and other unique circumstances. This inherited history, exclusive to an organization, is the source of benefit that provides value. In other words, these historical circumstances are valuable because they are rare and impossible to imitate by other organizations. Barney (1995) uses Caterpillar's unique opportunity to become the sole supplier of some specialized equipment to allied forces in the Second World War to account for the company's long-term success. This argument also bears a resemblance to Selznick's (1949) claim that organizations and their identities are infused with value, carriers of cultural-cognitive elements of institutions (Scott, 2001) and constructed from available patterns that can provide a competitive advantage to an organization.

Most 'western history' draws from an ontology of rationality and progress that defines the western cultural account, a term used by Meyer et al. (1987) to describe the emphasis placed on the rationality and agency of individual choice in western culture. The western cultural account is infused with "'values' that influence individuals to be assertive and achievement oriented [thereby] undercutting the possibilities for immersing individuality in a community" (Meyer et al., 1987: 21). The logical temporal extension of the western cultural account is to see western history as a somewhat orderly and linear unfolding of events in a teleological sequence of rational progress.

Western history, thus, is a way of apprehending ways of living with direct implications from the past grounded in peculiar understanding of the world inherited from the Enlightenment and the idea of progress. From an ontological perspective, western history treats the past as singular and unitary, independent of cultural differences. As the past is what is disconnected and inaccessible from the present, it appears objective in that the past happens to others, and there is very little connection between the people of today and those described in past accounts. In other words, there is a deliberate separation between the present and the past. This separation is, in fact, what makes western history possible, because it is about describing the other. That is, western history is always a narrative about someone or something else in the past. A western perspective on history emphasizes a stable concrete past reality which can be interpreted and reinterpreted in the present by social actors and can come to influence structures and behaviors in the present. This universalist approach to history has been detrimental to those groups who, in the past, lacked agency and legitimacy in the eyes of the dominant culture such as indigenous peoples in North America whose experiences we now discuss.

Indigenous peoples

Although Marsden (1991) elaborated on the term 'indigenous' to embody general non-western practices native to a particular place, we define indigenous peoples as those individuals and groups who were part of the first modern indigenous movements. These people, in particular, sought to challenge the ideas associated with colonization in North America, Australia and New Zealand (Minde, 2008). Unfortunately, colonial history has not been kind to indigenous peoples. For example, indigenous peoples in North America, and especially Canada, were forced to send their children to schools run by missionaries. At these schools, "whites tried to assimilate them [indigenous children] into a society that was not ready to receive them, while taking away all the skills necessary to function in their own society" (Gagné, 1998: 363). In addition, colonial settlers implemented a system of dependence centered on the control of resources and the enforcement of colonial standards. Cycles of grief, loss of culture and loss of independence promptly led to the loss of self-sufficiency.

For more than a century, many westerners in North America have contributed to the colonization and stigmatization of indigenous nations and their peoples. The North American Indian was first perceived as a 'savage'. Other noteworthy contemporary stigmas include 'substance abusers', 'cigarette sellers', 'benefiters of taxpayers', 'poachers' and 'casino operators'. Indigenous peoples, over time and in concert with the degrading socioeconomic conditions in many communities, became victims of abuse and struggled to preserve their identities. The consequence has been the psychological and physiological trauma of indigenous peoples.

This western history has reinforced various stereotypes and stigmas about what constitutes indigeneity, as many of these historical narratives are still used by many in North America. Nevertheless, there is more interest and curiosity about indigeneity around the world. Indigenous peoples remain resilient and strong. Indigenous nations have endured to maintain their rich cultures and unique traditions (Love, 2019). Differences in pre-and post-colonial experiences have led indigenous groups to express unique characteristics in terms of distinctive ways of defining themselves and their relation to their past. This richness has become a source of intrigue for us, especially within the context of reconciliation in Canada.[1] From 'savages' to 'victims' and, today, as 'cultural agents', indigenous peoples and their organizations offer a great platform to generate new knowledge about the relevance of the past in organization studies.

The problem with history for indigenous nations

History, in the western cultural account, is problematic for indigenous peoples. Indigenous peoples had independent and strong cultures and beliefs long before the arrival of westerners. Colonial governments, however, imposed their own historical perspectives by disseminating their own stories and propagating western accounts about indigenous peoples. These western historical narratives have survived and today exist as history within socially constructed western beliefs.

The power and influence to shape the past and construct historical narratives should not be taken for granted. For instance, through its laws, Canada's federal government has, and continues to, dictate who is and who is not indigenous based on its own historical definition of a status Indian. In the context of colonization, this history is reinforced in the present by those with a vested interest in consolidating their dominance and control. Western history, in the eyes of indigenous peoples, is a mechanism of domination and an effective tool to control the present and dictate the future. For them, western history consists of a few critical periods central to supporting a dominant narrative that are made up of prejudicial *facts* and western *truths*.

The construction of history by early colonialists has had serious consequences for indigenous peoples around the world, and we argue that the past cannot be the simple conclusions of a few western historians and their narratives. In the case of indigenous peoples, more hurtful than history itself has been the fact that those historical narratives have been so widely disseminated in a variety of media such as books, pictures, paintings and movies that they have become ingrained in the collective consciousness of society. These depictions were not chosen by chance (King, 2013) but were crafted to justify acts of violence and domination; they established a normative view about the past informed by prejudice and neglect of indigenous worldviews and ways of living, with direct implications for the development of social policies and programs for cultural assimilation. Western history has allocated credit to westerners as race was, and still is, a criterion in the creation of western history (King, 2013). Indigenous peoples around the world are, therefore, unable to rely on western history and possess a very different perspective of what the past actually entails.

We advocate for an alternative understanding of the past informed by indigenous worldviews. Our proposal is for organizational scholars, when talking about the past, to embrace perspectives other than those proposed by western philosophers and western historical theorists. Although we embrace the contributions of Foucault, Lévi-Strauss and others, for instance, we argue for particularism and suggest considering organizational phenomena via relevant factors in specific contexts. This would allow for a more critical and less universal perspective on contemporary organizations and encourage the inclusion of non-western worldviews.

Translating indigenous knowledge

Indigenous nations experienced very different pre-colonial ways of life (e.g. nomads vs. sedentary), as well as noteworthy differences in living habits due to ecology and the vastness of the landscape. And, although there seems to be a common thread in terms of spiritual worldview and attitude towards the world (Chapman, McCaskill and Newhouse, 1991), time spent in indigenous communities emphasizes that each community has various traditions, languages and indigenous identities.

Yet, it is difficult to translate and engage with indigenous knowledge because this requires tacit understandings about these ways of being to be surfaced and made explicit. Indigenous knowledge is unfamiliar because history has limited indigenous peoples' participation and engagement in contemporary research.

Also, because many earlier attempts to study indigenous peoples devalued indigenous knowledge, communities are today reluctant to share their information with researchers and remain sceptical and hesitant to accept outsiders.[2]

Indigenous communities are mnemonic communities. That is, indigenous peoples constitute their organization, community and themselves through acts of remembering and forgetting (Rowlinson et al., 2010). When thinking through the thoughts of past actors (Collingwood and Knox, 1946), indigenous peoples remember as members of a group (Olick, 1999) in terms of a shared, yet dynamic, past.

Indigenous organizations are unique. Located within their *reserves*,[3] these organizations mostly employ people from the community and seek guidance from community elders. Via this cultural embeddedness, many organizations come to reflect the norms and values of their nation's past. In other words, organizations are important elements of both the past and the present. We were welcomed in different types of organizations including band councils, on-*reserve* schools, health organizations, commercial credit organizations, just to name a few. With this privilege, we listened to stories and captured ways in which the past was understood and conceptualized in relation to organizations.

Western perspectives about history assume that historical interpretations based on written text are more reliable and accurate than those that rely exclusively on oral narratives (Hill, 1988). However, we contend that national archives are biased and insist that a greater sensitivity to the context in which the past occurs, via those key insiders who carry it with them, can offer a better appreciation of the past and a counter-narrative to the dominant perspective. Stories told by indigenous peoples echo older narratives and offer a relevant platform to connect the past to contemporary indigenous organizations.

We endeavored to elicit the views and understandings about the past that indigenous peoples themselves felt relevant based on their subjective human experience of remembering. Indigenous peoples, and especially elders, are known storytellers rooted in a documented oral tradition. Because the reconstruction of the past adapts images of ancient facts to present beliefs (Halbwachs, 1992), remembering can be defined as a body of knowledge, an attribute and a process (Wertsch and Roediger III, 2008). Our objective was to discover the past from stories told in the present (Gioia, Corley and Fabbri, 2002).

The past as related and circular

Western historians define the past as "a state of affairs of some social complexity existing over a period long enough to make it intelligible, a period now gone by, but remembered" (Pocock, 1962: 211). Even though awareness of events that took place in the past tends to be commonplace to most human societies, we cannot assume from this that all societies view and understand the past the same way. In fact, the concept of temporality for indigenous peoples differs quite significantly from that for the western world. That is, knowledge about the past is relational. It is not owned by anybody, but exists in complex relationships which are essential to both identity and culture. For instance, land is considered by many indigenous peoples as the voice of their ancestors that cannot be distinguished; earth, rivers, sky, rocks, trees are the means through which the past is expressed (Létourneau, 2017).

The relationship between people and nature is at the foundation of indigenous worldviews. Participation in the world for indigenous peoples presumes a spiritual contract with animals, land and the cosmos (Cajete, 2000). Pidgeon (2019: 426) argues that, 'indigenous knowledge … recognizes the inherent "relatedness" and "interconnectedness" of all living things'. This 'interconnectedness' signifies that the world extends beyond the earth, and people are required to participate in this world (Gladstone, 2018). The lack of separation between these components has traditionally led to a more interconnected understanding of the past, which means that, for the past to exist in the future, it must account for and include this entire way of knowing. This embeddedness is essential for traditional beliefs to exist in the present and make their way into the future.

For indigenous peoples, time is not linear. Indigenous communities/nations are connected to their past through a circular ontology. Past, present and future co-exist in an oral tradition via stories. The 'seventh generation' principle, often linked to ancient Iroquois philosophy, connects past, present and future through decision-making. More specifically, decisions made today should relate to the past and result in future benefits in seven generations. This philosophy applies as much to building and managing future relationships as it does to healing due to trauma. Indigenous philosophy prescribes that its peoples participate in a broader world, where the different elements of this world come to support the needs of its peoples (Gladstone, 2018) in the past, present and future. In other words, all things in life are related in a sacred manner through their duties and responsibilities according to their nature at the time of creation (Chapman et al., 1991) and through time.

Past occurrences

Western history has significantly understated the trauma directly caused by colonization. Trauma has led to the disturbance of knowledge on different scales for indigenous communities while also affecting how and what they remember. In fact, according to Gagné (1998), collective trauma can have a dramatic effect on future generations, as the trauma becomes embedded in society through time. More specifically, trauma has threatened oral traditions by decimating entire families, not only causing the premature loss of culture, but also, for some, affecting their willingness and ability to remember the past ("What past? We all went to residential school"). From an ontological point of view, colonization and contact created a historical injunction against indigenous ways of remembering that renders the past not easily accessible for many indigenous communities today.

Traditional indigenous knowledge, however, still exists in and through storytelling. The structure of collective memory based on an oral tradition allows the continuous revision of the stories and narratives about the past and the incorporation of evolving interpretations into the knowledge base of a society (Innis, 1986).

Through time, this knowledge is passed on and recreated. Elders are considered 'custodians of traditions' (Dacin, Dacin & Kent, 2019) and as knowledge keepers; they pass down stories and lessons from the past to younger generations. Those stories themselves are built on other stories that were themselves passed down by elders from previous, older generations. These historical narratives are different from western stories because they usually do not include specific, documented events, but often exist in metaphors, visions and ways of being. The amalgamation of such stories through a lifetime, coupled with being firmly engaged in the past, gives a particular individual the wisdom to become an elder and to help others connect with their past. Elders are, in fact, key to making the past exist in the present and live in the future. They do this by telling stories about past occurrences.

The term past occurrences was defined by a Cree elder as the collection of individual memories about the past that exist in stories held by members of a community and passed on over time, linking the past, present and future. For an indigenous community, past occurrences generate dissimilar historical narratives and yet work to convey a rich identity and a set of assumptions in the present. Although colonization has created a somewhat shared experience among indigenous peoples, traumatic breaks in the past are often unique to each indigenous community. Some were spared much, whereas others were not. In other words, interpretations of both traditional (how we were prior to colonization) and more contemporary (how we are after colonization) pasts have led indigenous communities to remember differently. These past occurrences act as a bridge between these periods. Still, for those elders that we've had the chance to listen to, although the exact terminology can at times vary, the concept of past occurrences, for most, embeds the present and future within a pre-colonial past. As this 'distant' past mostly exists in the orality of elders and not in written documents, the past itself is dynamic.

Owing to their relational and circular attributes, we present past occurrences as a counter-narrative to western history. Past occurrences are expressed in stories and exist within a circular ontology where natural and spiritual elements relate to each other and through time. As suggested by King (2013), we propose using concentric circles in a continuous spiral to illustrate this, where both present and future become an extension of the past, and where each circle can only be understood within the context of the others via a 'flowy progression'. In locating a specific spot on the spiral, these stories by elders move from one point to another and from one circle to another. Ways of being, ways of knowing, concrete worldviews and templates about how to live in the present stem from these stories and constitute a complete system of related elements. These past occurrences have allowed indigenous identities and cultures to strive and endure by maintaining who they always were. In other words, indigenous peoples (metaphorically) do not need to remember. Their past ways are always firmly rooted today. Time is therefore transformative; past occurrences speak loudly about cycles of perpetuation of the past, present and future.

We contend that thinking about past occurrences is substantially different from western history. Oral traditions of storytelling for indigenous peoples do not exist in books or archives: they exist in people. Although similar to western oral histories, another difference is that past occurrences are not about 'others': they are about 'themselves' in the past and in reflections of the present and the future. Past occurrences are not made up of specific events or a few critical periods. In fact, indigenous ancestors are not distinct from present people as the present embodies those that were 'here' in the past. The western functionalist perspective on history as *truths* or as *facts* is, therefore, unknown to elders as they literally personify various pasts and their wisdom. Elders share their wisdom directly from the past. By framing the present through continuous historical roots, past occurrences provide the means for indigenous peoples to spiritually live their pasts in the present.

Post-colonial history, cultural capital and authenticity

We recognize that theorizing past occurrences as a virginal and untainted indigenous approach to the past is not possible. The effects of colonization and colonial policies in indigenous identity and worldviews cannot be disregarded and need to be incorporated into a more complete understanding of the complexity of indigenous approaches to the past. Structural anthropology popularized the distinction between history and myth as two rival approaches to the past. As the argument goes, illiterate societies rely on mythical explanations of the world that emphasize continuity with the past, whereas literate societies approach the past from a historical point of view grounded on discontinuity and separation between past and present (Lévi-Strauss, 1966). We argue that these ideal-typical approaches do not reflect the complexity of post-colonial modes of historical consciousness for indigenous peoples and we advocate for a more profound understanding of the ways in which a mythic-historical consciousness (Hill, 1988) affects the way indigenous peoples understand themselves and take action in the world. In addition, we contend that this hybrid form of historical consciousness is not exclusive to indigenous peoples but is becoming widespread as global forces have been fostering the increasing tribalism of society (McLuhan, 2013).

Suddaby, Ganzin and Minkus (2017) have recently argued that we are witnessing the re-enchantment of society, where craft, based on authentic means of production, seem to be making its way back to replace more hyperrational approaches of profit maximization and economies of scale. Authenticity, which can translate to remaining true to established norms, values and expectations (Suddaby et al., 2017), as well as to history and identity (Suddaby and Foster, 2017), challenges the leading discourse of legitimacy which is founded on reflecting external norms, values and expectations (Suchman, 1995). Indigenous nations were traditionally organized on a barter system where access to resources fueled the development of specialized expertise. In contrast, for westerners, legitimacy became the driving force behind generating as much as possible for as many as possible via mass production.

However, the emergence of a discourse around authenticity as a counterclaim to the idea of legitimacy is in itself a product of western history and western modes of engaging with the past. The introduction of writing and the particular modes of reflexivity associated with it freezes time and opens it up for appraisal (Innis, 1986). The discursive articulation of the past disconnected from the lived tradition of oral societies promotes a disjunction in history that allows the past to be objectified and reflected upon (Giddens, 1984). It is through the engagement of indigenous peoples with western modes of thinking about the past, imposed or otherwise, that contemporary forms of indigenous historical consciousness emerge. The development of these distinct modes of reflexivity and temporal distancing provides for the heightened objectification of the past and allows indigenous peoples to approach their pasts as cultural tools (Swidler, 1986) that could be mobilized at will for different purposes.

Hence, a distinct resource that indigenous organizations and entrepreneurs have at their disposal is the unique knowledge of their own cultures. This cultural capital is a precious resource, exclusive to each indigenous community, transcending the present and spawned from past occurrences as carriers of tradition. Many indigenous communities have actually learned to exploit this valuable, rare and inimitable resource (Barney, 1995) by developing core competencies in the production of authentic goods. Cultural authenticity can add value to art, music and craft (Harrington, Birmingham and Stewart, 2017). For instance, Adrian Stimson, an artist and a member of the Siksika Nation, has depicted, through his paintings, bison in imagined landscapes to evoke ideas of cultural fragility, resilience and nostalgia. In one of his latest artistic performance, Stimson looked at identity construction via the hybridization of the Indian, the cowboy, the shaman and Two Spirit being. In another example, Unikkaaqtuat, a major multidisciplinary production blending circus arts, music, theatre and video projection, highlights the Inuit people, their traditions and vision for the future through a collaborative and mutually respectful process bringing Inuit and non-Inuit artists together.

In addition, some indigenous organizations more than others have developed core capabilities in exploiting their cultural capital via unique modes of organizing. Maskwacis Cultural College, for instance—a college in a Cree community—advances and preserves indigenous forms of life and thinking in order to remember dreams and visions for future generations. Cultural authenticity is also applicable to other industries. For instance, it is captured in a Wendat community at the Hotel-Musée Premières-Nations (First Nations Hotel Museum). In attracting outside guests, the hotel regularly provides access to storytellers and proud guardians of ancestral wisdom to share the myths and legends of the Wendat people. These accounts are told through stories and objects imbued with tangible memories exploring the themes of territory, memory and knowledge. The past is indeed an endogenous, invisible and intangible resource for indigenous organizations that can be accessed through past occurrences and strategically managed as a source of competitive advantage.

If society is indeed re-enchanting, we suggest that revisiting the ways that indigenous peoples authentically organize and produce in harmony with both the natural and spiritual world can rehumanize organizations. If, in fact, we are witnessing a return to tribalism (McLuhan, 2013), this provides a platform for indigenous organizations to express their own idiosyncratic values via their deeply embedded ways of being and doing. Considering the increasing interest in indigenous cultures—as culture agents—indigenous organizations can utilize this capital in an effort to move away from universal lines of western history towards a more pointed, circular, relational and authentic past. We argue that authenticity draws on the culture and heritage of indigenous peoples and, as cultural capital, it can be accessed in past occurrences. We also suggest that indigenous organizations can gain from embedding authenticity in most, if not all, business practices and functions, including governance structures, leadership style and even marketing strategies.

Conclusion

The intent of this paper has been to draw attention to the problem with the current leading perspective of western history in organization studies and to present a theoretically rich yet varied approach. For many outside the dominant mainstream society, ontological assumptions of the past do not reside in common and *universal* functionalist and positivist beliefs, but instead live in more relational and circular forms. Rich in culture, indigenous organizations offer a unique setting to examine how the past can be strategically used in the future.

The way that indigenous organizations connect with their past and re-enact their past occurrences entails engaging with those who have direct contact with the past. As 'custodians of traditions' (Dacin, Dacin & Kent, 2019), elders and their stories provide a rich alternative to western history by including feelings, places, worldviews, as they relate to the wisdom of different pasts. Hence, the past is not fixed and is a product of continuous, ongoing relations. The treatment of elders as valuable knowledge carriers is shared by most indigenous cultures and is still central to most nations today. This is in stark contrast with how westerners care for their elderly, where retirement and nursing homes are often used as outlets to effectively deal with the burden that older generations place on society.

Owing to the many stigmas, indigenous communities often display limited social capital, as their organizations lack reputational assets. In addition, basic factors of production such as land, people, information and financial capital are not always readily available. Many indigenous nations have been stripped from much of their traditional land, and, thanks to residential schools, most do not wish to develop their skills in educational institutions operated by outsiders. When it comes to information, a major problem for indigenous communities is connectivity. Capital is also difficult to attract. As building relationships with outsiders is challenging, attracting external capital from both private and public sectors is not always easy. Yet, cultural capital is a critical and available resource that can be drawn from past occurrences and used in the production of authentic goods. We argue that possessing core competencies in exploiting cultural capital and in generating authenticity is a valuable source of competitive advantage for contemporary indigenous organizations.

Although translating traditional knowledge is difficult, it provides a relevant platform to question what many have accepted as taken-for-granted universal theories. Implicit in this chapter is an appreciation for the richness and relevance of indigenous cultures and their potential to contribute to both the historicization and indigenization of organizational studies. In fact, with this research context, we hope not only to generate new theories about organizations, but also to suggest ways of redefining existing relationships between indigenous communities and the dominant western culture.

Notes

1 In June 2015, the Truth and Reconciliation Commission of Canada suggested 94 'calls to action' regarding reconciliation between Canadians and indigenous peoples.
2 Access to indigenous communities was enabled by existing relationships between the lead author and the various communities.
3 A *reserve* is a territorial designation for the land where indigenous communities have quasi-governmental status.

References

Anderson, B. (1983). *Imagined communities: Reflections on the origin and spread of nationalism.* London: Verso.
Anteby, M. and Molnár, V. (2012). Collective memory meets organizational identity: Remembering to forget in a firm's rhetorical history. *Academy of Management Journal,* 55 (3): 515–540.
Barney, J.B. (1995). Looking inside for competitive advantage. *The Academy of Management Executive,* 9 (4): 49–61.
Cajete, G. (2000). *Native science: Natural laws of interdependence.* Santa Fe, NM: Clear Light.
Chapman, I., McCaskill, D. and Newhouse, D. (1991). Management in contemporary aboriginal organizations. *Canadian Journal of Native Studies,* 11 (2): 333–349.
Clark, P. and Rowlinson, M. (2004). The treatment of history in organisation studies: Towards an 'historic turn'? *Business History,* 46 (3): 331–352.
Collingwood, R.G. and Knox, T.M. (1946). *The idea of history.* Oxford: Clarendon Press.
Coraiola, D.M. and Murcia, M.J. (2020). From organizational learning to organizational mnemonics: Redrawing the boundaries of the field. *Management Learning,* 51 (2): 227–240.
Dacin, M. T., Dacin, P. A., & Kent, D. (2019). Tradition in organizations: A custodianship framework. *Academy of Management Annals,* 13 (1), 342–373.
Foster, W.M., Coraiola, D.M., Suddaby, R., Kroezen, J. and Chandler, D. (2017). The strategic use of historical narratives: A theoretical framework. *Business History,* 59 (8): 1176–1200.
Foster, W.M., Suddaby, R., Minkus, A. and Wiebe, E. (2011). History as social memory assets: The example of Tim Hortons. *Management & Organizational History,* 6 (1): 10–20.
Gagné, M.-A. (1998). The role of dependency and colonialism in generating trauma in First Nations citizens. In Danieli, Y. (ed.), *International handbook of multigenerational legacies of trauma.* New York: Plenum Press, 355–372.
Giddens, A. (1984). *The constitution of society: Outline of the theory of structuration.* Cambridge: Polity.

Gioia, D.A., Corley, K.G. and Fabbri, T. (2002). Revising the past (while thinking in the future perfect tense). *Journal of Organizational Change Management*, 15 (6): 622–634.

Gladstone J. (2018). All my relations: An inquiry into a spirit of a Native American philosophy of business. *American Indian Quarterly*, 42 (2): 191–214.

Godfrey, P.C., Hassard, J., O'Connor, E.S., Rowlinson, M. and Ruef, M. (2016). What is organizational history? Toward a creative synthesis of history and organization studies. *Academy of Management Review*, 41 (4): 590–608.

Halbwachs, M. (1992). *On collective memory*. Chicago: University of Chicago Press.

Harrington, C.F., Birmingham, C. and Stewart, D. (2017). American Indian entrepreneurship. In Kennedy, D.M., Harrington, C.F., Verbos, A.K., Stewart, D., Glastone, J.S. and Clarkson, G. (eds), *American Indian business principles and practices*. Seattle, WA: University of Washington Press, 27–45.

Hatch, M.J. and Schultz, M. (2017). Toward a theory of using history authentically: Historicizing in the Carlsberg Group. *Administrative Science Quarterly*, 62 (4): 657–697.

Hill, J. (1988). *Rethinking history and myth: Indigenous South American perspectives on the past*. Urbana: University of Illinois Press.

Innis, H.A. (1986). *Empire and communications*. Washington, DC: Rowman & Littlefield.

Kieser, A. (1994). Why organization theory needs historical analyses—And how this should be performed. *Organization Science*, 5 (4): 608–620.

King, T. (2013). *The inconvenient Indian: A curious account of native people in North America*. Toronto, ON: Anchor Canada.

Kipping, M. and Üsdiken, B. (2014). History in organization and management theory: More than meets the eye. *The Academy of Management Annals*, 8 (1): 535–588.

Létourneau, J-F. (2017). *Le territoire dans les veines*. Montréal, QC: Mémoire D'Encrier.

Lévi-Strauss, C. (1966). *The savage mind*. Chicago: University of Chicago Press.

Love, T.R. (2019). Indigenous knowledges, priorities and processes in qualitative organization and management research: State of the field. *Qualitative Research in Organizations and Management: An International Journal*, 15 (1): 6–20.

Maclean, M., Harvey, C. and Clegg, S.R. (2016). Conceptualizing historical organization studies. *Academy of Management Review*, 41 (4): 609–632.

Marsden, D. (1991). Indigenous management. *International Journal of Human Resource Management*, 2 (1): 21–38.

McLuhan, M. (2013). *Understanding media: The extensions of man*. Berkeley, CA: Gingko Press.

Meyer, J.W, Boli, J. and Thomas, G.M. (1987). Ontology and rationalization in the Western cultural account. In Thomas, G.M., Meyer, J.W., Ramirez, F.O. and Boli, J. (eds), *Institutional Structure: Constituting State Society and the Individual*. Newbury Park, CA: Sage, 12–40.

Mills, A.J., Suddaby, R., Foster, W.M. and Durepos, G. (2016). Re-visiting the historic turn 10 years later: current debates in management and organizational history—an introduction. *Management & Organizational History*, 11 (2): 67–76.

Minde, H. (2008). *Indigenous peoples: Self-determination, knowledge and indigeneity*. Delft: Eburon.

Olick, J.K. (1999). Collective memory: The two cultures. *Sociological Theory*, 17 (3): 333–348.

Ortner, S.B. (1984). Theory in anthropology since the sixties. *Comparative Studies in Society and History*, 26 (1): 126–166.

Pidgeon, M. (2019). Moving between theory and practice within an Indigenous research paradigm. *Qualitative Research*, 19 (4): 418–436.

Pocock, J.G.A. (1962). The origins of study of the past: A comparative approach. *Comparative Studies in Society and History*, 4 (2): 209–246.

Rowlinson, M., Booth, C., Clark, P., Delahaye, A. and Procter, S. (2010). Social remembering and organizational memory. *Organization Studies*, 31 (1): 69–87.

Said, E.W. (1979). *Orientalism*. New York: Vintage Books.

Schultz, M. and Hernes, T. (2013). A temporal perspective on organizational identity. *Organization Science*, 24 (1): 1–21.

Scott, W.R. (2001). *Institutions and organizations* (2nd edn). Thousand Oaks, CA: Sage.

Selznick, P. (1949). *TVA and the grass roots: A study in the sociology of formal organization*. Berkeley: University of California Press.

Suchman, M.C. (1995). Managing legitimacy: Strategic and institutional approaches. *Academy of Management Review*, 20 (3): 571–610.

Suddaby, R. (2016). Toward a historical consciousness: Following the historic turn in management thought. *M@n@gement: Revue officielle de l'Association Internationale de Management Stratégique*, 19 (1): 46–60.

Suddaby, R. and Foster, W.M. (2017). History and organizational change. *Journal of Management*, 43 (1): 19–38.

Suddaby, R., Foster, W.M. and Quinn Trank, C. (2010). Rhetorical history as a source of competitive advantage. In Baum, J.A.C. and Lampel, J. (eds), *Advances in strategic management: The globalization of strategy research*. Bingley: Emerald, 147–173.

Suddaby, R., Ganzin, M. and Minkus, A. (2017). Craft, magic and the re-enchantment of the world. *European Management Journal*, 35 (3): 285–296.

Swidler, A. (1986). Culture in action: Symbols and strategies. *American Sociological Review*, 51 (2): 273–286.

Tennent, K.D., Gillett, A.G. and Foster, W.M. (2020). Developing historical consciousness in management learners. *Management Learning*, 51 (1), 73–88.

Vaara, E. and Lamberg, J.-A. (2016). Taking historical embeddedness seriously: Three historical approaches to advance strategy process and practice research. *Academy of Management Review*, 41 (4): 633–657.

Voronov, M., De Clercq, D. and Hinings, C.R. (2013). Conformity and distinctiveness in a global institutional framework: The legitimation of Ontario fine wine. *Journal of Management Studies*, 50 (4): 607–645.

Wadhwani, R.D., Suddaby, R., Mordhorst, M. and Popp, A. (2018). History as organizing: Uses of the past in organization studies. *Organization Studies*, 39 (12): 1663–1683.

Wanderley, S. and Barros, A. (2019). Decoloniality, geopolitics of knowledge and historic turn: Towards a Latin American agenda. *Management & Organizational History*, 14 (1): 79–97.

Wertsch, J.V. and Roediger III, H.L. (2008). Collective memory: Conceptual foundations and theoretical approaches. *Memory*, 16 (3): 318–326.

Zald, M.N. (1993). Organization studies as a scientific and humanistic enterprise: Toward a reconceptualization of the foundations of the field. *Organization Science*, 4 (4): 513–528.

PART III
Theoretical applications

7
THE CANADIAN ALOUETTE WOMEN
Reclaiming their space

Stefanie Ruel, Linda Dyer and Albert J. Mills

Introduction

The starting block for the race to space is often recognized as the launch of the Union of Soviet Socialist Republics' (U.S.S.R) Sputnik satellite in 1957, and the response by the United States (U.S.) with their Mercury and Apollo programs that sent White[1] men[2] into space and then to the moon (Launius, 2007). The White men involved in this Cold War race have been accorded an almost exclusive voice in space organizational histories and in the popular media (De Groot, 2006; Launius, 2005; 2007). We contend, along with others (Ruel, Mills and Helms Mills, 2019; Ruel, Mills and Thomas, 2018; Shetterly, 2016), that these histories cannot and must not be solely about and by these White men, that there had to be many complex[3] individuals involved in the global Cold War space race. Notably, the Canadian Cold War experience made important contributions to space and its exploration. The Canadian military and eventually Canadian privately owned companies were responsible through the phases of design, manufacturing, testing, launch and operations for the successful Alouette I and II satellite missions. These Canadian scientific satellites marked Canada as the third space-faring nation during this Cold War space race (Godefroy, 2011).

Just as in the U.S., Canadian men were at the center of this space race also. The Canadian focus has been on the '100' men who contributed to the Alouette program as witnessed by historical artifacts and archival evidence. Silence surrounding the women involved in these Alouette missions appears to maintain their 'work sleep[ing] in the forgotten' (Olsen, 1978: 11). We argue in this chapter that these Alouette women and their work must be raised out of this sleep and that they must be incorporated within the 'social circulation [...] connections among past, present and future' (Jones Royster and Kirsch, 2012: 23). Our attempts to establish these connections are in line with the notion of pluralistic understanding advocated by

Maclean, Harvey and Clegg (2016). To this end, we ask, how are Canadian Alouette women remembered? And what are some of the discursive processes involved in this gendered remembering?

The notion of gendered remembering includes men's recollection of institutional traditions (Hobsbawm and Ranger, 1983), along with women's 'fingerprints upon the handles of history' (Jones Royster and Kirsch, 2012: 10). With gendered remembering, we move beyond the past as 'a realistic record of every event and experience in time' (Suddaby, Foster and Quinn Trank, 2010: 152), refocusing our lens on everyday, complex Alouette individuals and their use of organizational histories in the present. With respect to discursive processes, we are concerned specifically with antenarratives (Boje, Haley and Saylors, 2016) circulating around Alouette women. Antenarratives are 'not yet fully-formed narratives, but rather pieces of organizational discourse that help to construct identities and interests' (Boje et al., 2016: 391). Antenarratives and their subjective interests are not fictional tales; they are reflective of processes that embrace critical imagination, in the sense that antenarratives provide us with an avenue to 'making connections and seeing possibility [...] in remaking interpretive frameworks' (Royster, 2000: 83). Some of the literature on collective memory tells us that histories are focused on 'what is remembered, not on what is never acknowledged' (Anteby and Molnár, 2012: 531) and that archival silences with respect to women ensure 'not simply invisibility but erasure' (Hunter, 2017: 203). With our work, we are interested in elevating antenarratives that appear to be 'never acknowledged', in particular those surrounding Alouette women, such that these women can be part of gendered remembering in organizational space histories.

We collected stories, narratives, media reports, and photographic images from both Canadian and American-based archival sites to be able to reconstruct this gendered Alouette remembering. We embraced a postmodern approach to these archives (Mills and Helms Mills, 2018), noting that 'narratives form in strategic context' (Boje et al., 2016: 392). We also interviewed surviving team members, transposing their recollections with archival data. We have to date found more than 120 Canadian women who were involved in the Alouette I and II satellites. It is beyond the scope of this chapter, however, to reproduce how each of these women is remembered and the discursive processes surrounding them. We focus, rather, on some of these Alouette women, notably Doris Jelly, Elinor Bachand, Beverly Fulton, Phyllis Timleck, Pat Butler, Ethel Moore and Audrey Scott, and on the discursive processes that surround them. We applied a subset of elements from the generative moments heuristic to these collected data, reproducing antenarratives centered around gendered identities, seeking to see these anew, feeling despair and movement, and playing with artifacts (Dutton and Carlsen, 2011). By doing so, we are contributing to the development of feminist historiography and to the undoing of silences.

We begin by presenting the theoretical framing for this study, looking at silences, antenarratives and gendered remembering. We then consider our methodology, built on the generative moments heuristic applied to archival documents and semi-structured interviews. We then present our findings and analysis. We close with a brief word on our study's contributions.

Theoretical framework: Silences, antenarratives, gendered remembering

We acknowledge that there are important gendered subtexts in organizational histories that need to be surfaced, in line with Allen's (1986) views on feminist histories and the silencing of the marginalized. This acknowledgement is achieved by looking at the concepts of silences, antenarratives as discursive processes and gendered remembering as an antithesis to collective memories, which we examine in turn below.

Silences

Organizational silence is more than the absence of voice, where voice is understood to be 'members of an organization express[ing] their views in an attempt to change organizational circumstances' (Knoll et al., 2016: 162). Voice has achieved conceptual maturity in various fields, including human resources management, organizational behavior and psychology. Some (Knoll et al., 2016) argue that silence has not achieved such conceptual maturity, whereas those focused on power and power relations in institutions, such as Clegg, Courpasson and Phillips (2006: 180) and their 'sounds of silence', dispute this characterization.

There are different aspects to consider in a study focused on silence that need to be teased apart, including who is practicing such silence and where silence occurs – that is, an employee or an employer, and their respective genders and other intersectional identities (Collins and Bilge, 2016) along with contexts. Foucault (1984) explains silence as being things that are not said, declined to be said or forbidden to be said. He calls on the discretion of the speaker to know the boundaries 'that function alongside the things said [...] There is not one but many silences' (Foucault, 1984: 343–348). Embracing this notion of plural silences, we acknowledge that they can exist across different contexts, where these contexts can be organizational, ethical, behavioral, writing or archival, to name just a few. Silences in organizations can be defined as the suppression or withholding of genuine expression (Knoll et al., 2016). Harlos (2016: 346) considered employee silences within the context of ethical concerns as 'a person's withholding of genuine expression about behavioral, cognitive and/or affective evaluations of organizational circumstances to persons perceived capable of effecting change or redress'. Foucault (1984: 59), within the context of sex, likens silences as 'an affirmation of nonexistence, and, by implication, an admission that there was nothing to say about such things, nothing to see, and nothing to know'. Olsen (1978), in the context of writing, builds her understanding of unnatural silences along hidden silences 'as work aborted, deferred, denied – hidden by the work which does come to fruition' (Olsen, 1978: 8). She also talks to censorship silences where the censurer can be the government, publishers, religion or even the self, with 'deletions, omissions, abandonment of the medium; [...] paralyzing of capacity' (ibid.: 9). These hidden and censorship silences in particular are imbued with power, where the marginalized writer remains in the void between creativity and life. Finally, within the context of histories, Carter (2006: 220) states that archival 'silence is equated with oblivion'. Hunter (2017: 208), drawing from Michel-Rolph Trouillot, likens historical silences to 'the power of historians to silence during the moment of creating retrospective significance'.

The practice of silences in the context of organizations can be categorized as a behavior inviting us to look at the role of emotions and practices of resistance. Psychologists and sociologists have argued that the practice of silences can come at a considerable physiological and psychological cost when one actively inhibits the expression of one's thoughts, emotions and behaviors (John and Gross, 2004; Pennebaker, 1989; Winnicott, 1960). Some have also argued that the practice of silences is indicative of a passive coping strategy (Tankirk and Richters, 2007). When researchers look to employees as a collective practicing silences, they refer to collective silences coalescing into organizational silence (Knoll et al., 2016). For example, Knoll et al. (2016) looked at collective sexual objectification in the historical airline industry where women are asked to practice caring activities and be glamorous sex objects as a collective while hiding behind a veneer of appropriate service industry standards (see also Mills, 1997; Mills and Helms Mills, 2006). Others question the overall negative framing of employee silences and archival silences in particular. They emphasize that such practices of silences can be influenced by and within power relations, being used as forms of resistance (Bies, 2009; Carter, 2006; Donaghey et al., 2011; Foucault, 1988) or as defensive workplace practices (Bowen and Blackmon, 2003).

There are various typologies and taxonomies for these 'many silences'. Harlos (1998) and Harlos and Pinder (1999) suggested two types of organizational silence in ethical practices: quiescent silence, which is fear- or anger-based, and acquiescent silence, which is futility- or resignation-based. Kurzon (2007), considering silences in social interaction or in interpersonal communication practices, builds on previous work on silences to present conversation silences where one does not speak and allows the other person in the conversation to speak. There are also thematic silences which relate to women not being given a voice until the 1960s. Kurzon (2007) includes textual silences, where one reads in silence or says a silent prayer. He closes his taxonomy with situational silences, where, in a large group of people, one practices rhetorical control (Kurzon, 2007). He underscores the importance of understanding influences from intentional silences and unintentional silences, psychological presence or non-presence where one withdraws from interactions, social norms and rules from the social code, and a need to consider the amount of people involved in social interactions (Kurzon, 2007).

Such 'rule[s] of silence' (Foucault, 1983: 128) and the state of research into silences underline a need to consider individuals, power relations and the contexts in which silences are practiced. We also need to move beyond organizational boundaries towards historical, creative and cultural influences (Allen, 1986; Harlos, 2016; Hunter, 2017; Knoll et al., 2016). Our understanding of silences, as Harlos (2016) points out, within ontological and epistemological concerns of 'knowing' silences is a reflection of the complexities of the self and of the self interacting with others. Harlos (2016) also invites researchers to move away from what she calls traditional work into areas that incorporate researcher and researched. Hunter (2017: 208) underlines that, as historians, 'we are forced […] to narrate and imagine the worlds and feelings of our subjects'. We are then less concerned with paradigmatic boundaries, looking more to the complexity of individuals as they interact with others, the power relations that are embedded in these social interactions and cultural influences, as well as the reflexivity of researchers.

We build our understanding of silences in this study as one that embraces Olsen's (1978) hidden and censorship silences. These hidden and censorship silences are influenced by life happening (Olsen, 1978) – in the sense of time and lack thereof – along with various life experiences, such as the cultural domination of, and systemic discrimination against, North American women during the Cold War era (Ruel et al., 2019; Runté and Mills, 2006), that are involved. These individuals who 'struggle for existence' (Olsen, 1978: 11) can and do leave traces via tales and myths, or antenarratives. We turn to these discursive processes next as part of our theoretical framework.

Antenarratives

Antenarratives are not necessarily linear, with a beginning, a middle and an end (Boje, 2014). They are rather indicative of 'dynamic processes of negotiating inter-relationships' (Boje et al., 2016: 393). Antenarratives are not fully formed stories, in the sense that they are fragmented, sometimes incoherent and may be speculations. Boje et al. (2016) present four specific antenarrative processes: they (1) emerge before grand narratives take form; (2) represent a deeper structure beneath these grand narratives; (3) reoccur, in a cycle of sorts, in events through time; and (4) are the 'between' of individual's stories and the organization's long-lived grand narratives. Boje et al. (2016), we believe, focused on the spoken or textual word in these fragmented, nonlinear stories and tales and did not consider photographic images and their influence as possible storytelling vehicles. In this work, we incorporate photographs as part of the dynamic processes involved in social interactions and as part of these 'in-between' narratives.

Given these characteristics of antenarratives, we acknowledge that they can reflect critical imagination on the part of the researched and of the researcher in the sense that they can be influenced by an individual's critical sensemaking processes (Helms Mills, Thurlow and Mills, 2010; Weick, Sutcliffe and Obstfeld, 2005). Sensemaking,

> unfolds as a sequence in which people concerned with identity in the social reality of other actors engage [in] ongoing circumstances from which they

extract cues and make plausible sense retrospectively, while enacting more or less order into those ongoing circumstances.

(Weick et al., 2005: 409)

We come to understand 'how different meanings are assigned to the same event' (Helms Mills et al., 2010: 183) by our sensemaking and its seven sociopsychological properties. Critical sensemaking, building on this notion of Weickian sensemaking, addresses some key areas of sensemaking that can be overlooked. Mills and Helms Mills (2004) notably folded power and gender into Weickian sensemaking. Critical sensemaking, a theoretical and analytical method, embraces power relations and context, along with identities. Furthermore, critical sensemaking looks to plausibility, rather than accuracy, in line with Weick's sensemaking (Helms Mills et al., 2010). An example of critical sensemaking includes, interestingly for this study on Alouette women, Hartt, Helms Mills and Mills's (2012) dual ANTi-History and critical sensemaking framework applied to archival materials. The interpretation of these materials supports the notion that history is socially constructed storytelling with respect to gender relations.

One premise of critical sensemaking is that social realities and interactions cannot be understood without looking at discursive practices such as antenarratives. Focusing on antenarratives and critical sensemaking leads us to reveal constraints the individual may face and incites them to 'seek out familiar solutions that have worked in the past […] [that] maintain the social status quo' (Helms Mills and Mills, 2009: 175). These familiar solutions can be influenced, in part, by institutional and cultural rules and meta-rules (Mills and Murgatroyd, 1991), such as women leaving work to marry and raise children (Ruel et al., 2019), and by social values (Unger, 1987a; 1987b), such as the historical belief that women were not technically/scientifically inclined (Hacker, 1989). These rules and social values are an integral part of the influences on the complex individuals within organizations and in their storytelling (Boje et al., 2016).

These antenarratives and critical sensemaking that surround such discursive processes guide us also to think 'about the silent in that time of the twelve-hour-a-day, six-day work week' (Olsen, 1978: 11). We must then consider the guiding hand of critical imagination in the sense that we build on these fragments of tales and stories, recognizing the cultural and social boundaries erected by larger systems of exclusion and domination. In this effort to recognize this guiding hand, we turn now to the notion of gender and gendered remembering.

Gendered remembering

'Doing gender', according to West and Zimmerman (1987: 126), is a 'complex of socially guided perceptual, interactional, and micropolitical activities that cast particular pursuits as expressions of masculine and feminine 'natures''. By embracing this notion, we are focusing on both interactional and institutional contexts where we 'do gender', as representing 'the most fundamental divisions of society' (West and Zimmerman, 1987: 126). 'Doing gender' provides such an 'interactional scaffolding of social structure, along with a built-in mechanism of social control' (West and Zimmerman, 1987: 147). Such mechanisms of social control and, we would add, performance are 'fundamental in forming the social nature and ideals of individuals' (Anderson, 2016: 175).

We acknowledge this gendered scaffolding and social control, and that we 'do gender' in an ongoing fashion in a particular context. Knowing 'your gendered place', within such scaffolding and social control, is reflective of ongoing power relations. For example, a woman who chooses to work in a masculine-dominated context, such as the space industry, might find herself walking a tightrope between 'doing' her feminine gender while also, at times, being accepted as an 'honorary man' in social interactions (Ruel, 2019). American and Russian Cold War space histories – along with the few Canadian Cold War space histories – perpetuate another aspect of this 'doing gender' spectrum beyond the feminine; that is, these histories talk extensively to the masculine hero rhetoric (Launius, 2005; Ruel et al., 2019). Such hero rhetorics are indicative of masculine/masculinities norms (Connell, 2005; Hearn, 2000; Knights, 2019) that are performed as both a meta-rule and as a social value. These norms are not only experienced and performed by the men in this industry, but also by the women who are embedded in such a context.

The various complex aspects, including meta-rules and social values, involved in 'knowing your gendered place', we argue, can also be practiced and reflected in acts of organizational remembering. The problem to date, however, is that organizational remembering or collective memory is focused on representing linear and, in some cases, factual accounts of past events by homogeneous individuals that form a collective. Notably, one definition of collective memory is the 'reconstruction of the past that adapts images of ancient facts to present beliefs' (Anteby and Molnár, 2012: 517). These collective memories are process-based and dynamic, where events are chosen that reflect the homogeneous collective (Casey and Olivera, 2011). Organizational mnemonics (Zerubavel, 1996), a branch of collective memories, are concerned with how organizational collectives establish a collective identity such that this identity provides boundaries that define the social institution (Coraiola et al., 2018). These social institutions are represented by social actors who collectively remember and share their memories of successes, practices and collective meaning-making, along with collectively forgetting the past (Coraiola et al., 2018). Organizational mnemonics rely, in part, on collective memories of 'the specific social and historical contexts of organizational memory' (Rowlinson et al., 2010: 69) that are not necessarily 'true' or objectively accurate. What is troublesome here is that, although organizational mnemonics acknowledge that memories can be influenced 'by the relations actors establish with other field-level actors' (Coraiola et al., 2018: 52), where these social actors can be the state, professions or social movements (Coraiola et al., 2018), the underlying assumption is that these actors are homogeneous and are a collective that shares a similar identity. In other words, in these constructions of remembering, management and organizational studies tend to embrace homogeneous, neutral concepts, such as 'collective', 'actors', 'community' and so on. Such neutral treatments remove questions and influences of 'doing gender' and of intersectional identities, such as ethnicity, race, sexuality and so on, as well as the exclusionary order that these intersecting identities can (re)create (Crenshaw, 1989, 1991).

More than 40 years of research have shown that the organization is not neutral or homogeneous when it comes to embedded complex individuals. 'Doing gender' is a social reality that needs to be addressed in organizational studies and, in particular, historical organizational studies. As a case in point, Kanter (1977: 43) underlines with respect to the concept of managers that:

> a 'masculine ethic' of rationality and reason can be identified in the early image of managers. This 'masculine ethic' elevates the traits assumed to belong to men with educational advantages to necessities for effective organizations: a tough-minded approach to problems [...] to set aside personal, emotional considerations in the interests of task accomplishment.

Furthermore, we see that, in certain organizational contexts, such as in science, technology, engineering and mathematics (STEM) contexts, collective memories are imbued with masculine/masculinities notions (Ruel, 2019; Watts, 2010). In contrast, when we talk of a collective and collective memories that are predominantly women's, this is historically linked to and gains legitimacy with feminist movements and the universal experience of subordination, as Joan Wallach Scott (2011) points out. Research on collectives and collective memories in contexts where there are token women (Kanter, 1977) underscores for us that these women have difficult choices to make with respect to the (re)creation of collective memories: they must either take gendered steps to assimilate into this collective, or walk a fine-gendered line, or recognize that they can be isolated from this collective (Bowen and Blackmon, 2003; Ruel, 2019; Watts, 2010).

Given our focus on organizational histories and archives, we must also acknowledge Harris (2001), who moves away from Derrida's binary opposition of remembering and forgetting in archives. Harris (2001: 6) embraces rather 'imagining' and the intertwined nature of remembering and forgetting:

> there is no remembering without forgetting. There is no remembering which cannot become forgetting. Forgetting can become a deferred remembering. Forgetting can be a way of remembering. They open out of each other, light becoming darkness, darkness becoming light. And dancing between remembering and forgetting, at once spanning them and within each, is imagining.

With respect to this archival dance in the 'imagining' and applying it to space organizational histories, Miller and Olivera (2006) looked at the National

Aeronautics and Space Administration (NASA) and its difficulties in keeping track of incident reports (i.e. some misfiled, no indexes, etc.). They offered two interpretations for this collective forgetting: intentional or unintentional processes that were influenced by a politics of forgetting (Nissley and Casey, 2002); or intentional, organized forgetting – that is, strategic forgetting (Casey and Olivera, 2011). These purposeful actions, we argue, are more layered than a question of intent or non-intent. This is similar to the notion of silences, as we discussed previously, that is beyond such questions of intent. Reaching into the Harris archival dance as a cue, the first author recalls having to produce these NASA incident reports, without having any training on how to complete them, along with juggling two missions and multiple international stakeholders and managing home responsibilities (that is, four children). There was no strategic or political intent in forgetting that she can recall; it was, anecdotally for her, an experience in lack of training and of time, and of being spread too thin across multiple responsibilities. Importantly, she also now retrospectively recognizes that she embraced hidden and self-censorship silences for fear of gendered reprisals from her masculine-/masculinities-dominated context. Her silences with respect to NASA incident reports for her missions include her embracing critical sensemaking – identities including gender, power relations, retrospective, plausibility and so on – and imagining. By doing so, she moves across a spectrum of productive and oppressive power relations, as opposed to binary representations.

In light of these insights and what we know of 'doing gender', we believe we need to recontextualize and reclaim nuanced understanding of power relations in such gendered space contexts, and the influences on remembering and forgetting in organizational space histories. In Anteby and Molnár's (2012) work within the aerospace industry, they underlined that shared beliefs of what should be remembered and what is forgotten are two sides of the same coin, in line with Harris's (2001) work. Importantly, Anteby and Molnár (2012: 532) define this relationship across remembering and forgetting as 'who we were not … [and] … who we are'. In our recontextualized understandings of women in the space industry and the stories that surround them, we note that they face important challenges of being either assimilated, walking a fine-gendered line or being left on the fringes. In other words, women and the antenarratives that surround them may appear for a time to be part of 'who we are' while also residing in 'who we were not'. These women might also embrace hidden and censorship silences, inviting this dance between gendered remembering and forgetting to continue via antenarratives that bubble to the surface. These marginal, fragmented tales may be reproduced by others, men included. It is left to those in the present and the future to shape and reshape these tales and stories. Some throw out those stories and antenarratives that do not reflect a homogeneous collective in organizational histories. We are advocating with our work to move the fragmented stories and tales surrounding women in the space industry into productive power relations such that we can embrace pluralistic understandings of 'who we were not' and 'who we are' in organizational space histories.

Methodology

We present in our methodology the nature and the method of data collection that we used. We then move to our data analysis framework, with the goal of answering our research questions: How are Canadian Alouette women remembered? What are some of the discursive processes involved in this gendered remembering?

Nature of data and method of data collection

The body of evidence in this study relies on four sources: Library and Archives Canada's Alouette I and II collection of documents; NASA's national headquarters' archives of Alouette I and II documents; the Friends of Communications Research Centre (CRC) organization; and semi-structured interviews with individuals who worked on these Alouette missions.

The Library and Archives Canada hold an extensive number of documents, well over 1500, focused on Alouette I and II. Within these documents, we found three major fonds created and housed under the following individuals: John H. Chapman, Colin Franklin and Curtis Yool. The first two individuals were senior executives and managers for these two missions, and Mr. Yool was responsible for taking and collecting photographs of various events in and around Alouette I and II. These archival documents include annual reports, summary and full reports of events, meeting minutes, media reports, celebration and commemorative notes, technical mission-specific documents and so on. Importantly, we found extensive formal organizational charts dating from 1958 until the end of the 1960s, outlining positions, roles and responsibilities of key personnel involved in these missions. We also found a number of personal notes and letters between various individuals, providing insight into social interactions at the time.

As for the NASA headquarters archives, there were no significant individuals attributed to the files that housed the Alouette I and II mission information. In fact, the first author found an interesting contrast between the Canadian archives and the U.S. archives: the personal touches, such as correspondence, notes to secretaries, personal letters, pictures of local events and so on, were present throughout the Canadian archive, whereas the U.S. archives were sanitized to such an extent that it was difficult to find any one individual within these archives.

The Friends of CRC have both a web-based presence and monthly meetings where former employees and those interested in the work of CRC are invited to support various activities. Through their web presence and through a presentation made by the first author at one of these monthly meetings, we were able to connect with a number of individuals who worked on Alouette I and II.

We conducted interviews with some of the Alouette members of the 'farm team' (transcript, James Mondo)[4] and uncovered additional personal photographic images and stories that individuals consented to share. The semi-structured interviews consisted of collecting various fragments of historical narratives along with pictures and notes taken at the time. These interviews were audio recorded and transcribed. In one instance, the first and second authors took copious notes instead of recording the interview, at the participant's request. These notes were later transcribed into a combined narrative.

We did face a dilemma about anonymizing our various informants. Our research intent is to write these Alouette women back into space histories. It is interesting that we promised confidentiality to the men we interviewed, such that their identities are concealed here by pseudonyms, but we do not conceal the identities of the women named in their reminiscences. The woman whom we have been able to interview thus far, notably Doris Jelly, gave her written consent to reveal her identity. As this research continues, we will continue to seek consent from the Alouette women to reveal their identities.

Data analysis framework

The generative moments heuristic (Dutton and Carlsen, 2011) permitted us to focus on the Canadian Alouette women and antenarratives, while also melding in the dominant class of men who contributed to these missions. Critical imagination, an important influence on the generative moments heuristic, guided us in the gendered remembering surrounding these Alouette individuals. We were able to acknowledge the 'contentious' nature of history, which is not as well defined as others would have us believe (Clark and Rowlinson, 2004), and focused our analysis on historical silences surrounding the women's contributions to the Alouette missions.

We evoked Dutton and Carlsen's (2011) five themes in the generative moments heuristic: seeing anew, feeling despair and movement, daring to engage, inter-relating, and playing with artifacts. We chose to focus on seeing anew, feeling despair and movement, and playing with artifacts, as we explain below. *Seeing anew* pulls on critical imagination and enables the creation of new questions and conversations. For example, the organizational charts we found in archives clearly identified women as 'Miss' or 'Mrs', even when some of these women had PhDs. We showed these organizational charts to some of the individuals we interviewed, along with some pictures found in archives that had no names associated to them. Some of these images included a 'space princess', where a woman was crowned at a monthly beauty pageant event, and what one of our interviewees (emphatically) called 'a wife' accompanying her husband to a scientific conference. Looking back at these organizational charts and at these images, the interviewees and the interviewers were challenged to see these artifacts anew, reflecting social values and organizational rules of the 1960s and transposing them to contemporary values and rules in such a way to assess them anew.

Feeling despair and movement incorporates feelings into embodied knowing, acknowledging emotions in gendered remembering. Returning to our example, the first author was initially surprised at the use of 'Miss' or 'Mrs' and the vehemence of our interviewee calling the woman pictured 'a wife'. This surprise led to her reflecting on her embodied experiences of the space industry in the 20th and 21st centuries, notably how she had been positioned and affectionally named a 'space princess' by her colleagues and then feeling despair at how this had positioned her below her counterparts, who were all men. The importance of this aspect of the generative moments speaks to not only the interviewee's feelings, but also the interviewer's movement through her own emotions and her embodied experiences of knowing.

Finally, *playing with artifacts* materializes data as 'symbols that store insights ... propel[ing] understanding and growth' (Dutton and Carlsen, 2011: 216). Photographic images and antenarratives became our site of play, where we offered counterclaims to refute the masculine-centric collective Alouette stories. Our goal, to be clear, was not to diminish the role the men played in these missions; our goal was to propel Alouette women into the present and the future. Playing with artifacts became a possible source of inspirational gendered remembering in which these Alouette women and their roles were no longer 'sleeping in the forgotten' and no longer lost to the hidden and censorship silences.

We focused on these three aspects of generative moments to recreate possibilities of knowing and of learning. These possibilities reside for us in liminal spaces, pushing idea change through relational stories. For example, in one interview, Doris Jelly talked about her start as a student in the Alouette program. She also shared more recent (1970s) space responsibilities, including her work on the Hermes satellite (an experimental communications satellite). The ultimate goal of Hermes was to set up telemedicine services to the Canadian North. Ms. Jelly spent considerable time explaining the mission and sharing pictures of herself interacting with various stakeholders on this mission. During her fragmented storytelling, the first author had moments of knowing and learning with respect to her own work on communications satellites for the North. The first author went so far as to state to Ms. Jelly that she would have loved to have met her 20 years ago, and that, if she had, the first author might have navigated her job and role in the contemporary space industry in a different fashion. This social interaction and the web of power relations pushed gendered remembering to an unexpected, liminal space of knowing, not only for the first author, but also for the second author who was present for this interview. We three embraced this web of plausibility, bringing forward this experience to the present. In other words, we acknowledge that we were influenced with and by our interactions with the various Alouette individuals.

Findings and analysis

The surfacing of antenarratives surrounding the Canadian Alouette I and II satellite missions and the women involved in these missions reflects a multitude of complex organizations and gendered individuals. Notably, these two satellites were designed, constructed and operated via the Defence and Research Telecommunications Establishment (DRTE), reporting to the Canadian Minister of Defence (DRTE, 1960a). A mix of public companies, including the Cosmic Ray Section of the National Research Council (Chapman, 1964), private companies, including De Havilland Aircraft Co., RCA Victor Co. Ltd, Sinclair Radio Laboratories and Spar Aerospace (DRTE, 1972), and international companies, including the

NASA-provided launch and Goddard Space Flight Center (NASA, 1962), all contributed to these missions. These organizations are important to recognize here given the fragmented stories surrounding who were involved in these missions (Godefroy, 2011) and the many antenarratives that took form in these different contexts.

Focusing on DRTE, through our archival search we uncovered men and women who worked in various capacities on Alouette I, including 35 engineers, 17 physicists and more than 100 support staff (Chapman, 1964; DRTE, 1960b; 1972). Although enumeration of these types of quantitative data reflects more of a modernist approach to archival research (Mills and Helms Mills, 2018), we approach archival data as postmodernists. This implies that we are concerned with the 'how' of the collection of artifacts, including judging and imagining the discourses in those collections (Mills and Helms Mills, 2018).

To this end, from the first and third authors' previous work on the U.S. space industry (Ruel et al., 2019), they learned that there was a proliferation of 'space princesses' across U.S. space organizations. These space princesses were representative of what women were 'supposed' to be like in the context of this industry, as representatives of the feminine ideal. Drawing on this knowledge, we did find one Canadian media report, reproduced in Figure 7.1, that is similar to antenarratives surrounding the U.S.-based space princesses.

FIGURE 7.1 Canadian space princess (*The Ottawa Citizen*, 1961)

We acknowledge that this Canadian space princess, an unnamed secretary working at DRTE, symbolizes one 'how' of the gendered remembering around Alouette. It is also important to underline that this is the only image of an Alouette woman available in the public domain. Through our interviews, we found that space princesses were indeed more prevalent than what was initially found in archival boxes from Library and Archives Canada. From the chairman of the Friends of CRC John Brebner's private photographic collection and subsequent conversations, we learned that, as a way to 'keep things interesting' for the people working on these missions, the DRTE held beauty pageants regularly (see Figure 7.2). Brebner also shared with us that images of women would also appear in slide carousels, as a way to break the monotony of calculations and technical drawings.

These particular antenarratives are but one example of how Canadian Alouette women are remembered. Drawing inspiration for seeing anew and feeling despair for this way of remembering these women and their mission contributions, we looked to instances of gendered remembering focused on men, hoping to achieve some movement away from these representations of the feminine in space. Canadian men were indeed reproduced extensively through images and media reports that we found in archives, and through various images shared by our interviewees. These Canadian men were often portrayed as being serious and hardworking and interacting with space hardware, as reflected in Figure 7.3. Imagine for a moment what the Alouette antenarratives surrounding women in Figures 7.4 and 7.5, from Brebner's personal collection, could tell us about women working on these missions.

We learned recently through *Hidden Figures* (Shetterly, 2016) that Black women played an integral role in getting U.S. White men to the moon. These Black

FIGURE 7.2 More Canadian space princesses (Brebner, 2014)

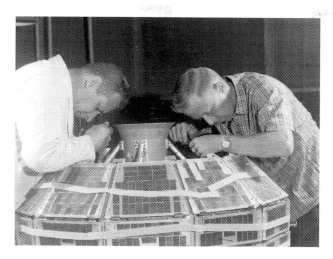

FIGURE 7.3 DRTE men interacting with Alouette artifact (Brebner, 2014)

FIGURE 7.4 Human computer (Brebner, 2014)

women acted as human computers, or mathematical wizards, taking on complex and detailed orbital calculations. In the case of Alouette women, we learned of the presence of such human computers working on these Canadian Alouette missions (Figure 7.4). We also learned of women's responsibilities as scalers (Figure 7.5). At the time, we were not certain what the archival documents were telling us with respect to these scalers. One of our interviewees (Dean Lorie)[5] helped us decipher what was being said and shown in photographic images about these women scalers. Lorie shared his own antenarratives surrounding these women scalers, reconstituted here as a flowing story:

FIGURE 7.5 Two DRTE scalers (Brebner, 2014)

DEAN LORIE: The scalers weren't hired to do research. They were hired to pick parameters off the ionograms. For example, they might pick several points along the X trace on an ionogram. These would be fed into a computer by a scientist and the electron density from the satellite height down to the height of the maximum density of the F2 layer calculated. There were about 4 or 5 ladies working on contract to 'scale' (i.e. get information from) the ionograms. If she were scaling ionograms, there should also be a projector containing a roll of film with the ionograms on it. This was 40 to 50 years ago so, except for Elinor [Bachand], I can't even remember their names. The lady I referred to, Elinor Bachand, was special. Elinor was special because she was fast and accurate. She investigated large numbers of ionograms looking for a particular feature. I wanted to make her a co-author on some papers but was told that because she was a contract employee she couldn't be an author or even acknowledged.

INTERVIEWER: When you say pass on the information so that a scientist can feed it into a computer, do you mean these scalers would use punch cards to capture the data and then give the punch cards to the scientist (like you)?

DEAN LORIE: You are correct. The ionograms were projected onto a screen and cross hairs were clicked on the point of interest and the coordinates transferred to punch cards.

The presence of these women scalers and their work appear to lie in the hidden and censorship silences, supported by their employment status as temporary, contractual employees. We recognized, upon analyzing these antenarratives and Dean Lorie's expression of surprise that we were interested in these scalers, that these women scalers were more than what the objective past was telling us. Today, notably, these women scalers would be recognized as technologists or technicians fulfilling key satellite data mission responsibilities. By seeing anew and holding onto a movement forward, we are breaking these historical silences in such a way to bring at least Elinor Bachand into the present, to celebrate her contributions on these missions and to inspire current women data mission specialists.

We were excited about the possibilities with this movement forward, and once again we turned to Dean Lorie to help us understand what some other fragments were telling us, reproduced here again as a story that lives in the antenarratives' 'in between':

> Mr. Petri and Miss Fulton asked for the latest roll-off curves on the low band sounder aerial. The most recent figure from the Sinclair Radio Lab is approx. 36db attenuation at 0.5MC/sec [...] Dr. Warren's group would study the present antenna characteristics.
>
> *(Barry, 1960)*

DEAN LORIE: I don't know why Len [Petri] and Bev [Fulton] wanted the roll-off curves; possibly because of some research Len wanted to do. The Alouette and ISIS satellites had two crossed dipoles, a short one for the lower frequencies and a long one for the higher frequencies. I think this quote must be before the launch of Alouette 1 because I think the crossover frequency was higher than 0.5 MHz (this is an old quote because we don't use MC/sec anymore.) Eldon Warren was our group leader. I guess he was involved in designing the best antenna for ionospheric studies. There weren't that many women that worked on the science [side]. Phyllis Timleck and I and a summer student [Doris Jelly] did some statistics on ground reflected echoes from Alouette 1 and 2. Bev [Fulton] must have been an engineer but I don't know where she is or what happened to her.

We found other instances of Beverly Fulton's presence in technical meetings, working on the science side of the Alouette mission, given the scientific quotes we can attribute to her. What is surprising in some of these documents is that she was part of technical discussions, which must have been meetings full of men, and yet another individual (James Mando) could not remember if there were any women involved in any of the technical meetings: 'there were probably secretaries in the meetings but not sure'. We probed further with Mando, asking about one particular scientist who was a mentor for Doris Jelly (see Figure 7.6).

We attempted to recreate relational stories for Mando, to instigate idea change, by asking if the name Moira Dunbar meant something to him: 'Moira Dunbar was quite well known. Notable scientist in Arctic research but not on Alouette. I used to hear about Moira but I don't think I ever met her'. This movement away from Alouette meetings and further discussions about the first author's experience in the Canadian space industry appeared to help Mando make important links with respect to women's roles on Alouette missions. Three such Mando antenarratives, including Figure 7.7, are shared here:

JAMES MANDO: [In 1957, there were] lots of women in various functions but not yet secretaries. There was Pat Butler, photography, and Ethel Moore produced illustrations and engineering drawings. [The] photography and drafting were

FIGURE 7.6 Doris Jelly (center) pictured with co-workers at DRTE (Jelly, 2019)

FIGURE 7.7 Pat Butler, photographer (Brebner, 2014)

really important; Ethel [Moore] had all the schematics produced for Alouette 1 […] If we didn't have the photographs and illustrations, don't know what we would have done!

While preparing to go to Vandenberg [Airforce Base, for launch in 1962], Frank Davies' secretary [Audrey] Scott had been watching the goings on and absolutely wanted to go with them. Davies said no – he got very nervous about this group of young men (20 somethings) letting loose. A male secretary was sent instead which raised eyebrows by NASA (couldn't believe that a man was a secretary!)

Why was Mando initially steadfast in his gendered remembering that there must have been women but he couldn't recall their presence in meetings? Perhaps he experienced 'introspective certainty' (Nisbett and Wilson, 1977: 255) about the absence of women as the Alouette technical events were salient in his perceptions and memories. In other words, women scientists might run counter to a plausible cultural rule in this man's recollection of institutional traditions (Hobsbawm and Ranger, 1983). Mando did have 'direct access to a storehouse of private knowledge' (Nisbett and Wilson, 1977: 255) and personal facts about the Alouette missions, hence his confidence that no women could be recalled as being present. When we directly asked about the Alouette women, his a priori rules and meta-rules in his particular context made him confident that there would have been none present.

It is also plausible that, at the time of the missions, the gender of team members was not seen as relevant to Mando's tasks and plans, and so attributions of gender to work done did not occur. When asked to recall the presence of team members, he simply relied on the perceived likelihood that there would have been women present. Furthermore, because we were asking about events that occurred more than 50 years ago, it is also likely that Mando would have been relying on representativeness as opposed to actual memories. Representativeness is used here in the sense that, if an individual is, say, a librarian, one would compare his information about the individual with the contents of his stereotype concerning librarians (Tversky and Kahneman, 1974). Cues that we provided through our relational stories, such as talking about Doris Jelly and Moira Dunbar, about the relevance of gender allowed him to reclassify his memories of the team members as men or women. Thus, his gendered remembering and the accompanying silences were not cases of intentional vs. unintentional practices, as Miller and Olivera (2006) would have us believe. Rather, it is plausible that Mando did not know about the women because they were not encoded in terms of gender in his memories of Alouette events.

Conclusion

There is a need, as Godfrey et al. (2016: 599) state, for there to be an 'entwining of history with morality and social impact'. The need to recognize 'doing gender' in space organizations, as one such morality and social impact study, guided our investigation into the Alouette I and II satellite missions and the hidden and censorship silences that have been carried through time. The grand narratives of the '100' men are central to the rhetoric of a 'teleology of success' (Suddaby et al., 2010: 161) for these Alouette missions. These meta-narratives propelled us forward to see these missions anew, to seek movement forward and to play with cultural artifacts to re-imagine what the gendered historical heritage could be with respect to Alouette.

In this study, we do not wish to undo the work of these '100' men. We are looking to unravel the institutional traditions around focusing only on these '100' and to consider various discursive processes, grounded in Boje et al.'s (2016) antenarratives and in the addition of photographic images, to our understanding of antenarratives. Through a framework of silences, antenarratives and gendered remembering, we presented how Canadian Alouette women's 'sleeping in the forgotten' can be undone such that a broader understanding of who they were and what their contributions were can be part of space organizational histories. With this gendered remembering study, we are making a contribution to the development of feminist historiography by subverting normative, masculine/masculinities-centric collective understandings of stories and embracing partial tales to bring some of these Alouette women to the fore.

Acknowledgement

The authors wish to thank Concordia University and the Social Sciences and Humanities Research Council for their generous funding of this research.

Notes

1. We recognize the sociopolitical characterizations of race, gender, class, etc., that are produced through discourses. To this end, we capitalize the 'White' and 'Black' races but leave 'woman' and 'men' uncapitalized.
2. The terms 'women' and 'men' encompass the feminine and masculine normative cisgender experiences that are attributable to these social positions and how gender is 'done' (West and Zimmerman, 1987). In other words, women and men are created and recreated through social interactions (West and Zimmerman, 1987).
3. We use 'complex' to reflect a lens of 'mutual construction […] [across] people's lives and identities [that] are generally shaped by many factors in diverse and mutually influencing ways' (Collins and Bilge, 2016: 26).
4. This is a pseudonym to protect the participant's identity.
5. This is a pseudonym to protect the participant's identity.

References

Allen, J. (1986). Evidence and silence: Feminism and the limits of history. In Pateman, C. and Gross, E. (eds.) *Feminist challenges: Social and political theory.* Sydney: Allen & Urwin, 173–189.

Anderson, K.L. (2016). *Thinking about sociology: A critical introduction* (2nd ed.). Oxford: Oxford University Press.

Anteby, M. and Molnár, V. (2012). Collective memory meets organizational identity: Remembering to forget in a firm's rhetorical history. *Academy of Management Journal,* 55 (3): 515–540.

Barry, J.N. (1960). *Topside Sounder coordination meeting: Electonics Lab, Nov. 30 1960* (Box MG 31 J 43 Vol. 11, File Satellite S-27: Satellite Coordination Meetings). Library and Archives Canada.

Bies, R.J. (2009). Sounds of silence: Identifying new motives. In Greenberg, J. and Edwards, M. (eds.), *Voice and silence in organizations*. Bingley: Emerald, 175–202.

Boje, D.M. (2014). *Storytelling organizational practice*. London: Routledge.

Boje, D.M., Haley, U.C.V. and Saylors, R. (2016). Antenarratives of organizational change: The microstoria of Burger King's storytelling in space, time and strategic context. *Human Relations*, 69 (2): 391–418.

Bowen, F. and Blackmon, K. (2003). Spirals of silence: The dynamic effects of diversity on organizational voice. *Journal of Management Studies*, 40 (6): 1393–1417.

Brebner, J. (2014). Private collection of photographic images: Alouette I, Alouette II, and ISIS [Photographic Images].

Carter, R.G.S. (2006). Of things said and unsaid: Power, archival silences, and power in silence. *Archivaria*, Spring (61): 215–233.

Casey, A.J. and Olivera, F. (2011). Reflections on organizational memory and forgetting. *Journal of Management Inquiry*, 20 (3): 305–310.

Chapman, J.H. (1964). Chapman, J.H. 'The Alouette Satellite', Jan. 1964: *The Alouette Satellite, for presentation to the Royal Canadian Institute, 18 January 1964* (MG 31 J43 Vol. 1). Ottawa: author; Library and Archives Canada.

Clark, P. and Rowlinson, M. (2004). The treatment of history in organisation studies: Towards an 'historic turn'? *Business History*, 46 (3): 331–352.

Clegg, S.R., Courpasson, D. and Phillips, N. (2006). *Power and organizations*. London: Sage.

Collins, P.H. and Bilge, S. (2016). *Intersectionality*. Oxford: Polity.

Connell, R.W. (2005). Change among the gatekeepers: Men, masculinities, and gender equality in the global arena. *Signs*, 30 (3): 1801–1825.

Coraiola, D.M., Suddaby, R. and Foster, W.M. (2018). Organizational fields as mnemonic communities. In Gluckler, J. (ed.), *Knowledge and institutions*. New York: Springer, 45–68.

Crenshaw, K. (1989). Demarginalizing the intersection of race and sex: A black feminist critique of antidiscrimination doctrine, feminist theory and antiracist politics. *University of Chicago Legal Forum*, 1: 139–167.

Crenshaw, K. (1991). Mapping the margins: Intersectionality, identity politics, and violence against women of color. *Stanford Law Review*, 43 (6): 1241–1299.

Defence and Research Telecommunications Establishment [DRTE]. (1960a). *DRTE Organization, 1960* (MG31-J43 (MSS1960) Vol. 3, file 3–27). Ottawa: Author; Library and Archives Canada.

DRTE. (1960b). *DRTE scientific and administrative organization guides, 1960–1965* (MG 31 J43 Vol. 3, File 3–27). Ottawa: Author; Library and Archives Canada.

DRTE. (1972). *10th anniversary of Alouette I: Invitation list* (RG 97, Acc 1985–1986/638, Box 13). Ottawa: Author; Library and Archives Canada.

De Groot, G.J. (2006). *Dark side of the moon: The magnificent madness of the American lunar quest*. New York: New York University Press.

Donaghey, J., Cullinane, N., Dundon, T. and Wilkinson, A. (2011). Re-conceptualising employee silence: Problems and prognosis. *Work, Employment and Society*, 25 (1): 51–67.

Dutton, J.E. and Carlsen, A. (2011). Seeing, feeling, daring, interrelating and playing: Exploring themes in generative moments. In Carlsen, A. and Dutton, J.E. (eds.), *Research alive: Exploring generative moments in doing qualitative research*. Copenhagen: Copenhagen Business School Press, 214–235.

Foucault, M. (1983). Afterword: The subject and power. In Dreyfus, H.L. and Rabinow, P. (eds.), *Michel Foucault: Beyond structuralism and hermeneutics* (2nd ed.). Chicago: University of Chicago Press, 208–226.

Foucault, M. (1984). We 'other Victorians'. In Rabinow, P. (ed.), *The Foucault reader*. New York: Pantheon Books, 292–300.

Foucault, M. (1988). *Politics philosophy culture: Interviews and other writings 1977–1984*. London: Routledge.
Godefroy, A.B. (2011). *Defence and discovery: Canada's military space program, 1945–74*. Vancouver, BC: UBC Press.
Godfrey, P.C., Hassard, J., O'Connor, E.S., Rowlinson, M. and Ruef, M. (2016). What is organizational history? Toward a creative synthesis of history and organization studies. *Academy of Management Review*, 41 (4): 590–608.
Hacker, S.L. (1989). *Pleasure, power and technology: Some tales of gender, engineering, and the cooperative workplace*. Sydney: Unwin Hyman.
Harlos, K. (1998). *Organizational injustice and its resistance using voice and silence*. Vancouver: University of British Columbia.
Harlos, K. (2016). Employee silence in the context of unethical behavior at work: A commentary. *German Journal of Human Resource Management*, 30 (3–4): 345–355.
Harlos, K. and Pinder, C. (1999). Patterns of organizational injustice: A taxonomy of what employees regard as unjust. In *Advances in Qualitative Organizational Research*, 2. Greenwich, CT: JAI Press, 97–125.
Harris, V. (2001). Seeing (in) blindness: South Africa, archives and passion for justice. *Archifacts*, October, 1–13.
Hartt, C., Helms Mills, J. and Mills, A.J. (2012). Reading between the lines: Gender, work and history: The case of the Nova Scotia Teachers' Union. *Journal of Management History*, 18 (1): 82–95.
Hearn, J. (2000). Is masculinity dead? A critique of the concept of masculinity/masculinities. In Mac An Ghaill, M. (ed.), *Understanding masculinities*. Maidenhead: Open University Press, 202–217.
Helms Mills, J. and Mills, A. J. (2009). Critical sensemaking and workplace inequities. In Özbilgin, M. (ed.), *Equality, diversity and inclusion at work: A research companion*. Cheltenham: Edward Elgar, 171–178.
Helms Mills, J., Thurlow, A. and Mills, A.J. (2010). Making sense of sensemaking: The critical sensemaking approach. *Qualitative Research in Organizations and Management: An International Journal*, 5 (2): 182–195.
Hobsbawm, E. and Ranger, T. (1983). *The invention of tradition*. Cambridge: Cambridge University Press.
Hunter, K.M. (2017). Silence in noisy archives: Reflections on Judith Allen's 'evidence and silence - feminism and the limits of history' (1986) in the era of mass digitisation. *Australian Feminist Studies*, 32 (91–92): 202–212.
Jelly, D. (2019). Private collection of photographic images: Alouette I, Alouette II, and ISIS.
John, O.P. and Gross, J.J. (2004). Healthy and unhealthy emotion regulation: Personality processes, individual differences, and life span development. *Journal of Personality*, 72 (6): 1301–1334.
Jones Royster, J. and Kirsch, G.E. (2012). *Feminist rhetorical practices: New horizons for rhetoric, composition, and literacy studies*. Carbondale, IL: Southern Illinois University Press.
Kanter, R.M. (1977). *Men and women of the corporation*. New York: Basic Books.
Knights, D. (2019). Gender still at work: Interrogating identity in discourses and practices of masculinity. *Gender, Work and Organization*, 26 (1): 18–30.
Knoll, M., Wegge, J., Unterrainer, C., Silva, S. and Jønsson, T. (2016). Is our knowledge of voice and silence in organizations growing? Building bridges and (re) discovering opportunities. *German Journal of Human Resource Management*, 30 (3–4): 161–194.
Kurzon, D. (2007). Towards a typology of silence. *Journal of Pragmatics*, 39 (10): 1673–1688.
Launius, R.D. (2005). *Heroes in a vacuum: The Apollo astronaut as cultural icon*. American Institute of Aeronautics and Astronautics Aerospace Sciences Meeting and Exhibit, Reno, 13.

Launius, R.D. (2007). What are turning points in history, and what were they for the space age? In Dick, S.J. and Launius, R.D. (eds.), *Societal impact of spaceflight*. Washington, DC: NASA, 19–39.

Maclean, M., Harvey, C. and Clegg, S.R. (2016). Conceptualizing historical organization studies. *Academy of Management Review*, 41 (4): 609–632.

Miller, S.B. and Olivera, F. (2006). *The memory of mishaps in NASA*. Academy of Management Annual Meeting 2006, Atlanta, GA.

Mills, A.J. (1997). Dueling discourses – Desexualization versus eroticism in the corporate framing of female sexuality in the British airline industry, 1945–60. In Prasad, P., Mills, A. J., Elmes, M. and Prasad, A. (eds.), *Managing the organizational melting pot: Dilemmas of workplace diversity*. London: Sage, 171–198.

Mills, A.J. and Helms Mills, J. (2004). When plausibility fails: Towards a critical sensemaking approach to resistance. In Thomas, R., Mills, A.J. and Helms Mills, J. (eds.), *Identity politics at work: Resisting gender, gendering resistance*. London: Routledge, 139–157.

Mills, A.J. and Helms Mills, J. (2006). Masculinity and the making of Trans-Canada Air Lines, 1938–1940: A feminist poststructuralist account. *Canadian Journal of Administrative Sciences*, 23 (1): 34–44.

Mills, A.J. and Helms Mills, J. (2018). Archival research. In Cassell, C., Cunliffe, A. and Grandy, G. (eds.), *The Sage handbook of qualitative research methods in business and management*. London: Sage, 32–46.

Mills, A.J. and Murgatroyd, S.J. (1991). *Organizational rules: A framework for understanding organizations*. Maidenhead: Open University Press.

NASA. (1962). *NASA Facts: Alouette – Canada's first satellite* (MG 31 J 43 Vol. 11, File Alouette 1 NASA Facts). U.S. Government Printing Office; Library and Archives Canada.

Nisbett, R.E. and Wilson, T.D. (1977). Telling more than we can know: Verbal reports on mental processes. *Psychological Review*, 84 (3): 231–259.

Nissley, N. and Casey, A. (2002). Viewing corporate museums through the paradigmatic lens of organizational memory: The politics of the exhibition. *British Journal of Management*, 13 (1): 35–45.

Olsen, T. (1978). *Silences*. New York: Delacorte Press/Seymour Lawrence.

Ottawa Citizen, The (1961). Canada 'Sputnik' world's least-heralded. *The Ottawa Citizen*. Library and Archives Canada.

Pennebaker, J.W. (1989). Confession, inhibition, and disease. In Berkowitz, L. (ed.), *Advances in experimental social psychology*, 22. San Diego: Academic Press, 211–244.

Rowlinson, M., Booth, C., Clark, P., Delahaye, A. and Procter, S. (2010). Social remembering and organizational memory. *Organization Studies*, 31 (1): 69–87.

Royster, J.J. (2000). *Traces of a stream: Literacy and social change among African American women*. Pittsburgh, PA: University of Pittsburgh Press.

Ruel, S. (2019). *STEM-professional women's exclusion in the Canadian space industry: Anchor points and intersectionality at the margins of space*. Bingley: Emerald.

Ruel, S., Mills, A.J. and Helms Mills, J. (2019). Gendering multi-voiced histories of the North American space industry: The GMRD white women. *Journal of Management History*, 25 (3): 464–492.

Ruel, S., Mills, A.J. and Thomas, J.L. (2018). Intersectionality at work: The case of Ruth Bates Harris and NASA. *Ephemera*, 18 (1): 17–49.

Runté, M. and Mills, A.J. (2006). Cold War, chilly climate: Exploring the roots of gendered discourse in organization and management theory. *Human Relations*, 59 (5): 695–720.

Shetterly, M.L. (2016). *Hidden figures: The American dream and the untold story of the Black women mathematicians who helped win the space race*. New York: William Morrow.

Suddaby, R., Foster, W.M. and Quinn Trank, C. (2010). Rhetorical history as a source of competitive advantage. In Baum, J.A.C. and Lampel, J. (eds.), *The Globalization of strategy research*, 27. London: Emerald, 147–173.

Tankirk, M. and Richters, A. (2007). Silence as a coping strategy: The case of refugee women in the Netherlands from South-Sudan who experienced sexual violence in the context of war. In Drozdek, B. and Wilson, J.P. (eds.), *Voices of trauma: Treating psychological trauma across cultures*. New York: Springer, 191–210.

Tversky, A. and Kahneman, D. (1974). Judgment under uncertainty: Heuristics and biases. *Science*, 185 (4157): 1124–1131.

Unger, R.M. (1987a). *Plasticity into power*. Cambridge: Cambridge University Press.

Unger, R.M. (1987b). *Social theory: Its situation and its task*. Cambridge: Cambridge University Press.

Wallach Scott, J. (2011). *The fantasy of feminist history*. Durham, NC: Duke University Press.

Watts, J.H. (2010). 'Now you see me, now you don't': The visibility paradox for women in a male-dominated profession. In Lewis, P. and Simpson, R. (eds.), *Revealing and concealing gender*. Basingstoke: Palgrave Macmillan, 175–193.

Weick, K.E., Sutcliffe, K.M. and Obstfeld, D. (2005). Organizing and the process of sensemaking. *Organization Science*, 16 (4): 409–421.

West, C. and Zimmerman, D.H. (1987). Doing gender. *Gender and Society*, 1 (2): 125–151.

Winnicott, D.W. (1960). Ego distortion in terms of true and false self. In *The maturational processes and the facilitating environment: Studies in the theory of emotional development*. Madison, CT: International Universities Press, 139–152.

Zerubavel, E. (1996). Social memories: Steps to a sociology of the past. *Qualitative Sociology*, 19 (3): 283–299.

8

THE ENDURING PRESENCE OF THE FOUNDER

A historical and interdisciplinary perspective on the organizational identity of collection museums

Sonia Coman and Andrea Casey

Overview

Repositories of an individual's drive to accumulate 'everything' in a 'place of all times that is itself outside of time' (Foucault, 1985: 26), collection museums are microcosms—or *heterotopias*, to use Foucault's term—whose organizing principle is dictated largely by the collector-founder, specifically by her or his collecting choices, all informed by her or his intellectual curiosity, worldview, and attitude towards the market. The art market, understood here as the ensemble of agents and venues where art is bought and sold, relies not only on the availability of art for sale and purchase, but also on sociopolitical and sociocultural codes that shape the interactions between relevant agents (seller, buyer, and any intermediaries). In that sense, our understanding of an art market is premised on the notion of 'art world' as defined by Becker (1982: x): 'the network of people whose cooperative activity, organised via their joint knowledge of conventional means of doing things, produce(s) the kind of art works that art world is noted for'. Conceptualized within this framework, art markets are inextricably linked to their geographical and cultural place as well as to their moment in history. Collectors can follow the market or purchase against the grain of market trends. Either way, a collector's attitude towards the market and her or his sense of self, influenced by cultural place and moment in time, will shape the identity of the collection and, to various extents, the market itself.

Essentially modern in their taxonomic and systemic nature, art museums and exhibitions are also strongly related to fairs, especially when they emerged in the 19th-century Euro-American world (Bennett, 1995). As part of the world of spectacle, art museums become what they are through successive implementations of tactics of display. In the case of museums with a unique founder, referred to as 'museum[s] of one's own' by art historian Anne Higonnet (2009: 1), the organization's ontological aspect of display is intertwined with the collector-founder's self-image and self-fashioning, created in part to speak to stakeholders and the public. That is especially the case with corporate museums (Castellani and Rossato, 2012) and collection museums (born out of private collections). If these collection museums become part of significant public spaces, such as the Freer Gallery of Art in the Smithsonian Institution in Washington, DC, they can play important roles in shaping the culture of a nation or society. Whether collection museums or corporate ones, museums are frequently used to highlight and provide knowledge about the past of a country or an organization, including critical events or social issues, and have the potential to facilitate change in how these issues or events are interpreted in the present and the future.

The purpose of this research is to explore how the identity of a collection museum evolves and to what extent such museums retain ontological allegiance to the collector-turned-founder, perhaps sustaining salient aspects of her or his identity. It also addresses to what extent the identity of the museum evolves through interaction of the presence of the founder with other factors such as the changing sociocultural norms of the art market, the country of origin, and other stakeholders, including the museum visitors themselves.

Under the umbrella of multidisciplinary literature on institutional 'ghosts' (Orr, 2014; Orr and Bennett, 2017: 16), collective memory, history as discourse (Barthes, 1984; Jenkins, 1991), and organizational identity, this chapter addresses how founders of art museums shape the identity of their cultural organization and continue to exert influence over the museum's decisions and discourse. By focusing on the presence of the founder in exhibitions—definable as sociocultural events as well as organizations in and of themselves—we can trace the presence of the founder's taste as a force, whether conservative or radical, in the changing discourse on the arts that he or she patronized. For example, does the museum install its permanent collection galleries in a fashion that reflects how the founder displayed her or his collection at home? Also, does the founder's taste play a role in the museum's choices of loans for temporary exhibitions? Such investigations can inform our understanding of the continuing impact of a founder's aesthetic identity on the evolution of the organizational identity of the museum.

As part of this investigation, we explore the mechanisms by which the founder's identity, as it influences the evolution of the identity of the collection, becomes a barometer of change in art-historical discourse and a criterion in the museum's acquisition philosophies. When a private collection becomes a public gift, the art is not only withdrawn from its commodity phase, but it is also institutionalized. Complementing the objects' institutionalization is the canonization of the founder's collecting choices, which resulted from a triangulation of personal taste, acquisition of knowledge, market availability, and her or his cultural moment in time. To what extent are the museum's subsequent purchases and loans impacted by the organization's internal canon—that is, the founder's model of collecting, as it becomes part of the organizational identity of the museum? Often equipped with teams of curators divided by specialization, museums part with the organic mode of acquisition that often characterizes private collecting. Nonetheless, certain tenets—such as privileging certain media or seeking objects of cross-cultural encounter—can be, and often are, transmitted from the founder to subsequent directors and curators of the museum, potentially sustaining the organizational identity of the museum.

These aspects of the founder's tastes and model of collecting are often commemorated through stories told in the museum, as well as in exhibitions and historical documents. In the art history and museum studies literature, there is growing scholarship on founders' and curators' aesthetic identities. These studies typically explore how such identities, from within the museum, contribute to the formation and/or revision of discourses on the arts (Bennett, 1995; Elsner, 1997; Holladay and Kopper, 2008), but rarely focus on how these identities shape the museum as organization. The relationship between organizational identity and memory (Anteby and Molnár, 2012; Casey, 2019; Hatch and Schultz, 2017; Schultz and Hernes, 2013) offers insights into these processes and provides components of a theoretical framework which, combined with theories derived from humanities scholarship in the history of collecting and the history of art history, helps illuminate how the identity of the museum evolves over time and influences subsequent additions, as well as how the stories of the additions are told. This chapter offers a theoretical framework grounded in organizational identity (Albert and Whetten, 1985), collective memory (Schwartz, 2000; 2005; 2015), and the history of collecting to explore these relationships.

This chapter contributes to theorizing about the role of the founder in organizational identity, theories of the history of collecting, and the field of museum practice. First, the role of the founder and her or his influence on organizational identity processes over time have been proposed in much of the theory and research on organizational identity from both the social actor perspective (Albert and Whetten, 1985; Whetten, 2006) and the social constructionist perspective (Hatch and Schultz, 2017; Casey, 2019). Yet assumptions about the nature of the founder's influence, its power over time, and its interaction with changing sociocultural norms have not been the focus of empirical studies. They have instead been part of the theorizing on organizational identity and have emerged as secondary findings in empirical studies. This study chose a unique setting—that is, the collection museum—as its context and analyzed the results of a historical case study of the Freer Gallery of Art to study the presence of the founder over time and its influence on the museum and its actions related to exhibiting, collecting, and so on. The exploration integrates theories of collective memory, which offer nuanced insights into the relationship between identity, history, and memory.

This investigation also provides a more in-depth example of how archival methods used in art history can be integrated with methods such as social network analysis to theorize about the presence of the founder in the organizational identity of a collection museum and the interactions between the founder, the museum, and the art markets in which they exist. This novel approach to case study research has the potential to offer unique insights into other organizational constructs.

In addition, this research contributes to the humanities literature on the history of collecting and on how museums evolve in relationship to art markets and the legacy of the founder's interests. How the founder influences the collection over time has been suggested in studies of museums and collections (Findlen, 1989; Preziosi, 1996; McClellan, 2008; Higonnet, 2009; Hill, 2012), and yet there is little empirical research to understand this role and its influence on how collections are expanded, displayed, and represented over time.

Finally, this research has implications for museum practice. Museums that are public spaces play critical roles in creating and, at times, recreating or sustaining the identity of a collective such as a society, country, or organization. Whose stories are told and which stories are not told in exhibitions (Nissley and Casey, 2002) can influence both the organization itself as well as the stakeholders with which it interacts.

The structure of this chapter is shown in Figure 8.1. First, we discuss the relevant theoretical and empirical literature on organizational identity, focusing on the potential role of the founder in the evolution of organizational identity, then the relevant literature on collective memory, followed by literature on the history of art collecting. Next, we present our methodology, particularly our focus on historical case studies and primary sources, combined with a multidisciplinary approach. We then provide an overview of a previously conducted historical case study that serves as the focus for our analysis. Our analysis of the findings of this case study are then explored through a multidisciplinary lens.

Theoretical framework

Organizational identity

Organizational identity was initially conceptualized by Albert and Whetten (1985: 265; original emphasis) as the features of an organization that meet the following criteria: 'the essence of the organization: *the criterion of claimed central character*', 'that distinguish the organization from others with which it may be compared: *the criterion of claimed distinctiveness*', and 'that exhibit some degree of sameness or continuity over time: *the criterion of claimed temporal continuity*'. They further noted that, 'for the purposes of defining organizational identity as a scientific concept, we treat

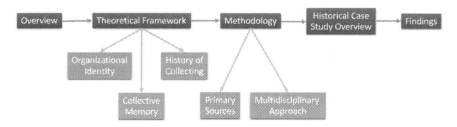

FIGURE 8.1 Overview of research process

the criteria of central character, distinctiveness and temporal continuity as each necessary and as a set sufficient' (Albert and Whetten, 1985: 265). These features are often referred to as CED (central, enduring, and distinctive) features that answer the basic question, 'Who are we' as an organization (Whetten and Mackey, 2002)?

Albert and Whetten's definition is grounded in institutional theory and frames organizations as legal or social actors in societies. The CED features of the organization, formed through the connection of the founder and the history of the organization over time, are 'reflected in its unique pattern of binding commitments' (Whetten, 2006: 220). Organizational identity as a coherent set of claims constitutes 'historical frames of reference' (Whetten, 2006: 223) and can emerge during crises or fork-in-the-road events (Whetten, 2006), or decisions to guide the organization and its future actions.

Since its inception, the majority of the theoretical and empirical work on organizational identity has taken a social constructionist approach (Corley et al., 2006) with the assumption that organizational identity evolves over time to meet critical changes in the environment (Corley and Gioia, 2004; Gioia, Schultz and Corley, 2000; Hatch and Schultz, 1997; 2000; 2002; Ravasi and Schultz, 2006) and history is reconstructed to meet the needs of the present (Gioia et al., 2000). The degree to which organizational identity evolves or changes over time has been the most debated component in the definition of organizational identity. More recently, there has been a move towards integrating these views with the idea that the organizational identity claims provide sense-giving as organizational members make sense of their work and the mission of the organization. In this process, the labels representing organizational identity may stay the same, and yet the meaning may evolve over time and with different groups of organizational members and stakeholders (Gioia, Patvardhan, Hamilton and Corley, 2013).

The role of history and collective memory in organizational identity processes has been explored (Anteby and Molnár, 2012; Casey, 2019; Hatch and Schultz, 2017; Ravasi and Schultz, 2006; Schultz and Hernes, 2013) from both the social actor and the social constructionist perspectives of organizational identity using concepts such as memory, legacy (Ravasi and Schultz, 2006), history (Ravasi, Rindova and Stigliani, 2019), material memory (Ravasi et al., 2019), historicizing (Hatch and Schultz, 2017), tradition, memory forms (Schultz and Hernes, 2013), heritage (Stigliani and Ravasi, 2007), and cultural practices (Hatch and Schultz, 2017), and yet the role of memory and history in organizational identity is relatively underdeveloped (Casey, 2019). In general, social constructionist perspectives on organizational identity have drawn upon revisionist history perspectives on collective memory theories that assert that history is reconstructed and managed by those in power to meet the needs of the present (Gioia et al., 2000; Ravasi and Schultz, 2006). For example, Zundel, Holt, and Popp (2016) theorized that managers use their organization's history as well as that of the external environment to manage organizational identity claims, particularly during periods of rapid change or uncertainty. Similarly, others (Suddaby, Foster and Quinn Trank, 2010) have proposed a rhetorical history perspective on how managers interpret and shape the meaning of the past. Frequently, rhetorical history is discussed in terms of stories from an organization's history that are 're-remembered' (Suddaby et al., 2016) in identity work. Others (Anteby and Molnár, 2012) have studied what is forgotten to facilitate how organizational identity is sustained over time.

Those theorists taking a social actor approach consider history from the perspective of the unique binding commitments that are sustained over time (Whetten, 2006). In more recent research on organizational identity and history, there has been an evolution of the perspective on history, with research reflecting the importance of authenticity in using history (Hatch and Schultz, 2017). In addition, Ravasi et al.'s (2019: 1) research on 'history, material memory, and the temporality identity construction' in the context of corporate museums proposes the concept of historical imperative that moves away from some of the ideas of rhetorical strategic construction (Suddaby et al., 2010: 45) and instead asserts that history may be reconstructed at times, but that this 'reconstruction is bounded by the material memory that it draws upon and the mnemonic practices and expectations of relevant audiences'.

Collective memory

Organizational stories about the founder and her or his life are a critical component of museum displays (Casey and Byington, 2013; Ravasi et al., 2019; Stigliani and Ravasi, 2007). The events selected, why they are considered significant, and how the stories of the events are constructed often highlight organizational identity claims. These phenomena are often investigated through the extensive literature on collective memory.

This chapter draws from the robust sociological literature on collective memory (Halbwachs, 1950/1980; Olick, Vinitzky-Seroussi and Levy, 2011; Schwartz, 2000; 2005; 2015). This literature is grounded in the seminal work of Maurice Halbwachs (1950/1980). Halbwachs, as a student of Durkheim, built on the ideas of collective representation and social facts to define the concepts of collective memory. Halbwachs also proposed the relationship between identity and memory, individual or collective, suggesting that identity was core to what was remembered.

Schwartz addressed the different approaches to collective memory, from more traditionalist views to the revisionist approach, where images and commemoration of historical figures and events are reconfigured to respond to current issues, with remembering of the past being shaped by those in power (Casey, 2019). Schwartz (2016: 18) noted the limitations of revisionist approaches in asserting that the distortion or malleable nature of memory is limited by 'reality's constraint on the malleability of perception'.

Schwartz proposed a compromise between these approaches. He suggested that the two central components of collective memory are history and commemoration (Schwartz, 2000; 2005; 2015). Commemoration is the process of remembering together (Schwartz, 2000). In organizations, commemoration often includes stories of founders and critical parts of their lives in relationship to the organization and its work. Stories or narratives of an organization's past are an essential part of the life of an organization (Martin, Feldman, Hatch and Sitkin, 1983), and research has focused on their significance in constructing the organization's present and future actions (Casey, 1997). How stories are selected for an exhibition and how they are presented reflect aspects of the organization's identity (Casey and Byington, 2013; Nissley and Casey, 2002). Schwartz theorized history as external to a group, a process of 'establishing and propagating of facts about the past' (Schwartz, 2008: 76). He asserted that the essence of history stabilizes through evidence over time. He defined collective memory as 'the representation of the past embodied in *both* historical evidence and commemorative symbolism' (ibid.: 9). History and commemoration have unique and different functions in collective memory, with history providing facts about the 'causes and consequences of events', whereas the critical events that are selected for commemoration are chosen through the 'community's distinctive values' and identity (Schwartz, 2010: 620). Schwartz (2005) proposed a dynamic tension between history and commemoration in that commemoration cannot stray too far from the historical evidence.

Similarly, recent empirical research on organizational identity and history has found that identity claims emerge in stories of critical events and of the founder. The identity claims that surface in these stories provide a broad, stable, yet to some degree adaptable, meaning foundation for organizational identity, as long as authenticity in the history is preserved (Hatch and Schultz, 2017). Whetten (2006: 221) theorized that critical founding events are 'institutional reminders of significant organizing choices' and 'binding commitments' or 'morals embedded in well-told stories of the defining moments of an organization's history'. The dynamic tension between commemoration and history as proposed by Schwartz (2005) is similar to the tension between historical imperatives and ideas about rhetorical history (Ravasi et al., 2019) and the importance of authenticity in the historicizing process in organizations (Hatch and Schultz, 2017).

History of collecting

A subfield at the intersection of art history, cultural sociology, and cultural anthropology, the history of collecting aims to understand influential individuals, institutions, and events that changed the course of how art was marketed, collected, and displayed. It also aims to shed light on the underlying sociopolitical and cultural structures that support or alter different models of collecting. Methodologically, the field combines historiography with critical discourse analysis. Given how significantly patterns of collecting affect the discourse about art, especially in terms of canons of value and hierarchy, studies in the history of collecting often also provide contributions to the relatively young field of the history of art history. Collectors—especially museum founders—have historically been central to these literatures. This chapter draws on them by extracting theoretical insight into the relationship between founders and museums' organizational identities from the findings of various relevant historical case studies (on Sir Hans Sloane, Charles Lang Freer, Isabella Stewart Gardner, etc.).

Numerous studies have concluded that the blueprint for the collection museum is the early modern cabinet of curiosities, or *kunstkammer*; they also imply that the founder is akin to a father figure (Elsner, 1997; Higonnet, 2009; Pomian, 1990). What complicate this approach are the numerous—and historically significant—cases in which the founder is a woman. Studies dedicated to such cases, from patronesses of the arts such as Caterina de Medici to women founders in the modern period such as Isabella Stewart Gardner, draw on gender studies and women's studies literatures to reconstruct the personae of female founders and to understand their challenges and accomplishments within the contexts of their respective periods (Hawley, Campbell and Wood, 2014; Hill, 2012; Holladay and Kopper, 2008; Tomas, 2017; Vrachopoulos and Angeline, 2005). Even with case studies that explore male founders, such as Charles Lang Freer or William and Henry Walters, we observe that those studies that engaged substantively with theoretical frameworks drawn from multiple literatures, from political historiography to women's studies, lead to the most accurate sociopolitical and psychological picture of the founder's presence in the organizational identity of the art museum.

Methodology

We combine methods from art history, cultural sociology, and organizational studies, with an emphasis on historical case studies. Methodologically, historical case studies can contribute significantly to the theoretical toolbox of organizational studies owing to the advantages of the most basic of humanities methods, namely a combination of historiography and content analysis. In the realm of art museums and exhibitions, historical case studies offer the possibility of longitudinal scrutiny. They also provide information on how taste was sedimented and disseminated and on how founder-sanctioned labels and brands were adopted and legitimized.

For the purposes of this chapter, we analyzed a recently completed study of a historical case, namely the collection of American industrialist Charles Lang Freer (1854–1919), which became, in 1923, the first art museum on the campus of the Smithsonian Institution in Washington, DC (Coman, 2021). A collection museum with a strong founder figure, the Freer Gallery of Art represents an ideal case study not only because of its unique trajectory from private collection to public institution, but also because of its extremely rare archival repository, containing thousands of materials that allowed the researcher to retrace the museum's institutional history from before it was even founded. In addition, we relied on the extensive historical research conducted by the first author for her forthcoming book in the subfields of the history of Japanese art history and the history of collecting.

The Freer case relied on two methodological choices essential to examining a historical case: (a) use of primary sources and (b) the integration of several disciplinary angles in a hybrid methodology tailored to the specificity of the case being investigated. We suggest that these two methodological approaches are also central to what makes a historical case study valuable for organizational studies, in that it encourages accuracy and innovation in data analysis.

Primary sources

Primary sources are invaluable in tracing the presence of the founder figure in the institutional identity of collection museums, because they provide, quite literally, time-stamped cross-sections of the organization, which can be analyzed cumulatively, leading to a 'big picture' of the institution's evolution, complete with its milestones and internal eras. In this context, the milestones may or may not be public-facing events, such as a centennial celebration, and oftentimes are intraorganizational changes, such as new leadership, or little-known external events that deeply affect the identity of the organization, albeit indirectly. For example, the dedication of a monument in Japan in 1930 honoring Freer's championing of an 18th-century Japanese potter reinforced, for key stakeholders such as fellow collectors and those theorizing Japanese art, the 'Freer' brand of the then-young Freer Gallery of Art.

Multidisciplinary approach

A multi- and interdisciplinary angle is instrumental in shedding light on aspects of a historical case that might remain hidden if the methodology were homogeneously historiographical. Specifically, sociological and anthropological methods and tools complement classical historical analysis. For example, in the Freer Gallery of Art case study, the first author made extensive use of social network analysis. Combining quantitative and qualitative analyses, the study repurposed the primary-source data to generate Freer's social network inasmuch as it pertained to his collecting activity, visualizing his overlapping social and professional circles that greatly influenced his aesthetic preferences and collecting choices. From color-coding different categories of network actors to ranking them by degree or betweenness centrality, basic social network analysis tools revealed important and surprising facts that would not have otherwise come to the surface. For example, Freer's ties with cultural institutions and holders of public office, preceding his gift to the Smithsonian in 1906, prepared the ground not only for Freer's commitment to public giving, but also for the interinstitutional ties of the future Smithsonian museum (Coman, 2021). In addition to images of the network, this study also entailed the preparation of an interactive representation of the collector-founder's social network (using R, Gephi, and Tableau). Methodologically, the advantage of the interactive version is that specific network actors or groupings thereof could be isolated and analyzed separately, leading to more insight into the complexity of the different voices that played a role in the collector's choices.

Historical case study overview

The historical case study we are using has already been conducted and is now forthcoming as a book (Coman, 2021). This book examines the role of a collector's social circles in shaping her or his aesthetic taste and collecting choices. It investigates the effect of such relationships as collections transition from private to public and from personal taste to institutional discourse. To address these issues, the book weaves a 'biography' of the collection of Japanese ceramics amassed by Detroit-based industrialist Charles Lang Freer. Through visual and historiographical analyses and methods tailored from sociology, the book analyzes three interrelated threads in the collection's life: first, Freer's purchasing behavior as shaped by his sociality with trusted dealers, artist friends, and fellow collectors; second, the aesthetic affinity that Freer sought to establish between Japanese ceramics and other artifacts in his collection, across mediums and cultures; and third, the ways in which Freer's collection, following its integration in the Smithsonian's Freer Gallery, continued to influence taste and discourse over generations of connoisseurs, collectors, and ceramists. The book adopts a global and comparative approach to understand how Japanese ceramics, as a category, were conceptualized and classified in Freer's time and to then map Freer's collection onto that blueprint, thereby creating a 'period portrait' of the collection. Finally, the book contrasts that portrait with subsequent and current understandings of the collection, revealing multiple layers of shifting categorizations. This cross-section sheds light on how discourse on Japanese ceramics, and by implication on Japanese arts at large, changed from the first wave of Japonisme in the mid-19th century to the present day. The book proposes that Freer's Japanese ceramics represented a microcosm that not only mirrored, but also influenced, the mutations occurring over time in transcultural conceptualizations and hierarchies of East Asian art.

The last chapter of the book completes the collection's 'biography' by examining its 'afterlives' following the collector's death and the collection's new status within the Smithsonian's National Museum of Asian Art. Covering the period between 1919 (the year of Freer's death) and 1930 (the year of the momentous dedication of a Freer monument in Kyoto), the chapter shows that the collection continued to be examined and enjoyed within Freer's paradigm of aesthetic affinity, while curators and visitors took it in other directions as well, from reattributing individual pieces to using them as models for American art pottery. Furthermore, it discusses a couple of cases in which Freer's collecting decisions in the field of Japanese ceramics were invoked to substantiate certain tenets of Japanese art history. In that, the chapter investigates how the collection was used as narrative and as tool for positioning.

Freer's enduring influence is rooted in the nature of his cosmopolitan social network. In the social network graph of Figure 8.2, created through qualitative and quantitative data analysis, the members of Freer's network are ordered in counterclockwise fashion, by degree—namely, by the number of connections that each actor had within the network. The graph color-codes the types of network

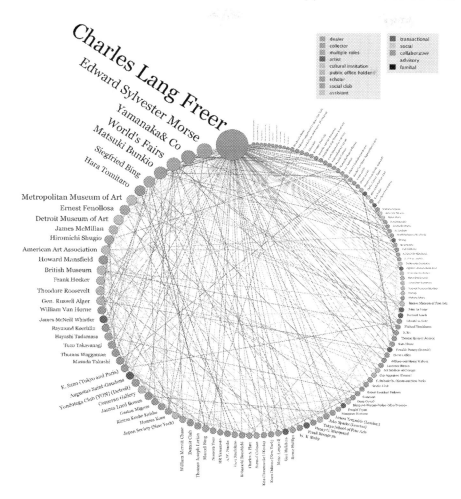

FIGURE 8.2 Social network graph

members and the types of relationships among them. This coding made it possible to get a sense of which roles and types dominated the network. Accordingly, dealers and fellow collectors dominate the social landscape of Freer's collecting. In this context, Freer's Japanese ceramics assumed the role of 'boundary objects', meaning cultural products of great interpretive plasticity that functioned as currency in transcultural exchanges of knowledge and power (Star and Griesemer, 1989).

If this network appears to be an essentially private one, the high numbers of cultural institutions and holders of public office within it tell a different story—that of a collection on the cusp of the personal and the institutional. Freer was connected with the major art institutions of his day. He corresponded with curators who provided connoisseurial evaluations of his purchases and he occasionally lent objects from his collection to exhibiting institutions. The American public office holders in Freer's network were at the intersection of the political and the military. General Russell Alger was instrumental in connecting Freer with President Roosevelt, who then supported Freer's efforts to ensure the ideal home for his collections in the nation's capital. Freer was also acquainted with influential Japanese officials, all involved in Japan's various processes of cultural reformation and restructuring during the Meiji period (1868–1912). These circles, both in the U.S. and in Japan, strengthened Freer's growing reputation and contributed to the canonical status of the Freer Gallery of Art and its collections, nascent in the museum's first couple of decades (Coman, 2021).

The essentially social nature of Freer's collecting can be characterized as 'aesthetic socializing' (Ikegami, 2005). The notion of aesthetic socializing, developed in relation to the sociability integral to cultural practices during Japan's Edo period (1615–1868), is applicable to this late 19th-century moment, too, and especially in the case of Freer, who sought beauty in the objects and situations with which he surrounded himself. Freer and his dealers and fellow collectors circulated in newly invented spaces of social power. In Japan, new 'influencers' such as Hara Tomitaro and Masuda Takashi, whose power did not derive from the pre-Meiji social system but from newly available types of entrepreneurship, forged new networks of cultural influence, notably by bringing in foreigners such as the antiquarian Edward Sylvester Morse, poet and philosopher Ernest Fenollosa, and Freer himself. Such spaces were enabled by processes of aesthetic socializing in which the practices of tea and of art collecting played key roles in the admittance and legitimation of members of new elite circles. Through similar mechanisms, such new spaces emerged outside Japan as well—for example, in Toledo, Ohio, or Detroit, Michigan, where the train and automotive industries opened up new sources of wealth. Freer once wrote that America needed a cure for its materialism, for which cosmopolitanism was partly to blame; Freer seemed to have thought that the cure was none other than the power of subtly beautiful art, enjoyed in the company of friends, to emotionally activate the inner universe of the individual (Coman, 2021).

The aesthetic nature of the collector's interest in Japanese ceramics—as opposed to a historical or archaeological interest—has been evoked as a core tenet of the mission of the Freer Gallery of Art since its inception. As Freer once dictated to his assistant, Katherine Nash Rhoades, who would later assume a curatorial position in the gallery, 'The pure emotion of the observer should be his first sensation—later as his interest deepens he should be given free access to the research and opinions of authoritative critics' (Freer and Sackler Archives, as cited in Coman, 2021). It was precisely this sentiment that another one of the first curators of the Freer Gallery of Art, Grace Dunham Guest, highlighted in her article titled, tellingly, 'Freer Gallery Is Arranged to Please Both Historical and Aesthetic Sensibilities' (Guest, 1927). There, she explained that curators 'compose their exhibitions as to give the observer the highest aesthetic pleasure of which he is capable, and at the same time, the most exact and scholarly information at their command' (Guest, 1927). Similarly, some scholars today argue that emotion and affect are core components of assignments of value in both ethics and aesthetics. For example, philosopher Jesse Prinz (2011) identified two stages of aesthetic appreciation, namely the subjective 'response stage', followed by the more epistemologically grounded 'assessment' stage. This notion of a two-step process of art reception brings to mind Freer's aforementioned notion of the ideal mode of looking at art, entailing an unmediated emotional reaction followed by instruction. For Freer and his generation, however, such notions sprang from the Emersonian belief in self-reliance and intuition—a belief that guided Freer in his collecting choices. In line with this mission to grant visitors the chance of an unmediated emotional and aesthetic response, the Freer Gallery of Art, in the 1920s and 1930s, sold 'gallery books' that included tombstone information for each displayed object, curatorial comments, and even a suggested viewing order. These gallery books 'freed' objects of the need for adjacent labels, ensuring that expert commentary could be made available after the visitor had an opportunity to experience the objects in and of themselves (Coman, 2021).

Katherine Rhoades and Grace Guest were working under the supervision of the first director of the Freer Gallery of Art, John Ellerton Lodge, whom Freer himself met in 1916 at the Museum of Fine Arts in Boston. Lodge's ties to Boston ran deep: the son of an influential Massachusetts senator, Lodge became affiliated with the Museum of Fine Arts when he was in his 30s, first as the assistant of writer and curator Okakura Kakuzo, then as curator of the Asian art department. Lodge was so attached to his Boston base that he maintained concurrent appointments at the Museum of Fine Arts and the newly opened Freer Gallery of Art until 1931. Lodge's stewardship epitomized the creative tension, mentioned earlier, between old/Bostonian and new/extra-Bostonian cultural centers. Also, it represented a continuation of Freer's longstanding ties to Bostonian East Asianists such as the aforementioned Morse and Fenollosa, who commented extensively on Freer's Japanese collections. Building on this legacy, Lodge was invested in ensuring the status and popularity of the new museum. According to the reports he submitted to the Smithsonian, the Freer consistently averaged 111,500 visitors per year from 1923 to 1927 (about a fourth of the average annual attendance at the much larger and much older Museum of Fine Arts in Boston); the Freer's many visitors had the opportunity to see a portion of Freer's collections, including displays of his Japanese ceramics, whose visibility contributed to their gradual acquisition of canonical status (Coman, 2021).

Freer himself sketched the early plans for the new museum, after research visits to already extant museums, and shared his ideas with the architect of the future museum, Charles Platt, who was a close friend. If one were to compare Freer's sketches with the actual museum plan at the time of its opening, it would become clear that both plans assigned galleries for Japanese pottery and painting that were to be situated across from galleries of Chinese art, in a similar fashion to 19th-century European displays of Asian art, which Freer would have seen in Paris in 1900, the year of the World's Fair. Also similar in both plans was the placement of the Peacock Room—a cornerstone of the museum, encapsulating Freer's journey to discovering Asian art and appreciating it in relation to the art of other cultures (Glazer and Meyer, 2017). Designed by American expatriate artist James McNeill Whistler for a London patron, Leyland, the Peacock Room combined Japoniste painting, Arts and Crafts furnishings, and East Asian ceramics; it was part of private collections in London and in Detroit and, ultimately, found its home in a public museum, the Freer Gallery of Art. In Whistler's eyes and in Leyland's home, the Peacock Room displayed Chinese blue-and-white porcelain, whereas, in Freer's Detroit home and subsequently in the new museum, it featured Japanese stoneware from Freer's collection. The difference in taste between Whistler and Freer and between a blue-and-white Peacock Room and an earth-toned tea-ware one continues to fascinate museum visitors to this day (Coman, 2021).

Freer's collecting actively participated in the formation of certain brands, such as those of early-modern Japanese potters Kenzan and Kōetsu (Wilson, 2001). Potters such as Kōetsu gained increasing prominence in the second half of the 19th century, when notions of art and art history were (re)invented in Japan. Freer's dealers mentioned Kōetsu as a strategy to market both the potter and themselves as connoisseurs and purveyors. Posthumously, Freer became increasingly known as a pioneering proponent of a group of painters, calligraphers, and potters to whom the label 'Rinpa' was ascribed and whose origins were traced back to Kōetsu and his collaborators, notably the painter Sōtatsu. In the 1920s and 1930s, making efforts to advertise Freer's association with Kōetsu and Rinpa was a group of Kyoto-based dealers and collectors, all participants in the Kōetsukai, an annual tea ceremony honoring Kōetsu at the artist's family temple in Kyoto. Of this group, the art collector and Mitsui businessman Masuda Takashi was the most salient voice. This unofficial campaign was crowned, in 1930, by the dedication of a Freer monument at Kōetsuji, the Buddhist temple dedicated to Kōetsu. Cultural influencers such as the Kōetsukai and Masuda contributed to the canonization of Freer's collecting choices. This canonization complemented the institutionalization of Freer's Japanese ceramics and contributed to similar canonizing processes for makers such as Kōetsu that Freer privileged in his collecting. As an 'institutional ghost', and through the efforts of transnational cultural brokers, Freer's vision continued to exert influence on emergent narratives of Japanese art (Coman, 2021).

Findings

It appears that what makes founders remain present, as it were, in collection museums, as opposed to other types of museums, is the connection between the original collector and her or his 'things' (used here in the Heideggerian sense). Bylaws and monetary endowments preserve the founder legally, but it is the founder's personal identity, as reflected in the collection, that ensures the survival and longevity of the founder figure in the organization's memory and identity.

As illustrated in Figure 8.3, the core identity of a collection museum, defined as a previously private collection that becomes institutionalized and public, derives from the combined attributes and values of the collection and its original collector.

FIGURE 8.3 Attributes and values of collector, collection, and collection museum

We were able to conclude, based on the historical case study we have analyzed, that the identities of collector and collection are the result of the creative tension between the collector's personal taste and the influence of the collector's network of providers and advisors on her or his collecting choices. As such, the collection museum preserves, in its institutional memory, the blueprint of the genesis of the collection and of the founder's cultural and aesthetic profile. Thus understood, the collection museum develops in directions that may or may not coincide with this initial, core identity, depending on its subsequent directors, curators, and projects, but—as illustrated in Figure 8.3—the external legitimization of the founder figure and of the collection, by entities that are predominantly independent of the museum itself, preserves and reinforces the presence of the founder in the institution's memory and values. In the historic case study we analyzed, the fact that the Masuda circle in Japan invoked Freer's focus on collecting Kōetsu in order to legitimize Kōetsu's status as a symbol of Japanese art had the double effect of reinforcing Freer's identity and recommending Freer and his collection museum as arbiters of taste in the larger Japanese art field. Ultimately, we suggest that it is the combination of the founder's identity, preserved in the institutional memory of the museum, on the one hand, and the external invocation and legitimization of the founder's choices, on the other, that contribute most significantly to the survival and longevity of the founder's presence in the organizational identity of the museum.

The consequences of our conclusion are manifold and warrant further study. Is the historical connection to the founder an inescapable characteristic of the collection museum? Is it a limiting factor? If later museum administrations decide to 'free' the collection museum of the founder's legacy, what kinds of changes are necessary, and how do they affect the institution's organizational identity? Whether continuing the trajectory charted by the founder or breaking with the founder's legacy, subsequent developments in the identity of a collection museum appear to necessarily relate to the founder and her or his core collection as a referent.

The practical implications of this paradigm can become useful conceptual tools for professionals in the museum field. As storytelling emerges as a central device for museums to communicate with stakeholders and the public, the narrative of the continuous presence of the founder's identity can take many forms, from a 'secret' playfully hidden in plain sight to a featured story. In either case, it is a powerful asset.

References

Albert, S. and Whetten, D.A. (1985). Organizational identity. In Cummings, L.L. and Staw, B.M. (eds.), *Research in organizational behavior*. Greenwich, CT: JAI Press, 263–295.

Anteby, M. and Molnár, V. (2012). Collective memory meets organizational identity: Remembering to forget in a firm's rhetorical history. *Academy of Management Journal*, 55 (3): 515–540.

Barthes, R. (1984). The discourse of history. In *The rustle of language*. New York: Hill & Wang.

Becker, H. (1982.) *Art worlds*. Berkeley, CA: University of California Press.

Bennett, T. (1995). *The birth of the museum: History, theory, politics*. New York: Taylor & Francis.

Casey, A. (1997). Collective memory in organizations. In Walsh, J. and Huff, A. (eds.), *Advances in strategic management 14: Organizational learning and strategic management*. Greenwich, CT: JAI Press, 111–151.

Casey, A. (2019). *Organizational identity and memory: A multidisciplinary approach*. London: Routledge.

Casey, A. and Byington, L. (2013). *Nike: A case study of identity claims in a complex global world*. Paper presented at the Annual Meeting of the Academy of Management, Orlando, FL.

Castellani, P. and Rossato, C. (2012). On the communication value of the company museum and archives. *Journal of Communication Management*, 18 (3): 240–253.

Coman, S. (2021). *The sociocultural matrix of Charles Lang Freer's Japanese ceramics: From individual taste to public discourse*. Forthcoming.

Corley, K.G. and Gioia, D.A. (2004). Identity ambiguity and change in the wake of a corporate spin-off. *Administrative Science Quarterly*, 49 (2): 173–208.

Corley, K.G., Harquail, C.V., Pratt, M.G., Glynn, M.A., Fiol, C.M. and Hatch, M.J. (2006). Guiding organizational identity through aged adolescence. *Journal of Management Inquiry*, 15 (2): 85–99.

Elsner, J. (1997). A collector's model of desire: The house and museum of Sir John Sloane. In Elsner, J. and Cardinal, R. (eds.), *Cultures of collecting*. London: Reaktion Books, 155–176.

Findlen, P. (1989). The museum: Its classical etymology and Renaissance genealogy. *Journal of the History of Collections*, 1 (1): 59–78.

Foucault, M. (1985). Of other spaces: Utopias and heterotopias. *Diacritics*, 16 (1): 22–27.

Gioia, D., Patvardhan, S., Hamilton, A. and Corley, K. (2013). Organizational identity formation and change. *Academy of Management Annals*, 7 (1): 123–193.

Gioia, D.A., Schultz, M. and Corley, K.G. (2000). Organizational identity, image, and adaptive instability. *Academy of Management Review*, 25 (1): 63–81.

Gioia, D.A. and Thomas, J.B. (1996). Identity, image, and issue interpretation: Sensemaking during strategic change in academia. *Administrative Science Quarterly*, 41 (3): 370–403.

Glazer, L. and Meyer, A. (2017). *Charles Lang Freer: A cosmopolitan life*. Washington, DC: Smithsonian.

Guest, G.D. (1927). Freer Gallery is arranged to please both historical and aesthetic sensibilities. *The United States Daily*, July 9.
Halbwachs, M. (1980[1950]). *The collective memory* (F.J. Ditter, Jr. and V.Y. Ditter, Trans.). New York: Harper & Row.
Hatch, M.J. and Schultz, M. (1997). Relations between organizational culture, identity, and image. *European Journal of Marketing*, 31 (5): 356–365.
Hatch, M.J. and Schultz, M. (2000). Scaling the tower of Babel: Relational differences between identity, image and culture in organizations. In Schultz, M., Hatch, M.J. and Larsen, M. (eds.), *The expressive organization: Linking identity, reputation, and the corporate brand*. Oxford: Oxford University Press, 11–35.
Hatch, M.J. and Schultz, M. (2002). The dynamics of organizational identity. *Human Relations*, 55 (8): 989–1018.
Hatch, M.J. and Schultz, M. (2017). Toward a theory of using history authentically: Historicizing in the Carlsberg Group. *Administrative Science Quarterly*, 62 (4): 657–697.
Hawley, A., Campbell, R. and Wood, A. (2014). *Isabella Stewart Gardner Museum: Daring by design*. New York: Skira Rizzoli.
Higonnet, A. (2009). *A museum of one's own: Private collecting, public gift*. New York: Periscope.
Hill, K. (2012). *Museums and biographies: Stories, objects, identities*. Suffolk, UK: Boydell Press.
Holladay, W. and Kopper, P. (2008). *A museum of their own: National Museum of Women in the Arts*. New York: Abbeville.
Ikegami, E. (2005). *Bonds of civility: Aesthetic networks and the political origins of Japanese culture*. Cambridge: Cambridge University Press.
Jenkins, K. (1991). *Re-thinking history*. New York: Routledge.
Martin, J., Feldman, M.S., Hatch, M.J. and Sitkin, S.B. (1983). The uniqueness paradox in organizational stories. *Administrative Science Quarterly*, 28 (3): 438–453.
McClellan, A. (2008). *The art museum from Boullée to Bilbao*. Los Angeles, CA: University of California Press.
Nissley, N. and Casey, A. (2002). The politics of the exhibition: Viewing corporate museums through the paradigmatic lens of organizational memory. *British Journal of Management*, 13 (S2): S35–S44.
Olick, J.K., Vinitzky-Seroussi, V. and Levy, D. (2011). Introduction. In Olick, J.K., Vinitzky-Seroussi, V. and Levy, D. (eds.), *The collective memory reader*. New York: Oxford University Press, 3–62.
Orr, K. (2014). Local government chief executives' everyday hauntings: Towards a theory of organizational ghosts. *Organization Studies*, 35 (7): 1041–1061.
Orr, K. and Bennett, M. (2017). Powerful storytelling: Leadership narratives from UK local government chief executives. *Local Government Review* (Dec.), 13–16. Retrieved from www.questia.com/magazine/1G1-516449087/powerful-storytelling-leadership-narratives-from
Pomian, K. (1990). *Collectors and curiosities: Paris and Venice, 1500–1800*. Cambridge: Blackwell.
Preziosi, D. (1996). Art, art history, and museology. *Museum Anthropology*, 20 (2): 5–6.
Prinz, J. (2011). Emotion and aesthetic value. In Schellekens, E. and Goldie, P. (eds.), *The aesthetic mind: philosophy and psychology*. Oxford: Oxford University Press, 71–88.
Ravasi, D., Rindova, V. and Stigliani, I. (2019). The stuff of legend: History, material memory, and the temporality of identity construction. *Academy of Management Journal*, 62 (5): 1523–1555.
Ravasi, D. and Schultz, M. (2006). Responding to organizational identity threats: Exploring the role of organizational culture. *Academy of Management Journal*, 49 (3): 433–458.
Schultz, M. and Hernes, T. (2013). A temporal perspective on organizational identity. *Organization Science*, 24 (1): 1–21.

Schwartz, B. (2000). *Abraham Lincoln and the forge of national memory*. Chicago, IL: University of Chicago Press.
Schwartz, B. (2005). The new Gettysburg address: Fusing history and memory. *Poetics*, 33 (1): 63–79.
Schwartz, B. (2008). Collective memory and abortive commemoration: Presidents' day and the American holiday calendar. *Social Research*, 75 (1): 75–110.
Schwartz, B. (2010). Culture and collective memory: Comparative perspectives. In Grindstaff, L., Lo, M.-C. M. and Hall, J. R. (eds.), *Handbook of cultural sociology* (2nd edn). London: Routledge, 619–628.
Schwartz, B. (2015). Commemoration. In Wright, J.D. (ed.), *International encyclopedia of the social and behavioral sciences* (2nd ed.). Cambridge: Elsevier, 235–242.
Schwartz, B. (2016). Rethinking the concept of collective memory. In Tota, T. and Hagen, T. (eds.), *Routledge international handbook of memory studies*. London: Routledge, 9–21.
Star, S. and Griesemer, J. (1989). Ecology, 'translations' and boundary objects: Amateurs and professionals in Berkeley's Museum of Vertebrate Zoology, 1907–39. *Social Studies of Science*, 19 (3): 387–420.
Stigliani, I. and Ravasi, D. (2007). Organizational artefacts and the expression of identity in corporate museums at Alfa-Romeo, Kartell, and Piaggio. In Lerpold, L., Ravasi, D., van Rekom, J. and Soenen, G. (eds.), *Organizational identity in practice*. London: Routledge, 197–214.
Suddaby, R., Foster, W.M. and Quinn Trank, C. (2010). Rhetorical history as a source of competitive advantage. In Baum, J.A.C. and Lampel, J. (eds.), *Globalization of strategy research*, 27. London: Emerald, 147–173.
Suddaby, R., Foster, W.M. and Quinn Trank, C. (2016). Re-Membering: Rhetorical history as identity-work. In *The Oxford handbook of organizational identity*. Oxford: Oxford University Press, 297–316.
Tomas, N. (2017). *The Medici women: Gender and power in renaissance Florence*. New York: Taylor & Francis.
Vrachopoulos, T. and Angeline, J.D. (2005). *Hilla Rebay, art patroness and founder of the Guggenheim Museum of Art*. New York: Edwin Mellen Press.
Whetten, D. A. (2006). Albert and Whetten revisited: Strengthening the concept of organizational identity. *Journal of Management Inquiry*, 15 (3): 219–234.
Whetten, D.A. and Mackey, A. (2002). A social actor conception of organizational identity and its implications for the study of organizational reputation. *Business and Society*, 41 (4): 393–414.
Wilson, R. (2001). *The potter's brush*. Washington, DC: Smithsonian Institution.
Zundel, M., Holt, R. and Popp, A. (2016). Using history in the creation of organizational identity. *Management & Organizational History*, 11 (2): 211–235.

9

INSTITUTIONAL ENTREPRENEURSHIP AND THE FIELD OF POWER

The emergence of the global hotel industry

Mairi Maclean, Charles Harvey and Roy Suddaby

Introduction

Institutional entrepreneurship as a field of academic enquiry is focused on the roles played by individual agents and agents acting in concert in promoting institutional change. From Bourdieu (1993; 1996), we infer that contests for institutional change are played out in the field of power, the integrative social domain that brings together powerful actors from different walks of life – business, politics, government agencies, media and the law – to affect changes in laws, regulations and conventions (Maclean and Harvey, 2019; Maclean, Harvey and Press, 2006). Institutional entrepreneurs pursue institutional change directly using legal or quasi-legal means by persuading others to act according to their interests through social influence or lobbying, often forming issue-based coalitions in pursuit of specific institutional goals (Wijen and Ansari, 2006). Hence, we define institutional entrepreneurship as the skilful actions taken by an individual actor or coalition of actors to affect changes in the informal or formal rules governing a field for personal or collective advantage.

There is little agreement on the processes commonly at work in institutional entrepreneurship and the ways in which these play out in different contexts. However, without some measure of agreement on the specific mechanisms whereby institutional entrepreneurs effect change in different arenas, it is difficult to generalize about strategy and tactics, let alone the outcomes of attempts to disrupt the status quo. The actual work of institutional entrepreneurship in its fine-grained detail is often glossed over. What is missing is research on collective endeavours, on emergent processes involving a range of actors in building momentum for institutional change (Aldrich, 2011; Maguire, Hardy and Lawrence, 2004; Lawrence and Phillips, 2004). It is in this aspect that Bourdieu's construct of the field of power adds value to the theory of institutional entrepreneurship.

Here, the emphasis is on interactions between elite actors with different types and amounts of capital who combine their efforts to press for institutional change (Harvey and Maclean, 2008). In what follows, we build on Bourdieu's ideas to identify three processes of institutional entrepreneurship – field formation, coalition building and rhetorical agency – at work in early phase globalization, when home-country firms seek to extend their operational reach into multiple host countries.

The historical research conducted to refine our thinking on institutional entrepreneurship and early phase globalization is focused on the role played by Conrad Hilton with others at home and abroad in the emergence of the global hotel industry between 1946 and 1967 (Maclean, Harvey, Suddaby and O'Gorman, 2018). In 1946, the hotel industry was highly fragmented, nationally and internationally, with low concentration ratios and few recognized brands or chains. Today, the industry is concentrated and globalized, heavily branded, and dominated by large enterprises with multiple sub-brands competing in different market segments (Contractor and Kunda, 1998; Davé, 1984; Dunning and McQueen, 1981). We show that this transition was the outcome of collective endeavours by business, political and social elites focused on the twin goals of economic prosperity and political stability. Hilton rose to prominence within the field by generating and applying the social, symbolic and cultural capital needed to secure the support of stakeholders at home and operate effectively within host-country fields of power (Harvey, Maclean, Gordon and Shaw, 2011).

Our study begins with the formation of the Hilton Hotels Corporation (HHC) in 1946, when the Western world was under threat from the political and military expansionism of Soviet Russia (Merrill, 2006). In this context, Hilton carved out market-leading positions for his hotels at home and abroad, notably through the incorporation in 1948 of Hilton Hotels International (HHI) as a wholly owned subsidiary of HHC. Hilton sought to expand the boundaries of the luxury hotel business into uncharted territory through a global strategy that identified the quest for world peace and prosperity with hotel construction. In doing so, he engaged in pioneering entrepreneurial processes of global diffusion of rationalized management templates. His success led to the flotation in 1964 of HHI as an independent company listed on the New York Stock Exchange (NYSE), the Hilton International Company (HIC). In 1967 HHI merged with Transworld Airlines (TWA), which grew as an operationally independent subsidiary of its new parent.

In examining the role of Conrad Hilton as an innovative entrepreneur engaged with others in multidimensional activities in the field of power, we pose two guiding research questions. First, what are the core processes of institutional entrepreneurship practised by Hilton in actualizing his vision of a globally connected hotel field? In short, what did it take to get the new field going? Second, alert to the importance of context to entrepreneurial endeavour, how far were these processes modified to suit transnational fora? In what follows, we review the literature on institutional entrepreneurship in the context of the field of power, exploring the role of rhetorical legitimacy seeking in creating a new industry. The next section is methodological, explaining our research process and documentary sources. In our empirical section, we draw on rich archival material to explore the entrepreneurial processes of field formation, coalition building and rhetorical agency that Hilton employed to drive the political and organizational 'horizon of expectation' (Koselleck, 2004: 255) and achieve desired outcomes. We discuss our findings and consider their implications for the theory and practice of institutional entrepreneurship within the field of power.

Institutional entrepreneurship and industry emergence

Institutional agency and the field of power

Drawing on the work of Eisenstadt (1980), DiMaggio (1988) conceptualized institutional entrepreneurship as a means of bringing agency back into the study of institutional change (Battilana, Leca and Boxenbaum, 2009; Garud, Hardy and Maguire, 2007). DiMaggio argued that institutional accounts had neglected the role of agency, disregarding the lived experience of individual agents who perform institution building. More recently, other commentators have suggested that this absence of individual actors from institutional research persists (Lawrence, Suddaby and Leca, 2011), echoing the charge made by some entrepreneurship scholars that researchers overlook the behaviour of actual entrepreneurs (Meyer, 2009; Zahra and Wright, 2011).

Institutional theory similarly fails to recognize the importance of power in institutional processes (DiMaggio, 1991). Yet to instigate new institutional arrangements requires power as well as agency. Despite widespread familiarity among institutional theorists with the theoretical universe constructed by Bourdieu (1990; 1993), researchers have largely failed to engage with the concept of the field of power, according insufficient scrutiny to how, in practice, 'institutional entrepreneurs define, legitimate, combat or coopt rivals, and succeed in their institutional projects' (Rao, 1994: 41). The field of power and its configuration are critical to institutional entrepreneurs, who draw on their interpersonal skills to form elite coalitions and interact with diverse types of resource holder, including local authorities, dignitaries or government agencies, whose support they require and with whom they must build alliances, often in highly ambiguous contexts (Maclean, Harvey and Chia, 2010). This applies especially to those entrepreneurs operating in nascent industries that suffer the 'liabilities of newness' (Aldrich and Fiol, 1994: 663). Learning to interact skilfully in the field of power can enhance an actor's status and positioning within an organizational field. Adept interaction entails framing and directing agendas while allowing others to believe they are in command of shared collaborative action to create a new type of value (Fligstein, 2001). Such processes determine allocative outcomes by influencing 'the reward structure in the economy' and are inherently political, eliciting the backing of internal and external constituencies (Baumol, 1990: 894).

This chapter brings together the concepts of institutional entrepreneurship and the field of power to explore them in conjunction with a rich empirical case. Given that the rules of entrepreneurship vary from context to context (Baumol, 1990), and that entrepreneurs 'respond differently to the incentives provided by formal institutions depending on different cultural settings' (Li and Zahra, 2012: 95), it follows that the field of power is likely to be subject to varying influences and constraints and, hence, differently configured when couched in diverse geographic locales and legal jurisdictions (Lamoreaux, Raff and Temin, 2007). Reputation is socially constructed and is linked to the relative standing of an actor or organization in the opinion of relevant stakeholders, who vary according to geographic locality (Rindova, Williamson, Petkova and Sever, 2005). Reputation is, therefore, open to manipulation by means of the selection and exchange of information through the exploitation of media channels, the cultivation of celebrity and the dissemination of narratives in selected contexts (Guthey, Clark and Jackson, 2009; Rindova, Pollock and Hayward, 2006).

Rhetorical legitimacy seeking

Barthes (1989) writes that language is power, but that we misrecognize it, perceiving it instead as something neutral. In an organizational world that is increasingly 'text laden' (Suddaby and Greenwood, 2005: 61), it makes sense that discourse is formative of new institutional realities, and that the agentic use of narratives might be instrumental in the processes that facilitate the emergence of new industries (Lawrence and Phillips, 2004; Munir and Phillips, 2005). Entrepreneurs who aspire to create a new industry have to work with the existing institutional environment within which their ideas are situated, while reframing it (Hargadon and Douglas, 2001). The activities of entrepreneurs with large-scale ambitions are located within broader societal discourses, with which they must resonate to attract resources and legitimacy (Downing, 2005). The accounts entrepreneurs purvey perform a crucial task in smoothing the processes that facilitate the establishment of new industries (Martens, Jennings and Jennings, 2007). The route to instigating a new industry lies not only in the employment of social skill, but also in the use of rhetoric and persuasion that influence access to resources (Rindova et al., 2006). In seeking to create a new global hotel industry consonant with US values in an uncertain environment, Hilton may be seen to engage in 'rhetorical institutionalism' (Greene, 2004). Green and Li (2011: 1662) define this as 'the deployment of linguistic approaches in general and rhetorical insights in particular to explain how institutions both constrain and enable agency'.

Hilton's agentic form of rhetorical institutionalism might be described more accurately as 'rhetorical agency' (Geisler, 2009): 'a communicative process of ... advocacy on issues of public importance' (Greene, 2004: 188). Rhetorical agency entails the deployment of arguments to persuade others of the correctness of a proposition or course of action. Charismatic entrepreneurs deploy rhetorical techniques to alter social norms. Rhetorical agency can help construct social reality as leading players in a given organizational field wrestle for the right to determine meaning (Berger and Luckmann, 1966). In this sense, it is an overtly political process, whereby politically motivated symbolic accounts that combine fact with fiction are advanced for legitimation purposes, amplifying desirable features of the focal actor or organization in the minds of resource holders while downplaying others. Rhetorical agency can thus enhance the reputation and competitive advantage of an organization by emphasizing its distinctiveness in the eyes of relevant constituencies (Rindova et al., 2006).

The need to make an organization prominent and identifiable is all the more acute in unstructured situations of industry emergence, where institutional entrepreneurs are concerned with 'framing the unknown in such a way that it becomes believable' (Aldrich and Fiol, 1994: 651). Founders who employ narratives couched in symbolic language are likely to acquire legitimation more swiftly than those who do not (Maclean, Harvey and Chia, 2012). Stories form the 'currency of communications to a wider public' and have the capacity to elucidate events and phenomena, enabling a persuasive vision of an emergent field to be articulated to build credibility (Aldrich and Fiol, 1994: 652). Once a convincing frame has been conceived, institutional entrepreneurs employ their social and narrative skills to advance that frame and its attendant social order (Fligstein, 2001). However, social reality is constituted not by *individual* texts or stories in isolation, but by a *corpus* of texts, produced in physical form and made available to wider publics (Maclean, Harvey, Golant and Sillince, 2020; Taylor, Cooren, Giroux and Robichaud, 1996). Thus, essential to the instigation of a new industry are 'structured collections of texts' that are 'inscribed – spoken, written, or depicted in some way', which inform the norms that mould opinions and interpretations of actors in the wider field (Phillips et al., 2004: 638, 636).

The rhetorical strategies of institutional entrepreneurs are bound up with dynamic processes of legitimation and delegitimation (Erkama and Vaara, 2010). To be deemed legitimate, the activities of a new organization, industry or field must be recognized as 'desirable, proper, or appropriate' within a broader societal value system with which they are consonant (Suchman, 1995: 574). Hence, rhetorical strategies comprise 'the deliberate use of persuasive language to legitimate or resist an innovation by constructing congruence or incongruence' (Suddaby and Greenwood, 2005: 41). Institutional entrepreneurs who promote accounts that conform to wider canonical discourses are more likely to attract legitimacy and influence outcomes in accordance with their interests than those who do not. Through rhetorical legitimation strategies, 'skilful cultural operatives' (Rao, 1994: 31) elicit commitment from diverse audiences to legitimate particular projects. The stories they tell are also performative (Goffman, 1959). In this regard, empirical research that explores the link between symbolic action in the form of public speeches and material outcomes in the field of power, including resource acquisition and market penetration, are lacking. This chapter helps to address this gap.

Research process

The methodology employed here, in keeping with the motivation of this edited collection, is that of historical organization studies: organizational research that draws extensively on historical data, methods and knowledge to explore, refine and develop theoretical ideas and conceptual insights (Maclean, Harvey and Clegg, 2016; 2017). Research of this type seeks to enrich understanding of historical, contemporary and future-directed social realities through analysis of the emergence, transformation and meaning of organizational and institutional phenomena (Maclean, Harvey, Sillince and Golant, 2014; 2018). Fieldwork sites are selected primarily on the basis of the availability of subject-relevant data sources and the 'rich, real-world context in which the phenomena occur' (Eisenhardt and Graebner, 2007: 25). To examine historical cases over an extended timeframe allows the life cycle of the focal organization to be studied in its entirety, set in historical context over the *longue durée*, with the benefit of historical perspective (Braudel, 1980). In this case, we set out to locate archival data on pioneering entrepreneurs involved in early phase globalization in the decades following World War II. We were drawn to Hilton given the pre-existing research interests of one team member aware of his role in the internationalization of the US hotel industry. Our choice was confirmed on gaining access to his extensive personal and business records. Hilton's public speeches, personal and business papers and private letters conjure up a coherent 'symbolic universe' (Rao, 1994: 31) conducive to exploring the link between symbolic action in the form of published scripts and outcomes in the field of power (Santos and Eisenhardt, 2009). The richness of the archival material upon which we draw permits exploration of processes of industry emergence (Rindova and Kotha, 2001), under-investigated in the literature.

The Hilton papers held at the University of Houston are extensive, comprising printed series of president's letters, annual reports and accounts, a large collection of photographs and miscellany, an oral history series, and 345 boxes of business and personal papers containing about 4,500 folders, most with multiple documents. The archive is only partially catalogued. Extensive searches are required to collate documents relating to particular topics. Our own search strategy, executed during two extended visits by three researchers, focused on gathering data relating to the development of HHI/HIC from the incorporation of HHC in 1946 to Hilton's withdrawal from day-to-day management in 1969.

On return from Houston, we classified all material collected from the archive according to its purpose and subject matter. We took an early decision to examine the data from the perspective of institutional entrepreneurship and the emergence of the global hotel industry. We organized and interrogated the data with a view to uncovering the entrepreneurial processes at play to overcome resistance to the creation of a multinational organization. We searched for longitudinal patterns in the documentary record while engaging in deductive theorizing. We extracted data relating to hotel negotiations, costs, ownership, project development and key protagonists, enabling us to explore issues relating to entry barriers, market access and fields of power (see Table 9.1). We classified and coded each of 62 public speeches given by Conrad Hilton between 1950 and 1965, enabling us to isolate recurrent themes, arguments and rhetorical techniques (Berg, 2009).

Further readings led to our identifying three core entrepreneurial processes at play. These are field formation, coalition building and rhetorical agency. Early phase globalization is facilitated by institutional changes in home and host countries. We therefore consider how these processes were applied both nationally and transnationally in terms of transferring Hilton's repertoire into host countries (Drori, Honig and Wright, 2009: 1008; Li and Zahra, 2012). *Field formation* has to do with imagining and identifying a new business model that yields competitive advantage, enabling first-movers to profit from early intervention (Agarwal and Braguinsky, 2015). We define field formation as *the process of shaping operational logics and common practices within the field*. Coalition building concerns forming and exploiting elite relationships and assembling resources to realize a particular vision while maximizing capital, power and standing (Baumol and Strom, 2007). This entails *closely associating influential actors with the ambitions of the organization.* Rhetorical agency involves legitimizing new markets and practices to convince stakeholders of the virtues of innovative templates and practices. In early globalization, the intention is to convince domestic stakeholders, including shareholders, financiers, customers

TABLE 9.1 Entry barriers and time to opening in Europe, the Middle East and Africa (EMEA)

Hotels and year of project initiation	Entry barriers	Time from project initiation to hotel opening		
		First wave (initiated 1948–55)	Second wave (initiated 1956–63)	Total number
Athens (1950), London (1952), Rome (1950), Paris (1955), Brussels (1960)	High	N = 4 Mean = 152 months	N = 1 Mean = 81 months	5
Berlin (1954), Cairo (1952), Tehran (1954), Amsterdam (1954), Rotterdam (1954), Paris Orly Airport (1959), Kuwait (1961)	Medium	N = 5 Mean = 84 months	N = 2 Mean = 74 months	7
Madrid (1948), Istanbul (1950), Tunisia (1960), Tel Aviv (1960), Rabat (1961), Cyprus (1962), Malta (1963)	Low	N = 2 Mean = 54 months	N = 5 Mean = 59 months	7
Overall mean scores		103.4 months	65.6 months	N = 19 Mean = 87.5

*Europe, the Middle East and Africa

and political leaders, that setting up operations abroad is desirable and legitimate. In host countries, the aspiration is to reduce resistance to access by suggesting that all parties share cognate values and goals. Rhetorical agency in a transnational context therefore entails the use of discourse to achieve value congruence, aligning host communities with the beliefs and objectives of foreign-owned ventures and ways of doing business (Greene, 2004; Martens et al., 2007).

Institutional entrepreneurship in practice

The empirical focus of this chapter is the emergence in the two decades after World War II of the global hotel industry, now dominated by large multi-chain, multi-brand corporations, including Accor, Hilton Worldwide, InterContinental and Marriott International, that compete across multiple segments of the market (Dunning and McQueen, 1981). Branded hotel chains had existed in the US and Europe before 1945, but on a relatively small scale and largely confined within national boundaries (Haynes, 1952; Rushmore and Baum, 2002). Following the incorporation of pioneering companies such as Hilton (1946) and Sheraton (1947), the industry became progressively more concentrated, integrated and international (Contractor and Kunda, 1998). In the case of Hilton, domestic and international growth proceeded simultaneously. On incorporation in 1946, HHC brought together nine affiliated but independently owned and operated hotels (HIA, 1946). Incorporation and listing on the NYSE gave access to the capital needed to realize Hilton's vision of a worldwide hotel chain united by common standards and facilitated by advances in transport, communications and organizational practices. In 1947, he entered into negotiations to lease and operate his first international hotel, the Caribe Hilton, owned and built by the Puerto Rican government to attract US tourists. HHI was incorporated in 1948 as a wholly owned subsidiary of HHC (HIA, 1948).

The landmark Caribe Hilton opened for business in 1949, but, over the next few years, domestic growth outran international growth. Hilton acquired his flagship property, the Waldorf Astoria hotel in New York, in 1949, and in 1954 he took over the 11 hotels in the Statler chain (HIA, 1954a). New hotels were planned for under-provisioned major cities, and a new sub-brand chain of Hilton Inns, initiated in 1957, introduced a new concept, the airport hotel (HIA, 1958a). Room capacity within the US quadrupled between 1947 and 1967. The pattern of growth at HHI differed markedly. Slow growth in the early 1950s was followed by a growth spurt in the late 1950s that accelerated into the 1960s. HHI was floated on the NYSE as an independent company in 1964 as HIC (HIA, 1964a). HIC merged with TWA in 1967 to realize operational synergies (HIA, 1967), by which time it had nearly as many hotels as HHC and half its room capacity.

Field formation

The emergence of the global hotel industry as a new institutional field following World War II depended on proving and disseminating a raft of innovative business ideas, practices and standards (Davé, 1984; Dunning and McQueen, 1981). Institutional change is 'the product of endogenous forces that are associated with the historical evolution of the field itself' (Leblebici et al., 1991: 360). HHI was one of two pioneers responsible for the rapid formation of the field. The other was the InterContinental Hotel Corporation (ICH), a subsidiary of Pan American World Airlines (Pan Am) set up in 1947 to facilitate the development of tourism in Latin America (Davé, 1984). Both companies had the endorsement of the US government, which recognized its foreign policy goals might be furthered through private-sector involvement in international economic development (Davé, 1984; Djelic, 1998; Hilton, 1957; Wharton, 2001): Pan Am/ICH in Latin America, and Hilton in Europe, under the aegis of the European Recovery Program (ERP; HIA, 1961). Both companies recognized the impetus given to business travel and tourism by the competitive strength of US companies, rising US living standards and increased market accessibility following advances in air travel. Although establishing a nascent industry 'is risky business under any conditions' (Aldrich and Fiol, 1994: 645), HHI and ICH realized that the risks associated with hotel building abroad might be mitigated by securing host-country participation in local companies formed to build and harvest rents from hotel properties (Davé, 1984; Dunning and McQueen, 1981).

Hilton's international blueprint was formed in 1947 following an approach from the Puerto Rican government, keen to open a new hotel in San Juan to boost tourism. Constrained by the capital requirements of domestic expansion, Hilton proposed the hotel should be built and owned by the Puerto Rica Development Corporation (PRDC) to architectural and design standards set by HHI (Hilton, 1957). Entrepreneurial rewards are fundamental to industry evolution and determine the 'rules of the game' (Baumol, 1990: 907). On completion, PRDC leased the hotel to HHI for 20 years and was paid two-thirds of gross operating profit as rent. HHI provided the working capital to underwrite operations and received one-third of gross profit in exchange for entrepreneurial and management services (HIA, 1958b).

The Caribe Hilton was an instant commercial success and, for Hilton, constituted an ideal type that he replicated in other international locations (HIA, 1964b). Entrepreneurs engaged in nascent ventures 'typically lack a clear view of industry structure', being without established patterns to follow (Maguire, Hardy and Lawrence, 2004; Santos and Eisenhardt, 2009: 644). However, conceiving a blueprint gave Hilton a model to replicate elsewhere, reducing uncertainty while enabling him to '*claim* a new and distinct market space' (Santos and Eisenhardt, 2009: 648). His international hotels were architecturally modern, offering a range of American comforts and services and occupying prime city sites. They stood out from the competition, embraced high standards, symbolized confidence in the future (Wharton, 2001) and were presented as mutually beneficial partnerships between host country and HHI (HIA, 1964b). The host country gained from the Hilton brand, operational expertise, group services such as reservations and marketing, employment opportunities, training and development of local staff, foreign currency earnings from tourism and business travellers, and improved local infrastructure (Porter, 2000). HHI gained by securing market access and opportunities for profit without risking large amounts of capital, creating the potential for rapid growth on a global basis (Dunning and McQueen, 1981).

ICH initially grew more rapidly than HHI by taking on management contracts with old hotels struggling for business. Management contracts, which paid the operator negotiated percentages of revenues and profit, had an advantage over leasing in not requiring provision of working capital and so were less risky. Reduced risk had to be traded off against profit potential and degree of control (DeRoos, 2010). ICH advanced by assuming management contracts for newly built hotels in partnership with host-country consortia, taking an equity stake, albeit reluctantly, in owning companies when necessary to secure the deal (Davé, 1984). HHI tried to stick to its policy of only contracting for new-build hotels in choice locations on the profit-sharing lease-and-operate model, without equity participation in owning companies. This stance softened only in the late 1950s, when Hilton's senior team at HHI persuaded him to negotiate management contract deals when 'flexibility in the matter is absolutely indicated', although he stuck to the view that the 'basic pattern of our contract is by now pretty well known ... a management contract will no doubt meet with resistance and suspicion' (HIA, 1959a: 1). Eventually, as the two competitors battled to secure deals between themselves and new entrants such as Sheraton, the management contract model became the norm (DeRoos, 2010; Garud, Jain and Kumaraswamy, 2002). HHI, moreover, was obliged to relax its no equity participation stance to secure operating rights in prestigious locations such as London, Paris and Brussels (HIA, 1965).

At home, Hilton's directors and stockholders were alert to the dangers of operating overseas, especially in the war-ravaged countries of Europe (Hilton, 1957; Magdoff, 1969). Risk aversion, according to Curt Strand, former president of HIC, was pronounced at HHI, confirmed by the expropriation of assets following the 1959 Cuban revolution (HIA, 1992; 1993). Only when early ventures proved successful did the appetite to move more quickly increase, underlining the importance of early wins (Rao, 1994). Yet gaining access to host-country markets was not straightforward. Entry barriers, the height of which was determined by differing combinations of political and competitor resistance, had to be surmounted. Political resistance assumed many forms and included withholding permissions to operate, planning restrictions, currency and other controls (HIA, 1950a; 1951; 1954b; 1959b). Competitor resistance took the form of political lobbying to deny market entry and subversive measures to restrict access to resources, including sites and finance (HIA, 1964c). In EMEA, the higher the barrier to entry, the longer it took to get a project started (see Table 9.1). In capital cities where suitable sites were scarce and competitor resistance was acute, early wave projects often stalled for years before permissions were granted and controls relaxed. When competitor resistance was high, but a government was anxious to secure a new American-operated hotel, as in Berlin, projects progressed more speedily. If competitor resistance was negligible and the host government positive, as in Spain and Turkey, early phase projects progressed apace (Rosendorf, 2014; Wharton, 2001). The same pattern persisted in the second wave of project development at HHI. What was different now was that economic growth had generated a higher level of prosperity, and host governments and investors were increasingly familiar with the Hilton business model and the benefits it afforded (Porter, 2000). Playing host to US-operated hotels that brought tourists and business travellers in their wake had become the norm (Rao, 2004), emblematic of 'the cumulative way in which entrepreneurial activity plays a role in reshaping the larger environmental context' (Aldrich and Fiol, 1994: 647).

Coalition building

Critical to the emergence of a new global industry is access to markets and resources in host countries (Huntingdon, 1973). In 1948, at the behest of the European Cooperation Agency (ECA), charged with implementing the ERP, Hilton travelled to Europe to assess the possibilities for building new hotels on the profit-sharing lease-and-operate model pioneered in Puerto Rico. He witnessed economic dislocation in London, Paris, Rome and Madrid, but reasoned that, with US financial and technical support, the European economy would improve (Hilton, 1957). He had recruited John Houser the previous April as executive vice-president charged with growing HHI (HIA, 1958c). Houser remained in post until 1958, when he ceded his responsibilities to Bob Caverly, assisted from 1961 by Curt Strand. In 1964, Strand replaced Caverly as vice-president when HHI morphed into HIC (HIA, 1992). As Aldrich and Fiol (1994: 649) stress, the 'sites within which renegotiations of meaning take place' are social contexts, and the reports and letters from Houser, Caverly and Strand to Hilton, and Hilton's personal correspondence, provide rich data on how these actors deployed interpersonal skills to gain access to host countries around the world. A standard pattern emerged. At home, Hilton was assiduous in forming alliances with politicians, officials and business leaders with a common interest in opening up new markets (HIA, 1960a). They would exert subtle pressure in host countries to help resolve problems. In Istanbul and Berlin, ECA officials and diplomats in Washington and in-country worked hand in glove with local politicians and officials to bring projects to fruition (HIA, 1950b; Wharton, 2001: 77–80). Within host countries, a similar alliancing strategy prevailed. To overcome obstacles and effect institutional change, HHI/HIC formed elite coalitions to incorporate subsidiaries, acquire choice sites, secure building and operating permits, form financial consortia, reach agreement for the remission of profits, procure import licences, access foreign currency, and a host of other matters, some of which required legal or regulatory changes (HIA, 1950a; 1951; 1954b; 1959b). Interacting with host-country elites proved a powerful legitimating strategy, enhancing the organization's reputation while improving access to local resources (Rindova et al., 2005). In countries where power was concentrated, issue resolution was relatively straightforward, as in Iran, where the Shah gifted a large tract of land for the hotel, and a top official,

Jeafar Behbehanian, was assigned to smooth the way for Hilton (HIA, 1959c). In countries where power was more diffuse and factions vied for control, such as Italy, progress was stuttering. Here, pressure from US officials and Pietro Romani, Italy's high commissioner for tourism, helped win project approval in 1954 after four years of negotiation, but even then repeated obstructions delayed completion until 1963 (HIA, 1954b).

In EMEA, where HHI/HIC opened 19 hotels between 1953 and 1967, the general strategy of forming elite coalitions to overcome difficulties within host countries was attuned to local circumstances. Hilton successfully implemented his preferred lease-and-operate model in a large majority of cases. The attractiveness of the Hilton brand gave him reputational advantage and negotiating power with high-status actors that he exploited to good effect. This advantage diminished as new competitors such as Sheraton entered the field (Davé, 1984). In a large majority of countries, Hilton avoided making a significant capital investment to add a new hotel to the HHI/HIC chain. Host governments and business elites preferred local ownership because it gave them a secure, long-term stake in the action. For governments, the main benefits stemmed from tourism and business travel boosting economic growth, local employment and the balance of payments (Behrman, 1971). For business elites, it provided a platform for the future within the hotel industry while integrating them into the emerging global community of capitalism. The exceptions came in developed European countries still reeling from war, where capital was scarce. In London, where the Board of Trade held final say on major capital projects, it was only when Hilton's partners, Charles Clore and Jack Cotton, persuaded him to make an equity investment in the owning company that the deadlock was broken (HIA, 1963a). The same applied in Paris, where agreement to finance the Hilton Inn at Orly Airport finally secured the prize of a downtown hotel funded by a consortium led by property developer Joseph Vaturi (HIA, 1960b). London and Paris, like Brussels, where Hilton financed the entire project, had such positive profit forecasts that Hilton abandoned his scruples on investing capital overseas (HIA, 1963b).

Rhetorical agency

Conrad Hilton prized effective communication. He courted celebrity and, throughout his career, was aware of the value of good publicity in creating business opportunities while predisposing key audiences in his favour (Gamson, 1994). He was meticulous in managing his image as a prayerful patriot who prized American democratic values, free enterprise and the right to own property (Rindova et al., 2005). The story he told of himself was of a man who kept his word, who was striving to improve the world not just for his own benefit, but also for others, at home and abroad (Hilton, 1957). His self-narrative chimed with the moral values of core constituencies (Fligstein, 2001). The scripts he propagated drew on the legitimating 'macro-cultural discourse' of the 'American dream' (Holt, 2004). He attributed his success to the self-reliance that stemmed from the Catholic faith instilled in him by his mother, and to being raised in a large frontier family in New Mexico. In his autobiography, *Be My Guest*, and biographical notes issued on demand to the media (HIA, 1954c), he portrays himself as a man of his times, inviting readers to react to him positively as a protagonist at the centre of the epic drama of US history.

As a public figure, Hilton attained his apogee in the 1950s. He was identified as 'the man who bought the Waldorf' and, after acquiring the Statler group in 1954, as 'the greatest hotelier in the world' (HIA, 1963c). He enhanced his prominence by being photographed with royalty, political leaders, the Pope, film stars and high-status actors (Rindova et al., 2005). He derived prestige from playing host to President Eisenhower and other US political leaders at Washington prayer breakfasts, and the famous prayer he authored, *America on Its Knees*, was circulated throughout the US in magazines and newspapers (HIA, 1954d). His life story featured in *Time* magazine. In short, through a skilful blend of public relations and symbolic association, Hilton engendered the 'social proof' that marked him out as a glamorous figure at the head of a successful company, leading the way in forging the global hotel industry (Rao, Greve and Davis, 2001).

Celebrity provided Hilton with the requisite platform to exercise rhetorical agency (Gamson, 1994). He was in demand as a public speaker and, through his speeches, had the opportunity to influence public opinion at home and abroad. Between 1950 and 1965, he gave 62 speeches, many of which were printed, circulated and reported in newspapers. The longest and most dramatic speeches, 28 with a mean length of 3,000 words, were overtly political. The remainder, including 21 hotel openings, were shorter (mean length 1,500 words) and less contentious.

In his political speeches, Hilton emphasized five core themes, which together made a consistent, distinctive argument on how to defeat communism. Three of these themes were derived from the contemporary discourse of anticommunism (Haynes, 1996; Heale, 1990). The need to combat Soviet expansionism echoed the Truman doctrine (Merrill, 2006); the case for US economic aid to distressed European economies restated that made to Congress in support of the ERP (Stanford, 1982); and the notion that US companies should become agents of international economic development was supportive of the urgings of the US government (Djelic, 1998; Magdoff, 1969). Two of Hilton's themes, however, had greater specificity. First, he identified hotel development as a potent weapon in the fight against communism (Rosendorf, 2014). Hotels boosted travel, trade, communication and cooperation across national boundaries and should be welcomed as a force for economic integration, peace and unity. 'World peace through international trade and travel' became HIC's strapline, and the theme became a favourite not just of Hilton's political speeches, but also of hotel openings at home and abroad, whose launch events helped legitimize the emergent field in the minds of influential third parties (Rao, 1994; Rindova et al., 2005). Second, Hilton urged that the struggle against communism was ideological. He followed the Catholic Church in denouncing communism as 'faithless', standing in monolithic opposition to those who cherished individual freedoms (Haynes, 1996). This led him to identify all communities of faith as potential allies, irrespective of national differences in governance, institutions and culture (Rosendorf, 2014).

Communication is fundamental to institutionalization (Suddaby, 2011). In Hilton's case, rhetorical agency functioned as an indirect but critical process of institutional entrepreneurship (Green and Li, 2011). It differentiated Hilton from his competitors by distinguishing him as a visionary leader committed to a noble cause, enhancing his social capital and helping convince others of the wisdom of investing in hotels, travel and tourism. At home, he won the support of fellow directors, investors, politicians and officials for investment in foreign hotels in politically high-risk countries. It is noteworthy that substantial funding was provided by the ECA to build Hilton hotels in Istanbul ($2 million; 30% of cost) and Berlin ($4.5 million; 65% of cost) on the perceived 'front line' against communism (HIA, 1950b; Wharton, 2001: 70). In host countries, the messages conveyed in Hilton's speeches resonated with assorted political and business leaders, and, in EMEA, HHI was treated preferentially over rivals InterContinental and Sheraton. His framing of the struggle against communism as opposition to faithlessness found favour in disparate regimes. In Iran, the Shah personally selected Hilton as a business partner, and, in Egypt, he had the support of General Nasser following his overthrow of the monarchy in 1952. Rhetorical agency helped dissipate host-country concerns about US omnipotence by focusing on a common enemy, shared values and the mutual benefits of hotels, tourism and business travel.

Discussion and conclusion

This chapter brings together the concepts of institutional entrepreneurship and the field of power, exploring them from the vantage point of a rich historical case. This reveals how Conrad Hilton, together with other elite actors at home and overseas, helped construct and legitimize the emergent global hotel industry, best depicted as an episode of collective agency in which Hilton played a leading role.

At the outset, we posed two research questions. The first relates to the core entrepreneurial processes of institutional entrepreneurship employed by Hilton in enacting his vision of a globally networked hotel industry. In answer, we propose that three key entrepreneurial processes proved critical to the emergence of the new industry: field formation, coalition building and rhetorical agency. Our second question relates to the adaptation of these processes when implemented transnationally.

In terms of field formation, we have demonstrated that Hilton, constrained by the risk aversion and domestic priorities of his board, developed a new template of multinational hotel company development, the profit-sharing lease-and-operate model, helping to shape the emergent global hotel industry by allying local ownership with international branding. In this regard, Hilton is really one of the first entrepreneurs to engage in processes of global diffusion of rationalized management templates, coordinating activities through cross-border exchanges and interactions.

He varied his repertoire or 'tool kit' so that each hotel exuded its national cultural heritage while achieving agreed specifications, uniting American and host-country architects and designers in joint project teams to blend the modern and luxurious with indigenous styles (Drori et al., 2009; Wharton, 2001). Time to opening varied by size of entry barriers encountered (see Table 9.1).

In terms of coalition building, we have shown that, domestically, Hilton collaborated with airlines, travel companies and influential third parties. In a cross-border context, he engaged in each case with a unique set of networks and relationships involving host-country politicians, officials and business elites to secure market access.

Finally, with respect to rhetorical agency, we have shown how the scripts Hilton propagated enabled him to impose a coherent vision that resonated with American societal values. Legitimacy claiming entails 'targeted and even manipulative rhetoric', within which repetition forms a powerful legitimating mechanism (Erkama and Vaara, 2010: 817). The five key themes that Hilton underscored in speeches, letters and prayers forged a consistent vision of a 'symbolic universe' imbued with meaning, which stakeholders were invited to buy into (Rao, 1994: 31). Domestic stakeholders were encouraged to see international hotels as playing a vital role in fostering free enterprise and democracy and forming a key plank in the battle against communism (Rosendorf, 2014). Stakeholders abroad were invited to recognize international hotels as a vital means of economic development and prosperity. Individual speeches were tailored to their audiences. The core messages, however, remained constant, marrying symbolic association with public relations in a manner that confirms Aldrich and Fiol's (1994: 666) insight that the 'social construction of organizational reality involved in building a new industry requires meaning-making on a grand scale'. The symbolic action of rhetorical agency paid dividends in terms of actual outcomes in diverse fields of power. Hilton's interpretation of the uncertain times in which he lived was crucial to his agency. The extensive meaning-making in which he engaged helped reduce ambiguity in unpredictable environments, as demonstrated by the extraordinary proliferation of hotels in disparate parts of the world.

Our study makes a contribution to theory by bringing together the concepts of institutional entrepreneurship and the field of power to explore their role in the emergence of a new global industry. Skilful actors are continuously 'pushing the limits of current rules that produce order' (Fligstein, 2001: 117). Key to realizing Hilton's vision of creating a global hotel industry to promote economic integration by supporting business travel and tourism was the need to construct markets across borders. A core insight of Santos and Eisenhardt (2009: 645) is that 'power is the unifying boundary logic'. The cross-border nature of our study enables us to explore the field of power not as a single, relatively abstract entity as it is often presented (Bourdieu, 1993; 1996), but rather as plural and variegated in the form of multiple, actual *fields of power* couched within different regimes and jurisdictions in which Hilton flexibly forged alliances with powerful others. He did so by tailoring his approach to the field of power in question, partnering with private and public entities while retaining the same template. Our case, therefore, underscores the fact that the composition of actors in any field of power – local, national or transnational – varies by prevailing governance regime, requiring adaptability from institutional entrepreneurs who engage with them. The multidimensional nature of diverse fields of power was heightened because they were further differentiated by their need and desire to attract American business, such that less developed countries displayed greater alacrity in welcoming Hilton's overtures than more developed ones. The implications of our research into Hilton's overseas activities are that our understanding of the field of power requires reconceptualization as something altogether more pluralistic, multidimensional and specific than commonly presented. Our research therefore adds to the work of Santos and Eisenhardt (2009) in underlining that power in general, and the field of power in particular, manifests differently in ambiguous settings, exacting differing responses from entrepreneurs.

We have also sought to make a methodological contribution in this chapter. The longitudinal nature of our study enables us to view Hilton's entrepreneurial activities holistically, set in their historical context. As Suddaby and Greenwood (2009: 186) argue, 'institutions are the outcome, not of discrete choices between alternative arrangements, but rather of long stretches of sedimentation in which the overt features of an organizational form are the product of complex layers of historical conflicts, crises and erosions'. Viewing the global hotel industry in historical perspective casts light on the manner in which it developed in the long run, emphasizing articulations and connections. This is especially valuable in a situation of industry emergence and evolution, affording fresh insights which might be lacking in an ahistorical account. Our view is that there is a place for in-depth historical cases, carefully selected and contextualized, as a source of fresh theoretical insights and construct development, micro observation proving critical to macro understanding. Hilton's role as an institutional entrepreneur in helping forge the global hotel industry, we suggest, warrants this level of attention.

References

Agarwal, R. and Braguinsky, S. (2015). Industry evolution and entrepreneurship: Steven Klepper's contributions to industrial organization, strategy, technological change, and entrepreneurship. *Strategic Entrepreneurship Journal*, 9 (4): 380–397.

Aldrich, H.E. (2011). Heroes, villains and fools: institutional entrepreneurship, NOT institutional entrepreneurs. *Entrepreneurship Research Journal*, 1 (2): 1–4.

Aldrich, H.E. and Fiol, C.M. (1994). Fools rush in? The institutional context of industry creation. *Academy of Management Review*, 19 (4): 645–670.

Barthes, R. (1989). *The rustle of language*. Berkeley, CA: University of California Press.

Battilana, J., Leca, B. and Boxenbaum, E. (2009). How actors change institutions: towards a theory of institutional entrepreneurship. *Academy of Management Annals*, 3 (1): 65–107.

Baumol, W. (1990). Entrepreneurship: productive, unproductive and destructive. *Journal of Political Economy*, 98 (3): 893–921.

Baumol, W. and Strom, R.J. (2007). Entrepreneurship and economic growth. *Strategic Entrepreneurship Journal*, 1 (3–4): 233–237.

Behrman, J.N. (1971). *International business and governments*. New York: McGraw-Hill.
Berg, B.L. (2009). *Qualitative research methods for the social sciences* (7th edn). Boston, MA: Allyn & Bacon.
Berger, P. and Luckmann, T. (1966). *The social construction of reality: A treatise in the sociology of knowledge*. London: Penguin.
Bourdieu, P. (1990). *The logic of practice*. Cambridge: Polity.
Bourdieu, P. (1993). *The field of cultural production*. Cambridge: Polity.
Bourdieu, P. (1996). *The state nobility: Elite schools in the field of power*. Cambridge: Polity.
Braudel, F. (1980). *On history*. Chicago: University of Chicago Press.
Contractor, F.J. and Kunda, S.K. (1998). Modal choice in a world of alliances: Analyzing organizational forms in the international hotel sector. *Journal of International Business Studies*, 29 (2): 325–357.
Davé, U. (1984). US multinational involvement in the international hotel sector – an analysis. *Service Industries Journal*, 4 (1): 48–63.
DeRoos, J.A. (2010). Hotel management contracts – past, present and future. *Cornell Hospitality Quarterly*, 51 (1): 68–80.
DiMaggio, P.J. (1988). Interest and agency in institutional theory. In Zucker, L.G. (ed.), *Institutional patterns and organizations: Culture and environment*. Cambridge, MA: Ballinger, 3–22.
DiMaggio, P.J. (1991). Introduction. In Powell, W.W. and DiMaggio, P.J. (eds), *The new institutionalism in organizational analysis*. Chicago, IL: University of Chicago Press, 1–38.
DiMaggio, P.J., Powell, W.W. (1983). The iron cage revisited: institutional isomorphism and collective rationality in organizational fields. *American Sociological Review*, 48 (2): 147–160.
Djelic, M.-L. (1998). *Exporting the American model*. Oxford: Oxford University Press.
Downing, S. (2005). The social construction of entrepreneurship: narrative and dramatic processes in the coproduction of organizations and identities. *Entrepreneurship, Theory and Practice*, 29 (March): 185–204.
Drori, I., Honig, B. and Wright, M. (2009). Transnational entrepreneurs. *Entrepreneurship Theory and Practice*, 33 (September): 1001–1022.
Dunning, J.H. and McQueen, M. (1981). The eclectic theory of international production: a case study of the international hotel industry. *Managerial and Decision Economics*, 2 (4): 197–210.
Eisenhardt, K.M. and Graebner, M.E. (2007). Theory building from cases: Opportunities and challenges. *Academy of Management Journal*, 50 (1): 25–32.
Eisenstadt, S.N. (1980). Cultural orientations, institutional entrepreneurs and social change: Comparative analyses of traditional civilizations. *American Journal of Sociology*, 85 (4): 840–869.
Erkama, N. and Vaara, E. (2010). Struggles over legitimacy in global organizational restructuring: A rhetorical perspective on legitimation strategies and dynamics in a shutdown case. *Organization Studies*, 31 (7): 813–839.
Fligstein, N. (2001). Social skill and the theory of fields. *Sociological Theory*, 19 (2): 105–125.
Gamson, J. (1994). *Claims to fame: Celebrity in contemporary America*. Berkeley: University of California Press.
Garud, R., Hardy, C. and Maguire, S. (2007). Institutional entrepreneurship as embedded agency: An introduction to the special issue. *Organization Studies*, 28 (7): 957–969.
Garud, R., Jain, S. and Kumaraswamy, A. (2002). Institutional entrepreneurship in the sponsorship of common technological standards: The case of Sun Microsystems and Java. *Academy of Management Journal*, 45 (1): 196–214.
Geisler, C. (2009). How ought we to understand the concept of rhetorical agency? Report from the ARS. *Rhetoric Society Quarterly*, 34 (3): 9–17.

Goffman, E. (1959). *The presentation of self in everyday life*. New York: Anchor Books.
Green, S.E. and Li, Y. (2011). Rhetorical institutionalism: Language, agency, and structure in institutional theory since Alvesson 1993. *Journal of Management Studies*, 48 (7): 1662–1697.
Greene, R.W. (2004). Rhetoric and capitalism: Rhetorical agency as communicative labor. *Philosophy and Rhetoric*, 37 (3): 188–206.
Guthey, E., Clark, T. and Jackson, B. (2009). *Demystifying celebrity*. London: Routledge.
Hardy, C. and Maguire, S. (2008). Institutional entrepreneurship. In Greenwood, R., Oliver, C., Sahlin, K. and Suddaby, R. (eds), *Sage handbook of organizational institutionalism*. London: Sage, 198–217.
Hargadon, A.B. and Douglas, Y. (2001). When innovations meet institutions: Edison and the design of the electric light. *Administrative Science Quarterly*, 46 (3): 476–501.
Harvey, C. and Maclean, M. (2008). Capital theory and the dynamics of elite business networks in Britain and France. *The Sociological Review*, 56 (s.1): 105–120.
Harvey, C., Maclean, M., Gordon, J. and Shaw, E. (2011). Andrew Carnegie and the foundations of contemporary entrepreneurial philanthropy. *Business History*, 53 (3): 424–448.
Haveman, H.A., Habinek, J. and Goodman, L.A. (2012). How entrepreneurship evolves: The founders of new magazines in American, 1741–1860. *Administrative Science Quarterly*, 57 (4): 585–624.
Haynes, J.E. (1996). *Red menace or Red scare? American anticommunism in the Cold War era*. Chicago: Ivan R. Dee.
Haynes, W.A. (1952). *An economic analysis of the American hotel industry*. Baltimore: Catholic University of America Press.
Heale, M.J. (1990). *American anticommunism: Combating the enemy within, 1930–1970*. Baltimore: Johns Hopkins University Press.
Hilton, C. (1957). *Be my guest*. New York: Prentice Hall.
HIA [Hotel Industry Archive]. (1946). HHC [Hilton Hotels Corporation]/ARA [Annual Report and Accounts]/Annual report.
HIA. (1948). HHC/ARA/Annual report.
HIA. (1950a). HIC [Hilton International Co.]/Box 1/Letter reviewing developments in Europe from J. Houser in Nice, France to C.N Hilton in Beverly Hills, CA, 20 September.
HIA. (1950b). HIC/Box 1/Letter from J.W, Houser in Istanbul to C.N Hilton in Beverly Hills, CA, 27 August.
HIA. (1951). HIC/Box 1/Letter reviewing developments in Europe from J.W, Houser in Rome, Italy to C.N Hilton in Beverly Hills, CA, 15 July.
HIA. (1954a). HHC/ARA/Annual report.
HIA. (1954b). HIC/Box 1/Letter reviewing international developments from J. Houser in New York to C.N Hilton in Beverly Hills, California, July 16.
HIA. (1954c). HHC/Box 196/Conrad Nicholson Hilton: President, Hilton Hotels Corporation, January.
HIA. (1954d). HHC/Box 10/Article and photograph of C.N. Hilton with President Eisenhower, *International Christian Leadership Bulletin*, May.
HIA. (1958a). HHC/ARA/Annual report.
HIA. (1958b). HIC/Box 4/Summary of Hilton Hotels International Inc. basic agreement, prepared by Gregory Dillon, January 12.
HIA. (1958c). HIC/Box 2/HHI press release announcing retirement of J.W. Houser detailing career and achievements, December 9.
HIA. (1959a). HIC/Box 2/Letter from C.N. Hilton to R.J. Caverly, May 5.

HIA. (1959b). HIC/Box 2/Letter reviewing international developments from R.J. Caverly in New York to C.N. Hilton in Beverly Hills, CA, March 23.
HIA. (1959c). HIC/Box 2/Memorandum on Tehran recommending signature of MoU with Pahlavi Foundation prepared for C.N. Hilton by R.J. Caverly, 31 October 1959.
HIA. (1960a). HHC/Box 74/Letter from C.N. Hilton to Ambassador J.P. Kennedy pledging his support for his son, recently elected US President, November 16.
HIA. (1960b). HIC/Box 1/Letter from R.J. Caverly to Gus Killenberg of Harris, Kerr, Forster & Co. stockbrokers on HIC strategy and tactics, October 14.
HIA. (1961). HHC/ARA/Hilton Hotels Corporation: the years ahead, special letter to shareholders from Conrad N. Hilton, February 20.
HIA. (1963a). HHC/Box 124/Responses to speech given by British Chancellor of the Exchequer, R. Maudling, by C.N. Hilton and C. Clore, April 17.
HIA. (1963b). HHC/Box 172/Letter from R.J. Caverly in New York to C.N. Hilton in Beverly Hills, CA enclosing profit forecasts for hotels opening in 1963, March 28.
HIA. (1963c). HHC/Box 120/Article headline 'The World's Greatest Hotelier' in *The Citizen* newspaper, April 1.
HIA. (1964a). HIC/ARA/President's letter.
HIA. (1964b). HHC/Box 196/Conrad Nicholson Hilton: summary of operations and principles, April.
HIA. (1964c). HIC/Box 7/Translation of long article on Hilton in Europe under the headline 'Be Big' in *Der Spiegel*, August 4.
HIA. (1965). HIC/ARA/Annual report.
HIA. (1966). HIC/ARA/President's letter.
HIA. (1967). HHC/Box 212/Script for the Mike Douglas show, August 28.
HIA. (1992). OHC [Oral History Collection]/Part A Interview with Curt Strand, former president of Hilton International Co. conducted by Cathleen Baird, October 21.
HIA. (1993). OHC/ Part B Interview with Curt Strand, former president of Hilton International Co. conducted by Cathleen Baird, December 6.
Holt, D.B. (2004). *How brands become icons: The principles of cultural branding*. Boston, MA: Harvard Business Press.
Huntingdon, S.P. (1973). Transnational organizations in world politics. *World Politics*, 25 (3): 333–368.
Koselleck, R. (2004). *Futures past: On the semantics of historical time*. New York: Columbia University Press.
Lamoreaux, N.R., Raff, D.M.G. and Temin, P. (2007). Economic theory and business history. In Jones, G. and Zeitlin, J. (eds), *Oxford handbook of business history*. Oxford: Oxford University Press, 37–66.
Lawrence, T.B. and Phillips, N. (2004). From *Moby Dick* to *Free Willy*: Macro-cultural discourse and institutional entrepreneurship in emerging institutional fields. *Organization*, 11 (5): 689–711.
Lawrence, T. Suddaby, R. and Leca, B. (2011). Institutional work: refocusing institutional studies of organization. *Journal of Management Inquiry*, 20 (1): 52–58.
Leblebici, H., Salancik, G.R., Copay, A. and King, T. (1991). Institutional change and the transformation of interorganizational fields: An organizational history of the US radio broadcasting industry. *Administrative Science Quarterly*, 36 (3): 333–363.
Li, Y. and Zahra, S. (2012). Formal institutions, culture, and venture capital activity: A cross-country analysis. *Journal of Business Venturing*, 27 (1): 95–111.
Maclean, M. and Harvey, C. (2019). Pierre Bourdieu and elites: Making the hidden visible. In Pina Cunha, M. and Clegg, S.R. (eds), *Management, Organizations and Contemporary Social Theory*. London: Routledge, 99–114.

Maclean, M., Harvey, C. and Chia, R. (2010). Dominant corporate agents and the power elite in France and Britain. *Organization Studies*, 31 (3): 327–348.

Maclean, M., Harvey, C. and Chia, R. (2012). Sensemaking, storytelling and the legitimization of elite business careers. *Human Relations*, 65 (1): 17–40.

Maclean, M., Harvey, C. and Clegg, S.R. (2016). Conceptualizing historical organization studies. *Academy of Management Review*, 41 (4): 609–632.

Maclean, M., Harvey, C. and Clegg, S.R. (2017). Organization theory in Business and Management History: Current status and future prospects. *Business History Review*, 91 (3): 457–481.

Maclean, M., Harvey, C., Golant, B.D. and Sillince, J.A.A. (2020). The role of innovation narratives in accomplishing organizational ambidexterity. *Strategic Organization*. In press.

Maclean, M., Harvey, C. and Press, J. (2006). *Business elites and corporate governance in France and the UK*. Basingstoke: Palgrave Macmillan.

Maclean, M., Harvey, C., Sillince, J.A.A. and Golant, B.D. (2014). Living up to the past? ideological sensemaking in organizational transition. *Organization*, 21 (4): 543–567.

Maclean, M., Harvey, C., Sillince, J.A.A. and Golant, B.D. (2018). Intertextuality, rhetorical history and the uses of the past in organizational transition. *Organization Studies*, 39 (12): 1733–1755.

Maclean, M., Harvey, C., Suddaby, R. and O'Gorman, K. (2018). Political ideology and the discursive construction of the multinational hotel industry. *Human Relations*, 71 (6): 766–795.

Magdoff, H. (1969). *The age of imperialism: The economics of U.S. foreign policy*. New York: Monthly Review Press.

Maguire, S., Hardy, C. and Lawrence, T.B. (2004). Institutional entrepreneurship in emerging fields: HIV/AIDS treatment advocacy in Canada. *Academy of Management Journal*, 47 (5): 657–679.

Martens, M.L., Jennings, J.E. and Jennings, P.D. (2007). Do the stories they tell get them the money they need? The role of entrepreneurial narratives in resource acquisition. *Academy of Management Journal*, 50 (5): 1107–1132.

Merrill, D. (2006). The Truman doctrine: Containing communism and modernity. *Presidential Studies Quarterly*, 36 (1): 27–37.

Meyer, D. (2009). Commentary: On the integration of strategic management and entrepreneurship: views of a contrarian. *Entrepreneurship Theory and Practice*, 33 (January): 341–352.

Munir, K.A. and Phillips, N. (2005). The birth of the 'Kodak moment': Institutional entrepreneurship and the adoption of new technologies. *Organization Studies*, 26 (11): 1165–1687.

Phillips, N., Lawrence, T.B. and Hardy, C. (2004). Discourse and institutions. *Academy of Management Review*, 29 (4): 635–652.

Porter, M.E. (2000). Location, competition and economic development: Local clusters in a global economy. *Economic Development Quarterly*, 14 (1): 15–34.

Rao, H. (1994). The social construction of reputation: Certification contests, legitimation, and the survival of organizations in the American automobile industry, 1895–1912. *Strategic Management Journal*, 15 (S1): 29–44.

Rao, H. (2004). Institutional activism in the early American automobile industry. *Journal of Business Venturing*, 19 (3): 359–384.

Rao, H., Greve, H. and Davis, G. (2001). Fool's gold: social proof in the initiation and abandonment of coverage by Wall Street analysts. *Administrative Science Quarterly*, 46 (September): 502–526.

Rindova, V.P. and Kotha, S. (2001). Continuous 'morphing': Competing through dynamic capabilities, form and function. *Academy of Management Journal*, 44 (6): 1263–1280.

Rindova, V.P., Pollock, T.G. and Hayward, M.L.A. (2006). Celebrity firms: The social construction of market popularity. *Academy of Management Review*, 31 (1): 50–71.

Rindova, V.P., Williamson, I.O., Petkova, A.P. and Sever, J.M. (2005). Being good or being known: An empirical examination of the dimensions, antecedents, and consequences of organizational reputation. *Academy of Management Journal*, 48 (6): 1033–1049.

Rosendorf, N.M. (2014). *Franco sells Spain to America: Hollywood, tourism and public relations as postwar Spanish soft power*. Basingstoke: Palgrave Macmillan.

Rushmore, S. and Baum, E. (2002). The growth and development of the hotel-motel industry. *Appraisal Journal*, 70 (2): 148–162.

Santos, F.M. and Eisenhardt, K.M. (2009). Constructing markets and shaping boundaries: Entrepreneurial power in nascent fields. *Academy of Management Journal*, 52 (4): 643–671.

Stanford, W.F. (1982). The Marshall plan: Origins and implementation. Department of State Bulletin, June.

Suchman, M.C. (1995). Managing legitimacy: Strategic and institutional approaches. *Academy of Management Review*, 20 (3): 571–610.

Suddaby, R. (2010). Challenges for institutional theory. *Journal of Management Inquiry*, 19 (1): 14–20.

Suddaby, R. (2011). How communication institutionalizes: a response to Lammers. *Management Communication Quarterly*, 25 (1): 183–190.

Suddaby, R. and Greenwood, R. (2005). Rhetorical strategies of legitimacy. *Administrative Science Quarterly*, 50 (1): 35–67.

Suddaby, R. and Greenwood, R. (2009). Methological issues in researching institutional change. In Buchanan, D. (ed.), *The Sage handbook of organizational research methods*. London: Sage, 176–195.

Taylor, J.R., Cooren, F., Giroux, N. and Robichaud, D. (1996). The communicational basis of organization: Between the conversation and the text. *Communication Theory*, 6 (1): 1–39.

Wharton, A.J. (2001). *Building the Cold War: Hilton International Hotels and modern architecture*. Chicago: Chicago University Press.

Wijen, F. and Ansari, S. (2006). Overcoming inaction through collective institutional entrepreneurship: Insights from regime theory. *Organization Studies*, 28 (7): 1079–1100.

Zahra, S.A. and Wright, M. (2011). Entrepreneurship's next act. *Academy of Management Perspectives*, 25 (4): 67–83.

10

'REMEMBER MACKINTOSH!' HISTORICAL HOMOLOGY AND HISTORICAL AFFINITY IN THE DESIGN OF THE SCOTTISH PARLIAMENT BUILDING

Ron Kerr and Sarah Robinson

Introduction

How did a new national parliament come to be organized and designed in Edinburgh in the context of late 20th-century Scotland? What historical and symbolic resources were drawn on by the designers of the parliament? Why was a specific historical precedent used as a resource by the contemporary architect and his partners? To address these research questions, we draw on recent work on Bourdieu and historical research (Calhoun, 2003; Gorski, 2013) and extend it by introducing the concepts of *historical homology* and *historical affinity* to capture the striking affinity of disposition and ethos (Bourdieu, 1984) that connects two architects (one Scottish, one Catalan), situated in the field of cultural production, albeit almost a century apart. In so doing, we extend the growing literature on historical organization studies by developing a historical relational analysis that incorporates Bourdieu's historical sociology (Maclean, Harvey and Clegg, 2017) and demonstrates 'the importance of the past in shaping the present and influencing the future' (Kieser, 1994: 619).

First, to ground our study empirically, we need to explain why a new parliament came to be built in Scotland in 1999. That is, what were the social conditions of possibility of this building? In brief, by the late 20th century, there was an increasing misalignment between UK and Scottish politics: whereas Scotland returned a majority of Labour Party members to the UK Parliament, the Conservatives, as the majority party in England, continued to form the UK government from 1979 to 1997. Over this period, social and political pressure grew in Scotland for either a renewal of formal independence or for a devolved form of government within the UK that would address this 'democratic deficit' (Macwhirter, 1990: 21).

As a result of 20 years of campaigning by Scottish civil society organizations, a referendum on Scottish devolution was held in 1997,[1] with a vote in favour of the creation of a parliament with devolved legislative powers. After some debate about the repurposing of existing buildings, it was decided that the parliament's home would be a new building, 'an important symbol for Scotland' that 'should pay tribute to the Country's past achievements and signal its future aspirations' (quoting the design brief for the building, in Scottish Parliament Corporate Body, 1999: n.p.).[2]

As we shall show, the key contributors to the building's conception were, first, the late Donald Dewar, Secretary of State for Scotland (1997–1999) and then (1999–2000) First Minister of Scotland. Second, Catalan architect Enric Miralles, the building's principal designer; and, third, Scottish designer Charles Rennie Mackintosh (1868–1928). In his design sketches for the parliament, Miralles included a hand-written aide-memoire, 'Remember Mackintosh' (reproduced in Balfour, 2005), indicating his affinity with the work of Mackintosh. For Miralles, the new parliament would constitute a 'dialogue across time' with his predecessor (quoted in Glancey, 2003).

Our study therefore contributes to the development of Bourdieusian field theory in historical organization studies by introducing and applying the concept of historical homology. We do this in order to understand how agents in the field of cultural production draw on historical resources (the past) in designing and constructing symbolically important buildings, and in so doing contribute to the ongoing process of national identity formation (the *nationizing* process: Gorski, 2013).

National formation and fields of cultural production

National identity is 'something always in the making, never made' (Samuel, 1998: 22). Nations are neither essential nor primordial, but engendered in and by social fields (Bourdieu, 1985; Brubaker, 1996; Calhoun, 1993; Eyal, 2005). These fields form part of a national 'universe' of social spaces in which each field is constituted by 'a set of objective, historical relations between positions anchored in certain forms of power (or capital)' (Bourdieu and Wacquant, 1992: 16). In the Scottish case, the process of becoming the 'United Kingdom' as a political union after 1707 meant that national identification would be maintained, not by the state, but by the independent Scottish institutions: education, including the teaching of Scottish history and geography, religion (the Church of Scotland), Scots law, and the press, as well as by cultural fields, notably the academic field and the field of literary production (Brubaker, 1996; Bourdieu, 2014).

Fields of literary production have been central to the formation of peripheral national identities, as in Ireland and Latin America (Casanova, 2004). So, in mid-20th-century Scotland, modernist authors (e.g. Hugh MacDiarmid and Lewis Grassic Gibbon) created a 'Scots national aesthetic' by adapting the Scots language to write about the Scottish land and people (Casanova, 2004: 293–294). The Scottish intelligentsia then constituted these works as a 'Scottish literary renaissance' and, through their work in universities, literary reviews and so on, institutionalized a Scottish literary canon. The writers and intelligentsia thus contributed to the formation of a national literary field and so to the process of national identity formation (Preuss, 2012).

There is, however, an absence of theoretically informed studies of the design, construction and symbolic power of national parliament buildings. This chapter, therefore, contributes a socio-historical study of how a new parliament, intended as a symbol of the nation and its politics, came to be organized and designed in the context of late 20th-century Scotland, and the role of architects, their firms and their collaborators in this process. Our theoretical contribution to historical organization studies, then, is to introduce the concept of historical homology and develop the concept of historical affinity. Through these concepts, we extend Bourdieusian field theory by showing why and how an architect, active in the 1990s and occupying a position in the field of cultural production homologous to that of an architect a century earlier, will draw on and adapt the work of that particular predecessor in designing a new building, conceived as a 'dialogue across time'.

By using field analysis, we are able to identify opposing positions in the field, what Bourdieu calls *pôles* of cultural production (Bourdieu, 1993a). These are the *pole of mass production* and the *pole of restricted production* ('art for art's sake' being a key to recognizing a relatively autonomous field of artistic production: see Bourdieu, 1984; 2014). Paradoxically, architects in the mass-production sector are not usually recognized by name outside the field, whereas the 'artists' at the opposite, restricted, pole may well be popularly recognized as 'starchitects'. This is despite the fact that they are entirely dependent on state or corporate clients for work, or on commissions from the independently wealthy (Jones, 2011). However, the relationship between client and architect produces a 'dialectic of distinction' (Lipstadt, 2003: 402–403) that benefits both agents, helping them to accrue cultural capital in their respective social fields.

To get a preliminary idea of the 21st-century globalized field of architecture and its polarities, we can draw on literature on the professions. For example, Faulconbridge (2009) identifies two categories of dominant architectural firm: (1) global architectural firms, including Gensler, Aedas, Kajima, HOK, RTKL SOM, NBBJ, and (2) starchitect firms such as Foster & Partners, OMA (Rem Koolhass's Office for Metropolitan Architecture), Gehry Partners, Studio Daniel Libeskind and Zaha Hadid Architects. Generally speaking, the first group specialize in imposing corporate towers, whereas the latter focus on commissions for iconic buildings. However, this reconstruction of the contemporary architectural 'profession' as a field of cultural production omits the smaller, atelier firms, a group with high cultural capital that includes EMBT (Enric Miralles Benedetta Tagliabue). It also omits the many local firms such as RMJM in Scotland, who enter into partnerships with atelier firms in order to provide local knowledge.[3]

Then, in order to reconstruct a relational sociology of the field of cultural production at the turn of the 20th century, we turn to critic Hermann Muthesius (1902: 193–194), whose work allows us to situate the Art Nouveau movement, including Mackintosh and his collaborators, as a pan-European avant-garde

(Fowler, 1997) within the field of architecture and design (Mackintosh and his collaborators exhibited in Vienna, Munich, Turin, Venice, Moscow, Budapest, Dresden and Berlin). That is to say, in the period 1890–1910, the Mackintosh group occupied a distinctive avant-garde field position and embodied a particular *ethos* (Fowler, 1997), a belief that architecture should mediate nature and history (Eadie, 1990; Tagliabue, 2009), and that 'total design' should include every detail of a building's interior.

Yet behind these named architects are organizations, both formal and informal: the partnership of Honeyman, Keppie and Mackintosh, 1889–1913, and 'The Glasgow Four' group who met at the Glasgow School of Art (GSA; Mackintosh, Margaret Macdonald, Frances Macdonald, Herbert McNair). In the 1990s, EMBT partnered with RMJM, project managers and engineers. Each of these 'names' also represents an organization – a firm, an aesthetic movement, a political party – in relation to other organizations in their field and across fields.

A socio-historical approach

In order to address our three research questions (see the Introduction above), we followed Charle's socio-historical methods (Charle, 2013: 67–88), by identifying, first, our problematic – namely fields of cultural production in relation to the conditions of possibility for the building – and, second, our object of research, the Scottish parliament building itself. We then clarified the *scale of division* – the origin and construction of the Scottish parliament – and the *scale of time* – the period from 1997 to 2004, and how it related to the period of the Glasgow Style of design and architecture.

We then applied field theory to two 'synchronic slices' (Bourdieu, 1996: 141) to reconstruct the position of Mackintosh and his collaborators in the architectural field in Europe as it was in 1900–1910 and then the position of Miralles in the field as it was in 1990–2004. This allowed us to situate the dominant players in relation to the dominated, identifying the poles of mass/restricted production and attributing dispositions to social agents. By producing and superimposing two synchronic analyses, we were able to identify homologies of field position and affinity dispositions between agents in these temporally distant fields. We also identified the key role of the Secretary of State for Scotland, an agent in the political field, in commissioning the building.

Our data sources are primarily archival. Miralles died in 2000, before the building was completed, but his thinking on architecture can be pieced together from newspaper interviews and from digital archives, including that of Miralles's firm, EMBT. The website archive of the publishers Divisare (2010) includes a section on EMBT, including photos, sketches, landscape plans of the parliament, and reproductions of Miralles's handwritten notes from the original proposal. From LexisNexus (1997–2005), we drew on reports of public lectures given by Enric Miralles in Glasgow and Edinburgh (Linklater, 1998); for additional Miralles quotes, see Grigor (2001) and Balfour (2005). We also identified the online recording of a lecture on 'Mackintosh and Miralles' given by Benedetta Tagliabue (Miralles's widow) at the GSA in 2009 (Tagliabue, 2009). The lecture includes a discussion of Miralles's own slides prepared for a lecture given during the 1999 Mackintosh & Miralles exhibition at the Hunterian in Glasgow.

Two major public inquiry reports into the processes of design and construction are archived online: the first, by the Auditor General of Scotland (AGS, 2000), and, the second, more comprehensive, by Lord Fraser (Fraser, 2004). The final report is available on the Scottish parliament website, and full transcripts of interviews (prefixed 'Transcript'), written witness statements ('WS') and a wealth of supporting documents ('MS') can be found via a historic link to the British Library's UK Web Archive.[4] We also consulted a BBC TV documentary on the building's construction (BBC, 2005) and Susan Bain's account of the process (Bain, 2005), based on her experience as a member of the documentary team.

To situate Mackintosh in relation to his contemporaneous field, we draw, as noted above, on the survey of Mackintosh's work on the University of Glasgow website;[5] on Hermann Muthesius (1902: 1904–5),[6] who places Mackintosh in the context of European Art Nouveau; on Eadie's Marxian approach to the Glasgow Style (Eadie, 1990); and on Fowler's Bourdieusian approach to cultural production and, in particular, her identification of Art Nouveau as an avant-garde movement (Fowler, 1997).

Finally, we applied Bourdieu's concepts of symbolic, social and physical space (Bourdieu, 1993b; Kerr et al., 2016) to our data to show in finer detail how the design and construction of the building brought together historical and symbolic resources, situating it in the context of debates over history, politics and culture in Scotland that are central to the ongoing process of nationizing (Brubaker, 1996, Gorski, 2013).

Situating the parliament: The symbolic power of place

Why Edinburgh? Where in Edinburgh? Leveraging the power of symbolic space

The parliament would be situated in Edinburgh, Scotland's capital, where the Scottish parliament had its seat until the 1707 Union with England (the old parliament building is now occupied by law courts and the advocates' library; see Siebert, Wilson and Hamilton, 2017). But where in Edinburgh? The building would be both culturally and politically symbolic; however, the power to commission resided in the political field with Donald Dewar who, as Secretary of State for Scotland – that is, the UK government minister in charge of devolution – was in a unique albeit temporary position of authority in the political field, in that he would oversee the processes of transition to, and election of, a new parliament. In this interregnum, he was free to take decisions about the building, albeit with advice from the Scottish Office and following feasibility studies of the sites (Lord Elder, Dewar's special adviser, in Fraser, 2004: 210).

Dewar's decision was also informed by an understanding of the city's history and symbolic topography: how history is materially embodied in such a place.

However, until early 1998, the new parliament was expected to be in the former Royal High School (RHS), a neoclassical building situated on Calton Hill that dominates the north of the city. Indeed, the RHS had been prepared to house the Scottish parliament if the 1979 referendum on independence had succeeded. However, the suitability of the RHS came into question after Dewar visited the site in May 1998. There were concerns over issues of accessibility, over the cost of restoration and renovation and (for Dewar) its symbolic value for the independence movement (Fraser, 2004: 2.8) – a 'vigil for a Scottish parliament' had been held near the building from 1992 until 1997 (Ascherson, 2014). A second site, the nearby St Andrew's House, was also considered. Built in the late 1930s to house the Scottish Office (i.e. the office of the Secretary of State for Scotland) and situated on Calton Hill, close to the RHS, St Andrew's House presents a sort of massive cliff face looming over the lower levels of the city. According to Wendy Alexander (Dewar's special adviser), a parliament in St Andrew's House would be 'just an extension of the old Government of Scotland' (Transcript 29-10-2003 PM: 295) and not symbolic of a new beginning. Dewar also considered its design as 'somewhat fascist' (according to Gibbons, cited in Fraser, 2004: 714). Of the other contenders, Leith, the old dockyard area to the north of the city, was not central enough, and Haymarket, adjacent to the railway station of that name, held no symbolic resonance – and any building there would be sited above a complex of old railway tunnels (Sudjic and Jones, 2001).

However, the Holyrood site appealed to Dewar. He thought that it 'offered the chance of a modern building on a city-centre site' (Thomson, cited in Fraser, 2004: 168). He also liked 'the symbolism of the Parliament being juxtaposed with the Crown in the shape of Holyrood Palace, and partly also the symbolism of the Parliament being next to a mountain and open country' (Fraser, 2004: Transcript 03-02-2004 AM: 168). For Henry MacLeish (later Scottish First Minister), 'it had the magic of history, it had the magic of politics, it was a UN heritage site, it was at the bottom of the Royal Mile, it was in the centre of Edinburgh, the capital city' (Transcript 29-10-2003 AM: 392).

How the actual decision was made and who, apart from Dewar, was involved in making it were points of contention examined by the Fraser inquiry. However, Dewar had the power to decide and, in early 1999, he announced that the Holyrood site had been chosen.

Why Miralles? A dialectic of distinction

Having decided on the site, Dewar and his advisers drew up a competition design brief. This was framed in highly symbolic terms: '(the building) will be an important symbol for Scotland. It should pay tribute to the Country's past achievements and signal its future aspirations' (in Scottish Parliament Corporate Body, 1999: n.p.). The challenge to the architects was to use this brief to design a building that would bring together social and physical space, but was primarily driven by its symbolic and historical dimensions.

There were 70 competition entries; a long list of 12 was chosen by a six-member panel. This was chaired by Dewar (political field). It included two representatives from the field of architecture (Professors Joan O'Connor and Andy McMillan), two from the bureaucratic field (Robert Gordon and John Gibbons) and one from the media (Kirsty Wark). The 12 architects were invited to Edinburgh to present to the panel. According to Andy MacMillan, '[Miralles/EMBT] produced some leaves and stems, which he laid on a plan to show us how the building would sit in the Canongate but also sit in what he described as the land of Scotland'; Robert Gordon thought that '[Miralles's] grasp of the site and his understanding of what was wanted, his conceptual understanding, was fantastic' (Transcript 16-12-2003 AM: 337). After this round of presentations, a short list of five was produced.

The final round of interviews followed on 22 June 1998 in Glasgow. The five candidates were asked to each develop six boards outlining their approach and 'a concept design to show what their actual approach to that particular site and building would be' (MacMillan, 2003). The presentations were assessed by experts, with a consensus in favour of EMBT's conceptual approach. In contrast, the other competitors were considered to be too dominating and not sufficiently respectful of the site. The panel agreed. According to John Gibbons (cited in Fraser, 2004: 714):

> Three of the schemes were monolithic in character; they were large schemes, and part of the concept was that the architect saw these as large imposing schemes, in a sense, more in the direction of the symbol of the State.

On the other hand, Miralles's design 'was composed of smaller parts; it was a smaller scale, a more human scheme' (Transcript 25-11-2003 PM: 407).

This meant that Dewar and the panel rejected one of the world's major starchitects – Richard Meier, designer of the £1bn Getty Museum in Los Angeles – positioned at the pole of restricted production, but with symbolic capital outside the architectural field. Instead, the panel chose an avant-garde European architect who was also positioned at the pole of restricted production; however, although little known outside the field, he was accumulating high cultural capital within the field (MacMillan, in Fraser, 2004: 551). For panel member Joan O'Connor, '[Dewar's] heart was in developing a contemporary icon. He wanted to make a landmark building that would identify that particular moment in Scotland's history' (Fraser, 2004). The dialectic of distinction (Lipstadt, 2003) would, therefore, operate to reinforce Miralles's reputation within the European architectural field, while simultaneously reinforcing Dewar's, and the future Scottish government's, reputation as a European patron of the arts. As Lord Fraser remarked,

> Donald Dewar harboured an aspiration to be 'the most important patron of the architecture of government for 300 years' and it is not difficult to understand why he was so enthused by what Enric Miralles presented to him in concept.
>
> *(Fraser, 2004)*

So, Dewar felt an affinity for Miralles. But why did Miralles feel a historical affinity for Mackintosh?

Why Mackintosh? Homology and affinity of disposition.

We now, therefore, turn to the question of historical affinity – that is, why did Miralles evoke *Mackintosh*, rather than, for example, Scottish architect William Adam, whose 18th-century Baroque-Palladian architecture was the subject of Miralles's Master's degree (Grigor, 2001)?

To answer this question, we apply socio-historical field theory to identify the striking homologies of field position and habitus that create an affinity between Mackintosh and Miralles, albeit a century apart. That is, both occupied positions at the periphery of a European field (Fowler, 1997); both collaborated with personal and professional partners with a focus on the total design, including the craft aspects of the interior design process. This focus on design that can be mechanically reproduced suggests that both the Mackintosh group and Miralles–Tagliabue were aiming at a breakout from the pole of restricted production; in the Mackintosh case, this is particularly clear as regards interior design (see Eadie, 1990). In addition, both architects used the past as a resource – both interpreted the Scottish architectural tradition, translating historical features into contemporary styles (Art Nouveau for Mackintosh, post-modern for Miralles).

There are further affinities in relation to the field. Mackintosh and the Glasgow Style designers aligned themselves with the European avant-garde in order to manoeuvre around the dominance of the Edinburgh Royal Academy and its historicists and to accumulate social and cultural capital via Art Nouveau–Style Moderne–Secessionist design networks. Similarly, Miralles's firm, EMBT, was an atelier firm. Situated in Barcelona, it had no international offices, instead partnering with local firms to deliver projects; EMBT did not offer clients a decontextualized 'global' style, but something that would be contextually embedded – for example, the design for Utrecht town hall.

The Scottish parliament would, therefore, be a secular building, the site and design of which would draw on historical and symbolic resources to represent the nation and its politics. So, what resources did Miralles–Tagliabue draw on in their design? And how might the use of these resources be related to the work of Mackintosh and his collaborators?

Historical and symbolic resources

Historical affinities: Organic architecture

Conceptually, the Art Nouveau movement posited two fundamental categories: nature and history (Eadie, 1990: 1). Key artists were preoccupied with issues of historical evolution and with a search for origins, including the beginnings of vernacular forms. Mackintosh identified features of the Scottish vernacular in the form of the Scottish baronial, typically fortified houses with characteristic features:

towers, turrets and crow-stepped gables. He did this in order to escape the late 19th-century dominance of historicist eclecticism in monumental buildings, both secular and/or sacred.

For Miralles, the building and the land would be organically related: the winning design concept was developed in a watercolour sketch of twigs and leaves, cast down, as it were, on the land between Salisbury Crags and Edinburgh's Old Town. For Miralles (in Balfour, 2005: 35):

> the building of the parliament should sit in the place
> with same logic and delicacy that organizes vegetal forms
> leaves x trees
> had always been an example

In his initial concept, Miralles focused first on physical space: on the land (this is a powerful theme in the Scottish national literary field)[7] and on how the building might fit into the landscape. He noted that:

> The Parliament sits in the land.[8] We have the feeling that the building should be land, built out of land. To carve in the land the form of gathering people together ... Scotland is a land ... The land itself will be a material, a physical building material.
>
> *(EMBT, 1998: n.p.)*

Miralles's aim, as he explained in his handwritten notes on his sketches, was:

> *To balance*
> *land and city*
> *at the Parliament Building*
> *the iconography should come out of that...*
> *(in Balfour, 2005: 35)*

Here, Miralles's thinking was in line with Dewar's (see above): Miralles emphasizes the parliament's position, situated physically and symbolically between the city (the people, the citizenry) and the Royal Palace of Holyrood (the Crown, sovereignty), but not dominating, or being dominated by, either.

In concept, the building is organic, configured to the site, situated at the nexus of the urban and the natural, the civic and the royal. It testifies to the power of the symbolic to be reinterpreted and to mobilize. In so doing, it incorporates the role of the building materials into the iconography in relation to Scotland's history.

Historical iconography

The overall symbolism of the building – how it relates to the land, the palace, the city – contributes to the process of national identity construction. And, within the building itself, a certain historical continuity is asserted – or created – both in the return to Mackintosh (historical affinity) and in the iconographic details of the design: for Miralles, it was 'crucial to meditate on the iconography of our parliament' (in Balfour, 2005: 36). In the completed building, then, symbols and emblems are all around: saltires (the cross of St Andrew, patron saint of Scotland) are set into the ceiling of the foyer, although these could also be axes or seagull shapes – the flag shapes seem caught in an invisible wind. As for the vesica – oval shapes of the roof – these could be seen as stylized upturned boats or leaves (the land, natural forms), or as fish (icons of the early church; Jencks, 2005). There are also Scottish vernacular features such as crow-stepped gables and a knot garden, and columns and furniture that abstract away from natural forms – stylized leaves, stems, branches, twigs – in the style of Mackintosh and Macdonald (Tagliabue, 2009; Glendinning and MacKechnie, 2004).

The vaulted passages in the building and the use of light draw on the interior of the GSA, which in turn draws on the Scottish vernacular (the fortified house, for example) and on 'Scottish ways of building' (Tagliabue, Transcript 09-03-2004 pm: 510).

By focusing on light and openness, Miralles also evoked the Scottish Enlightenment of David Hume and Adam Smith, as expressed in Edwin Morgan's poem *Open the Doors!* (Morgan, 2004).

The GSA building was a competition winner. Mackintosh's winning design incorporated Mackintosh's adaptations of the vernacular: 'Scottish fortified tower houses of the 16th and 17th centuries are an important influence, with their small windows irregularly placed in sheer, forbidding walls, and their corbelled projections'.[9] The incorporation into the design of the shell of 17th-century Queensberry House brings specific historical resonance. According to MacMillan, Miralles 'had a very clear view he should keep Queensberry House, for instance, because of its historic association' (Transcript 29-10-2003 AM: 203).

The Marquis of Queensberry was one of the chief promoters of the Act of Union in 1707 that ended the old Scottish parliament. Incorporating the Scottish baronial-style Queensberry House therefore symbolized a sort of rebirth of an old democracy. As a 'reconvened' parliament, the new building also contains iconographic elements evoking the hall on the High Street where the old parliament, dissolved in 1707, assembled. These elements include the oak hammer-beam roof of the new debating chamber, which recalls the roof of the old parliament building, and the Arniston Stones, salvaged from the old parliament, which form a lintel above the door to the walkway leading to the debating chamber.

Outside, on the Canongate, the narrow street that runs down to Holyrood, the external wall of the parliament is inlaid with stones from around Scotland (marble, sandstone, granite, etc.), all except two of which are incised with quotations in the three languages of Scotland – Gaelic, Scots and English – from writers such as Burns, Scott and MacDiarmid. In reproducing the words of canonical poets and novelists, the parliament's creators pay homage to the role of the literary field in the production of national identity (Brubaker, 1996; Casanova, 2004, Sapiro, 2013), while leaving space for writers of the future to be included.

Historical affinity: Designing a different kind of monument

As we have seen, in choosing a site for the parliament, Dewar rejected the dominating position and monumental architecture of the RHS and St Andrew's House. In consultation with the panel, he also rejected the more monumental competition designs, including the Le Corbusier-influenced modernism of Benson and Forsythe, architects of the controversial National Museum of Scotland extension.

Dewar's view is encapsulated by Fraser in the final report of his inquiry: 'the idea that the Parliament should be a classical temple, were certainly not things that he thought' (Fraser, 2004: Transcript 03-02-2004 AM: 168). This echoes Mackintosh's rejection of historicist styles in an 1893 lecture: 'How absurd it is to see modern churches, theatres, banks, museums, exchanges, municipal buildings, art Galleries etc, etc made in imitation of Greek temples' (quoted by Dunlop, 2019: n.p.).

This rejection of the traditional architectures of power was very much in line with Miralles's vision for the parliament as a national symbol. As Benedetta Tagliabue remembered:

> I recall very clearly that Enric had this discussion with Donald Dewar saying that he did not want a building of power expressing the kind of arrogance of power. He wanted a building of power which would not have, for example, a central cupola or a central chamber. He wanted it to be more in relation to the landscape.
>
> *(Fraser, 2004: 173)*

The parallels with Mackintosh's GSA are again striking in terms of creating a place that fits its environment. The parliament building would be 'organic like a university campus' and 'not monumental ... the buildings like neighbors' (Miralles, 1997: n.p.).

There is also a parallel in terms of the philosophy of total design, evidenced in the craft aspects of the interior design where the parliamentary furniture abstracts away from natural forms – stylized leaves, stems, branches, twigs – in the style of Mackintosh and Macdonald (Tagliabue discusses this in her 2009 Glasgow lecture; see also Glendinning and MacKechnie, 2004: 181–184).

The parliament's work would be transparent to the public. In the chamber, there is no glass wall between the people and their representatives. This was deliberate: Miralles believed that, 'in parliamentary buildings nowadays we confuse the use of glass with transparency, and that is not what it is about at all' (O'Connor, Transcript 29-10-2003 AM: 927). For Miralles, quoted in Grigor (2001: n.p.): 'A parliament is neither a viewing room, nor an observatory'. Here we might contrast the use of glass in Rafael Vinoly's short-listed proposal for a huge glass dome for the Scottish parliament, in Norman Foster's Reichstag in Berlin, and in the glassed-in Welsh Senedd by Richard Rogers.

The shape of the debating chamber, as conceived by Miralles, took its form from Mackintosh's lecture theatre rather than from the confrontational cockpit of

Westminster. It gives form to an idea of the political as a process of a people seeking consensus (a 'European' idea of politics, as promoted by the Constitutional Convention). That is, as Tagliabue stated, 'The fundamental idea, which never changed, was to provide a Parliament which is not authoritarian but the reverse, democratic'.

Discussion

Structural homologies and historical affinities

Nationizing is a process of interpretation and reinterpretation of the past (Samuel, 1998) in which agents in fields of cultural and academic production play a central role (Casanova, 2004). In terms of Scotland, philosophers and historians have reconstructed the 'Scottish Enlightenment' as a phenomenon that places Scottish thinkers, peripherally situated geographically and politically, at the centre of 18th-century thought, while, as already noted, the role played by agents in the literary field in the processes of Scottish national identity formation has been particularly well studied (Preuss, 2012; Craig, 2018).[10] This is recognized at Holyrood, on the Canongate Wall, where Miralles and Tagliabue pay homage to the role of writers such as Scott, Burns and MacDiarmid in the production of Scottish national identity.

But Miralles and Tagliabue also 'dialogue with history' in terms of architecture. So, 'For Miralles, Scotland best expressed herself through the genius of her architects' (Grigor, 2001: n.p.). In designing the parliament, then, Miralles was explicitly concerned with history, believing that, 'Whatever kind of place it is we should be able to enter historical meaning' (in Linklater, 1998: n.p.). The new parliament would set up a dialogue across time and space, an 'extended conversation between the city, its citizens and the buildings' (Miralles, in Glancey, 2003: n.p.).

As a result, the building's symbolic power would paradoxically lie in its creators' refusal of monumentality and domination. This also meant that the parliament building would be of necessity idiosyncratic: 'in our days there does not exist an architecture of convention that connects buildings, forms and social meaning', and so, 'Each public building should develop its own iconography' (Miralles, in EMBT, 1998: n.p.; from the proposed team document). That is, Miralles rejected the architectural features traditionally associated with the projection of power: the poles of an axis model (see Dovey, 2014, on the Palace of Westminster), the enfilade model of Versailles (Giedion, 1970); indeed, he rejected the monumental approach altogether, whether neo-classical or Gothic or modernist. Like Mackintosh's GSA, his building would be 'a discontinuous, fractured work, open to many interpretations' (Crawford, 2018: 41).[11]

In terms of geography and cultural field topography, Glasgow (Mackintosh) and Barcelona (Gaudi) are homologous as peripheral cities. In both cases, however, avant-gardes in social and geographical peripheries became symbolic 'reference points' for the field. And this is again true in the 1990s. For example, in the course of an interview on Gaudi and Miralles, Colombian architect Felipe Mesa notes that, for his generation of Colombian architects, 'the cultural reference point was Spain, in particular Barcelona or Madrid'.[12]

The Art Nouveau of Mackintosh and Gaudi can be seen, in retrospect, as proto-modernist (Pevsner, 1936; 1969); that is, late-period Art Nouveau is moving away from curvilinear high Art Nouveau in the direction of modernist abstraction (Eadie, 1990). After World War I, Art Nouveau was replaced by Art Deco and modernism. This movement parallels in reverse how the post-modernism of Miralles moves out of – or on from – modernist abstraction (Miralles's attention to how a building fits into its surroundings can be seen as typically post-modern; see Jencks, 2005). That is, Mackintosh is moving towards abstraction, whereas Miralles is drawing back from abstraction. But there is an affinity here: both are interested in the aestheticization of organic form, in history, and in time (Eadie, 1990: 1). Enric Miralles was an artist 'who worked with the fluid form; concrete; with unusual shapes; with rich materials, but in a very simple form' (Gibbons, in Fraser, 2004: 470). His buildings, including the parliament, are organic. And Miralles's affinity with Mackintosh was noticed by the television presenter Kirsty Wark, particularly in relation to the 'delicate drawings of flowers and stems' (Wark, in Fraser, 2004: WS-1301 to 08).

However, in Miralles's parliament, the iconography is allusive. Symbolic forms are stylized and ambiguous: the leaves or upturned boats that form the roof; the diagonal crosses inset in the vaulted ceiling of the entrance hall that represent Scotland's emblematic national flag, although seen from some angles these shapes could be stylized seagulls. The transparent 'bottle' shapes inserted into the walls of the debating chamber: might these be stylized people overlooking the debates? Or, might they be (as Edinburgh wits prefer) whisky bottles, symbolic of Scotland's most valuable product?[13] Similarly, the shape of the windows in the MSPs' offices can be seen as blinds drawn back to let the light in or, more subversively, as hairdryers (emitting 'hot air' perhaps)?

The project was organized as a design collaboration between EMBT atelier and the Scottish firm RMJM, with the political client producing the design brief and commissioning the building. We next discuss the role of Donald Dewar and his position in the political field – how the dialectic of distinction operates in relation to the parliament.

Designing a national parliament

Dewar was a minister in the New Labour government at Westminster. However, as Secretary of State for Scotland and based in Edinburgh and Glasgow, he was somewhat detached, the designer of a new political field and able to leverage his interim position of strength. Dewar considered himself a Scottish 'cultural nationalist', an aficionado of Scottish art and Scottish vernacular architecture (McAlpine, 1999). He also felt an affinity with Catalonia, having visited Barcelona in 1998 and seeing there another a culturally distinct yet stateless European nation. For Kirsty

Wark, this also applied to Miralles, who: 'As a Catalan ... seemed to be in tune with the aspirations of a devolved Scottish Parliament operating within a European context' (in Fraser, 2004: WS-13-01 to 08). As Mick Duncan of RMJM states:

> the concept behind this building, which I think is absolutely wonderfully unique, that it was part of Scotland, not part of Edinburgh, and there was an integration between the land of Scotland and the building: highly important, very highly charged idea could only have been achieved on that site, and I think that this project shows a bond between the architect, the client and the land.
>
> *(Duncan, in Fraser, 2004: 314)*

But Dewar, as already noted, did not want the parliament to be a 'great monument to power'; he liked the idea of 'people sitting together', which, he thought, 'summed up the new way of consensual, accessible politics that the panel had been hoping to achieve' (Bain, 2005: 50). Miralles understood this vision: 'our proposal is that Scotland is a land, not a series of cities. It demands a construction that is not monumental in the classical sense' (quoted in McCrone, 2005: 6); so, what Miralles produced was 'Aggregated space... a space made of juxtaposed pieces without a preferred point of view' (Bourdieu, 1988: 562). He makes use of history and symbolism to open the future by leaving 'space for imagination' (Tagliabue, 2009: n.p.).

In the 1890s and 1990s, artistic avant-garde thinking in fields of architectural production was infused with a philosophical preoccupation with time. This is evident in, for example, the work of Bergson, mediated in Scotland through the work of Patrick Geddes (see Eadie, 1990), and Proust; and, in the later period, Blanchot and Bergson, as mediated by Deleuze. For Bergson, it is the present that (re)constructs the past ('the retrospective illusion'; see Bourdieu, 1988). So, for Mackintosh, seeking to escape historicism, the vernacular was something authentically Scottish that could be recuperated from the past. Mackintosh could also draw on the resurgence of interest in Celtic mysticism and symbolism, in which the meaning behind the form is suggested, not stated.[14] Both Mackintosh and Miralles could ask, in effect, what from the past speaks to the present, and what in the present speaks to the future? But, for Miralles, the second question is undecidable, and that is why Miralles is wary of the monumental in terms of place:

> it seems who speaks last is right. It appears that the latest building is the only that can be spoken of. For this reason it's difficult to make a leap forward in time and act as sensors of the future.
>
> *(Miralles and Tagliabue, 1999: n.p.)*

That is, Miralles did not want to design a monument that closes the past. He wanted to keep the future open, throughout the design process and in the process of construction. He wanted to leave the project open to contingency, to grow organically; there is no finality of meaning: 'a project is made of unconnected instants' (Miralles and Tagliabue, 1999: n.p.). The building, democracy, the nation are changing in ways we cannot predict, but may be able to detect:

> At times only the person who's capable of consistently starting and making the same movement seems to advance. This small vibration may say something about the future.
>
> *(Miralles and Tagliabue, 1999: n.p.)*

So, what Miralles offered Scotland was, we argue, a reinterpretation of the principles and ideas of Mackintosh, who had in turn reinterpreted the vernacular – not, however, reproducing the past, but synthesizing something 'new': providing a 'sensor of the future'.

Space, time and movement were entangled: the parliament is intended to be lived in, to be a working parliament, open to the people. It is designed for the walker: to be open, to be walked through, to be experienced physically and deciphered visually. For Miralles, 'Although the design is one of fluidity with shapes that direct the viewer through the architecture, the actual feeling of movement that pervades it can only be truly experienced as one moves within the space itself' (in Quiros, MaKenzie and McMurray, 2011: n.p.).

For Mackintosh (according to Eadie, 1990), nature and geometry are given articulation through the human imagination. This is what gives a building a 'practical necessity'. The parliament itself would be an *agora* or place of assembly, situated in a sort of natural amphitheatre, an extension of the land that sweeps down from Arthur's Seat, a social space in which people (*demos*) could gather together to discuss and decide, not a high place from which the powerful could look down on the people and decide for them.

However, although Miralles, based on historical homology and historical affinity, mobilized Mackintosh as a symbolic resource to construct a vision of a nation and a new politics, this vision of the political soon came into conflict with the politics of 'dissensus' – in particular over national independence – that emerged in/from the newly formed Scottish political field – a topic that will be dealt with elsewhere.

Conclusion

At the outset, we posed the following questions: How did a new national parliament come to be organized and designed in Edinburgh in the context of late 20th-century Scotland? What historical and symbolic resources were drawn on by the designers of the parliament? Why was a specific historical precedent used as a resource by the contemporary architect and his partners? In answering these questions, this chapter demonstrates the role of fields, and in particular fields of cultural production, in the ongoing process of national identity formation. In keeping with the overarching theme of this book, we have contributed to historical organization studies in the following ways. We introduced the concept of historical homology to demonstrate the importance of Scottish architecture in evoking nationhood in the new parliament's design.

We showed how, based on an affinity of position, disposition and ethos, the parliament's architects, Miralles and Tagliabue, translated the historical tradition of Mackintosh and Macdonald into a contemporary, European context. That is, we identified an affinity of habitus and an affinity of position and disposition that link the past (Mackintosh) with the present (Miralles).

We also introduced the concept of historical affinity to capture the relations between the two architects and other key players which allowed this to happen. In so doing, we contributed to historical organizational studies of space by adding the dimension of time to Bourdieu's physical, social and symbolic space, showing how the past is used by architects and politicians in the organization of a national democratic space, and how that space might speak to the future.

Notes

1. This was a 'dual referendum' which asked (1) whether a parliament should be set up (Yes, 75%), and (2) whether it should have power to raise taxes (Yes, 65%; Ascherson, 2014).
2. Based on the July 1997 White Paper section: A home fit for the Scottish parliament (Fraser, 2004: 2.9 2.10).
3. RMJM (international) designed the Glasgow Royal Concert Hall, Edinburgh Airport, Falkirk Wheel, Scottish Office Leith, Stirling and York campuses.
4. www.webarchive.org.uk/wayback/archive/20150401033631/http://www.holyroodinquiry.org/transcripts_documents.htm
5. www.mackintosh-architecture.gla.ac.uk/
6. www.mackintosh-architecture.gla.ac.uk/catalogue/name/?nid=MuthHer
7. For example, Lewis Grassick Gibbon's *A Scots Quair* and more, recently, *And the land lay still*, by James Robertson.
8. 'Sits' in the sense of 'meets'; in the original Spanish: *el Parliamento se reune en la Terra*.
9. www.mackintosh-architecture.gla.ac.uk/catalogue/browse/display/?rs=133&xml=des
10. See Ascherson's first-hand account of the 1997 dual-referendum campaign and the key role of cultural producers in this, including author William McIlvannie and traditional musicians and singers (2014).
11. www.parliament.scot/parliamentarybusiness/CurrentCommittees/109732.aspx
12. http://kvadratinterwoven.com/fan-club-series-enric-miralles
13. Kitsch emblems of Scotland – tartan, whisky, bagpipes, kilts – are absent except in the gift shop.
14. Lethaby (1892) was influential.

References

Ascherson, N. (2014). *Stone voices: The search for Scotland*. London: Granta Books.
Auditor General for Scotland (AGS). (2000). *Report: The new Scottish Parliament building*. Edinburgh: The Auditor General.
Bain, S. (2005). *Holyrood: The inside story*. Edinburgh: Edinburgh University Press.
Balfour, A. (2005). *Creating a Scottish parliament*. Edinburgh: Finlay Brown.
Bourdieu, P. (1984). *Questions de sociologie*. Paris: Editions de minuit.
Bourdieu, P. (1985). The social space and the genesis of groups. *Theory and Society*, 14 (6): 723–744.

Bourdieu, P. (1988). Flaubert's point of view. *Critical Inquiry*, 14 (3): 539–562.
Bourdieu, P. (1993a). *The field of cultural production*. Cambridge: Polity.
Bourdieu, P. (1993b). *La misère du monde*. Paris: Editions du Seuil.
Bourdieu, P. (1996). *The rules of art: Genesis and structure of the literary field*. Stanford: Stanford University Press.
Bourdieu, P. (2014). *On the state: Lectures at the Collège de France, 1989–1992*. Cambridge: Polity.
Bourdieu, P. and Wacquant, L.J. (1992). *An invitation to reflexive sociology*. Chicago: University of Chicago Press.
British Broadcasting Corporation (BBC). (2005). *The Holyrood files*, directed by Stuart Greig; available on DVD from BBC Scotland.
Brubaker, R. (1996). *Nationalism reframed*. Cambridge: Cambridge University Press.
Calhoun, C. (1993). Nationalism and ethnicity. *Annual Review of Sociology*, 19 (1): 211–239.
Calhoun, C. (2003). Why historical sociology? In Delanty, G. and Isin, E.F. (eds), *Handbook of historical sociology*. London: Sage, 383–394.
Casanova, P. (2004). *The world republic of letters*. Cambridge, MA: Harvard University Press.
Charle, C. (2013). Comparative and transnational history and the sociology of Pierre Bourdieu. In Gorski, P. (ed.), *Bourdieu and historical analysis*. Durham, NC: Duke University Press, 67–88.
Craig, C. (2018). *The Wealth of the Nation: Scotland, Culture and Independence*. Edinburgh: Edinburgh University Press.
Crawford, A. (2018[1995]). *Charles Rennie Mackintosh*. London: Thames & Hudson.
Divisare (2010). Miralles Tagiabue: The Scottish Parliament. https://divisare.com/projects/134155-miralles-tagliabue-embt-the-scottish-parliament
Dovey, K. (2014). *Framing places: Mediating power in built form*. London: Routledge.
Dunlop, Alan (2019). Evidence to the Scottish Parliament. www.parliament.scot/parliamentarybusiness/CurrentCommittees/109732.aspx
Eadie, W.P. (1990). *Movements of modernity: The case of Glasgow and Art Nouveau*. London: Routledge.
Enric Miralles Benedetta Tagliabue (EMBT). (1998). Scottish Parliament building proposed team. Pdf available at Scottish Parliament at www.parliament.scot>VisitorInformation>4.Enric_Miralles_Moya.pdf
Eyal, G. (2005). The making and breaking of the Czechoslovak political field. In Wacquant, L. (ed.), *Pierre Bourdieu and democratic politics*. Cambridge: Polity, 151–177.
Faulconbridge, J.R. (2009). The regulation of design in global architecture firms: Embedding and emplacing buildings. *Urban Studies*, 46 (12): 2537–2554.
Fowler, B. (1997). *Pierre Bourdieu and cultural theory: Critical investigations*. London: Sage.
Fraser (of Carmyllie), Lord. (2004). *The Holyrood inquiry*. Edinburgh: Scottish Parliament Corporate Body.
Giedion, S. (1970). *Space, time and architecture*. Cambridge, MA: Harvard University Press.
Glancey (2003). Homage to Catalonia. *The Guardian*. www.theguardian.com/artanddesign/2003/aug/11/architecture.regeneration
Glendinning, M. and MacKechnie, A. (2004). *Scottish architecture*. London: Thames & Hudson.
Gorski, P.S. (2013). Nation-ization struggles: A Bourdieusian theory of nationalism. In Gorski, P.S. (ed.). *Bourdieu and historical analysis*. Durham, NC: Duke University Press, 242–265.
Grigor, M. (2001). Ye of little faith. *Scotsman*. www.scotsman.com/business-2-15069/ye-of-little-faith-1-528599
Harvey, C., Press, J. and Maclean, M. (2011). William Morris, cultural leadership, and the dynamics of taste. *Business History Review*, 85 (2): 245–271.

Jencks, C. (2005). *The Scottish Parliament*. London: Scala.
Jones, P. (2011). *The sociology of architecture: Constructing identities*. Liverpool: Liverpool University Press.
Kerr, R. and Robinson, S. (2016). Architecture, symbolic capital and elite mobilisations: The case of the Royal Bank of Scotland corporate campus. *Organization*, 23 (5): 699–721.
Kerr, R., Robinson, S.K. and Elliott, C. (2016). Modernism, postmodernism, and corporate power: Historicizing the architectural typology of the corporate campus. *Management and Organizational History*, 11 (2): 123–146.
Kieser, A. (1994). Why organization theory needs historical analyses – And how this should be performed. *Organization Science*, 5 (4): 123–146.
Lethaby, W.R. (1892). *Architecture, mysticism and myth*. London: Macmillan.
Linklater, A. (1998). A glimpse inside the eye of Miralles. *The Herald*, October 5.
Lipstadt, H. (2003). Can 'art professions' be Bourdieuean fields of cultural production? The case of the architecture competition. *Cultural Studies*, 17 (3–4): 390–419.
Maclean, M., Harvey, C. and Clegg, S.R. (2017). Organization theory in business and management history: Present status and future prospects. *Business History Review*, 91 (3): 457–481.
Macwhirter, I. (1990). *After Doomsday*. Edinburgh: Unit for the Study of Government in Scotland, University of Edinburgh.
McAlpine, J. (1999). Nice Wark. *Sunday Times*, February 7.
McCrone, D. (2005). Cultural capital in an understated nation: The case of Scotland. *British Journal of Sociology*, 56 (1): 65–82.
Miralles, E. (1997). Mélanges. *Architecture d'aujourd'hui*, 312: 68–81.
Miralles, E. and Tagliabue, B. (1999). *Time architecture*. Barcelona: Editorial Gustavo Gili.
Morgan, E. (2004). *Open the doors!*www.scottishpoetrylibrary.org.uk/poetry/poems/opening-scottish-parliament-9-october-2004
Muthesius, H. (1902). Die Glasgower Kunstbewegung: Charles R. Mackintosh und Margaret Macdonald-Mackintosh. *Dekorative Kunst*: 193–221.
Pevsner, N. (1936). *Pioneers of the modern movement from William Morris to Walter Gropius*. London: Faber & Faber.
Pevsner, N. (1969). The sources of modern architecture and design. *Journal of Aesthetics and Art Criticism*, 28 (2): 259–260.
Preuss, S. (2012). *A Scottish national canon? Processes of literary canon formation in Scotland*. Heidelberg: Winter Verlag.
Quiros, L.D., MaKenzie, S. and McMurray, D. (2011) Enric Miralles: Architecture of time. www.quirpa.com/docs/architecture_of_time__enric_miralles.html
Samuel, R. (1998). *Island stories: Unravelling Britain* (Vol. 2). London: Verso.
Sapiro, G. (2013). Structural history and crisis analysis. In Gorski, P.S. (ed.), *Bourdieu and historical analysis*. Durham, NC: Duke University Press, 266–285.
Scottish Parliament Corporate Body. (1999). *Scottish Parliament: Research briefings: RN 99–11*. Edinburgh: Queen's Printer for Scotland.
Siebert, S., Wilson, F. and Hamilton, J. R. (2017). 'Devils may sit here': The role of enchantment in institutional maintenance. *Academy of Management Journal*, 60 (4): 1607–1632.
Sudjic, D. and Jones, H. (2001). *Architecture and democracy*. London: Lawrence King.
Tagliabue, B. (2009). Mackintosh and Miralles. www.gsa.ac.uk/life/gsa-events/events/b/benedetta-tagliabue/

11

INSTITUTIONAL CHANGE AS HISTORICAL CONFLUENCE

The development of the nursing profession in Japan

Ken Sakai

Introduction

This chapter identifies the connections between institutional work and institutional outcomes (Lawrence, Leca, and Zilber, 2013 ; Lawrence and Buchanan, 2017) through a historical organizational study of institutional change in Japanese nursing. Following DiMaggio's classic study (1988), explanations of endogenous institutional change have largely depended on the concept of institutional entrepreneurship (Fligstein, 1997), which refers to "the activities of actors who have an interest in particular institutional arrangements and who leverage resources to create new institutions or to transform existing ones" (Maguire, Hardy and Lawrence, 2004: 657). However, scholars have recently begun turning to the concept of institutional work, which can be defined as "the purposive action of individuals and organizations aimed at creating, maintaining, and disrupting institutions" (Lawrence and Suddaby, 2006: 215). Moreover, because institutional work typically focuses on the day-to-day activities of nameless actors rather than the overt success of prominent actors, it can "contribute to a move away from a concentrated, heroic, and successful conception of institutional agency" (Lawrence, Suddaby and Leca, 2009: 11)—that is, institutional entrepreneurship (Suddaby, 2010; Willmott, 2011).

Despite such expectations, studies of institutional work often fall into a voluntarist analysis of institutional change. In other words, institutional work analyses tend to follow a pattern: collective actors work together in a particular way to make systemic modifications incrementally that ultimately lead to significant institutional change. However, such linear connections between institutional work and institutional outcomes are reductive and seldom reflect the actual dynamics of institutional change (Lawrence et al., 2013). A key issue in such voluntarist analyses is that scholars tend to focus on powerful actors engaged in institutional work (Lawrence et al., 2013). Certainly, focusing on the intended strategies and actions of such actors simplifies the understanding of endogenous institutional change. In order to preclude such assumptions, this chapter investigates institutional change among Japanese nurses in the nineteenth and twentieth centuries who typically were "powerless, disenfranchised, and under-resourced" (Martí and Mair, 2009: 101). This state of affairs was generally accepted until the 1990s and 2000s, when nursing became a relatively powerful profession in the Japanese healthcare field.

In this chapter, I suggest that institutional change was not accomplished through the institutional work of nurses alone, but resulted from the confluence of multiple histories, including nurses' institutional work and the actions of adjacent actors such as doctors, policymakers, and medical equipment manufacturers. While emphasizing the role of the actors typically selected as protagonists of institutional change by scholars, this argument draws attention to the agency of other actors in the field. Although such actors should not be treated as muscular heroes beyond the influence of social regulations, their agency needs to be recognized. Whereas Lawrence et al. (2013) argue that retrospective accounts embedded in interviews and archival data have played a primary role in the linear connection between institutional work and institutional outcomes, this chapter suggests that historical organization studies can avoid such a simplified connection, even when utilizing interviews and archival data, by emphasizing the complexity of historical reality.

This chapter comprises four further sections. Through an overview of the treatment of agency in institutional theory, the next section establishes the importance of the concept of institutional work and identifies the research gap addressed in this chapter: namely, the direct connection between institutional work and institutional outcomes. The third section discusses the methodology and sources used in this chapter. The fourth section analyzes the connection between institutional work and institutional outcomes through a historical case study of Japanese nurses. The final section discusses the theoretical contributions of this chapter, as well as the challenges that need to be addressed in future studies.

Institutional work and agency

Neo-institutional theory has become a prevailing perspective in macro organization theory, revealing the propensity of modern organizational actors to follow socially legitimized orders in the organizational field, as well as the emergence of institutional isomorphism (DiMaggio and Powell, 1983). According to this logic, researchers have tended to depict organizations as puppets adopting structures and practices with little reflection. Consequently, the power relations embedded in such structures and practices are largely overlooked (Munir, 2015). The power upon which such analyses focus is systemic power, which "works through routine, ongoing practices to advantage particular groups without those groups necessarily establishing or maintaining those practices" (Lawrence, 2008: 174; see also Clegg, 1989; Lawrence and Buchanan, 2017; Lawrence, Winn and Jennings, 2001).

However, as institutional theorists shifted from a focus on isomorphism to institutional change, so institutional agency and episodic power were introduced into the literature on institutions. Episodic power refers to "relatively discrete, strategic acts of mobilization initiated by self-interested actors" (Lawrence et al., 2001: 629; see also Clegg, 1989; Lawrence and Buchanan, 2017). This shift saw a plethora of studies on the struggles of institutional entrepreneurs in changing institutional orders (DiMaggio, 1988; Garud, Jain and Kumaraswamy, 2002; Munir and Phillips, 2005). However, recently, such work has been criticized for treating a few actors as "hypermuscular supermen" (Suddaby, 2010: 15) with special social skills (Fligstein, 1997). In other words, explanations of institutional change as relying on institutional entrepreneurs have tended to fall into "voluntarism" (Willmott, 2011: 71).

In contrast, the concept of institutional work enables researchers to place greater focus on the day-to-day struggles of ordinary organizations or individuals rather than institutional entrepreneurs. Nevertheless, it has often been assumed that prominent and powerful actors—such as top executives or leaders—mainly engage in institutional work (Lawrence et al., 2013). For instance, Rojas (2010) shows how the institutional work of a college president provided them with the power necessary to restructure the organization and challenge the norms governing student conduct. Meanwhile, Kraatz (2009) emphasizes the role of an organizational leader in institutional work by linking Selznick's concept of institutional leadership with that of institutional work. Through a historical case study of South African mining employers, Hamann and Bertels (2018) reveal how employers use institutional work to enhance and maintain their advantageous position in an unequal social system.

Professionals are also commonly identified as engaging in institutional work (Lawrence et al., 2013). In fact, professions themselves are institutions (Muzio, Brock and Suddaby, 2013), and professionals have been observed to be "the most influential, contemporary crafters of institutions" (Scott, 2008: 223). Professionals can exert a profound change in the field because they hold dominant positions within the field of power (Maclean, Harvey and Chia, 2010). Indeed, referring to DiMaggio and Powell's (1983) classic argument, Suddaby and Viale (2011: 426) contend that, "the key mechanism through which professionals exert profound social change is by means of the prominent and powerful position that professionals often occupy within organizations and within organizational fields". Numerous studies on the way in which professionals engaged in institutional change have explicitly or implicitly assumed this premise (e.g. Greenwood, Suddaby and Hinings, 2002; Rao, Monin and Durand, 2003; Reay, Goodrick, Waldorff and Casebeer, 2017; Suddaby and Greenwood, 2005). Even studies of seemingly less powerful or subordinate professionals, such as nurses, have assumed that their actors can take strategic, purposeful, and continuous action (e.g. Reay, Golden-Biddle and Germann, 2006), not to mention elites such as doctors (e.g. Currie, Lockett, Finn, Martin and Waring, 2012; Reay et al., 2017).

As Willmott (2011) argues, institutional work should have been identified as an adequate path between extreme structural determinism (i.e., isomorphism in early neo-institutional theory) and voluntarism (i.e., institutional entrepreneurs). However, as indicated above, with the exception of a few historical studies—such as

Martí and Fernández (2013), who examined the institutional work in Holocaust resistance—the institutional work literature "tends to focus primarily on the actions of *powerful actors* in organizational fields with strong strategic intentions aimed at shaping existing institutions" (Lawrence and Buchanan, 2017: 499; italics added). As a result, extant studies tend to presume direct, linear connections between institutional work and institutional outcomes (Lawrence et al., 2013). Consequently, focusing on the variations of institutional work, these scholars have fallen into the trap of voluntarist analysis—in the manner typical of institutional entrepreneurship. Meanwhile, indirect and complex causalities producing institutional outcomes, including the unintended consequences of actors' actions, have been relatively overlooked (Lawrence and Buchanan, 2017). Scholars have generally assumed that institutional work is completed within a relatively short time. However, we intuitively know that real institutional dynamics are more complex, occurring over longer periods of time (Currie et al., 2012) and through interrelated influences, including the unintended consequences of other actors and impact of sociocultural change. Accordingly, this chapter seeks to identify and elucidate the connections between institutional work and institutional outcomes from this perspective.

Methodology and data analysis

In this chapter, I conduct a qualitative historical organizational study of institutional change in Japanese nursing, from its emergence in the 1880s to the present. Historical organization studies involve "organizational research that draws extensively on historical data, methods and knowledge, embedding organizing and organizations in their sociohistorical context to generate historically informed theoretical narratives attentive to both disciplines" (Maclean, Harvey and Clegg, 2016: 609). This case study was selected because of the recent rise in power and status of Japanese nursing professionals: where they were once "powerless, disenfranchised, and under-resourced" actors (Martí and Mair, 2009: 101), Japanese nurses have come to enjoy a relatively powerful position in the field of Japanese healthcare. This historical case makes it easier to identify historical factors other than the agentic work of Japanese nurses, thereby offering an opportunity for theoretical insight (Eisenhardt and Graebner, 2007) while avoiding the voluntarist explanation of institutional work.

Although Lawrence et al. (2013) warn that the retrospective nature of interviews and archival data can result in the presumption of a linear connection between institutional work and institutional outcomes, historical study can avoid such simplified causal explanations. One of the clear strengths of historical organization studies is longitudinal analysis of the complexities of organizational reality. Many scholars have acknowledged the importance of the historic turn in organizational studies (Clark and Rowlinson, 2004; Kieser, 1994; Maclean, Harvey and Clegg, 2017; Suddaby, Foster and Mills, 2014; Wadhwani and Bucheli, 2014; Hamann and Bertels, 2018). The linear connection between institutional work and institutional outcome is largely attributable to the assumed agency of historical actors rather than the type of data or way in which data are collected. The tendency of scholars to select and focus on a certain protagonist and their engagement in institutional work results in their underestimating the agency of other historical actors, thereby producing a linear connection between institutional work and institutional outcome. Recognizing the agency of related historical actors in analysis[1] introduces interesting and real historical complexity.

This chapter uses source criticism, triangulation, and hermeneutic interpretation (Kipping, Wadhwani and Bucheli, 2014) to reconstruct the history of Japanese nurses from the 1880s to the present. In addition to secondary sources, this chapter uses archival sources on nursing in Japan, government documents, and statistics. Archival sources were arranged chronologically, and the validity of each source was ensured by crosschecking sources. These sources are complemented by data on adjacent actors in the healthcare field, including doctors (some of whom also serve as executives in Japanese hospitals), policymakers, and medical equipment manufacturers. The chapter also considers the sociocultural shifts that influenced the healthcare field to contextualize the history of nursing in Japan (Hamann and Bertels, 2018).

I draw additionally on the transcripts of 21 oral history interviews conducted with 19 individuals between January 2016 and March 2020. In order to avoid hagiography, interviewees comprise practicing or former nurses as well as other medical professionals and related personnel: namely, eight nurses, two doctors, four medical office workers, an occupational therapist, a researcher focusing on Japanese nursing history, two former top executives from a surgical instrument manufacturer, and a former top executive of a medical equipment wholesaler. All relevant information from the 34 hours of recordings was transcribed verbatim. Rather than coding the interviews through software, I analyzed the interviews as complete narratives in order better to understand relationships between field and social contexts and reported events, actions, and developments (Currie, Finn and Martin, 2008). To assure validity, the interviews were compared with one another and read against secondary sources. Some unreliable sources were subsequently removed. All sources were reinterpreted and rearranged to create a consistent history of nursing in Japan.

Institutional change in Japanese nursing

In the late nineteenth century, assisting doctors constituted nurses' main task. This included managing their medical equipment and even performing housekeeping duties such as washing clothes and making tea (Kameyama, 1984; Tanaka, 2001). This continued after the Second World War (1939–1945), with nursing only gaining recognition as a bona fide profession during the 1990s. For instance, in 1990, a surgeon noted that Japanese surgeons and ordinary people regarded nurses as professionals on an almost equal footing with surgeons (Miyazaki, 1990). Moreover, three medical clerks interviewed in 2019 evaluated nursing as an important and powerful profession in the healthcare field (A.K., personal communication, August 14, 2019; S.S., personal communication, August 27, 2019; Y.S., personal communication, September 15, 2019). This section examines how this came about in greater detail.

The emergence of nurses and postwar reform

The nursing profession first emerged in Japan during the Meiji era (1868–1912; Ryder-Shimazaki, Koyama and Tanaka, 2018), when the Japanese government established a modern educational system for the learning of Western and particularly German-based medical practices (Hayashi, 1974). During this period, nurses had a lower social position and served as "handmaidens" to doctors (Currie et al., 2008: 543). Indeed, although a modern nursing school based on the ideas of Florence Nightingale was established in Tokyo in 1885, nursing education failed to gain traction in Japan. As a result of war and the spread of infectious diseases, the number of hospitals needed to be increased, and doctors needed many "handmaidens". Most nurses were poor, migrant girls from rural areas. That migrant girls depended on the decisions of their parents meant that they could not withdraw from the hospitals easily (Ryder-Shimazaki et al., 2018; Tanaka, 2001). Nurses were subordinate to doctors—their low social status compounded by traditional gender inequality in Japan (Kameyama, 1984; Kawashima, 1977; Tanaka, 2001). However, few questioned this state of affairs. For instance, in 1988, a retired Japanese nurse testified regarding her experiences working for a male physician in 1924: despite working long hours with insufficient rest and a belligerent boss, the nurses reportedly enjoyed their work (Takasu, 1988).

This situation changed with the outbreak of the Second World War. Although there were 4,858 hospitals and 199,831 beds in Japan in 1941, there were only 645 hospitals and 31,766 beds by 1945—the majority having been destroyed by fire. Doctors, nurses, medical equipment, and medicine were insufficient (Fukunaga, 2014). After the war, Crawford F. Sams (1902–1994), Colonel of the US Medical Corps and Chief of the Public Health and Welfare Section of General Headquarters (hereinafter, General Headquarters),[2] began reforming the Japanese medical system, modeling it after that of the US. Grace Elizabeth Alt (1905–1978) promoted these reforms in the nursing sector. Their first observation was that Japanese hospitals were unsanitary and lacked basic equipment and materials. These conditions were exacerbated by low levels of medical care and medical education. Moreover, because the nurses were busy helping doctors, patient care usually fell to family members (Fukunaga, 2014; Kawashima, 2014; Saiseikai Utsunomiya Hospital, 1957).

General Headquarters implemented several radical reforms (Ryder-Shimazaki et al., 2018; Shimazaki, 2011). The Japan Midwife, Nurse, and Public Health Nurse Association was established in 1946, changing its name to the Japanese Nursing Association in 1951. This was followed by the passing of the Act on Public Health Nurses, Midwives, and Nurses in 1948. Indispensable to addressing the rapid increase in demand for medical services in Japan, this Act formally recognized both registered and secondary nurses. Using secondary nurses—or *Otsu-Shu* in Japanese—who had a more basic level of nursing, enabled a more rapid buildup in nursing numbers (Tanaka, 2001). Accordingly, this chapter uses the term "registered nurses" to refer to nurses who had more thorough training; although subordinate to doctors, registered nurses had a higher status within the nursing field. Some registered nurses complained about this categorization, fearing that it would negatively impact nurses' social status. Nevertheless, the Act constitutes a watershed moment in Japanese nursing as it defined nurses as "a person under licensure from the Minister of Health and Welfare to provide medical treatment or assist in medical care for injured and ill persons or puerperal women, as a profession" (Japanese Law Translation, 2012). This definition confirms that nurses should not only assist doctors but also provide nursing care to patients. Thus, by fulfilling a unique function, nurses were no longer regarded as subordinate attendants of doctors—at least on paper. Moreover, in 1948, the Ministry of Health and Welfare founded a Nursing Division under the directorship of Seki Hora (1893–1980), a Japanese woman certified as a registered nurse in the US (Hokenshi Josanshi Kangoshi Ho 60 Nenshi Hensan Iinkai, 2009; Kusakari, Tamura and Yano, 2014).

Such reforms also signified the import of professional nursing identities from the US after the Second World War. However, conventional nursing identities and practices remained dominant, hindering the introduction of new practices and perspectives. Consequently, Japanese nurses continued serving as doctors' handmaidens or, at best, assistants (e.g. Kawashima, 1977). Aside from gender norms, two major factors suppressed the power of nurses in Japan: the immaturity of nursing education and the creation of the "assistant nurse" as a professional category.

First, Japan lacked a mature educational system for the training of nurses. Indeed, despite postwar reforms, General Headquarters, the Ministry of Health and Welfare, and prominent hospitals struggled to provide systematic nursing education. Nineteen schools for the training of registered nurses were certified in 1947, with the general curriculum enhanced in 1951. Additionally, some junior colleges and universities established nursing departments in the 1950s. However, most nursing schools were managed by large hospitals. As a result, curricula differed from one hospital to another, with content and practical training tailored to the specific requirements of the training hospital (Ujiie and Fukumoto, 2014). Thus, as their knowledge and expertise varied, nurses' claim to full professional standing was weakened, and their standing was slow to improve. In contrast, the medical educational system for the training of doctors was systematic, standardized, and based on US practices (Hayashi, 1974).

Second, the reconsideration of the Act on Public Health Nurses, Midwives, and Nurses in 1951 resulted in the creation of the "assistant nurse" as a professional category.[3] Registered nurses hoped for the abolition of the professional category of "secondary nurse" in order to raise the status of nursing. However, Japan urgently needed low-cost medical assistants owing to the increasing demand for medical services. Accordingly, the Japan Medical Association—the largest professional organization of doctors—requested that General Headquarters establish "assistant nurse" as a professional category. The category of "secondary nurse" was subsequently replaced by "assistant nurse" in 1951. Whereas becoming a registered nurse required at least 3 years of education after graduating from high school, assistant nurses required only 2 years of education after completing junior high school. As such, the category of assistant nursing met the needs of young girls who wanted to become "nurses" but did not have the financial or educational means to do so, as well as doctors' demands for low-cost assistants. Although the wage level of assistant nurses was lower than that of registered nurses, their scope of work and workload were almost the same as those of registered nurses (Hayashi, 2018; Kawashima, 2014; Tanaka, 2001; Ujiie and Fukumoto, 2014). Therefore, the category of assistant nurse hindered the professionalization of nurses, as well as attempts to improve their status (Kawashima, 1977).

Meanwhile, bolstered by the serious shortage of nurses, the dissatisfaction of nurses with their inferior work environment gradually emerged during the 1950s. As the demand for hospitals and beds increased rapidly after the Second World War, the government and General Headquarters sought to address the matter of inadequate care for inpatients provided by unlicensed attendants or family members. Accordingly, the Medical Care Act of 1948 stipulated that the distribution standard of nurses should follow a ratio of one nurse for every four inpatients. This was followed by the introduction of an incentive scheme designed to improve nursing services in 1950. Under this scheme, hospitals could receive additional medical funds from the government for following nursing rules, including the distribution standard (Tsunoda, 1997). However, the requirement for official nursing certification hindered some from entering the profession, resulting in Japanese hospitals suffering from chronic nursing shortages in the 1950s. As such, Japanese nursing was characterized by high workloads, poor working environments, and relatively low wages. For instance, in the 1950s, general nurses were required to live in hospital dormitories; if they wished to marry, they had to give up their careers. Nurses were also required to work more than ten night shifts a month, often alone (Sugaya, 1965). Whereas traditional feminine virtues of humility and modesty prevented nurses from demanding better working conditions and wages before the Second World War, this changed with emerging awareness of labor rights in the 1950s (Tanaka, 2014).

A significant number of nurses joined Japan's growing labor movement in the 1960s. The largescale labor movement initiated by the nurses of a hospital in the Niigata prefecture in 1968 spread across Japan. Despite the scope of such movements, hospital executives—primarily male doctors—resisted change and sustained the unequal power dynamics between nurses and doctors. Nevertheless, such movements gradually enhanced the confidence of nurses, who began to openly express their opinions regarding the need to improve working conditions. In doing so, many nurses began questioning conventional attitudes toward the behavior of nurses—that is, the widespread belief that, as humble Japanese women, nurses should refrain from voicing their opinions, especially regarding working conditions (Hashioka, 1998; Tanaka, 2014).

The unintended consequences of technological innovations

Technological innovations in the 1960s and 1970s also influenced the state of nursing in Japan. Technological innovations can be roughly divided into two categories: low-maintenance medical instruments and medical engineering equipment. First, as nurses primarily served as assistants to doctors, particularly in the management of medical tools—including sterilization and maintenance—the invention of low-maintenance medical instruments such as disposable syringes and stainless-steel surgical needles impacted nurses' workloads and practices (Miyahara, 2016). Disposable syringes were first introduced to Japan in 1963 by Terumo, a Japanese medical instrument manufacturer. Japanese aversion to waste hampered the spread of disposable syringes, but manufacturers emphasized patient safety, and this resulted in large hospitals adopting the technology in the early 1970s (Terumo, n.d.). As noted, the development of stainless-steel surgical needles also impacted nursing. Even in the 1950s, surgical needles around the world were made of iron treated with surface plating. Given the tendency of such materials to rust, nurses encountered difficulties in maintaining and preparing surgical needles. They had to select an appropriate rust-free needle based on the surgery type, remove the rust-preventing oil from the needle, and disinfect the tool before the surgery. After surgery, the nurses had to sterilize and reapply oil to prevent the needles from rusting. The time and energy required by this process was taken for granted by hospitals. This changed in 1961, when MANI, a Japanese medical manufacturing company, developed a series of stainless-steel surgical needles (Sakai, 2019).[4] In 1967, MANI launched disposable sterilized stainless-steel eyeless needles with sutures; this technology was later improved and relaunched in 1971. Such innovations reduced nurses' workloads, allowing nurses to reflect on their daily operations and amend them in practice (Miyahara, 2016).

Second, technological innovations in medical engineering equipment in the 1960s and 1970s impacted nursing practices, particularly in terms of nurses' responsibilities and the power relations between nurses and doctors. The diffusion of medical equipment in the 1960s and 1970s was particularly apparent in Japan's larger and wealthier hospitals (Kawahara and Suzuki, 2014). For instance, in 1966, 98.3% of hospitals with more than 100 beds had diagnostic X-ray devices, 84.1% had X-ray tomography devices, 24.2% had ultrasonic diagnostic equipment, 58.2% had fundus cameras, 40.7% had electroencephalographs, 96.3% had electrocardiographs, and 29.9% had devices for brain surgery (Yamashita, 2001). An unintended consequence of the rapid diffusion of such medical equipment was a sharp increase in the medical information that needed to be recorded. As doctors were too busy for such tasks, the recording of medical information was entrusted to nurses. Consequently, recording medical information became the primary task of nurses in large hospitals in the 1960s and 1970s. A survey of 330 registered nurses in seven hospitals in Tokyo in 1970 suggests that, although the primary duties of nurses were to "assist in the medical care" provided by doctors, measuring and recording patient symptoms became the core task of such assistance (Amano, 1972). Essentially, innovations in medical equipment changed the meaning of "assist in medical care": nurses gradually became the *partners* of doctors, who had to cooperate with nurses in order to accomplish their daily tasks. As such, power dynamics changed within the organizational field as nurses began to influence doctors' activities far more than they had before (Crozier and Friedberg, 1980).

The expansion of nursing education and social status

Although power relations gradually shifted in large hospitals during the 1970s, many doctors felt that the tasks of nurses should be dictated by doctors (Amano, 1972; Kawashima, 1977). In response to such attitudes, registered nurses in leadership positions began reforming formal rules and institutions through their own political networks. Such nurses generally obtained a Master's degree or doctorate from US or top-ranked Japanese universities and occupied important posts in the Nursing Division of the Ministry of Health and Welfare, as well as the Japan Nursing Association. In 1971, Shigeru Ishimoto was elected as a Diet member and organized the Parliamentary Group for Nursing Problems in 1973. With its membership including 157 Diet members, the group's support resulted in various improvements in the work environment of nurses, including raising the night-shift allowance. This political association has continued improving the social power of nurses in Japan since the 1970s. Leading nurses also compiled a set of rules and statistics in creating an intellectual infrastructure for nursing in Japan. Based on these intellectual achievements, high-ranking nurses revised nursing curricula— including for assistant nurses—and sought to expand the nursing departments of universities during the 1980s (Hokenshi Josanshi Kangoshi Ho 60 Nenshi Hensan Iinkai, 2009).

Although registered nurses had already begun exercising their voices in challenging the status quo, from the mid-1980s, their voices grew strong enough to be heard more widely—facilitating further change in nurses' professional identities and practices. This shift was the unintended consequence of several policies. During the 1970s, top hospital executives (who were also doctors) could increase the number of beds in order to expand their revenue. However, owing to concerns that the autonomous management of each hospital would result in an excessive increase in the number of beds, the Japanese government began limiting such increases. In 1985, the government enacted a law requiring that prefectures prepare medical plans. However, prefectural governments formulated their plans sequentially; for instance, Kanagawa Prefecture completed its plan in 1987, whereas Tokyo did not complete its plan until 1989. With all prefectures only having completed their plans in 1989, the time lag between the year in which the law was enacted and the year when its stipulations were met triggered a last-minute increase in the number of hospital beds (Yoshihara and Wada, 2008). Although the number of nurses also increased, most nurses felt that the disparity between the number of beds and the number of nurses had significantly increased their workload. Indeed, the number of nurses per 100 beds in Japanese hospitals was lower than those of other developed countries. According to the Ministry of Health, Labour and Welfare (2001), the figures in 1988 were 33.6 in Japan, 85.4 in the UK, and 134 in the US.[5] With the surge in beds triggering a backlash from general nurses (Sakai, 2019), the Japan Federation of Medical Workers' Unions started fighting for improvements in nursing conditions, collecting some 76,635 signatures in 1988 (Tanaka, 2014). This movement continued into the early 1990s, particularly after media outlets reported on nurses' poor working conditions. These dynamics undermined traditional notions of nurses as submissive in terms of their professional identities and practices. Japanese nurses began arguing that certain responsibilities were outside their purview and sought to delegate "peripheral duties" to others, such as pharmacists and clinical engineers, and focus on improving their daily operations (Okamoto, 1993).

Several politicians, the Nursing Division of the Ministry of Health and Welfare, and the Japanese Nursing Association also took action to increase the number of nurses and improve the quality of nursing in Japan. Consequently, the Act on Assurance of Work Forces of Nurses and Other Medical Experts was enacted in 1992. Thereafter, the number of universities with nursing departments increased from 12 in 1989 to 63 in 1998. This trend continued in the 2000s, growing from 104 in 2003 to 255 in 2017. The number of nursing graduate schools also increased steadily, with some 165 graduate schools offering Master's degrees in nursing in 2017, and 88 offered doctoral degrees (Ryder-Shimazaki et al., 2018). At the same time, the contents of basic nursing education began to include highly abstract arguments. For instance, the introduction of a basic textbook for nursing details a philosophical approach to nursing (e.g. Ryder-Shimazaki et al., 2018). The establishment of such higher, abstract nursing education improved nurses' awareness of their status as professionals.

These changes are reflected in Japanese academia. As Figure 11.1 shows, the number of academic papers on nursing and the percentage of papers including the term "professional" published in Japan also grew rapidly after the 2000s, indicating that interest in academism and professionalism among nurses increased significantly during this period.

The recognition of nurses' status and power in the 2000s

More recently, the registered nurses in the Ministry of Health, Labor and Welfare[6] and large hospitals have argued for greater autonomy for Japanese nurses, particularly with the emergence of an aging society (Ministry of Health, Labour and Welfare, 2003). These arguments have resonated with powerful politicians, facilitating the further expansion of nursing roles in Japan (Cabinet Office, 2009).

As a result, although the category of assistant nurse has not been abolished owing to the resistance of doctors, changes since the 1990s have expanded the power and

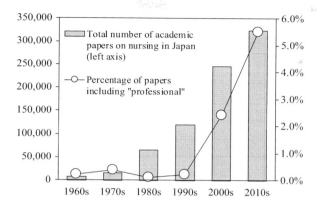

FIGURE 11.1 Changes in academism and professionalism in Japanese nursing, 1960s–2010s

Note: The original search term for "nursing" was "kango", and that for "professional" was "senmonshoku".

Source: Ichushi Web (the bibliographic database provided by the Japan Medical Abstracts Society). Retrieved from https://search.jamas.or.jp/, accessed April 8, 2020.

social status of nurses in Japan. In addition to being able to express their opinions openly, even in front of doctors, nurses have begun exercising their influence in medical services. Indeed, whereas a veteran nurse testified that her work involved providing both nursing care and assistance to doctors during the 2000s, even ordinary nurses have recognized their status as indispensable partners of doctors. For instance, having worked during the 2000s, a former nurse recalled how nurses established their specialties and a fair partnership with doctors:

> Doctors cure patients, but nurses observe them. For example, when patients, both mentally and physically damaged, are anxious about their illness and cannot eat or take a bath, they are not satisfied and do not get better. So, for example, nurses try to make food easy to eat and give patients a comfortable bed bath. Nurses also think of how to warm patients' bodies … The nurses were able to express opinions to the doctors. For example, when a doctor gave a wrong instruction, a nurse said, "Hey, is it all right?" or "Is it all right to omit this from the drip?" So, the nurses were asking the doctor directly. Yes, nurses and doctors were talking equally.
> *(Female former nurse, A.O., personal communication, September 16, 2019; translated from Japanese)*

According to another former nurse who worked in the 2000s, with the exception of assistant nurses, nurses and doctors respected each other (M.O., personal communication, October 25, 2019). These sources indicate that a significant number of nurses were able to enjoy professional status by the 2000s. In fact, for non-professional medical office workers in contemporary Japanese hospitals, nurses seem like dominant and powerful professionals. The three young medical office workers at relatively large hospitals interviewed for this study in 2019 reported that nurses enjoy a very high status as established professionals in their hospitals, as noted by the following excerpts from interviews with two medical office workers at different hospitals:

> I think doctors and nurses come in a set. They work very hard in the same tough situations. They are different from us and are on another level. They are at the top of the hospital. The other medical workers are in the middle. And we are at the bottom of the pyramid.
> *(Female medical office worker Y.S., personal communication, September 15, 2019; translated from Japanese)*

> I guess that nurses are treated favorably in hospitals. Their wage increase rate is higher than that of the other medical workers and ours. Regarding the relationships with the doctors, I don't feel doctors are much stronger than the nurses … Rather, I feel that what the nurses say becomes law in the hospital.
> *(Male medical office worker S.S., personal communication, August 27, 2019; translated from Japanese)*

Their testimonies suggest that Japanese nurses have successfully improved their power and status and have attained a high degree of institutional change.

Discussion and conclusion

This chapter demonstrates the historical complexities between institutional work and institutional outcome, making two contributions to the literature in doing so. The first of these is historical, the second theoretical. In providing a historical overview of the long-term development of Japanese nursing, this study will be of interest to historians interested in healthcare development. The institutionalized subordination of Japanese nurses changed with the professionalization of nursing in Japan. Although this institutional change was realized through the various actions of nurses, including improvement in their daily operations and discursive arguments for expanding their autonomy, sole reliance on the agentic work of nurses—the protagonists—is insufficient to explain these outcomes. Rather, it is necessary to consider institutional change as resulting from the confluence of multiple histories. Furthermore, although this study elucidates just one case, that of Japan, it is possible that many Western countries, including the UK and the US, that have experienced professionalization of nursing (Chua and Clegg, 1989; Apesoa-Varano, 2007) may have historical experiences very similar to those seen in Japan. Therefore, this chapter may also contribute to international comparative studies in the healthcare field.

This chapter's theoretical contribution is rooted in its historical analysis, particularly insofar as it underscores the need for a broader understanding of agency and historical dynamics in examining institutional work. The confluence of histories is a research perspective that acknowledges that any historical phenomenon is not a consequence of the intended and strategic actions of certain actors regarded as central by researchers, but a synthesis of various actions and actors. These actors maintain their agency to greater or lesser degrees, even when impacted by various institutionalized orders. This perspective resonates with the notion that historical events should be considered complex phenomena occurring in open systems (Bhaskar, 1978). However, it is important to note that, for historical organization studies, the critical elements of this open system are the actions of related actors, who have unique interests. The movement of these social elements is relatively unstable compared with natural elements. The careful consideration of such unstable elements results in a more appropriate explanation of institutional dynamics. As demonstrated in this chapter, the institutional work of Japanese nurses was possible through a system constituted through and shaped by the actions of other actors. For instance, a series of reforms by General Headquarters significantly impacted the logic and identity of nursing in postwar Japan. Meanwhile, technological innovations such as disposable syringes and stainless-steel surgical needles reduced the workload of nurses, enabling them to reflect on their daily operations. In this respect, medical equipment innovations unintentionally improved the position of nurses, particularly in terms of the power dynamic between doctors and nurses, as they became responsible for recording medical information. The improvement of the education system also bolstered the nursing profession in Japan. Although educational improvement was largely prompted by nurses' agentic work, the widespread movement for greater recognition and education was triggered by a government policy intended to control the number of beds in hospitals.

This chapter reveals a new means of examining the link between institutional work and institutional outcomes. Tacitly based on voluntarism, conventional explanations of institutional change typically emphasize the struggle of nurses, drawing a linear relationship between their institutional work and the broad institutional outcomes. In contrast, explanations reliant on determinism tend to focus on environmental factors or accidental events, overlooking the role or meaning of institutional work entirely. In underestimating human agency, such a view is inappropriate, particularly insofar as it returns to the static interpretations of early neo-institutional theory, in which power is crystallized into "logics" or "structures", and agency is overlooked (Clegg, 1989; Munir, 2015; Willmott, 2011). Therefore, as demonstrated in this chapter, a consideration of historical confluence suggests a means of avoiding the biases toward both voluntarism and determinism in explaining institutional changes.

Nevertheless, some challenges remain for future research. This chapter focuses on the circumstances in relatively large hospitals in Japan because of the availability of information. However, because, in small clinics, doctors are the employers of the nurses, the power and status of nurses still might not have improved adequately compared with in large hospitals (E.K., personal communication, January 31, 2020; K.T., personal communication, March 11, 2020). Additionally, the impact of the appearance of other medical professionals requires further investigation, as does the influence of nursing development and reform in other countries, particularly the US and Europe. Furthermore, other tributary histories might have flowed into the history of Japanese nursing development. In this way, any historical explanation should always be considered incomplete, and the concept of historical confluence can contribute by reminding us of this point.

Acknowledgments

I would like to acknowledge the helpful comments from colleagues at the Sub-theme 30 (Realizing the Potential of Historical Organization Studies) of EGOS, July 5–7, 2019, Edinburgh University. This work was supported by JSPS KAKENHI (grant number: JP 19K13784).

Notes

1 For examples, see Allison's (1971) third model or Crozier and Friedberg's (1980) political analysis. Whereas these studies focused on the organizational level, this chapter examines the organizational field level. Nonetheless, their perspectives and premises regarding human agency can be applied to the field level without issue.
2 According to the Bernard Becker Medical Library (2011, October 4), Crawford F. Sams was promoted to the rank of Colonel in August 1942 and Brigadier General in 1948.
3 The category of "assistant nurse" in Japan is similar to "licensed practical nurse" and "licensed vocational nurse" in the US and to "state enrolled nurse", which once existed in the UK. However, because the category is formally referred to as "assistant nurse" in Japan (Japanese Law Translation, 2012, October 31), this chapter uses the term "assistant nurse".
4 According to Inoue (1954), a stainless-steel surgical needle for ophthalmology known as a "revised type of Castroviejo" may have existed around 1954. However, the details of these needles are unclear. Numerous sources claim that MANI developed the first stainless-steel surgical needles.
5 These figures vary slightly by source but are consistent in that Japan's figures are lower than those of other developed countries.
6 In 2001, the official name of the Ministry of Health and Welfare was changed to the Ministry of Health, Labour and Welfare.

References

Allison, G.T. (1971). *Essence of decision: Explaining the Cuban missile crisis*. Boston, MA: Little, Brown.
Amano, M. (1972). Kangofu no rodo to ishiki [Professionalization of the nurse: A case study]. *Japanese Sociological Review*, 22 (3): 30–49.
Apesoa-Varano, E.C. (2007). Educated caring: The emergence of professional identity among nurses. *Qualitative Sociology*, 30: 249–274.
Bhaskar, R. (1978). *A realist theory of science*. Hassocks: Harvester Press.
Cabinet Office (2009). Dai 12 kai keizai zaisei shimon kaigi gijiroku [The minutes of the twelfth council on economic and fiscal policy]. www5.cao.go.jp/keizai-shimon/minutes/2009/0519/agenda.html
Chua, W.F. and Clegg, S.R. (1989). Contradictory couplings: Professional ideology in the organizational locales of nurse training. *Journal of Management Studies*, 26 (2): 103–127.

Clark, P. and Rowlinson, M. (2004). The treatment of history in organisation studies: Towards an 'historic turn'? *Business History*, 46 (3): 331–352.
Clegg, S.R. (1989). *Frameworks of power*. London: Sage.
Crozier, M. and Friedberg, E. (1980). *Actors and systems: The politics of collective action*. Chicago, IL: University of Chicago Press.
Currie, G., Finn, R. and Martin, G. (2008). Accounting for the 'dark side' of new organizational forms: The case of healthcare professionals. *Human Relations*, 61 (4): 539–564.
Currie, G., Lockett, A., Finn, R., Martin, G. and Waring, J. (2012). Institutional work to maintain professional power: Recreating the model of medical professionalism. *Organization Studies*, 33 (7): 937–962.
DiMaggio, P.J. (1988). Interest and agency in institutional theory. In Zucker, L.G. (ed.), *Institutional patterns and organizations: Culture and environment*. Cambridge, MA: Ballinger, 3–21.
DiMaggio, P.J. and Powell, W.W. (1983). The iron cage revisited: Institutional isomorphism and collective rationality in organizational fields. *American Sociological Review*, 48 (2): 147–160.
Eisenhardt, K.M. and Graebner, M.E. (2007). Theory building from cases: Opportunities and challenges. *Academy of Management Journal*, 50 (1): 25–32.
Fligstein, N. (1997). Social skill and institutional theory. *American Behavioral Scientist*, 40 (4): 397–405.
Fukunaga, H. (2014). *Nihon byoinshi* [The history of Japanese hospitals]. Tokyo: Pilar Press.
Garud, R., Jain, S. and Kumaraswamy, A. (2002). Institutional entrepreneurship in the sponsorship of common technological standards: The case of Sun Microsystems and Java. *Academy of Management Journal*, 45 (1): 196–214.
Greenwood, R., Suddaby, R. and Hinings, C.R. (2002). Theorizing change: The role of professional associations in the transformation of institutionalized fields. *Academy of Management Journal*, 45 (1): 58–80.
Hamann, R. and Bertels, S. (2018). The institutional work of exploitation: Employers' work to create and perpetuate inequality. *Journal of Management Studies*, 55 (3): 394–423.
Hashioka, T. (1998). Sengo no kango rodo undo ga shimeshita mono [What nurses' labor movements after the Second World War showed]. In Japan Society of Nursing History (ed.), *Kensho: Sengo kango no gojunen* [Verification: Fifty years of nursing after the Second World War]. Tokyo: Medical Friend, 174–194.
Hayashi, C. (2018). Junkangofu(shi) seido o kangaeru [Considering the assistant nurse system]. *The Journal of Japan Society of Nursing History*, 31 (2): 25–34.
Hayashi, S. (1974). *Shujutsu: Sono rekishi to tenkai [Surgery: The history and progress]*. Tokyo: NHK.
Hokenshi Josanshi Kangoshi Ho 60 Nenshi Hensan Iinkai [The compilation committee of the sixty-year history of Act on Public Health Nurses, Midwives, and Nurses]. (2009). *Hokenshi josanshi kangoshi ho 60 nenshi* [Sixty-year history of the Act on Public Health Nurses, Midwives, and Nurses]. Tokyo: Japanese Nursing Association.
Inoue, M. (1954). *Hakunaisho zen tekishutsu shujutsu* [Complete cataract removal]. Tokyo: Igakushoin.
Japanese Law Translation. (2012, October 31). Act on Public Health Nurses, Midwives, and Nurses. www.japaneselawtranslation.go.jp/
Kameyama, M. (1984). *Kindai nihon kangoshi 4: Kangofu to ishi* [History of modern Japanese nursing, volume 4: Nurses and doctors]. Tokyo: Domesu.
Kawahara, Y. and Suzuki, N. (2014). Shippei to tekunoroji no henka to kango [Changes in disease and technology in nursing]. In Japan Society of Nursing History (ed.), *Nihon no kango no ayumi* [The history of Japanese nursing]. Tokyo: Japanese Nursing Association, 111–128.

Kawashima, M. (1977). *Kango no jiritsu* [Independence of nurses]. Tokyo: Keiso Shobo.

Kawashima, M. (2014). Sengo kango no yoake [The dawn of nursing after the Second World War]. In Japan Society of Nursing History (ed.), *Nihon no kango no ayumi* [The history of Japanese nursing]. Tokyo: Japanese Nursing Association, 7–26.

Kieser, A. (1994). Why organization theory needs historical analyses—and how this should be performed. *Organization Science*, 5 (4): 608–620.

Kipping, M., Wadhwani, R.D. and Bucheli, M. (2014). Analyzing and interpreting historical sources: A basic methodology. In Bucheli, M. and Wadhwani, R.D. (eds.), *Organizations in time: History, theory, methods*. Oxford: Oxford University Press, 305–329.

Kraatz, M.S. (2009). Leadership as institutional work: A bridge to the other side. In Lawrence, T.B., Suddaby, R. and Leca, B. (eds.), *Institutional work: Actors and agency in institutional studies of organizations*. Cambridge: Cambridge University Press, 59–91.

Kusakari, J., Tamura, Y. and Yano, M. (2014). Hoken iryo seido to kango [The health and medical system and nursing]. In Japan Society of Nursing History (ed.), *Nihon no kango no ayumi* [The history of Japanese nursing]. Tokyo: Japanese Nursing Association, 43–72.

Lawrence, T.B. (2008). Power, institutions and organizations. In Greenwood, R., Oliver, C., Sahlin, K. and Suddaby, R. (eds.), *The Sage handbook of organizational institutionalism*. London: Sage, 170–197.

Lawrence, T.B. and Buchanan, S. (2017). Power, institutions and organizations. In Greenwood, R., Oliver, C., Lawrence, T.B. and Meyer, R.E. (eds.), *The Sage handbook of organizational institutionalism* (2nd edn). London: Sage, 477–506.

Lawrence, T.B., Leca, B. and Zilber, T.B. (2013). Institutional work: Current research, new directions and overlooked issues. *Organization studies*, 34 (8): 1023–1033.

Lawrence, T.B. and Suddaby, R. (2006). Institutions and institutional work. In Clegg, S.R., Hardy, C., Lawrence, T.B. and Nord, W.R. (eds.), *The Sage handbook of organization studies* (2nd ed.). London: Sage, 215–254.

Lawrence, T.B., Suddaby, R. and Leca, B. (2009). Introduction: Theorizing and studying institutional work. In Lawrence, T.B., Suddaby, R. and Leca, B. (eds.), *Institutional work: Actors and agency in institutional studies of organizations*. Cambridge: Cambridge University Press, 1–27.

Lawrence, T.B., Winn, M.I. and Jennings, P.D. (2001). The temporal dynamics of institutionalization. *Academy of Management Review*, 26 (4): 624–644.

Maclean, M., Harvey, C. and Chia, R. (2010). Dominant corporate agents and the power elite in France and Britain. *Organization Studies*, 31 (3): 327–348.

Maclean, M., Harvey, C. and Clegg, S.R. (2016). Conceptualizing historical organization studies. *Academy of Management Review*, 41 (4): 609–632.

Maclean, M., Harvey, C. and Clegg, S.R. (2017). Organization theory in business and management history: Present status and future prospects. *Business History Review*, 91 (3): 457–481.

Maguire, S., Hardy, C. and Lawrence, T.B. (2004). Institutional entrepreneurship in emerging fields: HIV/AIDS treatment advocacy in Canada. *Academy of Management Journal*, 47 (5): 657–679.

Martí, I. and Fernández, P. (2013). The institutional work of oppression and resistance: Learning from the holocaust. *Organization Studies*, 34 (8): 1195–1223.

Martí, I. and Mair, J. (2009). Bringing change into the lives of the poor: Entrepreneurship outside traditional boundaries. In Lawrence, T.B., Suddaby, R. and Leca, B. (eds.), *Institutional work: Actors and agency in institutional studies of organizations*. Cambridge: Cambridge University Press, 92–119.

Ministry of Health, Labour and Welfare (2001). *Iryo seido kaikaku no kadai to shiten: kaisetsu siryo hen* [Challenges and perspectives of healthcare reforms: Commentary and data]. Tokyo: Gyosei.

Ministry of Health, Labour and Welfare. (2003). Aratana kango no arikata ni kansuru kentokai hokokusho [Report from the Conference on the New Way of Nursing]. www.mhlw.go.jp/stf/shingi/other-isei_127284.html

Miyahara, T. (2016). Nihon ni okeru shujutsu kango no shinpo [The progress of operative nursing in Japan]. In Japan Operative Nursing Academy (ed.), *Shujutsu kango no rekishi* [The history of operative nursing]. Tokyo: Tokyo-Igakusha, 67–99.

Miyazaki, M. (1990) Shujutsubu kinmu kangofu no chii [The social position of operating nurses]. *The Japanese Journal of Operating Room Nursing*, 5 (8): 1.

Munir, K.A. (2015). A loss of power in institutional theory. *Journal of Management Inquiry*, 24 (1): 90–92.

Munir, K.A. and Phillips, N. (2005). The birth of the 'Kodak Moment': Institutional entrepreneurship and the adoption of new technologies. *Organization Studies*, 26 (11): 1665–1687.

Muzio, D., Brock, D.M. and Suddaby, R. (2013). Professions and institutional change: Towards an institutionalist sociology of the professions. *Journal of Management Studies*, 50 (5): 699–721.

Okamoto, T. (1993). Gyomu buntan niyoru kango gyomu kaizen no kangaekata [The way of thinking of improvement of nurses' daily operations by the division of duties]. *Kango Tenbo* [Nursing Perspective], 18 (2): 14–18.

Rao, H., Monin, P. and Durand, R. (2003). Institutional change in Toque Ville: Nouvelle cuisine as an identity movement in French gastronomy. *American Journal of Sociology*, 108 (4): 795–843.

Reay, T., Golden-Biddle, K. and Germann, K. (2006). Legitimizing a new role: Small wins and microprocesses of change. *Academy of Management Journal*, 49 (5): 977–998.

Reay, T., Goodrick, E., Waldorff, S.B. and Casebeer, A. (2017). Getting leopards to change their spots: Co-creating a new professional role identity. *Academy of Management Journal*, 60 (3): 1043–1070.

Rojas, F. (2010). Power through institutional work: Acquiring academic authority in the 1968 third world strike. *Academy of Management Journal*, 53 (6): 1263–1280.

Ryder-Shimazaki, R., Koyama, A. and Tanaka, S. (2018). *Kangogaku gairon* [An introduction to nursing] (4th edn). Tokyo: Ishiyaku.

Saiseikai Utsunomiya Hospital. (1957). *Soritsu 15 shunen kinenshi* [The memorial magazine of the 15th anniversary]. Tochigi, Japan: Saiseikai Utsunomiya Hospital.

Sakai, K. (2019). Thriving in the shadow of giants: The success of the Japanese surgical needle producer MANI, 1956–2016. *Business History*, 61 (3): 429–455.

Scott, W.R. (2008). Lords of the dance: Professionals as institutional agents. *Organization Studies*, 29 (2): 219–238.

Shimazaki, K. (2011). *Nihon no iryo: Seido to seisaku* [Health care in Japan: Institution and policies]. Tokyo: University of Tokyo Press.

Suddaby, R. (2010). Challenges for institutional theory. *Journal of Management Inquiry*, 19 (1): 14–20.

Suddaby, R., Foster, W.M. and Mills, A.J. (2014). Historical institutionalism. In Bucheli, M. and Wadhwani, R.D. (eds.), *Organizations in time: History, theory, methods*. Oxford: Oxford University Press, 100–123.

Suddaby, R. and Greenwood, R. (2005). Rhetorical strategies of legitimacy, *Administrative Science Quarterly*, 50 (1): 35–67.

Suddaby, R. and Viale, T. (2011). Professionals and field-level change: Institutional work and the professional project. *Current Sociology*, 59 (4): 423–442.

Sugaya, A. (1965). *Kangorodo no shomondai* [Various problems of nursing labor]. Tokyo: Igakushoin.

Takasu, F. (1988). Shujutsushitsu mukashi banashi 2 [The old stories of operating rooms No. 2]. *The Japanese Journal of Operating Room Nursing*, 3 (5): 72.
Tanaka. S. (2001). Senryoki ni okeru hokenfu josanpu kangofu ho no rippo katei [Legislation of the public health nurse, midwife, and nurse law during the occupation period]. *Kanagawa Law Review*, 34 (2): 441–505.
Tanaka, S. (2014). Kangoshi no seikatsu to rodo [Life and labor of nurses]. In Japan Society of Nursing History (ed.), *Nihon no kango no ayumi* [The history of Japanese nursing]. Tokyo: Japanese Nursing Association, 27–42.
Terumo. (n.d.). Terumo story since 1921. www.terumo.co.jp/terumostory/
The Bernard Becker Medical Library. (2011, October 4). Crawford F. Sams, in Washington University School of Medicine, Oral History Project. http://beckerexhibits.wustl.edu/oral/interviews/sams.html
Tsunoda, Y. (1997). Nihon ni okeru kangofu seisaku no rekishiteki tenkai [The policy evolution of nurses in Japan: An economic analysis]. *Iryo to Shakai* [Medical Treatment and Society], 6 (4): 86–106.
Ujiie, S. and Fukumoto, M. (2014). Kango kyoiku no hensen [The transition of education for nursing]. In Japan Society of Nursing History (ed.), *Nihon no kango no ayumi* [The history of Japanese nursing]. Tokyo: Japanese Nursing Association, 73–102.
Wadhwani, R.D. and Bucheli, M. (2014). The future of the past in management and organization studies. In Bucheli, M. and Wadhwani, R.D. (eds.), *Organizations in time: History, theory, methods*. Oxford: Oxford University Press, 3–30.
Willmott, H. (2011). 'Institutional work' for what? Problems and prospects of institutional theory. *Journal of Management Inquiry*, 20 (1): 67–72.
Yamashita, M. (2001). Sengo iryo gijutsu kakushinka ni okeru kango gyomu no hensenkatei [The changes in Japanese nursing care jobs under medical technological innovations from 1960s to 1970s]. *Osaka Economic Papers*, 51 (3): 114–130.
Yoshihara, K. and Wada, M. (2008). *Nihon iryo hoken seidoshi* [The history of the Japanese medical insurance system] (rev. edn). Tokyo: Toyo Keizai Shinpo Sha.

12

STUDYING THE PROCESSES OF MANAGERIAL LEGITIMACY AND CONTROL OF FORMER STATE-OWNED ENTERPRISES IN POST-COMMUNIST SOCIETIES

A longitudinal study

Anna Soulsby

The purpose of this chapter is to consider how power over the changing reputation of organizational actors can be used to develop control over organizational identity and establish managerial legitimacy. In the post-communist societies of Central and Eastern Europe, the process of the re-legitimization of management is an especially important and complex moral issue for the managers and owners of organizations. Those that have survived the privatization process of the early 1990s and the economic upheavals of the late 1990s now increasingly draw upon the pre-1989 and post-1989 history of the organizations as a legitimating resource. They are very aware of the cultural value as well as the economic value of tradition and reputation (Olins, 1989; Rowlinson, Booth, Clark, Delahaye and Procter, 2010; Zerubavel, 2003).

The role of stories in developing shared understanding and collective sense making is an important element in the developing legitimacy and acceptance (Boyce, 1995). An organization's past can be treated as a strategic resource where various organizational stakeholders can use stories from the past to attempt to package and repackage history, mediating and creating the organization's identity for both internal and external audiences (Ooi, 2001). In the case of post-communist societies, a particular problem is coming to terms with and evaluating the reputations and actions of past directors and managers who were key actors and had powerful roles in the life of the organization and the local community. Narrative accounts of historical actions and events within organizations (and the communities they are located within) can be utilized or manipulated by organizational actors such as managers to legitimate their behaviour and past and current strategic decisions. This chapter will explore the process of how managers can use narratives to construct and control the historical accounts of actions and events that they want to become part of the organization's established 'official history', both before and after the Velvet Revolution of 1989, the non-violent transition of power that took place in what was then Czechoslovakia. The chapter now proceeds as follows: the next section discusses the relationship between the pressures of the transition environment and the lax external political and economic controls that enabled managers to take advantage of the privatization process. Then, there is a description of the research design, the case study organization and the account of the rise and fall of a key organizational actor. This is followed by a conclusion and discussion.

The transition period, privatization and control over managers

After the revolution in 1989, the quick introduction of the market economy was seen as a vital part of the process of restoring democracy (e.g. Brom and Orenstein, 1994; Holy, 1996). The Czechoslovak government decided to approach microeconomic restructuring through voucher privatization (Dlouhý and Mládek, 1994; Gray, 1996; Hagopian, 1994; Makhija and Spiro, 2000; Spicer, McDermott and Kogut, 2000). The intention was to ensure a massive reallocation of public assets to the private sector in a very short period, partly to address the fear that members of the Communist Party or anti-change social forces might take back control (e.g. Mlčoch, 1998; Sachs, 1996: 29; Wheaton and Kavan, 1992: 127). The rapidity of legal change was intended to minimize the degree to which former *nomenklatura* were able to 'privatize' state assets to their own advantage (Brom and Orenstein, 1994: 94; Pearce and Branyiczki, 1993). The privatization process was supposed to create owners for former state-owned enterprises (SOEs), imposing the discipline of the market on decision-making and restructuring. However, the existing management continued to exercise high levels of discretion over strategic decision-making with consequences for the future ownership and governance of SOEs (Sanders, 2006).

After voucher privatization, large enterprises were mainly owned by investment privatization funds (IPFs). The IPFs were largely owned by commercial banks in which the state still had substantial ownership interests. However, an IPF could only own through the privatization process a maximum of 10% of any enterprise, and so the method created highly fragmented ownership structures. At the first meetings of enterprises' owners, the IPF representatives usually ended up holding a majority of board posts, including that of chairman. However, these representatives had little experience of managing enterprises (e.g. Brom and Orenstein, 1994; Lízal and Kočenda, 2001) and so mostly conceded to the expertise of internal management. Investors were attracted to invest in organizations that had insider management because they would understand the issues (Hingorani, Lehn and Makhija, 1997). As a result, the effectiveness of external scrutiny of decision-making remained low during this period (Lízal and Kočenda, 2001; Sanders, 2006). Another important factor for the organizational survival of the current managers of the SOEs was that the new boards needed to confirm the former *nomenklatura* managers in their positions so that they were able to put clear legal distance between themselves and their communist pasts. The current managers were invariably confirmed in their posts.

This period also saw a tacit continuation of soft budgets for privatized enterprises (Jackman, 1994). The semi-state-owned banks used their indirect ownership of many privatized enterprises as a strategic mechanism to shore up their own lending business. They had little interest in calling in bad loans or forcing the bankruptcy of badly performing enterprises (Coffee, 1996; Sanders, 2006). Many large privatized enterprises continued to suffer from economic inefficiencies. This was the time of the 'Wild East'. The rush to privatize enterprises had created a weak system of controls (Kenway and Klvacova, 1996; Mertlík, 1997; Pavlínek, 2002; Sanders, 2006). This was an institutional environment in which widespread abuse was evident in illegal privatization deals, insider trading and the 'tunnelling' of company assets by managers (Myant, 1999), an illegal practice whereby shareholders took out company assets or profits for their own benefit, leaving an empty corporate shell. In late 1997, as rumours of systematic corruption and evidence of 'cronyism' crept closer to the political centre, public and political pressure forced the resignation of the neo-liberal Klaus government. The political-economic crisis was a watershed in the Czech transitional process. The Czech economy went into recession, and the government made new commitments to privatize the remaining state holdings of bank assets and tighten the budget constraints on businesses.

The sudden economic and institutional changes had radical implications for the degree of strategic discretion that managers had exercised within the transition environment. The increase in the 'constraining' role of external factors was felt in the enterprises by the growing influence of shareholders. The tolerance of managerial corruption was becoming less acceptable, and the need to demonstrate managerial legitimacy was becoming imperative. By the early 2000s, societal pressure was building for greater transparency, and managers needed to demonstrate accountability (Sicakova-Beblava and Beblavy, 2016). The time of the Wild East was coming to an end.

Research design

The empirical basis for this chapter is an ongoing longitudinal study of organizations conducted by the author since 1992 in former SOEs in the Czech Republic (Clark and Soulsby, 1995; Soulsby and Clark 1996). In keeping with the overarching theme of historical organization studies (Maclean, Harvey and Clegg, 2016) within which this book is located, the longitudinal, processual nature of the study allows for the processes of decision-making to be located in a historical context. To follow a case study company for so long is arguably extremely rare in organization studies. Doing so, however, affords insights that can only be gleaned through consideration over a "long time span" (Braudel, 1980: 27). The organizations have gone through radical changes including privatization and changes in management and ownership. The focus of the research study has been to examine processes of change and the utilization of symbolic resources, such as narratives by managers to legitimate their actions and to respond to the challenges of the post-communist transition environment. The chapter draws on data from a project conducted through a 'punctuated longitudinal case study' research design (Soulsby and Clark, 2012). The authors have traced the processes of restructuring and change in a small number of Czech former SOEs since the first field visits in the wake of the collapse of communism.

Volnské Strojírny a Slévárny (Vols), the case study organization that forms the empirical basis for this chapter, was first visited by the author in 1992, with follow-up visits in 1993,1995, 1996, 1998, 2000, 2003, 2007 and 2011. All of the names used in the chapter are pseudonyms to preserve confidentiality (Saunders, Kitzinger and Kitzinger, 2015). This may be unusual in historical work; however, it is commonplace in organization studies. As this chapter is located in historical organization studies, the case study organization has been anonymized as stated. Each visit to Vols enabled the collection of a combination of real-time and retrospective data. The authors conducted semi-structured interviews with senior and middle managers, whose reflections on the current situation and storied accounts of the organization's histories constitute the basic qualitative data form in the project. The research project also comprises interviews with the new managers who took positions in Vols after it was acquired, including an interview with one of the new director-owners (part of a field visit to the new parent company in 2008). Table 12.1 gives the details of the respondents' positions and the year of the interviews. In addition, we gathered corporate documents (e.g. company annual reports) and materials from non-corporate sources, such as the Czech Commercial Register, newspaper reports and other electronic sources. The longitudinal nature of the research means that there is also an extensive collection of materials, including data from observation, photographs of the enterprise and town, maps and field notes from each visit.

The case study organization

Vols is an engineering company that was a former SOE. It is located in a small town in the Czech Republic, Volna. It is the only large employer in the town (the company logo is visible everywhere) and one of the largest in the region. The organization was established in 1948 for political reasons, and engineering production started in 1951. The strong links between the enterprise and the town meant that generations of managers and workers have spent their entire careers in the organization. One director noted, "many people started young in Vols at the same time and so have grown up together" (Mr BV, director of Mechanical Engineering Department, 1992 interview). A particular feature of organizational life in pre-1989 Czechoslovakia was the close relationship between the enterprises and the local communities. The managers and workers often lived in the same apartment blocks on the housing estates. Workers and managers often returned to their hometowns after training or studying and stayed with the same SOE for most of their working lives (Adam; 1987; Altmann, 1987; Clark and Soulsby, 1999a). After 1989, they no

Processes of managerial legitimacy 211

TABLE 12.1 Interviewees and other key actors

Number	Interviewees and key actors	Position	Year of interviews
1	AV	Vols commercial director	2007
2	BV	Director of Vols Mechanical Engineering Department	1992
3	CV	Vols personnel director	2007
4	DV	Head of Personnel Department, Vols	1992, 2000
5	EV	Vols director of strategy	1992, 1993, 1995, 2 interviews in 1996
6	FV	Vols finance director, 1985–1997, general director 1997–2002 ("the magician")	1996
7	GV	Vols deputy head of strategy	1992, 1993, 1995, 2 interviews in 1998
8	IV	Vols director of metallurgy, director of production	1992, 1998, 2003, 2007
9	JV	Vols director of finance	2007
10	LV	Vols head of economic planning	1992
11	MV	Vols head of sales and marketing	1992
12	VV	Vols senior marketing manager	2007
13	TS	Assistant to SS, the general director of Strojarstvo/chairman of Strojarstvo (relative of a shareholder/owner/director of Strojarstvo)	2007, 2008
14	HS	Chairman of Vols supervisory board Shareholder/owner/finance director of Strojarstvo	2008
15	KV	Vols director of finance (1998–2003)	Not interviewed
16	TV	Vols production director/ general director 1989–1997	Not interviewed
17	SF	Head of investment fund/chairman of board of Vols 1995	Not interviewed
18	SS	Shareholder/owner/chairman of board of Vols. Shareholder/owner/chairman of Strojarstvo directors	Not interviewed

longer had the certainty of a job for life with the enterprise. The actions and decisions of managers were visible and commented on within the wider community, because their and their families' lives were locked into the local society. This social interconnectedness has remained the case after the Velvet Revolution as generations of the same families have spent their working lives in the enterprise.

In 1990, Vols's senior managers were all former *nomenklatura* managers who had spent their whole careers within their enterprises. In the first place, these internal appointments to the large, soon-to-be-privatized enterprises assured some degree of continuity with the state socialist past, reproducing many established organizational values and practices. In fact, this managerial continuity was to prove attractive to potential investors (Hingorani, Lehn and Makhija, 1997). A characteristic of Vols management was an expressed commitment to the wider community and the families of employees. The managers started to restructure the organization in 1990, and privatization via the 'voucher method' was completed by 1994. The organization underwent restructuring, but it was through incremental change; the top management team usually preferred to manage through consensus. They were very aware of the potential damage to the town and their reputation if there were negative consequences. Vols's managers continued to adopt the structural and financial approach that reinforced their earlier actions taken on the grounds of social responsibility to the community; in 1997, Vols still employed approximately 80% of the 1993 numbers. The senior management team remained unchanged, and former *nomenklatura* managers continued to work side by side with former 'dissidents' with a shared view of the enterprise and its vital social role in the community.

However, by the late 1990s, the company started to have financial problems and was acquired by another Central European engineering company that had been a long-standing former customer. Since the acquisition by the new engineering company in 2002, the decisions of the directors and managers in the pre- and post-privatization periods have come under scrutiny as the managers have retired or left. In particular, the reputations of some directors who were originally regarded as 'heroes' have been re-evaluated in both the enterprise and the community. In the case of directors and managers in the period prior to 1989, there were some outstanding characters that wielded immense power as part of the Communist system, but were not seen as organizational 'heroes'. Other managers had powerful and influential 'unofficial' reputations as imaginative engineers or designers who were highly regarded but were not promoted because they did not engage in party politics or because the party barred them. Since 1989, some past directors, who were communists, are now acknowledged as excellent at directing the enterprise within the constraints of the pre-1989 period. However, other directors, whose reputations had been high in the 1990s, are now regarded with cynicism and disgust because they are seen as having enriched themselves at the expense of the organization. The account given below that forms the basis for this is one of the career of a man who spent the majority of his entire formal career in Vols. The account is constructed from the various sources cited above, which span the period 1992–2011.

The rise of "the magician"

Before the revolution in 1989, Vols was not in a bad economic situation. There was one major customer, the USSR, and they had no sales problems. There were opportunities for families to move to Volna and get an apartment because Vols was an important enterprise (Mr LV, head of Economic Planning Department, 1992 interview). As was normal at the time, the Communist Party formally controlled access to management positions through the *nomenklatura* system (Kaplan, 1987; Waller, 1993; Wheaton and Kavan 1992; Wolchik, 1991). In the view of one respondent (Mr LV, head of Economic Planning Department, 1992 interview):

> It was not possible to be a manager and not be member of the Communist Party. Careers and promotions were made through the Communist Party. There were many rules but they were not kept. People were not afraid just before the revolution because change was clearly imminent. The most important thing was the origin of the factory. It was established by government decision in the region; a bad decision for this type of production – a very good labour force, but no raw materials. The region was heavily influenced by Vols. Production was exported to 'the East', and this increased the prestige of the company – this was good for political reasons for the growth of the company – it attracted resources to support production. It was a successful factory, attracting many good workers; skill levels were good, workers were generally happy and working conditions 'friendly'. Relations worsened over time, as they did across Czechoslovakia.

Another director also commented that the prestige of Vols meant that membership of the Communist Party was a precondition for top management in Vols before 1989 (Mr FV, then finance director, 1996 interview):

> The Communist Party affected almost everyone in the country; everyone was scrutinized by the Communist Party, e.g. membership. When I started as the Director of Economy, I was not a member but it did not make any difference, I had to listen to their views. Communist Party control over the workplace lasted until 1989, and did not diminish before. Those who protested were a few in Prague, and then there was an overnight revolution. It was shock for some in Vols, but not for me. Many people left top positions after 1989. They voted, in some sense, on heads of department and those who were not trusted left their position.

Unlike other senior and middle managers who were voted out by the enterprise employees, Mr FV had stayed in his position in Vols. He had initially joined Vols in 1976 in the Research and Development section (part of the Technology Department). It was his first employment position. His career proceeded very rapidly within Vols. In 1981, he became the deputy assistant of the technical director. In July 1982, he had another promotion to become an assistant to the general director. In March 1983, he became the head of information technology and he replaced the previous director of economy (finance) in 1985.

Although Mr FV was known to be a member of the Communist Party, his financial skills meant that he was thought to be indispensable during the immediate post-revolutionary period when the survival of the enterprise was uncertain. Other respondents in the early 1990s commented on the high reputation he had within the enterprise as finance director. In 1992, Mr EV (the director of strategy) referred to him as "the magician" because of his ability to find the money to pay the enterprise's wages in the difficult early and mid-1990s. If the enterprise had collapsed then, the effect on the town would have been catastrophic, in terms not only of the local economy but also of social and welfare provision. According to another respondent in 1992, Mr DV (the head of the Personnel Department and a former dissident who had been appointed by Mr FV), "although Mr FV had been a communist, he had been expert in the right (organizational) position". In a 1996 interview, the finance director, Mr FV, said that he regarded it as an advantage for his career that he had been promoted steadily, "one degree at a time". His personal development was not in a single functional area because he had moved to different departments in the enterprise:

> It was also a very great advantage to have started in the Technology Department and learn the deep parts of the organization as an assistant of the production director, and as an assistant to the general director. I had a chance to learn about running the organization.

After 1989, the balance of power between the top management team had changed. The position of production director, held by Mr TV, who from 1989 to 1997 was also the general director, was now seen as less important by other directors and managers. Before 1989, the director of production was the most important person with the most important department, because only the "plan needed to be met, now the finance director was the most important" (Mr EV, 1992 interview). The enterprise had not yet been privatized, and although the general director was seen as being very protective of the workers, "he could not control the company so the company controlled itself" (Mr LV, head of Economic Planning Department, 1992 interview). In his view:

> The forces for change were Mr FV (the finance director) and Mr EV (the director of strategy). They are interested in changes and now thanks to them, others are. They are strong personalities and want change. Wanting is a most powerful force.

According to the Mr MV, head of sales and marketing (1992 interview), there would have been serious effects for the local economy, including social problems, if Vols collapsed.

> The enterprise needed to pay their suppliers in cash but there was a shortage; this was a Czech problem with all the firms facing cash shortages. The creative solutions found by the finance director included bartering with customers and

exchanging IOUs. The problem is acute because of breakdown of previously secure USSR markets and no longer having the backing of the state. They are now searching for new markets in countries that have money. There are barter deals with Russia, giving rolling mills equipment in exchange for railway tracks. The rails are melted down and reprocessed. This is profitable because of exchange rates. Barters and other deals Russian deals are a reflection of historical contacts. In Vols, there is lots of 'beer criticism' but Vols is very important in the community because of welfare etc.

Mr MV argued that the most powerful figure in the enterprise was the finance director because:

> Prices are the most important thing now. The main objective of the factory is not just to make money but to adopt a flexible approach to business – such flexibility needs monitoring and controlling – a big problem for finance and accounting.

The privatization of the enterprise was completed via the voucher method (Brom and Orenstein, 1994; Dlouhý and Mládek, 1994; Gray, 1996; Hagopian, 1994; Makhija and Spiro, 2000; Spicer, McDermott and Kogut, 2000), and the managers were focussed on maintaining the enterprise during the turbulence of the transition period. In 1993, there were 18,000 individual shareholders, but, by 1995, this had fallen to 16,000. The director of strategic planning, Mr EV and his deputy, Mr GV (interview, 1995), commented that:

> The majority of the volume of shares was now owned by eight investment funds. The most important fund was ABC, whose representative was the chairman of the board of directors of Vols, Mr SF. Formally, the fund and the consultants were independent, but they were chaired by the same person, Mr SF. About the relationship between the investment fund ABC and the consultancy activities regarding Vols, you can come to your own conclusions. Mr SF is on many boards of directors.

By the mid-1990s, there was emerging disagreement between the top management team. Mr FV, the finance director, commented in 1996 that he had been used to staying 2–3 years in each post and then moving on, but he had been in his current position a long time and now he felt "a little bored". He had always been motivated in his career by change and the realization of new ideas. He felt the post-communist system was more favourable for him, compared with the central planning system. He had many ideas, with the freedom to apply them. Before the revolution, they were forced to fulfil the plans of the ministry, and he had felt himself to be a "technical expert rather than an economic one". He was very direct as far as his future career was concerned; he saw two alternatives: he would either become the general director or join another enterprise and start from zero. He felt that it "would be just a matter of a few days or a week to get used to losing my friends, to overcome the painful reaction and start somewhere else". He believed that he would be able to get used to the change because he "can do new things and overcome problems, and after years [here] it would be something new". He commented:

> [I feel] too much, because I started my career in Vols; without Vols the infrastructure of this region would not exist. We are paying thousands of crowns per year to employees and they spend it in shops and on services; so without Vols the small firms could not exist. Vols is the most dominant enterprise in the region and has had the dominant role in the development of this region. I have had a chance because of Vols.

In 1997, the general director, Mr TV, a former communist who had been appointed by the other directors under the orders of the Communist Party in spring 1989, stood down. The top management team had started to divide between the former general director and his supporters who were in favour of an incremental approach to change and the other directors who were in favour of quicker changes under the strong leadership of the finance director (Clark and Soulsby, 1999b). Mr FV was promoted from the finance director to the general director. In the view of a director (appointed in 1990), Mr. IV, "the directors thought it was time for a change and Mr FV was much younger and had complete experience as an engineer and in finance".

The magician's "fall from grace"

In the late 1990s, Vols seemed to be surviving the pressures of the transition period, and, by becoming the general director, Mr FV had achieved the objective he had set for his career. Other managers apparently still held him in high regard. However, there were serious financial problems under the surface. The top management team moved to restructure the company, selling off non-assets, and reorganize the divisions into profit centres (Mr IV, interview 2007). Despite these moves, the company's sales fell, with a poor financial performance in 1999, and, by 2000, the company posted serious losses.

The managers were facing problems from the external environment, including increased competition in the engineering sector (Mr IV, interview 2007). The DEF bank, which had been the majority shareholder and had been mainly inactive in terms of corporate governance, went into bankruptcy in 2000. Another bank, GHI, reluctantly took over Vols's shares under pressure from the Czech government, and the debts were passed on to the Consolidation Fund. The GHI bank confirmed Mr FV in his position and insisted on Vols taking on more experienced directors but did not take an active interest in developing the strategy of the company (Kenway and Klvacova, 1996; Mertlík, 1997; Pavlínek, 2002; Sanders, 2006). This was a time when there were increasing internal clashes between the heads of the different divisions. According to the director of commerce, Mr AV (interview 2007):

> It was because no one in top management was directly controlling the company. Unlike Strojarstvo now, there was no upper hand. The owner was a bank, and they were only exercising control at the end of the year and they only looked at the money, this was their only point of evaluating the company.

Another senior manager, Mr VV (senior marketing manager, interview 2007) commented: "the biggest problem was that the top managers were here physically but this was only one of their jobs, they had no motivation to solve the problems".

The implication was that the managers had other business interests. The company tried to turn its fortunes around through cutting costs, but GHI bank would not invest in the company or settle its debts. Under the direction of Mr FV, the top management tried to cut costs. They cut production and started to sell off assets – for example, the local transport company, the accommodation hostel, the logistics building, a factory hall. However, there were increasing internal concerns and suspicions about how this was being done. One respondent, Mr IV, commented that he "did not want to be impolite" about the effect Mr FV's management had on the company, criticizing him for the loss of organizational advantage and the loss of designers and machines (interview 2007). The commercial director, Mr AV (interview 2007), commented that, during this time of uncertainty and lack of direction:

> In my opinion, this was the time when bad deals were made and the company lost money, e.g. such as selling the internal railway. Top management founded a (private) daughter company to operate the railway company. Vols repaired the locomotive engine for 1 million kc and sold it to the company for 200,000 kc. In fact, the company did not pay for the engine but said that it would make up the cost within the [pay it back by the cost of the monthly] transportation service it provided [to Vols]. Mr FV was the owner of the daughter – but not only him; other top managers were also founders of the private railway company.

In 2001, the power plant was being prepared for sale. This was the "period of the greatest instability for Vols" (Mr VV, senior marketing manager, worked in Vols for 33 years; 2007 interview). The commercial director, Mr AV, regarded it as extremely fortunate that the company had been eventually taken over:

> They [members of the TMT] also prepared other divisions of the factory for selling – e.g. the energy division. Luckily, they did not manage to sell them in time – in my view – if they had had six more months the energy division would have been sold, like Poldí Kladno [a famous steelworks that collapsed

into bankruptcy after privatization]. If others had controlled the division supplying energy, they would have been in a monopoly position regarding Vols. This is a strategic case. There are of course other things that were secrets – people made deals with 'under the table' money.

The personnel director, Mr CV (who had always worked at Vols, as had his parents; interview 2007) gave an account of what had happened to the organization's hotel and hinted at corruption by some senior managers:

> We had a hotel with 180 rooms, Hotel Volna, but they sold it in 2002 before Strojarstvo arrived – the contract had gone too far so it could not be saved. FV sold it for 14 million crowns, which is only the price of a house, and included the land around it. Officially, the entrepreneur was from Brno and owned a string of hotels. But, in the corporate register, if you find the firm, you can see the names of other owners, it is all publicly available information.

As a consequence of the cutbacks and assets, sales employees started to leave. People were aware of the actions of some of the top managers. The selling of company assets was not unusual in this time of the "Wild East" (Mlčoch, 1998). The commercial director, Mr AV, commented:

> Everyone knew about it but of course, people in lower positions were unable to influence what was going on. This was the situation in a number of Czech companies. There is excellent evidence; a number of companies went bankrupt for reasons very similar to the Vols case. Managers were not rich enough so they made 'bad' deals to make money for themselves. Same as in politics, people only have four years as a politician to make money. It happened everywhere, but in comparison with other companies, Vols never generated red numbers and there were no problems paying salaries.

In 2000, the general director started to look urgently for an external strategic investor. They approached a privatized CEE engineering company, Strojarstvo, a long-standing customer of Vols. Its former directors owned the company; they had acquired Strojarstvo as part of their own privatization process. According to one of the new director/owners, Mr HS, the general director of Vols and the finance director, approached their company to interest them in investment because they had failed to raise funds to buy out the company themselves. This was on the condition that they would keep their positions, but Strojarstvo was not interested in this.

In Volna and Vols, people had been aware of the economic crisis, and there was great fear that Vols would be broken up and asset-stripped, ceasing to exist as an engineering company. There were rumours circulating about organizations looking to buy Vols; there was great concern that a notorious asset-stripper was keen to acquire and break up Vols (Mr TS, interview 2007). According to Mr AV (commercial director, interview 2007): "Before Strojarstvo bought Vols, there was a wave of firing people. People did not know what the future of the company would be". In 2002, Strojarstvo bought the majority of shares from GHI bank and took over the management of the company after an extraordinary meeting of shareholders. According to a middle manager (Mr VV, 2007 interview):

> Before Strojarstvo entered the company, they were our best or very good customer; there was no other relation except as good customers. The top management and middle management knew Strojarstvo, but normal employees did not – they do not care, they only care about their jobs and want to go home.

The finance director of Vols (Mr JV, worked in Vols since 1993, and finance director since 2003; interview 2007) said:

> God bless the [acquiring] company! Because it left the company whole. Now it is clear that it was beneficial to have bought metallurgy and machines in the same company, because managers can co-operate together and it is all easier. Our relationships are more than just business. The Bank investment funds decided to select Strojarstvo and this was good for both the funds and Strojarstvo. There were several factors. First of all there were close relationships between the managers of Vols and Strojarstvo. Second, Strojarstvo had a lot of cash. They wanted to make a clever investment in another market. But very important was the close relationship between managers. We trusted each other. Vols managers could persuade Strojarstvo of the company's potential in its products and Strojarstvo managers trusted Vols' managers' internal knowledge of the company.

The finance director, Mr JV (interview 2007), also commented that local people were initially surprised by the acquisition: "at first it was a big surprise, of course, because people expected to be bought by a Western company, not an Eastern one. Eastern levels are seen as lower than here". After the extraordinary meeting of shareholders, the new owners moved quickly to appoint a new top management team. The new chairman of the board appointed a compatriot to the position of general director, and Mr FV left the company (Mr IV, interview 2007). Mr FV still runs the transport company in addition to the three pharmacies (Mr VV, interview 2007) and other companies he has shares in (as he did while general director of Vols).

It was no surprise to the managers of Vols that the well-regarded director of the production division, Mr IV, kept his position (until he retired in 2010). However, Vols managers were surprised that the new owners also kept the director of finance, Mr KV (1998–2003) in position. The commercial director commented, "But everyone and I were surprised that they kept the financial director from the former top management team – Mr KV – who was one of the bad people making decisions to sell off assets. This is a key position" (Mr AV, appointed in 2005, 2007 interview).

Initially, the new majority owners appointed their own choice of directors and managers to other senior positions. However, they did not understand the nature of Vols engineering activities and the investment required because of their different technical engineering background (Mr VV, interview 2007). The new owners then reorganized the Vols top management team with only two compatriots in position as directors. According to one of director/owners, Mr HS (finance director of Strojarstvo and member of Vols's supervisory board, 2008 interview), "they had to move very quickly to take Vols over because it was in a terrible state. They needed to prepare a revitalization plan as they had done for their own company in the 1990s". The chairman of Vols, Mr SS (and chairman of Strojarstvo), stated in the 2002 Vols annual report:

> Since the first round of the coupon privatization, the joint stock company Vols went through quite a complicated evolution when its management staff was varying more kinds of philosophical approach to control. As a result of such goings-on the new management in 2002 had to accept the auditor's comments and realize provisions for depreciation in the amount of 217.5 mill. CZK. The previous management took several very bad decisions that consequently the company had to cope with financially.

The new owners undertook a 6-month audit and stopped the selling of assets. After Vols's situation was "stabilized they wanted people back who knew the company because of a loss of know-how. I got word from the General Director (in 2005) that he wanted me back. The policy of Strojarstvo was to stop selling off the assets and go to for re-integration instead" (Mr VV, senior marketing manager, 2007 interview). In 2002 and 2003, the focus of the majority shareholders and managers was on restoring the company and restructuring it, both internally and within the Strojarstvo group of companies (Mr IV, Mr TS, interview 2007). In 2005, Strojarstvo obtained all of the remaining shares in Vols (Mr TS, interview 2007). In 2005, the owners appointed a new Czech general director (the former director of commerce, who came from Volna and who had worked in Vols since 1984). Only two of the directors were compatriots of the new owners, the technical director and the logistics director; all the other directors, with exception of the production director, Mr IV, were new appointments to their positions.

Although Vols had become a wholly owned subsidiary of Strojarstvo, the managers of Vols argued that there was still a lot of respect for the engineering heritage of Vols and its traditions. The new owners have maintained the social and welfare traditions and obligations of Vols. Mr TS commented that: "We have a strong social programme and it is a very clean company, we take care of our employees. Vols was a very important acquisition for us". In addition, Strojarstvo had also made substantial investment in local cultural artefacts and buildings in Volna – for example, refurbishing a castle and developing a museum. This echoed their own practice of maintaining social and welfare activities together with investing in cultural and heritage activities in their own local town and countryside (Mr TS, interview 2007).

Discussion and conclusion

There are two clear periods in the career of FV in Vols as presented by the respondents (Boyce, 1995; Ooi, 2001). In the 1990s narrative accounts, Mr FV was regarded with admiration as the "magician". He was seen as having the ability to help the enterprise survive the economic turbulence of the 1990s when other venerable state enterprises were failing – for example, Poldi Steelworks; he could find the money to pay suppliers and wages. At a time when the collapse of Vols would have been catastrophic for the local community – "Volna is Vols" – his creative approach made him the most powerful person in the organization. He had also forged a strong relationship with the other key director, Mr EV, the director for strategy. The other senior managers saw them as modernizers, key drivers for change and hungry for power. Mr FV's ambition to get to the top of the company was always very clear (interview 1996). While the organization was dependent upon him to survive, he was held in high esteem locally. However, when the economic crises of the late 1990s started to affect the Czech economy, his organizational reputation started to fall. This was especially the case as the other managers became aware of his decisions to sell off assets. The sale of the refurbished train and the enterprise hotel had caused great anger internally. There was growing disagreement between the managers, and key employees started to leave Vols.

In the second period, the mid-2000s, the organizational narrative about the career of the former general director had settled around a story with two aspects. First, respondents commented that he had been involved in selling company assets and had used his position to his financial advantage. The sales were seen as an underhand way to enrich himself and his family at the expense of Vols and Volna. Second, after the takeover by Strojarstvo in 2002, Mr FV's decisions were directly and openly criticized by the new chairman in the first annual report by the new owners. At this point, the official organizational narrative was now one where Mr FV was regarded (and presented) as an organizational 'villain'. Even though he was the one who had approached Strojarstvo, Strojarstvo was presented as the saviour of the company. He was viewed as disloyal and a poor director, because his decisions had placed the company and, thereby, the town in great danger. The new managers from Strojarstvo had taken on the task to restructure and save Vols. As time passes, these accounts of managers' actions, including the narratives of those regarded (labelled) as organizational 'villains' for the period between 1989 and the early 2000s, will be the ones to survive (Olins, 1989; Rowlinson et al., 2010; Zerubavel, 2003).

However, as other managers noted, the possibilities for organizational and personal corruption were built into the structures of the Czech privatization process. The determination of Czech governments to speed up the process of liberalization of markets and the privatization of enterprises in the 1990s led to problems of weak external restraints on managers and their behaviour (Lízal and Kočenda, 2001; Mlčoch, 1998; Sanders, 2006). The managers of state enterprises with inside knowledge could prepare the privatization projects with little interference. As an elite, they had the opportunity to maintain their societal position and to grow rich very quickly. There was a power vacuum because of the poor corporate governance exercised by the external shareholders in the form of the banks and investment funds (Lízal and Kočenda, 2001). There was no incentive, until the banking crisis of 1997, for shareholders to take an active part in the supervision of directors' decisions (Hingorani, Lehn, and Makhija, 1997). As seen above, some shareholders used their position of power in the enterprise to instruct the directors to use consultancy services provided by their own company. The 1990s was also a period of increasing economic divide, as managers started to take on more practices from the West – for example, rewarding themselves with higher pay and benefits. However, in societal terms of public acceptance of perceived unethical behaviour, from the start of the 2000s (and as accession to the European Union came closer), public concern about corruption rose up the Czech political agenda (Sicakova-Beblava and Beblavy, 2016).

Since the start of the 2000s, the owners of organizations have started to exert more control over their corporate image and brand. The preservation of archives and artefacts, together with sponsorship of local social and commemorative events, is regarded as an important part of the process of legitimation and of preserving connections with the organization's pre-1989 history and identity (Rowlinson et al., 2010). This is also seen in formal public documents – for example, annual reports – as well as in the development and reproduction of consistent official internal narrative accounts. For the managers and owners of privatized SOEs, who were part of the elite *nomenklatura*, the control of the 'official' history (Boyce, 1995; Ooi, 2001) is a way of legitimating their past activities, their acquisition of wealth and solidification of their post-communist social position.

References

Adam, J. (1987). Similarities and differences in the treatment of labour shortages. In Adam, J. (ed.), *Employment policies in the Soviet Union and Eastern Europe* (2nd edn.). London: Macmillan.

Altmann, F.-L. (1987). Employment policies in Czechoslovakia. In Adam, J. (ed.), *Employment policies in the Soviet Union and Eastern Europe* (2nd edn.). London: Macmillan.

Boyce, M.E. (1995). Collective centring and collective sense-making in the stories and storytelling of one organization. *Organization Studies*, 16 (1): 107–137.

Braudel, F. (1980). *On history*. Chicago: University of Chicago Press.

Brom, K. and Orenstein, M. (1994). The privatized sector in the Czech Republic: Government and bank control in a transitional economy. *Europe-Asia Studies*, 46 (6): 893–928.

Clark, E. and Soulsby, A. (1995). Transforming former state enterprises in the Czech Republic. *Organization Studies*, 16 (2): 215–242.

Clark, E. and Soulsby, A. (1998). Organization-community embeddedness: The social impact of enterprise restructuring in the post-communist Czech Republic. *Human Relations*, 51 (1): 25–50.

Clark, E. and Soulsby, A. (1999a). *Organizational change in post-communist Europe: Management and transformation in the Czech Republic*. London: Routledge.
Clark, E. and Soulsby, A. (1999b). The adoption of the multi-divisional form in large Czech enterprises: The role of economic, institutional and strategic choice factors. *Journal of Management Studies*, 36 (4): 535–559.
Coffee, J.C. (1996). Institutional investors in transitional economies: The Czech experience. In Frydman, R., Gray, C. W. and Rapaczynski, A. (eds), *Corporate governance in Central Europe and Russia*. Vol. 1, Budapest, London and New York: Central University Press.
Dlouhý, V. and Mládek, J. (1994). Privatization and corporate control in the Czech Republic. *Economic Policy*, 19 (9): 156–170.
Gray, C. (1996). In search of owners: Privatization and corporate governance in transition economies. *The World Bank Research Observer*, 11 (2): 179–197.
Hagopian, M.J. (1994). The engines of privatization: Investment funds and funds legislation in privatizing economies. *Northwestern Journal of International Law & Business*, 15 (1): 75–104.
Hingorani, A., Lehn, K. and Makhija, A.K. (1997). Investor behaviour in mass privatization: The case of Czech voucher scheme. *Journal of Financial Economics*, 44 (3): 346–396.
Holy, L. (1996). *The little Czech and the great Czech nation: National identity and the post-communist social transformation*. Cambridge: Cambridge University Press.
Jackman, R. (1994). Economic policy and employment in the transition economies of Central and Eastern Europe: What have we learned? *International Labour Review*, 133 (3): 327–345.
Kaplan, K. (1987). *The communist party in power: A profile of party politics in Czechoslovakia*. London: Westview.
Kenway, P. and Klvacova, E. (1996). The web of cross-ownership among Czech financial intermediaries: An assessment. *Europe-Asia Studies*, 48 (5): 797–809.
Lízal, L. and Kočenda, E. (2001). State of corruption in transition: Case of the Czech Republic. *Emerging Markets Review*, 2 (2): 137–159.
Maclean, M., Harvey, C., and Clegg, S.R. (2016). Conceptualizing historical organization studies. *Academy of Management Review*, 41 (4): 609–632.
Makhija, A.K. and Spiro, M. (2000). Ownership structure as determinant of firm value: Evidence from newly privatized Czech firms. *The Financial Review*, 35 (3): 1–32.
Mertlík, P. (1997). Czech privatization. *Eastern European Economics*, 35 (2): 64–83.
Mlčoch, L. (1998). Czech privatization: A criticism of misunderstood liberalism. *Journal of Business Ethics*, 17 (9–10): 951–959.
Myant, M. (1999). *Industrial competitiveness in East Central Europe*. Aldershot: Edward Elgar.
Ooi, C-S. (2001). Persuasive histories: Decentering, recentering and the emotional crafting of the past. *Journal of Organizational Change Management*, 15 (6): 606–621.
Olins, W. (1989). *Corporate identity*. London: Thames & Hudson.
Pavlínek, P. (2002). Domestic privatisation and its effects on industrial enterprises in East-Central Europe: Evidence from the Czech motor component industry. *Europe-Asia Studies*, 54 (7): 1127–1150.
Pearce, J. and Branyiczki, I. (1993). Revolutionizing bureaucracies: Managing change in Hungarian state-owned enterprises. *Journal of Organizational Change Management*, 6 (2): 53–64.
Rowlinson, M., Booth, C., Clark P., Delahaye, A., and Procter, S. (2010). Social remembering and organizational memory. *Organization Studies*, 31 (1): 69–87.
Sachs, J. (1996). The transition at mid-decade. *AEA Papers and Proceedings*, 86 (2): 128–133.
Sanders, M. (2006). *Privately managed privatisation in the Czech Republic: Lessons learned*. Arlington, VA: Jefferson Institute.

Saunders, B., Kitzinger, J., and Kitzinger, C. (2015). Anonymising interview data: Challenges and compromises in practice. *Qualitative Research*, 15 (5): 616–632.

Sicakova-Beblava, E. and Beblavy, M. (2016). Using government manifestos to analyse the political salience and shape of anti-corruption policies in the Czech Republic and Slovakia. *Policy Studies*, 37 (4): 295–313.

Soulsby, A. and Clark, E. (1996). The emergence of post-communist management in the Czech Republic. *Organization Studies*, 17 (2): 227–247.

Soulsby, A. and Clark, E. (2012). Theorizing process through punctuated longitudinal case study research: Narrative data and the problem of retrospection. In Welch, C. and Piekkari, R. (eds.), *Rethinking the case study approach in international business research*. Cheltenham: Edward Elgar, 277–300.

Spicer, A., McDermott, G.A., and Kogut, B. (2000). Entrepreneurship and privatization in Central Europe: The tenuous balance between destruction and creation. *Academy of Management Review*, 25 (3): 630–649.

Waller, M. (1993). *The end of the communist power monopoly*. Manchester: Manchester University Press.

Wheaton, B. and Kavan, Z. (1992). *The velvet revolution: Czechoslovakia, 1988–1991*. Oxford: Westview.

Wolchik, S.L. (1991). *Czechoslovakia in transition: Politics, economy and society*. London, Pinter.

Zerubavel, E. (2003). *Time maps: Collective memory and the social shape of the past*. Chicago: University of Chicago Press.

PART IV
Conclusion

13

AT THE INTERSECTION OF THEORY AND HISTORY

A research agenda for historical organization studies

Stewart R. Clegg, Roy Suddaby, Charles Harvey and Mairi Maclean

Introduction

In the preface to *The Order of Things*, Foucault (1970: xv) recites Jorge Luis Borges's fictional taxonomy of animals to capture the fragmentation and confusing arbitrariness of any culturally determined system of knowledge. Much the same confusion might arise by using the total knowledge of organization theory to construct a taxonomy of organizations, dividing them thus: (a) those belonging to the gods, (b) dead, (c) profitable (d) open systems, (e) machines, (f) positive, (g) processes, (h) cows, (i) emotional, (j) performing, (k), imagined, (l), mindsets, (m) enacted, embodied, embrained, (n) broken, (o) inimitable, (p) isomorphic, (q) occupying niches, (r) contingencies against dread, (s) structural adjustments, (t) broken hammers, (u) spider plants, (v) brains, (w) cages, (x) animals, (y) psychic structures and (z) classified elsewhere.

Fanciful? Not really. We have no doubt that each one of these terms might fruitfully be used to develop a whole panoply of theories about what organizations are. In fact, in every case, we can think of literatures that do precisely that. Indeed, they do precisely that and much more besides; the imaginaries of theory know no bounds. If we want to signify what an organization is, there are far too many ways of answering the question to satisfy a sober and disciplined mind. Such minds are too industriously proclaiming the verity of their schemas and casting scorn on those of others, thus showing the sobriety and discipline of the minds in question.

There is one ontological 'given' that constitutes all organizations. Their history. All 'organizations are complex structures-in-motion that are best conceptualized as historically constituted entities' (Clegg, 1981: 545). Odd then, is it not, that the historical facticity of organizations, however contested, is what anchors them in space and time yet is routinely discounted? Consider an indubitable aspect that all organizations share: they are a network of social relations that extend across space and through time. Given this, the historical situatedness of spatiality and temporality would seem to be a prominent feature. If history is one unifying constant in organization theory, then it is ironical that so much of that theory seems unfamiliar with its history.

That there is organization and are organizations is a simple fact of social life, wherever it might be situated. Just as there might be 8 million stories to be found in the city, so might there be in the organizations that make up the city (Silliphant, 1958). Some of the tales come extraordinarily well annotated, curated by archivists, whereas others may be just rumours, remembrances. There are, as Boje (2011) suggests, not only narratives but also antenarratives, fragments of stories, allusions. History is known through its telling and remembering as well as its re-membering and its forgetting. History translates a sense of the past in the present through accounts, be they oral traditions, organizational or legal accounts, accounts in the media or gossip, or simply what interviewees might tell us when we ask them specific questions. Any of these accounts both reveal and conceal data about the accounting and that which is accounted, as well as that which is not accounted. No authority resides in any single accounting; if it did, we would have to defer to various accounts far more than would be wise in scholarly terms. Just because a key figure, a very stable genius, for example, acting in a role in which considerable power is vested, provides an account of something, a wise person would not accept such an account at face value. They would cross-check accounts, review sources, document interpretations, build up a grid elaborating what is taken to be the reliability of the various sources consulted. They would situate the being, the character, of the object under study and those that populated it through a tapestry of sources.

The object of the organization is both a historical actor and actant; it is personified and instrumental; it is the voices and the voiceless of history, as well as those devices that dominated and liberated that which became that history. There are many histories, some official, some unofficial, others scurrilous and some imagined. Any actually existing organization contains myriad histories that situate it: founders' tales and creation myths; consultants' reports and survey responses; ethnographies and audits; video, audio and text-based accounts; tales of power as well as of troubled times; accounts of the subaltern as well as subaltern accounts; her story as well as his story; the good, the bad and the ugly.

Given the detritus of material sedimented in the structuring of relations, in devices developed, adopted and abandoned, in performances rated and appraised, in characters recalled and celebrated, as well as those condemned to be forgotten, leaving the barest traces, of designs superseded and inimitable capabilities in place and out of time, there is an infinite number of accounts; indeed, there are millions of stories.

Making sense of historical organization studies – an illustration

One of us (Clegg, 2017) published a contribution called 'The East India Company: The first modern multinational?' Three years later, in 2020, the author read a newly published book, *The Anarchy: The Relentless Rise of the East India Company* by

William Dalrymple (2019). Both contributions deal with the same phenomenon, the actually existing organization known as the East India Company, and both argue a similar thesis that, in Dalrymple's (2019: 396) words, 'the East India Company – the first great multinational corporation, and the first to run amok – was the ultimate model and prototype for many of today's joint stock companies'. He goes on to remark, in conclusion to his magisterial volume, how,

> Such was the disruption caused in eighteenth-century India by the advent of the East India Company that a whole new literary genre was invented to deal with it. This is the genre of moralizing histories known as The Book of Admonition, or *Ibrat-Nâma*. The admonitory purpose of these histories was put succinctly by Khair ud-Din Illahabadi, the author of the best known volume: *Az fâra-did-I sar -guzasht-i guzashtâgan, bar khud 'ibrat pazîrad'* – By considering these past lives, take heed for your own future.
>
> The East India Company remains history's most ominous warning about the potential for abuse of corporate power – and the insidious means by which the interests of shareholders can seemingly become those of the state. For, as recent American adventures in Iraq have shown, our world is far from post-imperial, and quite probably never will be. Instead, Empire is transforming itself into forms of global power that use campaign contributions and commercial lobbying, multinational finance systems and global markets, corporate influence and the predictive data harvesting of the new surveillance-capitalism rather than – or sometimes alongside – overt military conquest, occupation or direct economic domination to affect its ends.
>
> Four hundred and twenty years after its founding, the story of the East India Company has never been more current
>
> *(Dalrymple, 2019: 397)*

In telling his tale of power, Dalrymple deploys a huge variety of source material: he uses maps of eighteenth-century India, constructs a *dramatis personae* of the complex cast of characters that people his pages, as well as a grasp of the actants that aided and abetted their rise and fall, comprised of ships, forts, navigation devices, finances and banking systems, weapons, military strategies, famines, financial crises and much else. The book features ample illustrations, both literally and figuratively, of the people and places discussed, catalogues of manuscripts consulted in the Indian National Archives; the Company's official records; the private correspondence of many of its most famous actors; the poetry of Shah Alam; the Bengali poet Ganga Ram's *Maharashta Purana*; archives in the Punjab, England and Scotland, both public and private; materials from French, English, Tamil, Persian, Bengali and Urdu sources, as well as scholarly articles in journals of repute. The book teems with life and detail.

No one can read this astonishingly detailed work of history without being overawed by the sheer industry that the 6 long years, as well as the assistance the author had during that time, have been able to produce. Yet, the nearest that the author comes to offering a theory about the organization that he has so carefully studied comes in the last two pages. In many ways, the book is a testament to one part of the 'dual integrity' (Maclean, Harvey and Clegg, 2016) written about in the first chapter of this book, the methodological rigour (Maclean, Harvey and Stringfellow, 2017), the sound and robust investigatory procedures that characterize the best histories. History at its purest is written from the sources and the prodigious work required to digest and detail these sources, composing a narrative.

When Clegg wrote the paper on the East India Company that was published in 2017, he had consulted just a few primary sources and a selection of secondary sources but he was armed at the ready with a conceptual apparatus that he was able to draw on from a work he had completed on conceptualizing multinationals in a book on *Strategy: Theory & Practice* (Clegg, Schweitzer, Pitelis and Whittle, 2017). The research for that chapter provided a conceptual frame with which to view the East India Company. He began from the concepts and read the data through these, having a grid with which to make sense of those data consulted. He fashioned one part of dual integrity quite readily, having the resources to hand. A narrative was fashioned also, strung on the superstructure of the conceptual grid with a datum from here, a datum from there. The author is in no doubt that the grid came first, however; once the grid was extracted from the prior work on multinational strategy, the sensemaking was in place to arrange the data, as they were available through access to various secondary works, to construct the narrative. The East India paper was a work of history that approached its subject through a conceptual grid, as opposed to Dalrymple's (2019) approach through the archives.

These are two quite opposed ways of working; one privileges data, fragments, sources, carefully crafted into a narrative vibrant with detail and long in the recounting. The other privileges concepts and the grids that they can conjure and then searches for the data to illustrate the thesis. What dual integrity requires in its demands is the accomplishment of both practices: it must be able to achieve organizational mastery in narrating the sources into a ripping yarn, and that yarn should be woven into the weft and warp of a conceptual frame provided by detailed knowledge of disembedded and generalizing concepts as deployed across a variety of appropriate theoretical sources. Had the Dalrymple book been available in 2017, dual integrity could have been much better respected, which suggests that one fruitful avenue for historical organization studies is to work with our conceptual framing and with the detailed histories that mastery of the archives can produce. A single person does not have to do all the work, and a division of labour, whether explicit or implicit, that is respectfully constructed, can do much to advance dual integrity. There are many such admirable histories available that can be data for organization scholars.

A history of the present

There are many impediments to achieving dual integrity in organization studies. The most basic are assumptions about the ontology of cause and how to capture it epistemologically. Habermas (1972) wrote about knowledge interests. The knowledge interest in control has been accumulated over time in the field now known as organization studies. There are historical as well as contemporary reasons for this interest. The history of the present, Michel Foucault once remarked, is 'a history of the different modes by which, in our culture, human beings are made subjects' (1982: 208). We presume that many of our readers will be subjects of business schools much like those that employ the authors (Maclean, Harvey and Clegg, 2017). The business school, historically, had humble origins, in commercial colleges and trade schools, as a part of vocational education, before it was instituted as a part of the University of Pennsylvania in 1881. Once incorporated in the institution of the university, it became a part of an institutional nexus being forged from ideas about what constituted science, the professions and research. The origins of modern industrial capitalism in the United States are rooted in the last quarter of the nineteenth century and first quarter of the twentieth century. Part of that history was the colonization of capitalism's intermediary functionaries, the managers, by engineering discourse that promised to instil efficiency, equity and industrial harmony. The professional rhetoric of the new managerial project was largely constituted in terms of norms of technical rationality. The key conceptual idea of efficiency was one that readily translated seamlessly into the neo-classical economics and economic rationalism that would later come to dominate the business schools in the 1980s.

Management as a *profession* offered the promise of 'scientific modernity' – a rationally ordered world, populated by rational individuals capable of scientific analysis and modelling that could be put to practical use in conducting the affairs of men (all the early texts concerned with management students assumed that they would be men). In the conception of the nineteenth-century founders of the business school model, management as a profession would become an occupation that could claim both exclusive *expertise* in and an *ethical* ground for *efficiency in practice*. The expertise, especially after the widely circulated rhetoric of F.W. Taylor (1911), was to be premised on a rationality conceived as if it were a science, in which the ethical dimension of professionalism would derive from that science being applied in the service of efficiency.

The narratives of Taylorist rational efficiency were forged in a crucible in which control was sought over contingent variables that could be manipulated to enhance organizational outcomes of various sorts. There was a history, of sorts, to scientific management's manipulation of independent variables such as illumination (Hassard, 2012) in a causal context that strove to be experimental, using systematic variance to discover what became known much later, more broadly, as 'best practice'. Thinking of phenomena in this way prioritizes those variables that can be held to account, that can be manipulated, that can make a difference. To do so is to privilege a very specific conception of causality in which phenomena have to be seen to be related; must be seen to be related significantly and, importantly, to be subject to managerial control. That managerial control could be equated with efficiency was a notion that suffered repeated blows during the Depression era, before the Second World War revived it in its all-American guise.

The Second World War had a profound effect on the institutions of American life, including the business school. The United States won the war, it was widely assumed, not just because its forces were overwhelming and unblooded by campaigns on the Eastern Front, as were the German troops they faced, but because of the organizational expertise and precision of the planning for the Normandy landings. Moreover, although the other armies made some use of new social science techniques of personnel selection and training, none did so with the energy, efficiency, the sheer scale of resources, of the United States. From this energy and these investments, new research topics, approaches and funding developed rapidly, and massive new organizations mobilizing millions of people were constructed and experienced. In the post-war era, the realization was that the new society of the 'organization man' (Whyte 1960) required a commitment to technically rational management if it were to function effectively. Not surprisingly, many officers in the military assumed office in the corporations.

In the 1950s, the Ford Foundation and the Carnegie Corporation deployed extensive rhetorical and pecuniary resources in building a commitment in elite business schools to research-based, social science, quantitative disciplinary knowledge. Major book-length reports were published in 1959. Science was on the agenda, with the new science being behavioural. The times they were a-changing.

The times that were changing had historical specificity. In the English language, historical lags in translation from the German had made Max Weber's (1922; 1924; 1946; 1947; 1978) early twentieth-century posthumous writings late arriving foundations for post-war studies of organizations (Clegg, Courpasson and Phillips, 2006). His ideas became largely known in departments of sociology, where his ideas flourished in 1950s typological analyses of organizations (Gouldner, 1954). By the 1960s, Weber's interpretative and historically comparative sociology was increasingly challenged by theories of the social system (Parsons, 1951), with its functional prerequisites and pattern variables much better suited to the new science.

Science, the new science, was to be shown off at best through statistical data, factor analysis and regression equations. These were the foundations of the knowledge that put the business schools on a more professional and scientific footing by widespread recruitment of behavioural scientists from psychology, political science and economics, among other disciplines. The new science cast the die in favour of conceptions of causality in which ontogenetic conceptions, inhering in either the essence of a phenomenon or its history, were marginal (Khurana, 2007). The trajectory of business school development in an Anglosphere that was becoming ever more neo-liberal from the 1980s onwards ensured that quaint concerns with the history of phenomena remained, by and large, marginal. Henceforth, Max Weber and his heirs, for whom comparative histories were vital, were largely to be found elsewhere or, if the originals were cited, reduced to elements in 'classical theory' whose analyses of specific historical tendencies of bureaucracy, in Weber's case, were interpreted as essential, contingent dependent variable features of all organizations (Pugh and Hickson, 1976). Cross-sectional causality allowed for control of organizational design by adjusting the variables much as the Hawthorne researchers adjusted the levels of illumination. Causality, conceived in terms of spatially and temporally proximate variables, can be controlled and manipulated. To be able to exercise this control is important for any aspect of organizational design, at whatever level, be it psychological, organizational or strategic.

Structural causality, whether historical, ontogenetic or naturally tendential, is a very different concept to that of cross-sectional causality. Except in science fiction and those polities, organizations and forms of governmentality based on the possibility of such fictions, present designs cannot be redrawn in any causal way that controls the past as a manipulable variable. The past in the present can be undone by contestations based on other accounts; hence the importance of censorship in certain forms of organizational and other politics. The past *can* be made an open book; turning the page, consulting another source, gaining another interpretation make the past as infinite and as malleable as ingenuity will allow. It *cannot* be controlled in a simulacrum of physics envy. Hence, all that enter into historical approaches to organizations should leave notions of synchronous causality at the threshold. What is distinctive about the historical perspective is a conception of causality that is structural or genealogical. To articulate the challenge of dual integrity, causality has to be conceptually mapped and tapped through deep immersion in the historical constitutions of the field.

A history of the future? A current research agenda for historical organization studies

On the presumption that (a) the interest in control can be relaxed in favour of an interest in scholarship per se, scholarship that is disinterested in being a managerial accessory and (b) that such scholarship can be founded on non-presentist conceptions of causality, possibilities can be sketched for future research. These possibilities concern historical shifts in physical proximity, defined as 'the probability of people being in the same location during the same period of time' (Monge and Kirste, 1980: 110), whereby organizational proximity is 'the extent to which people in an organization share the same physical locations at the same time providing an opportunity or psychological obligation to engage in face-to-face communication' (Monge, Rothman, Eisenberg, Miller and Kirste, 1985: 1133). Thus defined, opportunity and psychological obligation are outcomes of proximity. The reason why people in an organization share the same physical locations at the same time is mainly to be found in task interdependence: 'the extent to which the items or elements upon which work is performed or the work processes themselves are interrelated so that changes in the state of one element affect the state of the others' (Scott and Davis, 2007: 126–127). Especially when interdependence is sequential or reciprocal (Thompson, 2007: 54–55), workers need to be physically proximate to perform their bodily embedded tasks.

These spatial relations are changing. With the advance of a globalizing economy, of outsourcing and of alliances, as well as of information technologies, an increasing number of people can or must collaborate at a distance. Not only that, the assumptions that have led to internal organizational spatial relations premised on open-plan offices, hot desking and close working in small meeting rooms are increasingly questionable. These questions of distance have achieved heightened acuity with the effects of the COVID-19 pandemic closing down a large part of economic activity and imposing rules of social distancing.

Self-regulation has historically become increasingly internalized, something on which both Foucault (1977) and Elias (1982) agree. Elias argues that longer and more complex chains of interdependence between people lead to greater self-regulation. Elsewhere, it has been suggested that this self-regulation may be because of enhanced proximity and visibility (Clegg and van Iterson, 2013). Where interdependence and its constraints remain invisible, the effect may be the reverse, a lessening of self-regulation. Making organizational structures more flexible and fluid transfers regulation from the disciplines of the organization to the discipline of the self. In an age when, as a result of lockdowns and social distancing, the lack of proximity with and spatial awareness of the others with whom one interacts is not just a matter of distance, as in supply chains, but also social distance that strives to minimize contiguity, these social changes, contingent on the pandemic spread of the corona virus, open possibilities for increasingly less self-regulated behaviour to occur, characterized by increasing levels of abuse, bullying and anger. These behaviours may be prompted by the increasing amounts of locked-down time together endured by people who might be better served by spatial and temporal separation (Cormack, 2020). They might also be a result of the increasing intermediation of social interaction by online channels.[1] Social distancing and its frustrations are also leading to increasing anti-social behaviour.[2] Indeed, in some jurisdictions, performative anger at the loss of liberties that state regulation of social distancing entails has created graphic images of armed insurrection entering forcefully into state assemblies that belie Weber's (1978) conception of the state as an organization with the legitimate monopoly of the means of violence.

The imposition of social distancing as a form of self-regulation in a time of pandemic creates the conditions for a natural historical comparative experiment. Has the virtual university created almost overnight led to increased or diminished civility in terms of interactions between students and between staff and students? How do these effects vary across different countries? Isolating and working from home are not available as options to all people. It depends on the kind of work they do; for instance, personal service work, body work and skin trades cannot be done in isolation (O'Neill, 1970; 1972). Homeless people and multi-occupancy tenancies cannot isolate. Total institutions such as prisons, cruise ships and aged care facilities cannot easily practise isolation as their design dictates congregation at key times, such as meal services.

Of course, COVID-19 opens up other avenues for research. The virus is widely argued to have spread from bats to wild animals sold in wet markets in Wuhan, where the purchasers and eaters of these animals provided hosts for the virus from whom it could spread in the human population. This suggests that, in a globalized world in which humans can move rapidly from one place to another, the variable development of the civilizing process in different places leaves humanity at risk from its least civilizationally self-regulating enclaves, such as wet markets, with wild animals captured for human consumption. That the consequences of this local niche in the civilizing process have produced a virus that has had the consequences of intensifying self-regulation through social distancing, with civilizational lag forcing civilizational processes elsewhere, is indeed ironical.

Infectious disease has been 'one of the fundamental parameters and determinants of human history' (McNeill 1998: 295), the greatest single cause of death around the world, with the present pandemic no exception. The extent of the pandemic, its origin in China and the hostility of its regime to inquiry into responsibilities and remedial actions suggests that the civilizing process remains acutely politically disaggregated. The existence of the wet markets and their captive species is in part attributed to the marginalization of peasants from large-scale industrial agrarianism. The rise of industrial-scale farming in China and the resulting marginalization of millions of smallholder farmers have meant that, in order to survive, those farmers that have been pushed out geographically to the margins of prime farming land live and work closer to uncultivable zones such as forests, where bats – reservoirs for coronaviruses – lurk and infect the animals that the farmers trap for sale in the market.

The COVID-19 virus has become an actant that connects those areas least civilizationally self-regulated with the furthest reaches of the civilizational process. The pandemic will accelerate or accentuate aspects of the civilizational processes it has made problematic. Britain's brief dalliance with herd immunity and the survival of the fittest philosophy that lay behind it, the increasing use of lockdown and social isolation, random acts of violence in resistance to self-regulation – through individual coughing and spitting in anger through to widespread armed and organized civil disobedience in the United States – demonstrate that there is much historical unevenness to be explained in the civilizing process (see van Krieken, 2019).

Beck (1992) published *The Risk Society* in the wake of Chernobyl; since that time, the veracity of his thesis that contemporary risks are global and respect no boundaries has been validated by the effects of tsunamis, volcanic ash clouds and, most recently, the effects of COVID-19. These events are examples of existential threats: they threaten life itself on a global scale. The Commission for the Future has reported that, 'The coronavirus pandemic, with its demand for unified global action, also presents an unprecedented chance for humanity to combine in solving its other shared threats'.[3] More than an opportunity for learning, COVID-19 offers also a wake-up call in relation to the necessity to prepare to deal with existential threats that can be plausibly foreshadowed but not forecasted.

The experience of the current global pandemic has revealed another important limitation of our current practices and theorizing. COVID-19 was not a completely unexpected event: the WHO had alerted world governments to the likelihood of a pandemic, especially in the aftermath of the SARS and MERS epidemics of the past decade. Moreover, even before COVID-19, contemporary society had known the devastating effect of HIV-caused AIDS, a 'slow-burn' pandemic causing tens of millions of fatalities around the planet.

Events such as COVID-19 are hardly 'Black Swan' events (Taleb, 2007) – that is, events which have enormous impact but are also very rare. They are predictable surprises (Watkins and Bazerman, 2003). Pandemics should not be unexpected; they have happened in the past and they will doubtless occur in the future, even if we do not know when. What makes a phenomenon such as COVID-19 problematic in terms of risk assessment is not the fact that it is totally unpredictable but that neither the specific characteristics of the phenomenon nor exactly when it might occur can be forecast based on past trends. Trends are by their very nature retrospective in character, as we review their causes by looking back to their origins. This high degree of uncertainty makes traditional risk management techniques, based on quantitative assessment and assumptions of linear causality, worthless.

If there are unprecedented opportunities for humanity to combine in the face of these threats, as the Commission for the Human Future suggests, they can only be achieved through organizational capabilities (Baker, 2020). However, much of organizational risk management is ritual in the face of endemic uncertainty about *what* will happen, *where* and *when,* as Pierides, Clegg and Cunha (2020) argue with reference to emergency management services. Invariably, planning is conducted for the events of prior emergencies, rather than the unknown unknowns of the future.

Many developed countries, such as the UK and USA, had developed very sophisticated pandemic response plans, based on the stockpiling of medical materials and the preparation of detailed protocols of actions. Yet, in the last couple of decades, various political pressures (ranging from calls for reducing public expenditures to the need to signal discontinuity with previous governments) have led to the dismantling of these risk management systems. The obvious consequence is that these countries have been severely affected by the virus diffusion. By contrast, countries which had directly suffered the effects of the SARS and MERS epidemics have arguably been much better prepared to deal with the threat, greatly reducing the first impact of the pandemic.

Management capabilities for coping with surprise and uncertainty on a system-redefining scale should not be reduced to planning and compliance; they should be understood as a suite of individual, organizational and inter-organizational knowledges, practices and attitudes developed historically. This understanding prompted a group of scholars within the field of historical organization studies to launch an essay competition in March 2020 inviting responses to the question, 'What lessons can history provide to companies and managers currently coping with the impact of COVID-19?' Forty-one essays were received, and the six best papers were published online. The winner, Siobhan Nelson, of the University of Toronto, in a wide-ranging study of the treatment of infectious diseases, draws three lessons from the history of nursing: first, go back to the basics of hygiene and infection control; second, innovate in the face of a new disease; third, prioritize support for front-line staff before, during and after a pandemic (Nelson, 2020). The need is to sustain robust healthcare systems. These systems, however, require a constant investment to be created, maintained and renewed. As such systems imply conspicuous investments, it is necessary to consider the need to maintain both their legitimacy and support. The more developed and sophisticated the system is, the more legitimacy its maintenance will require, which can be particularly problematic if its necessity is not perceived (Watkins and Bazerman, 2003).

Changes in social conceptions of distance are already emerging in post-virus China. Human contact is being minimized in service organizations; social relations are being authoritatively organized, medicalized and sanitized with wipes, mask and thermometers with spaces in which multiple occupancies occur being deep-cleaned (Moritz, 2020). Building and maintaining a collective capacity to manage the implications of catastrophic but unlikely risks require a consideration of a range of social and organizational issues, such as how social networks and global chains of interdependence operate and change historically over time, transforming the nature of power relations. The most fundamental aspects of being human, how we relate intimately to each other, are being challenged by responses to a mute coronavirus.

The implications of pandemic threats are well known. Chen, Lau, Woo and Yuen (2007) warned of the likelihood of COVID-1, known as SARS, reappearing. They concluded their analysis by saying that:

> Coronaviruses are well known to undergo genetic recombination ... which may lead to new genotypes and outbreaks. The presence of a large reservoir of SARS-CoV-like viruses in horseshoe bats, together with the culture of eating exotic mammals in southern China, is a time bomb. The possibility of the re-emergence of SARS and other novel viruses from animals or laboratories and therefore the need for preparedness should not be ignored.
>
> *(Chen et al., 2007: 683)*

The existence of scientific knowledge is insufficient to overcome various vulnerabilities of organizational sensemaking, including psychological dispositions, organizations' strategic preparedness and the political interests of organizational elites (Weick, 1995). That this is the case is especially evident at the level of state organization. The capacity of the state within differing political cultures, how quotidian community relations change and reflect ideologies about national identity and culture, as well as the role that technology plays in everyday life, all contribute to the kind of society we design through processes of inclusion and exclusion. The history of the organizational future is being accelerated now, as these words are being written. At its very centre will be profound questions about civilizing processes, social regulation and their organization that will predicate the history of the future.

Two actants, two major social disruptors. First, the East India Company, wreaking havoc on ancient civilizations in India (and in China with its trade in opium). In many ways, its effects were akin to a long-lasting virus in its impact on bodies, individual, political and cultural, causing intergenerational anarchy in those regimes it transformed. Second, another actant, this time a virus proper, that jumped species, upended much of the world, questioning the extent of civilizing processes, throwing institutions and organizations into disarray and posing major issues with which organizational history might engage. A few of the issues that arise have been lightly sketched. What is evident in all of the issues sketched is that the effects of these chains of asynchronous causality cannot be thought of other than in their historical sense; they are matters that impinge deeply on current taken-for-granted notions of what regulation through selves, organizations and institutions entails in a global world. These taken-for-granted notions have been laminated historically and are being tested and deconstructed immediately.

Conclusion

By the time this book is read, its readers will be living and making these future histories. To echo a memorable phrase, they will be doing so not under circumstances of their choosing, but under circumstances existing already, given and transmitted from the past (Marx, 1852). That is how futures are made. There is an element of 'living up to the past' in composing new futures, reimagining and elaborating what has gone before while, at times concomitantly, there is an element of breaking with the past (Maclean, Harvey, Sillince and Golant, 2014). What will be most interesting, to recall Marx once more, will be the extent to which the spirits of the past are conjured up, their slogans intact, in time-honoured disguise and borrowed language or the extent to which these are superseded by a 'new dawn' (Wordsworth, 1850).

Interest in the impact of differing temporal spans on organizations and organizing is growing (Schultz and Hernes, 2013), offering fertile ground for the development of historical organization studies. The temporal depths that shape organizational becoming have the power to upset conventional ordering, as Durepos and Vince point out in this volume (Chapter 3), engendering nonlinear narratives that suggest new relationships with past, present and future and the interplay between them. Under such circumstances, 'the logical carapace of Time is attacked; there is no longer a chrono-logy (if we may separate the two parts of the word)' (Barthes, 1989: 281). This creates the potential for 'the chain of the hours, the sequence of the years … to grow confused, and to break its ranks' (Proust, 1981 [1954]: 5). The reordering or shifting of elements occasioned in this way brings to the surface deep structures normally hidden from view. The cultural substrata that underpin organizations and societies run deep, serving as powerful impediments to, or enablers of, change. Like slow-moving glaciers, incremental change at this sedimentary level is difficult to discern. In delving into distant pasts, whether that of the East India Company or that of eighteenth-century church governance, we uncover not only crucible events but traces of the deeper institutional and historical processes that gave rise to them, extending the scope of explication. It is our hope in compiling this book that it will serve as a guide to signpost the way to the multifarious potentialities or 'efflorescences' that lie ahead (White, 1973), pointing the way to new worlds of enchantment. We wish its readers every success in their forays into historical organization studies that beckon.

Notes

1 www.news.com.au/national/cyber-abuse-up-by-50-percent-amid-covid19-restrictions/video/0e8534dc15a01707ab2e065cb6a14178
2 www.npr.org/sections/coronavirus-live-updates/2020/04/28/846684162/what-to-do-when-people-dont-practice-social-distancing
3 Commission for the Human Future, www.humansforsurvival.org/node/86; see full report at http://humansforsurvival.org/sites/default/files/CHF_Roundtable_Report_March_2020.pdf

References

Baker, D. (2020). Complexity in the future: Far-from-equilibrium systems and strategic Foresight. In *The 21st century singularity and global futures*. Springer: Cham, 397–417.
Barthes, R. (1989). *The rustle of language*. Berkeley, CA: University of California Press.
Beck, U. (1992). *Risk society: Towards a new modernity*. London: Sage.
Boje, D.M. (ed.) (2011). *Storytelling and the future of organizations: An antenarrative handbook*. London: Routledge.
Cheng, V.C., Lau, S.K., Woo, P.C. and Yuen, K.Y. (2007). Severe acute respiratory syndrome coronavirus as an agent of emerging and reemerging infection. *Clinical microbiology reviews*, 20 (4): 660–694.
Clegg, S. (2017). The East India Company: The first modern multinational? In *Research in the sociology of organizations (Volume 49): Multinational corporations and organization theory: Post millenium perspectives*. Bingley: Emerald, 43–67.
Clegg, S.R., Courpasson, D., and Phillips, N. (2006). *Power and organizations*. London: Sage.
Clegg, S.R. and van Iterson, A. (2013) The effects of liquefying place, time, and organizational boundaries on employee behavior: Lessons of classical sociology, *Management*, 16 (5): 621–635.
Clegg, S.R., Schweitzer, J., Pitelis, C., and Whittle, A. (2017). *Strategy: Theory & practice*. London: Sage.
Clegg, S.R. (1981). Organization and control. *Administrative Science Quarterly*, 26 (4): 545–562.
Cormack, L. (2020) Domestic violence victims seeking help rises 10 per cent after COVID-19 lockdown, *Sydney Morning Herald*, May 1. www.smh.com.au/national/nsw/domestic-violence-victims-seeking-help-rises-10-per-cent-after-covid-19-lockdown-20200501-p54oxt.html, accessed 18.05.20.
Dalrymple, W. (2019). *The anarchy: The relentless rise of the East India Company*. London: Bloomsbury.
Elias, N. (1982). *The civilizing process*. New York: Pantheon Books.
Foucault, M. (1970). *The order of things*. London: Routledge.
Foucault, M. (1977). *Discipline and punish*. London: Allen Lane.
Foucault, M. (1982). The subject and power. In Dreyfus, H.L. and Rabinow, P. (eds), *Michel Foucault: Beyond structuralism and hermeneutics*. Chicago: University of Chicago Press, 202–226.
Gouldner, A.W. (1954). *Patterns of industrial bureaucracy*. Glencoe: Free Press.
Habermas, J. (1972). *Knowledge and human interests*. London: John Wiley.

Hassard, J.S. (2012). Rethinking the Hawthorne Studies: The Western Electric research in its social, political and historical context. *Human Relations*, 65 (11): 1431–1461.

Khurana, R. (2007). *From higher aims to hired hands: The social transformation of American business schools and the unfulfilled promise of management as a profession.* Princeton: Princeton University Press.

Maclean, M., Harvey, C., and Clegg, S.R. (2016). Conceptualizing historical organization studies. *Academy of Management Review*, 41 (4): 609–632.

Maclean, M., Harvey, C., and Clegg, S.R. (2017). Organization theory in business and management history: Current status and future prospects. *Business History Review*, 91 (3): 457–481.

Maclean, M., Harvey, C., Sillince, J.A.A., and Golant, B.D. (2014). Living up to the past? Ideological sensemaking in organizational transition. *Organization*, 21 (4): 543–567.

Maclean, M., Harvey, C., and Stringfellow, L. (2017). Narrative, metaphor and the subjective understanding of historic identity transition. *Business History*, 59 (8): 1218–1241.

McNeill, W.H. (1998 [1976]). *Plagues and peoples.* New York: Anchor Press.

Marx, K. (1852) *The Eighteenth Brumaire of Louis Bonaparte*, Marx/Engels Internet Archive, accessed 18.05.20.

Monge, P.R. and Kirste, K.K. (1980). Measuring proximity in human organizations. *Social Psychology Quarterly*, 43 (1): 110–115.

Monge, P., Rothman, L.W., Eisenberg, E.M., Miller, K.E., and Kirste, K.K. (1985). The dynamics of organizational proximity. *Management Science*, 31 (9): 1129–1141.

Moritz, M. (2020) The business world can never go back to the way things were. *Financial Times*, May. www.ft.com/content/bc7cbed2-8bae-11ea-a109-483c62d17528, accessed 05.05.20.

Nelson, S. (2020). *Nursing infectious disease: A history with three lessons.* Available at: https://www.historylessonscovid.org/files/2/Nelson%20Nursing.pdf, accessed 21.05.20.

O'Neill, J. (1970). Sociology as a skin trade. *Sociological Inquiry*, 40 (1): 101–104.

O'Neill, J. (1972). *Sociology as a skin trade: Essays towards a reflexive sociology.* New York: Harper Torchbooks.

Parsons, T. (1951). *The social system.* London: Routledge.

Pierides, D., Clegg, S.R., and e Cunha, M.P. (2020). The emergency management paradox as ritual. *Research in the Sociology of Organizations.* In press.

Pugh, D.S. and Hickson, D.J. (1976). *Organizational structure in its context: The Aston Programme* (Vol. 1). Westmead: Saxon House.

Proust, M. (1981[1954]). *Remembrance of Things Past.* London: Penguin.

Schultz, M. and Hernes, T. (2013). A temporal perspective on organizational identity. *Organization Science*, 24 (1): 1–21.

Scott, W.R. and Davis, G.F. (2007). *Organizations and organizing.* Upper Saddle River: Pearson.

Silliphant, S. (1958). *Naked City* (writer, TV drama). New York: ABC TV.

Taleb, N.N. (2007). *The black swan: The impact of the highly improbable.* New York: Random House.

Taylor, F.W. (1911). *The principles of scientific management.* London: Pearson.

Thompson, J.D. (2007). *Organizations in action.* New Brunswick: Transaction.

van Krieken, R. (2019). Norbert Elias and organizational analysis: Towards process-figurational theory. In Clegg, S.R. and Pina e Cunha, M. (eds), *Management, organizations and contemporary social theory.* London: Routledge, 158–184.

Watkins, M.D. and Bazerman, M.H. (2003). Predictable surprises: The disasters you should have seen coming. *Harvard Business Review*, 81 (3): 72–80, 140.

Weber, M. (1922). *Wirtschaft und Gesellschaft: Grundriß der verstehenden Soziologie Studienausgabe.* Cologne/Berlin: Kiepenheuer & Witsch.

Weber, M. (1924). *Gesammelte Aufsätze zur Sozial- und Wirtschaftsgeschichte*. Tübingen: Mohr.
Weber, M. (1946). *From Max Weber: Essays in sociology*. New York: Oxford University Press.
Weber, M. (1947). *The theory of social and economic organization* (Trans. A.M. Henderson and T. Parsons). Oxford: Oxford University Press.
Weber, M. (1978). *Economy and society: An outline of interpretive sociology*. Berkeley, CA: University of California Press.
Weick, K.E. (1995). *Sensemaking in organizations*. Thousand Oaks, CA: Sage.
White, H. (1973). *Metahistory: The historical imagination in nineteenth century Europe*. Baltimore, MD: Johns Hopkins University Press.
Whyte, W.H. (1960). *The organization man*. Harmondsworth: Penguin.
Wordsworth, W. (1850), *The prelude or, growth of a poet's mind; an autobiographical poem*, Internet Archive (1 edn), London: Edward Moxon.

INDEX

abstraction 85, 182, 198
academia 47–52, 197–198, 234
Accor 156
accountability 30–31, 34–35, 48, 209
accounting 32–33, 228
actor-network theory 8
actual, domain of 81–82
Adam, W. 177
aesthetics 51, 140, 142–143, 182
affect 142; *see also* emotion
affinity, historical 170, 172, 177, 179–180, 184–185
agency 92; in composition 50–51; institutional 188–189, 192, 200–201; rhetorical 152–153, 155–156, 160–162
airlines 81, 110, 150, 156–157, 163
Albert, S. 134–135
Aldrich, H.E. 159, 163
Alexander, W. 175
Alford, R. 25
Alger, R. 142
Allen, J. 109
Alouette satellite missions 107–108, 116–126
Alt, G.E. 193
Alvesson, M. 48, 50–51
anonymity 117, 210
Anteby, M. 90, 115
antenarratives 108, 111, 115, 117–123, 126, 228
ANTi-History 8, 39, 112
Archer, M. 26
architecture 170–173, 175–185

archives 10, 95, 154, 191–192, 230; art history 133, 138; gender/silences 108; postmodern approach 119; remembering/forgetting/imagining 114–116; Scotland/England 32; serendipity/immersion 86–87
Aristotle 26
Aronson, E. 63
art 140–145, 172; history of collecting 137–138; market 131–134
Art Nouveau 172, 174, 177, 182
ascription, of metaphors 68
Asia, East 140, 143–144
associative mind 45
Australia 93
authenticity 98–100, 136–137
avant-garde 172–174, 176–177, 181, 183

Bachand, E. 122
Badham, R. 12
banks 208–209, 216–217, 219
Barcelona 181–182
Barney, J.B. 92
Barthes, R. 152
Bastien, F. 13
Bateson, M.C. 50–51
Beck, U. 235
Becker, H. 131
behavioral sciences 232
Behbehanian, J. 160
Belfrage, C. 83–85, 87
belief 27, 30, 48, 93
Bell, C. 59, 62

Berg, M. 47, 49
Bergson, H. 183
Berlin 158–159, 162
Bertels, S. 190
Bhaskar, R. 82
Black, M. 63
Black Swan events 236
Black women 120; *see also* gender; race
Blanchot, M. 183
Boddice, R. 49
Boje, D.M. 111, 126, 228
Bollas, C. 45, 49
Borges, J.L. 227
Boston, MA 143
Bourdieu, P. 8, 26, 43, 149–151, 170–172, 174, 185
Braudel, F. 10
Brebner, J. 120
Bridgman, T. 12
Bruce, K. 9
Brussels 158, 160
Burke, K. 69
Burns, T. 63
business schools 231–232

Canada 93, 113; Alouette women 107–108, 116–126
capitalism 30, 48, 160, 229, 231; *see also* globalization; neoliberalism
Caribe Hilton 156–157
Carlsen, A. 117
Carnegie Corporation 232
Carter, R.G.S. 110
case study research 133, 138–140, 191, 209–210
Casey, A. 14
Catalonia 170–171, 181–183
Caterpillar 92
Catholics 26–27, 34, 160–161
causality 60, 81–82, 91–92, 191, 230–233, 238
Caverly, B. 159
CED (central, enduring, and distinctive) features 135
celebrity 160–161
censorship 109–111, 115, 122, 233
ceramics 140–142, 144
change, institutional 149–151, 157, 188–190, 200
Chapman, J.H. 116
Charle, C. 173
Charmaz, K. 84
Cheng, V.C. 237
Chihadeh, C. 12
China 143–144, 234–235, 237

Christianity 26–27, 30–35
chronology 40–47, 49–50, 53, 238
Chrysty, G. 59
Church of England 26, 30–35
Church of Scotland 29–35, 171
civilizing process 235
Clegg, S.R. 4–5, 108–109, 228–230, 236
clock time 48–49
Clore, C. 160
coalition building 155, 159–160, 162
coding 84, 141, 192
Cold War 107, 111, 113, 150, 160–161
collecting, history of 137–138
collection museums 131–133, 138–145
collective memory 96, 108, 113–115, 133, 135–137
collector-founders 131–134, 138–139, 145
Collingwood, R.G. 6, 11
colonization 91, 93–94, 96–98
Coman, S. 14
commemoration 136–137, 222; *see also* memory
Commission for the Future 235–236
common law 35
Communications Research Centre (CRC) 116, 120
communion 27, 29
communism 161–163, 208–209, 212–216; *see also* post-communist societies
comparative history 30, 36
composition, by narrative 40, 45–47, 50–52
comprehension, by narrative 40, 43–44, 47–50
confidentiality 117, 210
confluence, historical 189, 200–201
consciousness, historical 77–78, 87–88, 91, 98
Conservative Party 170
construction, social 61, 80–81, 84, 135
context sensitivity 6
control 231, 233; former state-owned enterprise 207–209, 213–222; gender and 113
Coraiola, D.M. 13, 79–80
Corbin, J. 84
coronaviruses 234–238
corporate social responsibility (CSR) 8
corrective critique 69
corruption 209, 221–222
Cotton, J. 160
Courpasson, D. 109
COVID-19 234–238
creed 26
critical grounded theory (CGT) 83–88
critical history 11, 78–79, 81, 83, 85, 87

critical imagination 108, 111–112, 117
critical realism (CR) 78, 81–84, 87
critique, corrective v. debunking 69
Cuba 158
cultural capital 99–100
culture 237; indigenous 91–101; museums and 132, 144; organizational 58–62, 65–66
Cummings, S. 10, 12
Cunliffe, A.L. 46, 53
Czech Republic 209–210, 214–222
Czechoslovakia 208–209, 213

Dalrymple, W. 229–230
data 4–6, 10, 83–87, 116–117
De Certeau, M. 11–12
Decker, S. 84
deconstruction 78, 80–81
deduction 85
Defence and Research Telecommunications Establishment (DRTE) 118–122, 124
Deleuze, G. 7, 183
Derrida, J. 114
despair 117
determinism 190, 201
devolution 170–171, 174, 183
Dewar, D. 171, 174–178, 180, 182
DiMaggio, P.J. 151, 188, 190
disciplines, bridging 4, 16–17, 77, 139
discourse 71–72, 111–112, 152–153; see also language; narratives
discursive strategies 8
distancing, social 234–235, 237
diversity 8
doctors 190, 193–201
Domingues, J.M. 82
dreamworlds 45, 51
dual integrity 5, 9, 230, 233
Dunbar, M. 123, 125
Duncan, M. 183
Durepos, G. 7, 11–12, 238
Durkheim, E. 136
Dutton, J.E. 117
Dyer, L. 13

e Cunha, M.P. 236
Eadie, W.P. 174
East India Company 228–230, 237
Edinburgh 31, 170, 174–175, 183–184
Edinburgh Royal Academy 177
education 34–35; of managers 8–9, 58–59, 61, 70, 72; of nurses 193–195, 197–198
Egypt 162
Eisenhardt, K.M. 163–164
Eisenhower, D. 161

Eisenstadt, S.N. 151
Elias, N. 234
emancipation 86–88
embodied history 40, 43, 46–47, 50, 52
EMBT 172–173, 176–177, 182
emotion 41–47, 49–51, 53, 110, 117–118, 142
engineering 114, 123; former state-owned enterprises 210–212, 216, 218, 220; medical 196
England 30–35
Episcopalians 31
episodic power 189–190
epistemology 4, 9–10, 39, 77–79, 111, 231
ethnography 85–86
European Cooperation Agency (ECA) 159, 162
European Group for Organizational Studies (EGOS) 4
European Recovery Program (ERP) 157, 159, 161

faculty career achievement 47–52
faith 26–27, 30, 36, 160–162
Faulconbridge, J.R. 172
feminism 108–109, 126; see also gender
Fenollosa, E. 142–143
Fernández, P. 191
field: formation 155–159, 162; of power 149–155, 162–164; theory 171–173, 177, 184
Fiol, C.M. 159, 163
Fleming, J. 59
fluid metaphors 71
Ford Foundation 232
foregrounding 68
forgetting 7, 95, 113–115, 126
Foster, N. 180
Foster, W.M. 7, 13, 79, 90
Foucault, M. 25, 27, 30, 109, 131, 227, 231, 234
founder figures 131–134, 136–139, 144–146, 153
Fowler, B. 174
Franklin, C. 116
Fraser, Lord 176, 180
Freer Gallery of Art 132–133, 138–145
French, W. 59, 62
Freud, S. 64
Friedland, R. 25–26, 36
Fulton, B. 123

Gagné, M.-A. 96
Ganzin, M. 98
Gasparin, M. 8

Gaudi, A. 182
Geddes, P. 183
Geertz, C. 35
gender 81, 107–126, 138, 192–201; antenarratives 111–112; gendered remembering 112–115; methodology 116–117; silences 109–111; space industry 118–126
generative moments 117–118
Germany 28, 158–159, 162
ghosts, institutional 132, 144
Gibbons, J. 176
Giddens, A. 26
Glaser, B.G. 83–84
Glasgow School of Art (GSA) 173–174, 177, 179–181
Global South 8
globalization 154–160, 233–235
Godfrey, P.C. 125
Goffman, E. 28
Golant, B.D. 69
Gordon, R. 176
governance 34–35
Graham, H. 35–36
grand narratives 111, 125; *see also* narratives
Grant, D. 69
Green, S.E. 152
Green, W. 8
Greenwood, R. 164
grounded theory, critical 83–88
Guest, G.D. 142–143

Habermas, J. 231
Halbwachs, M. 136
Hall, E.T. 59–60, 64–65
Hamann, R. 190
Harlos, K. 109–111
Harris, V. 114–115
Hartt, C. 112
Harvey, C. 4–5, 8, 14, 108
Hauf, F. 83–85, 87
healthcare *see* nursing
Hellriegel, D. 59
Helms Mills, J. 7, 112
Herman, S. 59, 69
Hermes satellite 118
heterotopias 131
Higonnet, A. 131
Hilton, C. 150, 154–155, 157–164
Hilton Hotels Corporation (HHC) 150, 154, 156
Hilton Hotels International (HHI) 150, 154, 156–160, 162
Hilton International Company (HIC) 150, 154, 159–161

historical affinity 170, 172, 177, 179–180, 184–185
historical confluence 189, 200–201
historical consciousness 77–78, 87–88, 91, 98
historical homology 170–172, 177, 184
historical institutionalism 7
historical organization studies (HOS) 3–18, 201, 238–239; bridging disciplines 16–18; conceptual contributions 11–13; definition 3; disciplines/traditions 4, 90; methodology/epistemology 9–10, 29, 154, 189, 191, 230; principles 5–6; putting into action 6; reflexivity 41–46, 52–53; research agenda 233–238; theoretical applications 13–16
historical reflexivity *see* reflexivity
historicism, in architecture 178, 180, 183
historicization 3–5, 137
history 227–238; of collecting 137–138; collective memory 136–137; comparative 30, 36; critical 11, 78–79, 81, 83, 85, 87; embodied 40, 43, 46–47, 50, 52; as evaluating/explicating/conceptualizing/narrating 5; of the future? 233–238; *longue durée* 10, 154; of management education 8–9; of practices 27–28, 35–36; of the present 230–233; problematic for indigenous peoples 93–94; reconstructivist/deconstructivist ontologies 79–81; rhetorical 7, 136–137; theory and 6–7, 9
Holt, R. 135
Holyrood 175, 178–179, 181
homology 170–172, 177, 181, 184
hotel industry 150, 154, 156–164, 218
Houser, J. 159
hubris 63–64, 67
Hume, D. 179
Hunter, K.M. 110

ice cube model 61, 70
iceberg 57–72; as counter-metaphor 67–70; as generative metaphor 62–67; as sleeping metaphor 58–62
iconography 178–179, 181–182
identity 7; academic/professional 49–52; gendered 108, 113–114; indigenous 92–94, 96–99; museums/founders 131–133, 144–146; national 171–172, 178–181, 184–185, 237; organizational 132–138, 145
imagination, critical 108, 111–112, 117
incongruity, perspective by 69–70
India 8, 229, 237

indigenous peoples 91–101; 'past occurrences' 96–98; past as related/circular 95–96; post-colonial history, cultural capital, authenticity 98–100; problem with history 93–94; translating knowledge 94–95
induction 83, 85
industry emergence 151–153, 164
institutional change 149–151, 157, 188–190, 200
institutional entrepreneurship 149–151, 188, 190–191; industry emergence and 151–153; methodology 154; in practice 151–164
institutional 'ghosts' 132, 144
institutional logics 25–26
institutional work 188–191, 200–201
institutionalism: historical 7; rhetorical 152
InterContinental Hotel Corporation (ICH) 156–158, 162
interdependence 233–234, 237
interpretation 78, 87–88
intersectionality 114; see also gender; race; sexuality
interviews 27–28, 116–118, 189, 191–192
Inuit people 99
investment privatization funds (IPFs) 208, 215
Iran 159, 162
irony 68–69
Istanbul 159, 162
Italy 160

Janssens, M. 8
Japan 139–145, 189, 191–202; expansion of nurses' education/status 197–199; postwar reform 193–196; recognition of nurses' status/power 198–200; technology and 196–197
Jelly, D. 117–118, 120–125
Jessop, B. 84
Jones, G. 8
Jordanova, L. 30

Kanter, R.M. 114
Keenoy, T. 69
Keith, G.S. 34
Kerr, R. 15
Ketelaar, E. 86
Kieser, A. 90
King, T. 97
Kipping, M. 4
kirk sessions 31–34
Knoll, M. 110
knowing 77–79, 111, 117–118

knowing see also epistemology
knowledge, indigenous 94–96, 101
Kōetsu 144–145
Kraatz, M.S. 190
Kurzon, D. 110

labor 195–201, 210–213; institutional work 188–191, 200–201
Labour Party 170
Lakoff, G. 57
Lamberg, J.-A. 8, 92
Lancashire 27
language 152–153, 171; see also discourse
Latin America 157–158
Lau, S.K. 237
law 28, 35, 149
Lawrence, T.B. 189, 191
legitimation 98, 152–153, 155–156, 163, 207, 222, 237
Li, Y. 152
literacy 35
literature 171–172, 179
lock-down 234–235
Lodge, J.E. 143
London 158–160
longue durée 10, 154
Lounsbury, M. 25
Luyckx, J. 8

McKenzie, N.G. 8
Mackintosh, C.R. 171–174, 177, 179–182, 184–185
Maclean, M. 4–5, 8, 14, 108
MacLeish, H. 175
MacMillan, A. 176, 179
Madrid 159, 182
management 8–9, 114, 135, 231; contracts 158; former state-owned enterprises 207–222; iceberg metaphor 58–59, 61, 70, 72
Mando, J. 123–125
MANI 196
March, J.G. 70
Marriott International 156
Marsden, D. 92
Martí, I. 191
Marx, K. 238
Marxism 80
Maskwacis Cultural College 99
Massachusetts 143
Masuda Takashi 142, 144–145
mathematics 114, 121
Matsushita, K. 15
medicine see nursing
Meier, R. 176

Meiji era 142, 193
memorial inscriptions 28–29
memory 7, 9, 39; gendered remembering 108, 112–115, 118, 120, 125–126; indigenous peoples 95–96; museums and 133, 135–137; *see also* commemoration; forgetting
men *see* gender
Mesa, F. 182
metaphor 12, 57–72; counter- 67–70; generative 62–67; sleeping 58–62
methodology 9, 53, 83, 116–117, 173; art history 133, 138–139; critical grounded theory 83–84, 87–88; institutional entrepreneurship 154–156; institutional work 191–192; longitudinal 209–210; retroductive 84–87
Meyer, J.W. 92
Miller, S.B. 114, 125
Mills, A.J. 7, 13, 81, 86, 112
Minkus, A. 98
Miralles, E. 171, 173–185
mnemonics: organizational 113; *see also* memory
modernism, architectural 171, 180–182
modernity 64–65, 231
Molnár, V. 90, 115
monuments 144, 180–183
moral emotions 42
Morgan, E. 179
Morgan, G. 62
Morse, E.S. 142–143
Mullins, L. 59
Munslow, A. 78–79, 81
museums 131–134, 136, 138–146
Mutch, A. 8, 11, 26
Muthesius, H. 172, 174
myth 98

narratives 5, 146; antenarratives 108, 111, 115–123, 126, 228; de/constructivist approaches 80–81; of founders 136–137; founders' use of 152–153; organizational heroes/villains 221–222; of realization 43–50, 52; reflexive approaches 39–41; western/indigenous 95–97
NASA 114–116, 119, 125
Nasser, G.A. 162
national identity 171–172, 178–181, 184–185, 237
nature 177–178, 184
Nelson, S. 236
neoliberalism 47–50, 232
network analysis, social 139–142

New York Stock Exchange (NYSE) 150, 156
New Zealand 93
Newcastle 17
Nightingale, F. 193
nomenklatura 208, 211–213, 222
Nottinghamshire 32–33
nursing 189–202, 236; expansion of education/status 197–199; Japanese postwar reform 193–196; recognition of status/power 198–200; technology and 196–197

Ocasio, W. 25
O'Connor, J. 176
Olivera, F. 114, 125
Olsen, T. 109, 111
ontology 39, 111, 227, 230; critical realism 81–83; emancipatory 77–79, 87; indigenous 92, 96–97, 100; reconstructivist/deconstructivist 79–81
open systems 201
oral history 27, 192
oral tradition 95–97, 99
organization studies 3–6, 101, 209–210; gender and 113–114; historic turn 3, 17, 191; historical case studies 138–139; historical consciousness 77–78, 90–91; history of the present 230–233; iceberg metaphor 57, 61–62; of routines 27–28, 36; silences 109–110; theory 40–41, 52, 227–230
organizational identity 132–138, 145
organizational mnemonics 113
Oswick, C. 69

Pan American World Airlines (Pan Am) 157
pandemics 234–237
paradox 68–69
Paris 158–160
parishes 31–34, 36
parliament buildings 170–172, 174–175, 178–184
past: 'occurrences' 97–98; as related/circular 95–96; uses of 8, 77–78
path dependence 8
Perchard, A. 8
performance 27, 30, 35
performativity 50, 153
Phillips, N. 109
photography 111, 116, 118, 120–124, 126, 161
Pierides, D. 236
Pinder, C. 110
Pio, E. 8

place, identification with 28–29
Platt, C. 143
pluralistic understanding 5–6, 107, 115
Popp, A. 135
positivism 39, 82–84, 100
post-communist societies 207–222; transition/privatization 208–209; rise of "the magician" 212–216; magician's "fall from grace" 216–221
post-empiricists 80
postmodernism 40, 44, 80, 108, 119
Powell, W.W. 190
power: architectures of 180–181; field of 149–155, 162–164; gender relations, medical profession 189–190, 195–199; gender relations, space industry 110, 112–113, 115
practical realists 80
practices 25–26, 35–36, 110; ecclesiastical routines 31–34; governance/accountability 34–35; history of, challenges 27–28; religious 26–27, 29–30
practise, as verb 26
praxis 42
Presbyterians 27, 30–31, 34–35
Press, J. 8
Prinz, J. 143
privatization 207–209, 212, 220–222
professionals 15, 190, 198–200, 231
progress, as myth/assumption 43, 53, 91–92
Protestants 26, 30–35
Proust, M. 183
proximity 233–234
pubs 34
Puerto Rico 156–157, 159
Puerto Rico Development Corporation (PRDC) 157

Queensberry House 179
Quinn-Trank, C. 7, 90

race 94, 107, 114, 120
rationality 91–92, 114, 231; iceberg metaphor 63–66, 68–70; systems 60–61
Ravasi, D. 136
real: domain of 81–82; *see also* ontology
realism: critical 78, 81–84, 87; naïve 83; practical 80
realization, narratives of 43–50, 52
reconstructivist ontology 79–81
record keeping 29–30, 32–33
reflexivity 8, 39–53, 86, 99, 111; corporatized university 47–52; embodied history 46–47; iceberg metaphor 58;

narratives of realization 43–46; theory development 40–43
relationality 95–96
religion 26–27, 29–36, 160–161, 171
representational truth 6
representativeness 125
reputation 152, 159–160, 176, 207, 212, 221
research, meaningful 47–48, 50–52
research process *see* methodology
researcher 78–80, 87–88, 111
restricted production, pole of 172, 176–177
retroduction 82, 84–85
Reynolds, M. 44, 51
rhetorical agency 152–153, 155–156, 160–162
rhetorical history 7, 136–137
Rhoades, K.N. 142–143
Rick, T. 59
Ricoeur, P. 5
Rinpa 144
risk 158, 236
ritual 30, 35–36
RMJM 172–173, 182–183
Robinson, S. 15
Rogers, R. 180
Rojas, F. 190
Roman law 35
Romani, P. 160
Rome 159
Roosevelt, F.D. 142
routines 27–28, 30, 36; ecclesiastical 31–35
Rowlinson, M. 4, 6, 78, 86
Royal High School (RHS) 175
Ruel, S. 13
rules 28, 112–113, 117, 125, 197; of evidence 9
Russia 113, 150, 161, 215

Sachs, S. 8
St Andrew's House 175, 180
Sakai, K. 15
Sams, C.F. 193
Santos, F.M. 163–164
scalers 121–122
Schein, E. 60
Schinckus, C. 8
Schon, D. 58
Schwartz, B. 136–137
science 83, 114, 231–232, 237; historical studies as 5
Scotland 29–35, 170–178, 181–184
Scottish Enlightenment 181
Second World War 193, 231–232
Seeber, B.K. 47, 49

seeing anew 117
Seixas, P. 78
self-regulation 234–235
Selznick, P. 92
Senge, P. 60
Senior, B. 59
Sennett, R. 28
sensemaking 8, 111–112, 115
serendipity 86
sexuality 26, 109–110
Sheraton 156, 158, 160, 162
Siksika Nation 99
silences 109–110, 115, 117, 122
Sillince, J.A.A. 69
Slocum, J. 59
Smith, A. 179
Smithsonian Institution 132, 138–140, 143
Snell, K. 28
socialization 43–44, 46
Sōtatsu 144
Soulsby, A. 16
Soviet Union 107, 113, 150, 161, 212, 215
space industry 107, 113, 115, 117–121, 123–126
Spain 158–159, 182
Sputnik 107
state 234, 237
state-owned enterprises (SOEs) 208–210, 222
Stimson, A. 99
stories *see* narratives
Strand, C. 158–159
Strauss, A.L. 83–84
striking moments 44, 47–49
Strojarstvo 218–221
structuring structures 43
Stutz, C. 8
substance 26
Suddaby, R. 7, 14, 79, 90, 98, 164, 190
Sum, N.-L. 84
Sydney Harbour Bridge 17
Syed, J. 8
systems thinking 58, 60, 201

Tagliabue, B. 174, 180–181, 185
task interdependence 233–234
Taylor, F.W. 231
technology 233–234; as hubris 64; medical 196–197, 201; space industry 114, 122
Terumo 196
texts 152–153; *see also* discourse
theoretical fluency 6
theory 227–230; historical reflexivity 39–47, 52; history and 6–7, 9
thick description 7

Thornton, P. 25
time 40–53, 238; in corporatized university 47–52; historical reflexivity 43–47; as linear/circular 91–92, 96–97
Titanic 59, 63–64, 67, 69
Tomitaro, H. 142
tourism 156–160, 162
transactional model 8
Transworld Airlines (TWA) 150, 156
trauma 96–97
tribalism 100
tropes, counter- 69, 71–72
Trouillot, M.-R. 110
trust 6, 219
truth, representational 6
Turkey 158
Turner, M. 57
Turner, T. 33–34
Tyne Bridge 17

UK 170–171, 174, 198, 200, 235–236; *see also* England; Scotland
unconscious 45, 49, 64
Underdown, D. 35–36
Unikkaaqtuat 99
university: corporatized 47–52; nursing education 197–198; virtual 234
unsettling 42–44, 46–47, 49, 53
US 28, 142, 231–232, 235–236; gendered remembering 107, 113, 116, 119; institutional change 193–194, 198, 200; institutional entrepreneurship 154, 156–157, 159–164
Üsdiken, B. 4
USSR 107, 113, 150, 161, 212, 215

Vaara, E. 8, 92
Vaturi, J. 160
Velvet Revolution 208, 211
vernacular 177, 179, 182–184
Veyne, P. 30
Viale, T. 190
Vince, R. 11–12, 44, 51, 238
Vinoly, R. 180
viruses 234–238
visitations 29, 34–35
voice 109
voluntarism 188, 190, 201

Wadhwani, R.D. 8, 77, 84
Waldorf Astoria 156, 161
Wallach Scott, J. 114
war 193, 231–232
Wark, K. 182–183
Washington, DC 132, 138

Weber, M. 30, 232, 234
Weick, K. 72, 112
Welch, C. 87
Wendat people 99
West, C. 112
western assumptions 8, 91–100
wet markets 234–235
Whetten, D.A. 134–135, 137
Whistler, J.M. 144
White, H. 5, 9
White men 107, 120; *see also* gender; race
Whitman, J. 28
Willmott, H. 190

women *see* gender
Woo, P.C. 237
Woodforde, James 33
Woodman, R. 59
work 195–201, 210–213; institutional 188–191, 200–201
writing, the self 51–52

Yool, C. 116
Yuen, K.Y. 237

Zimmerman, D.H. 112
Zundel, M. 135

Printed in the United States
By Bookmasters